Norihiro Yagi won the 32nd Akatsuka Award for his debut work, *UNDEADMAN*, which appeared in *Monthly Shonen Jump* magazine and produced two sequels. His first serialized manga was his comedy *Angel Densetsu* (Angel Legend), which appeared in *Monthly Shonen Jump* from 1992 to 2000. His epic saga, *Claymore*, is running in *Monthly Jump Square* magazine.

In his spare time, Yagi enjoys things like the Japanese comedic duo Downtown, martial arts, games, driving, and hard rock music, but he doesn't consider these actual hobbies.

CLAYMORE VOL. 14
SHONEN JUMP ADVANCED Manga Edition

STORY AND ART BY
NORIHIRO YAGI

English Adaptation & Translation/Arashi Productions
Touch-up Art & Lettering/Sabrina Heep
Design/Izumi Evers
Editor/Leyla Aker

VP, Production/Alvin Lu
VP, Sales & Product Marketing/Gonzalo Ferreyra
VP, Creative/Linda Espinosa
Publisher/Hyoe Narita

Printed in the U.S.A.

Published by VIZ Media, LLC
P.O. Box 77010
San Francisco, CA 94107

10 9 8 7 6 5 4 3 2
First printing, March 2009
Second printing, February 2010

www.viz.com

RATED T+ FOR OLDER TEEN
PARENTAL ADVISORY
CLAYMORE is rated T+ for Older
Teen and is recommended for
ages 16 and up. This volume
contains realistic violence.
ratings.viz.com

THE WORLD'S MOST
CUTTING-EDGE MANGA
SHONEN JUMP ADVANCED
www.shonenjump.com

SHONEN JUMP ADVANCED Manga Edition

Claymore

クレイモア

Vol. 14
A Child Weapon

Story and Art by **Norihiro Yagi**

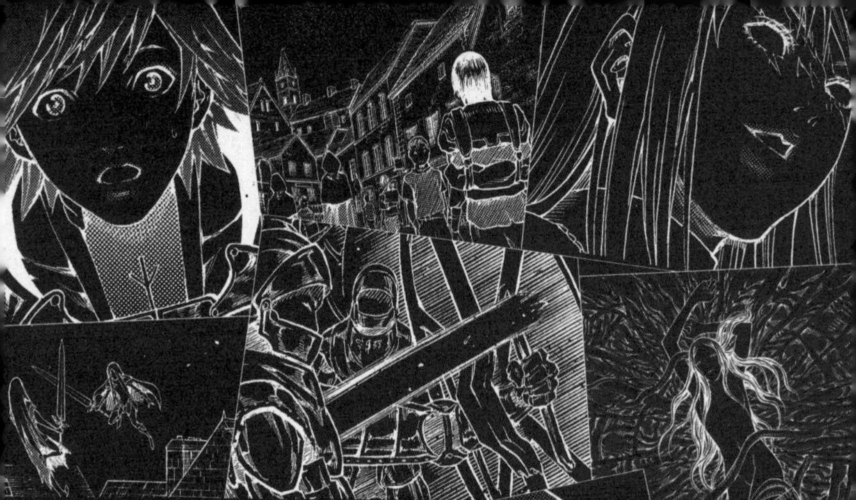

Seven years have passed since the Battle of the North, and Clare and her comrades have begun to act. Meanwhile, Clarice and Miata have received orders to hunt down the deserter Galatea. The two of them enter an unknown town...

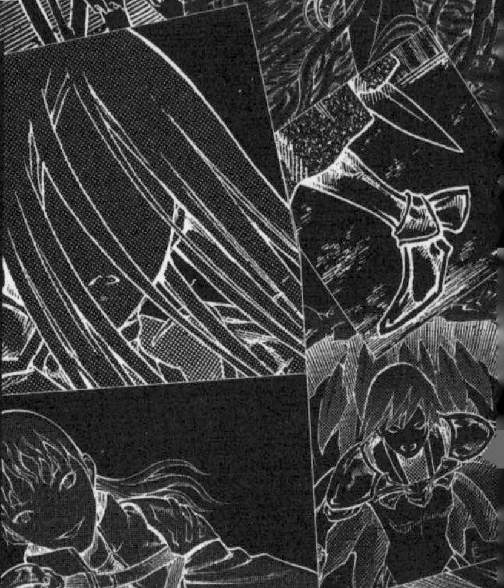

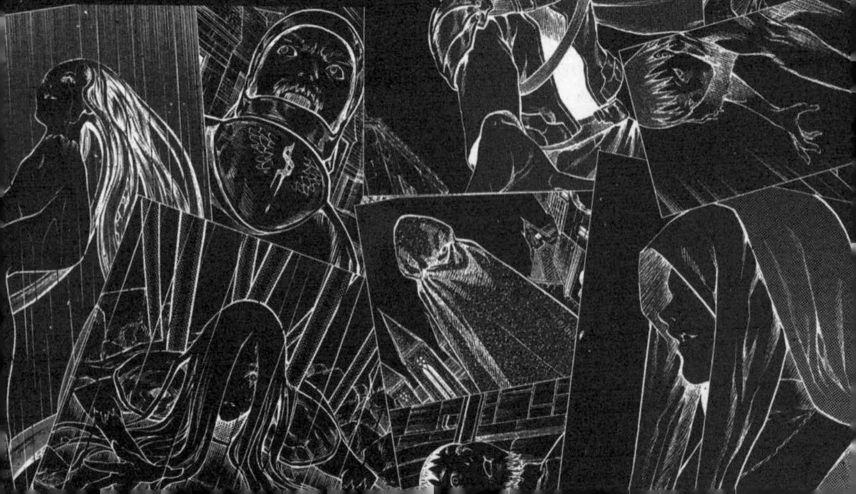

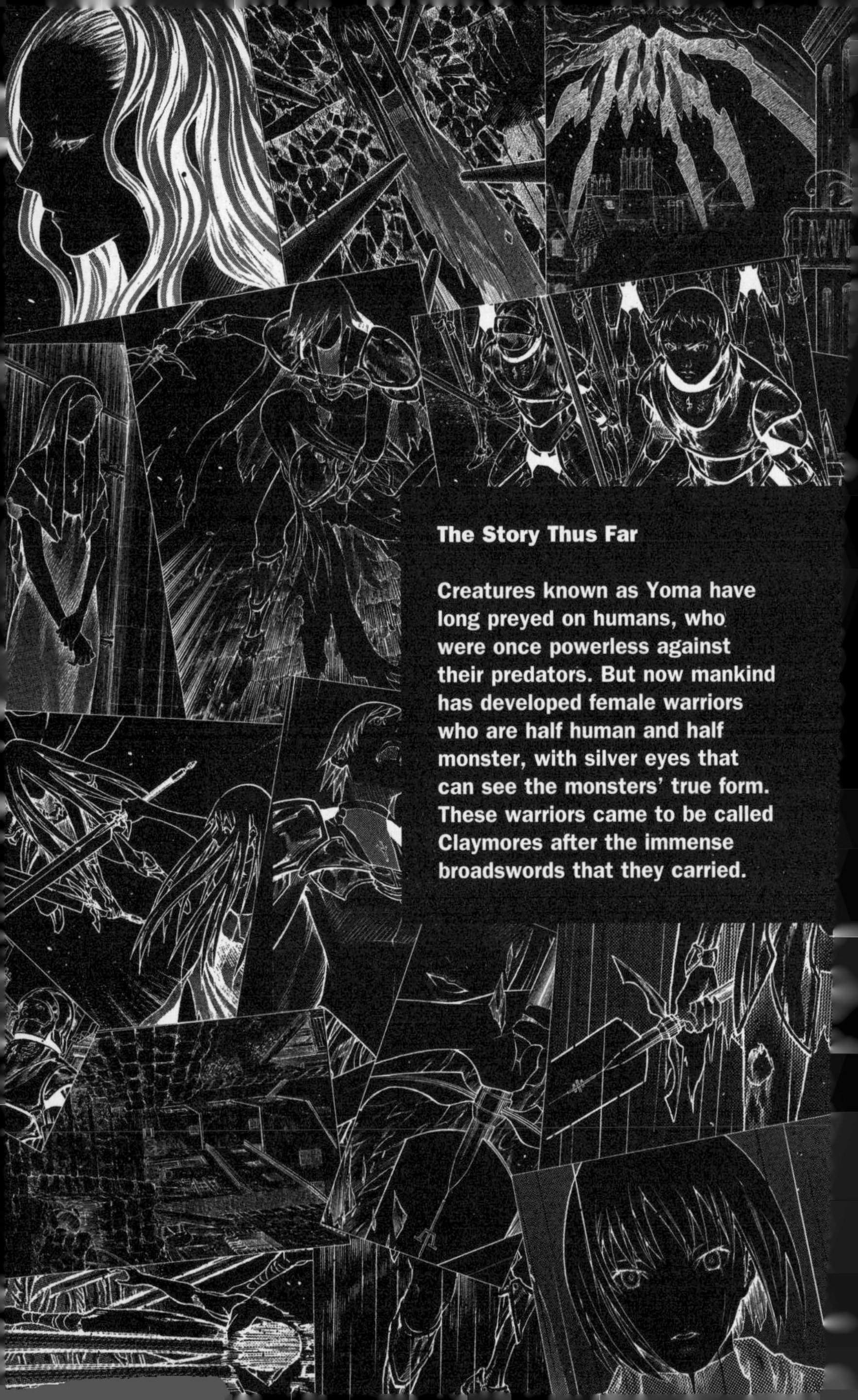

The Story Thus Far

Creatures known as Yoma have long preyed on humans, who were once powerless against their predators. But now mankind has developed female warriors who are half human and half monster, with silver eyes that can see the monsters' true form. These warriors came to be called Claymores after the immense broadswords that they carried.

クレイモア

Claymore

Vol. 14

CONTENTS

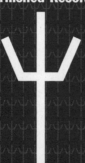

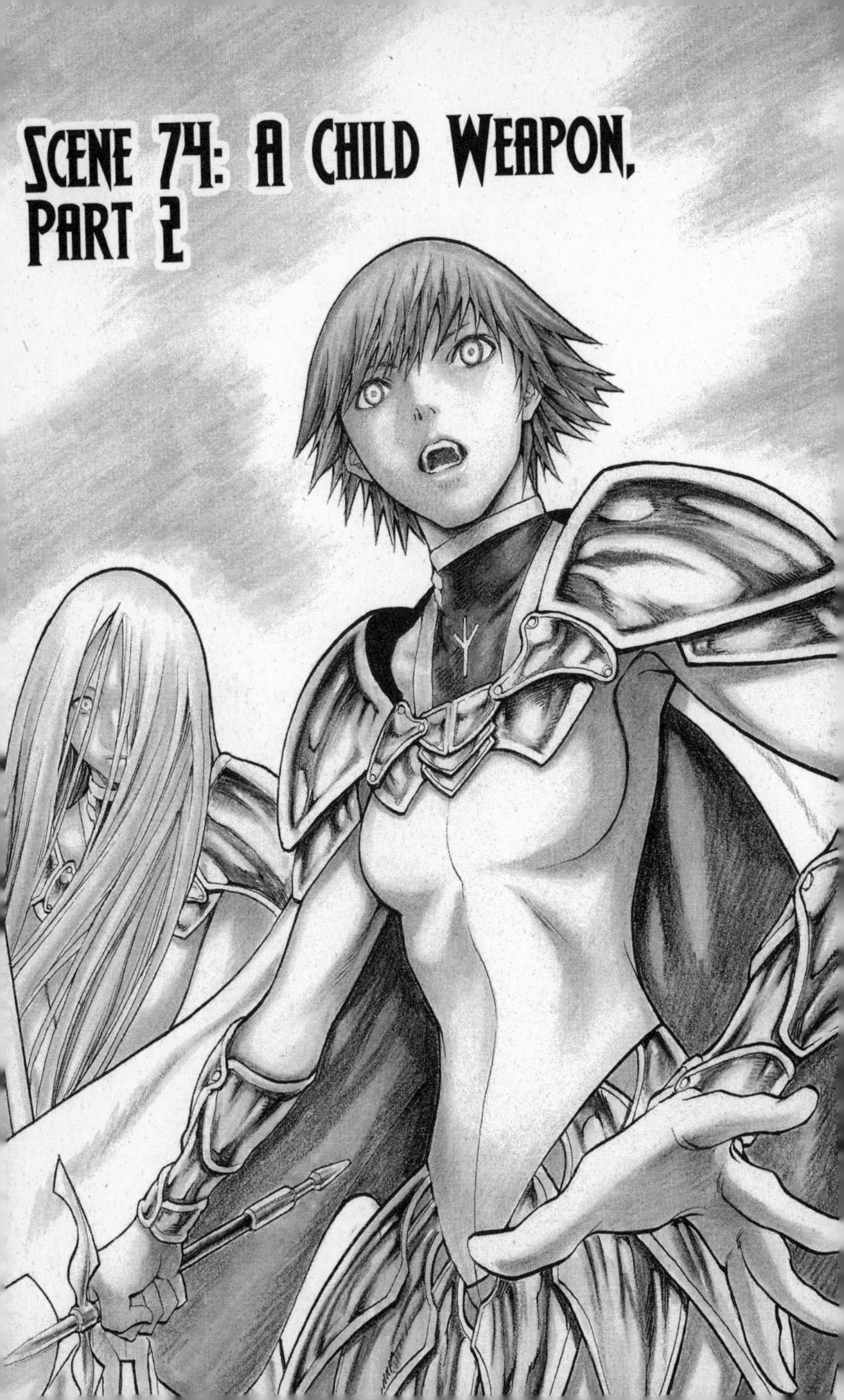
SCENE 74: A CHILD WEAPON,
PART 2

Claymore クレイモア

READ THIS WAY

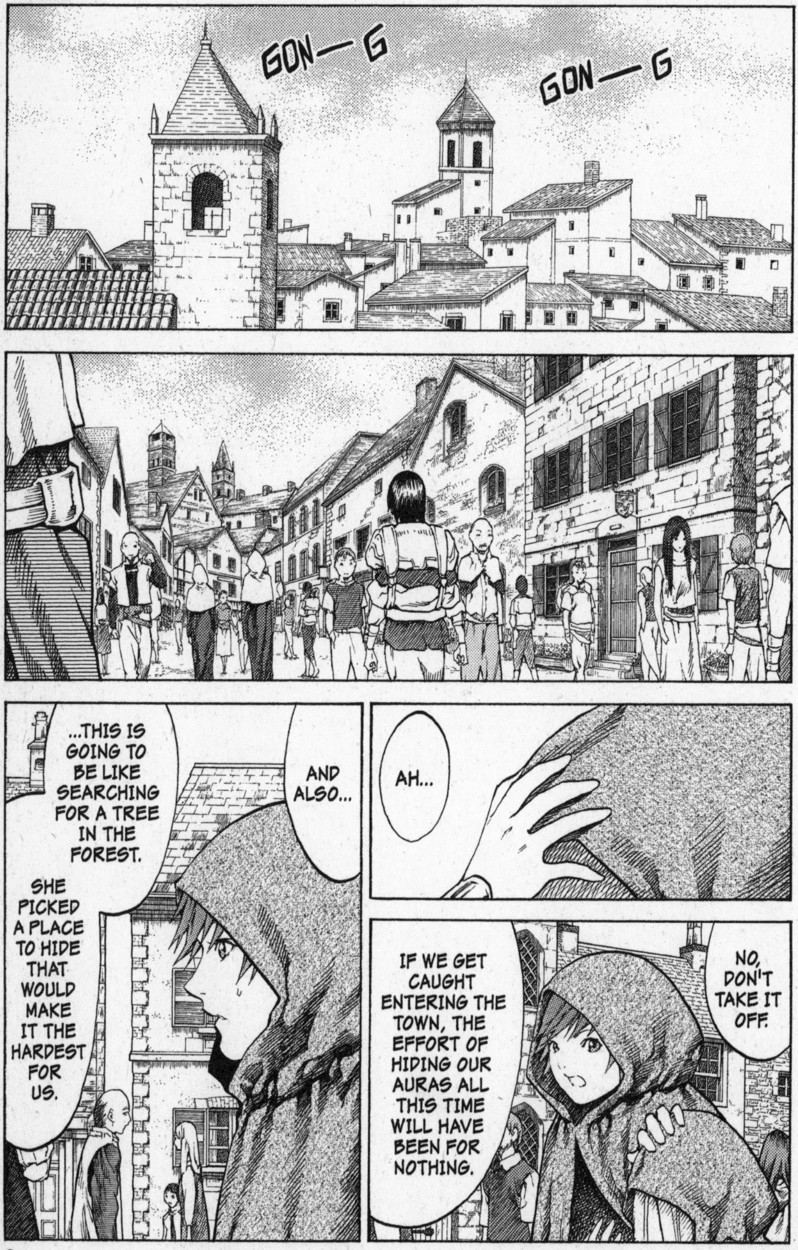

GON—G
GON—G
AH...
NO, DON'T TAKE IT OFF.
IF WE GET CAUGHT ENTERING THE TOWN, THE EFFORT OF HIDING OUR AURAS ALL THIS TIME WILL HAVE BEEN FOR NOTHING.
AND ALSO...
...THIS IS GOING TO BE LIKE SEARCHING FOR A TREE IN THE FOREST.
SHE PICKED A PLACE TO HIDE THAT WOULD MAKE IT THE HARDEST FOR US.

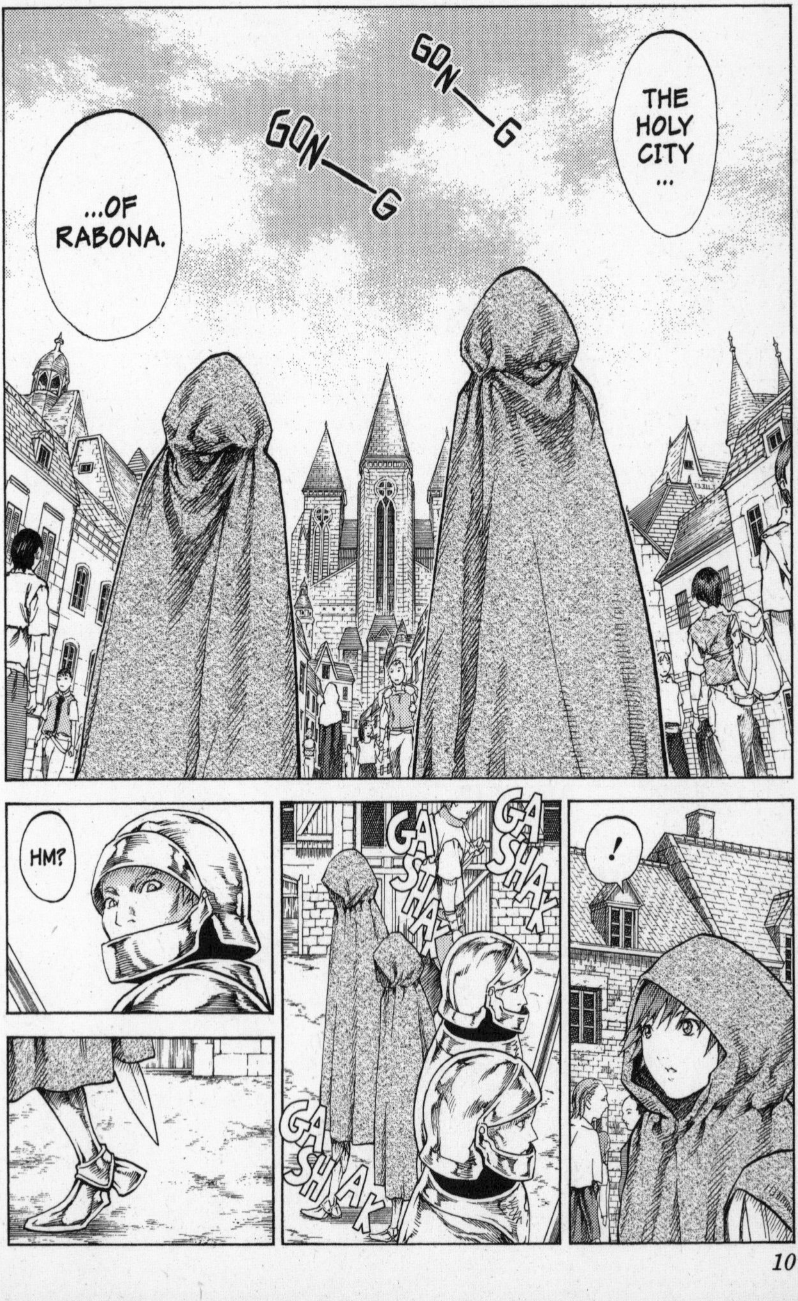
THE HOLY CITY ...
GON—G
GON—G
...OF RABONA.
!
GASHAK
GASHAK
GASHAK
HM?

READ THIS WAY

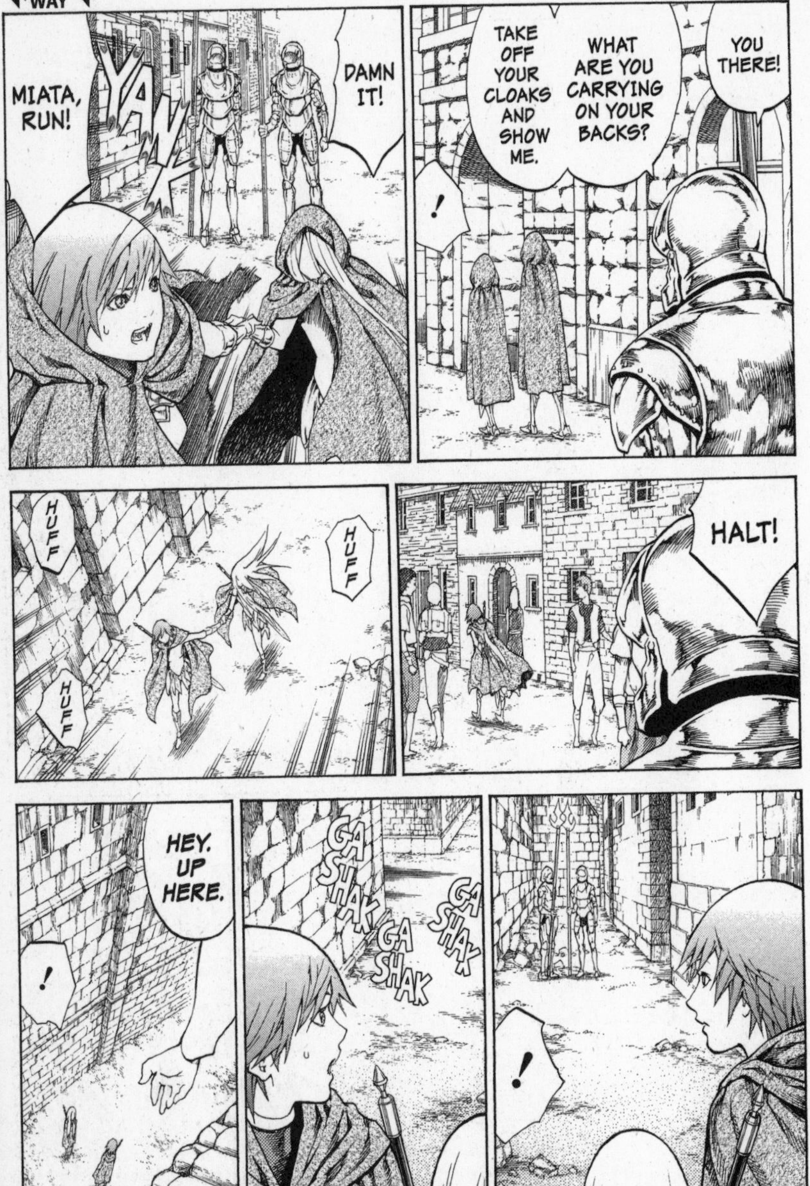

YOU THERE!
WHAT ARE YOU CARRYING ON YOUR BACKS?
TAKE OFF YOUR CLOAKS AND SHOW ME.
!
DAMN IT!
YANK
MIATA, RUN!
HALT!
HUFF
HUFF
HUFF
!
GA SHAK
GA SHAK
GA SHAK
HEY. UP HERE.
!

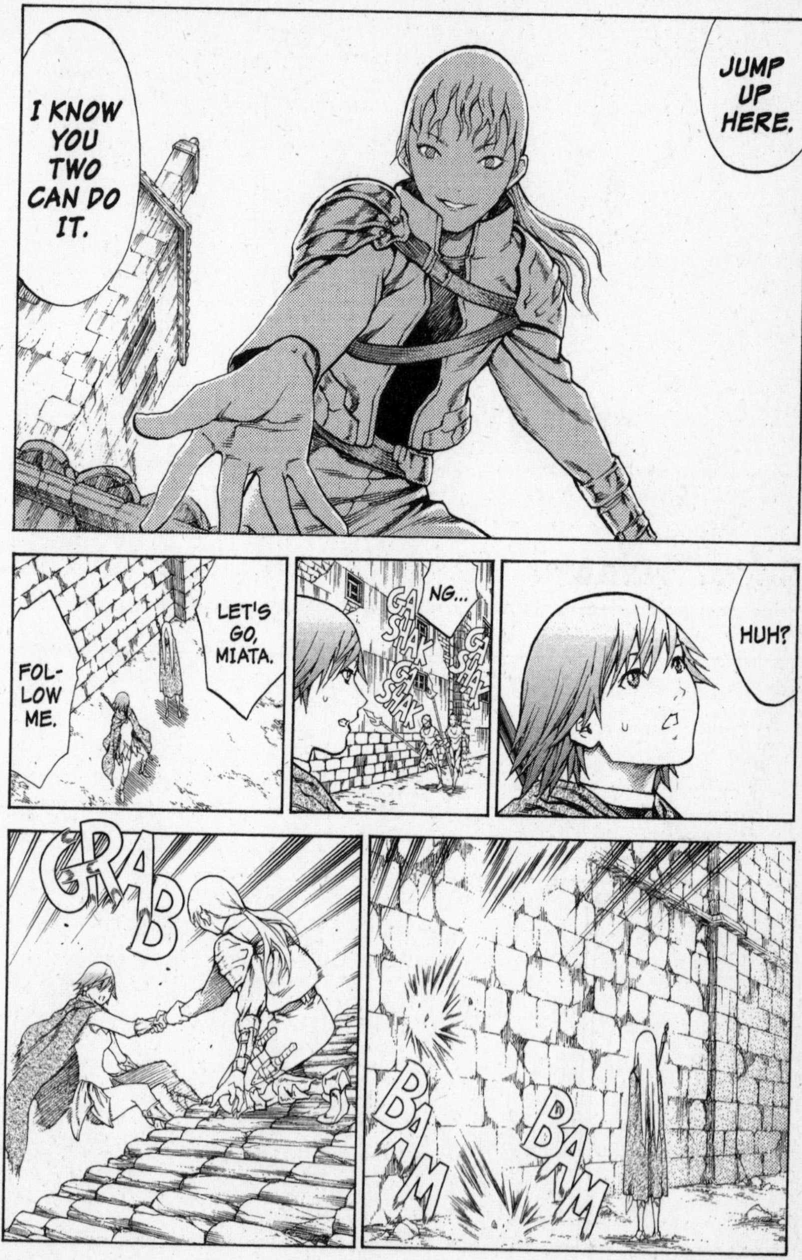
JUMP UP HERE.
I KNOW YOU TWO CAN DO IT.
HUH?
NG...
GA SHAK GA SHAK
GA SHAK
LET'S GO, MIATA.
FOL-LOW ME.
BAM
BAM
GRAB

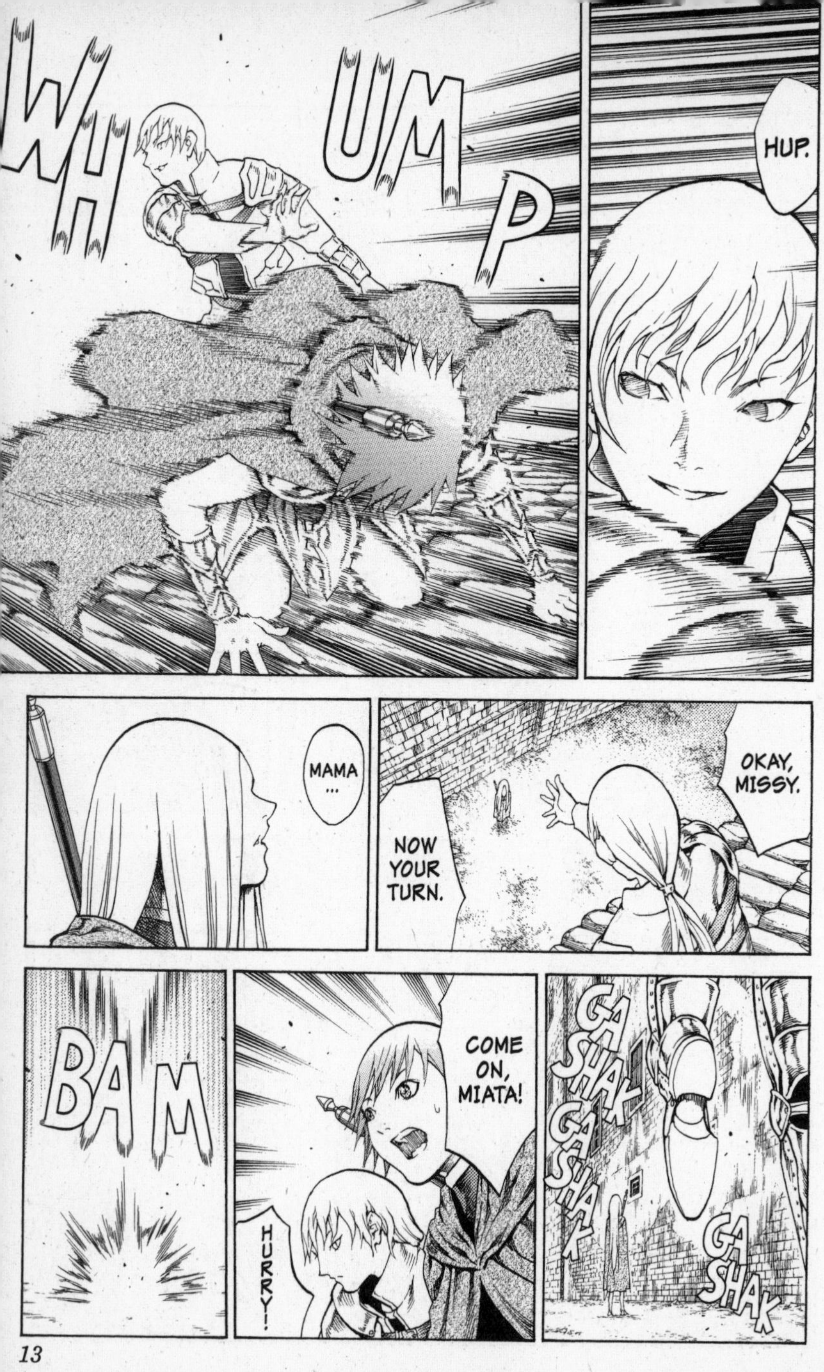
HUP.
WHUMP
OKAY, MISSY.
NOW YOUR TURN.
MAMA ...
GASHAK
GASHAK
GASHAK
COME ON, MIATA!
HURRY!
BAM

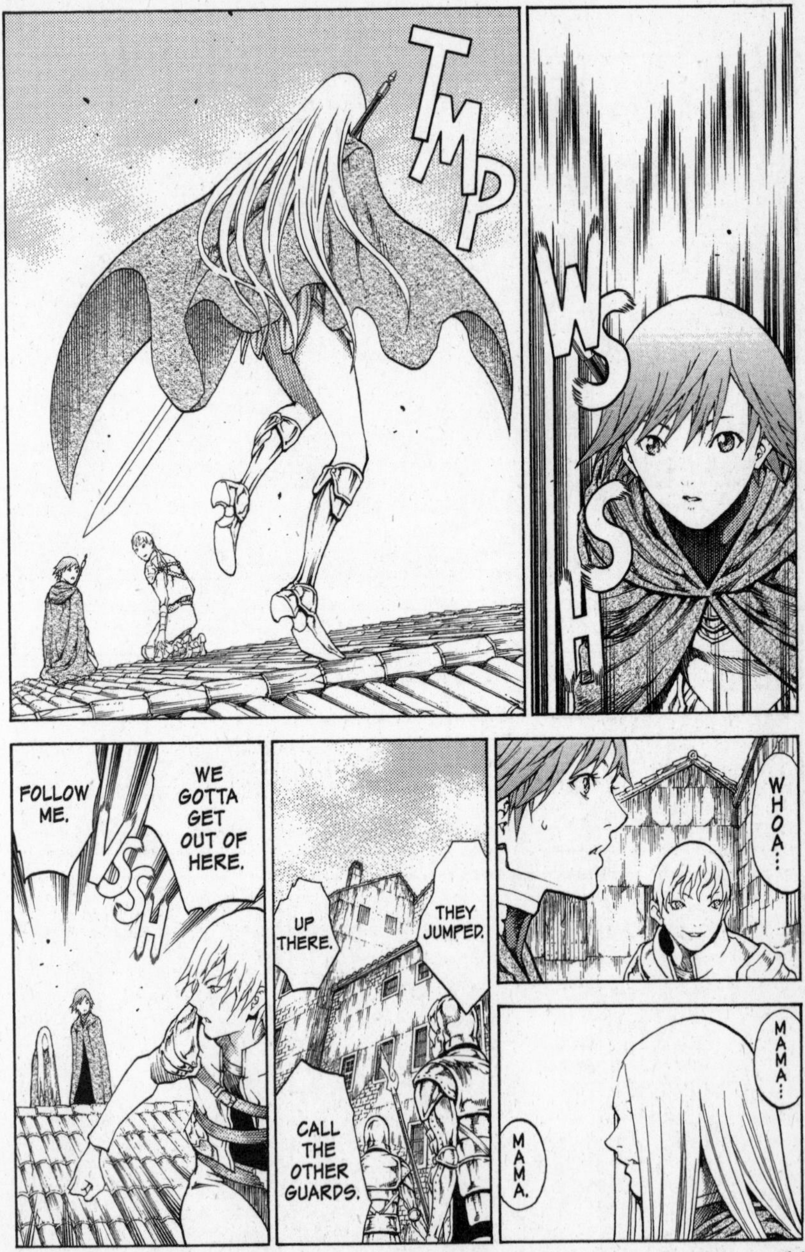
WSSH
TMP
WHOA...
MAMA...
MAMA.
THEY JUMPED.
UP THERE.
CALL THE OTHER GUARDS.
WE GOTTA GET OUT OF HERE.
FOLLOW ME.
VSSH

READ THIS WAY

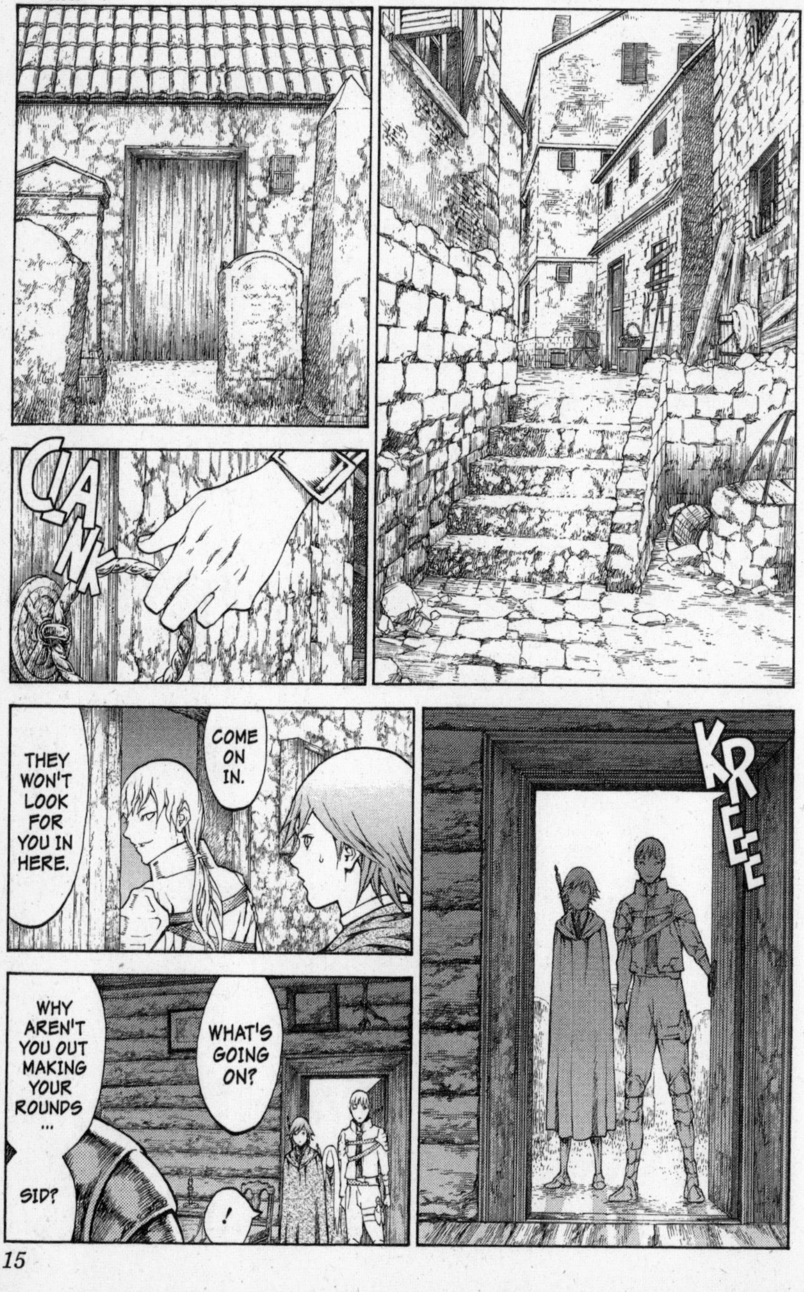
CLANK
KREEE
COME ON IN.
THEY WON'T LOOK FOR YOU IN HERE.
WHAT'S GOING ON?
WHY AREN'T YOU OUT MAKING YOUR ROUNDS...
!
SID?

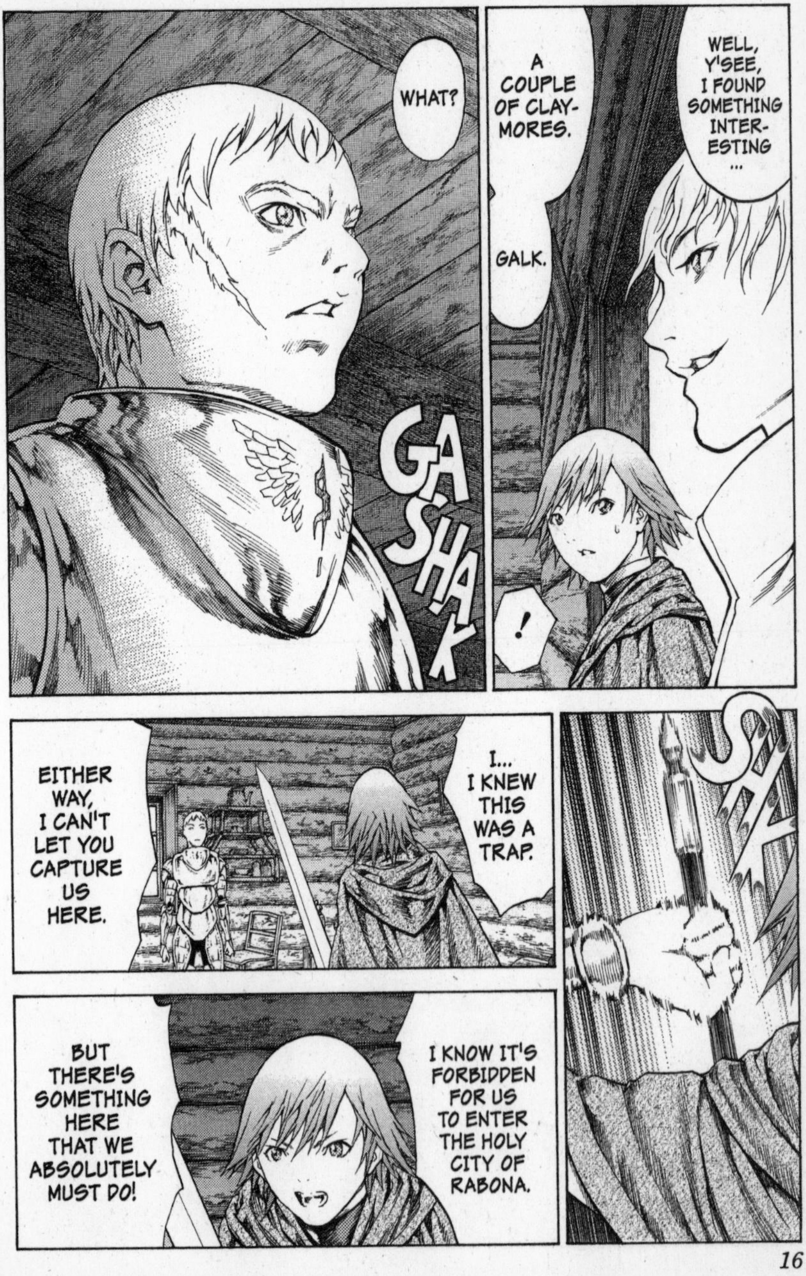
WELL, Y'SEE, I FOUND SOMETHING INTER-ESTING ...
A COUPLE OF CLAY-MORES.
GALK.
!
WHAT?
GASHAK
SHA
I... I KNEW THIS WAS A TRAP.
EITHER WAY, I CAN'T LET YOU CAPTURE US HERE.
I KNOW IT'S FORBIDDEN FOR US TO ENTER THE HOLY CITY OF RABONA.
BUT THERE'S SOMETHING HERE THAT WE ABSOLUTELY MUST DO!

READ THIS WAY

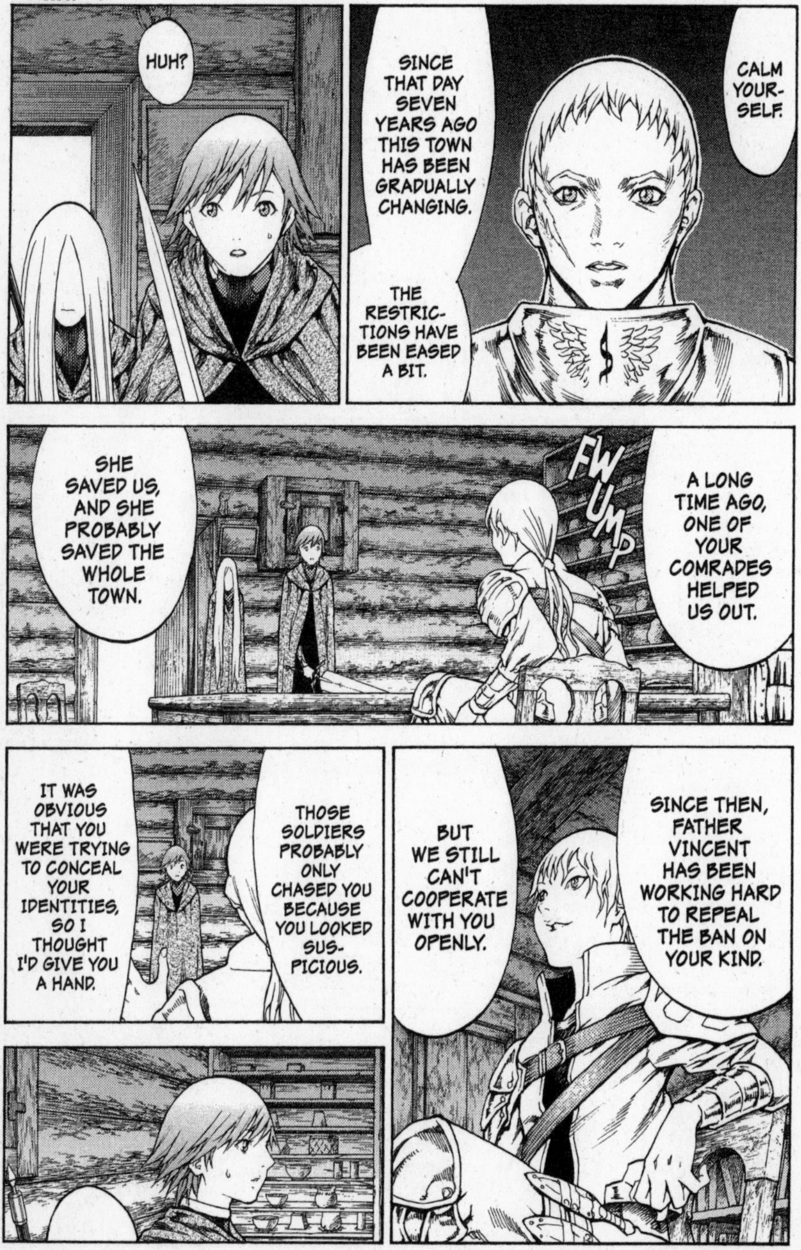

CALM YOURSELF.
SINCE THAT DAY SEVEN YEARS AGO THIS TOWN HAS BEEN GRADUALLY CHANGING.
THE RESTRICTIONS HAVE BEEN EASED A BIT.
HUH?
FWUMP
A LONG TIME AGO, ONE OF YOUR COMRADES HELPED US OUT.
SHE SAVED US, AND SHE PROBABLY SAVED THE WHOLE TOWN.
SINCE THEN, FATHER VINCENT HAS BEEN WORKING HARD TO REPEAL THE BAN ON YOUR KIND.
BUT WE STILL CAN'T COOPERATE WITH YOU OPENLY.
THOSE SOLDIERS PROBABLY ONLY CHASED YOU BECAUSE YOU LOOKED SUSPICIOUS.
IT WAS OBVIOUS THAT YOU WERE TRYING TO CONCEAL YOUR IDENTITIES, SO I THOUGHT I'D GIVE YOU A HAND.

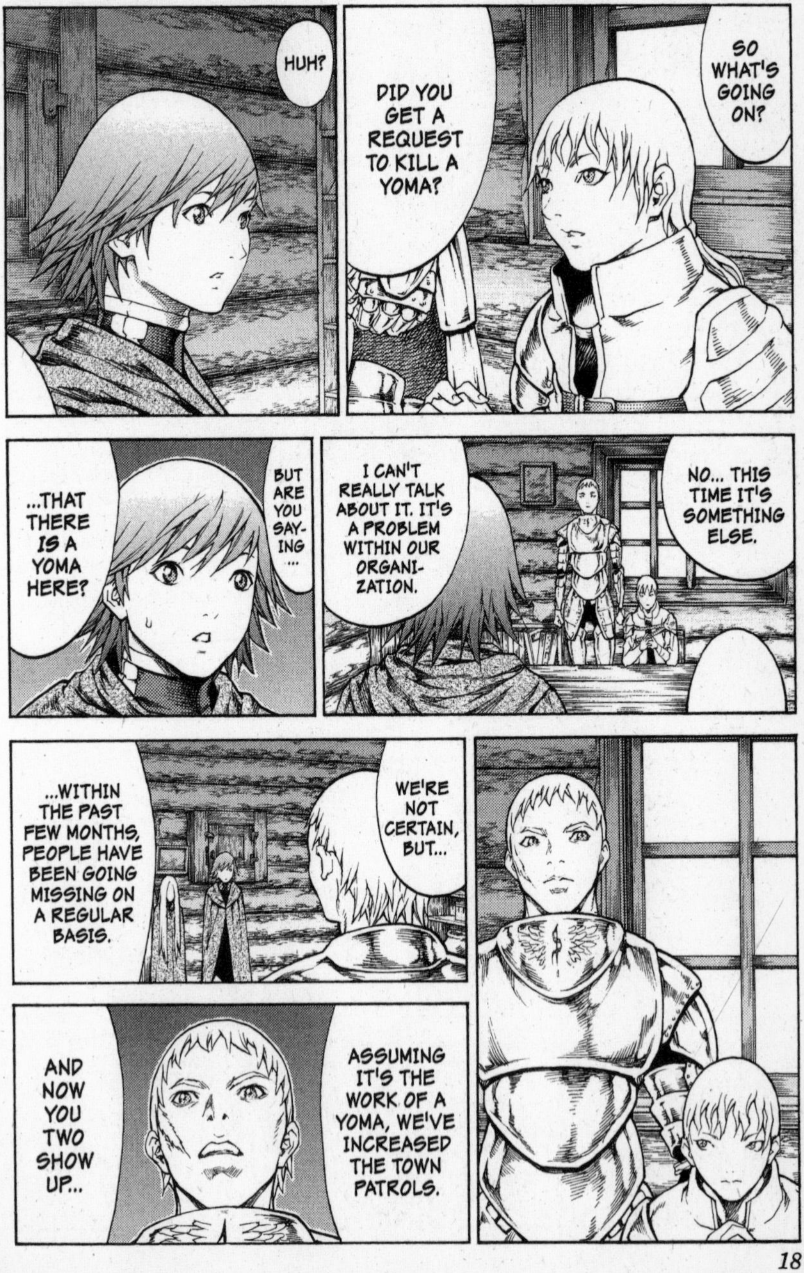
SO WHAT'S GOING ON?
DID YOU GET A REQUEST TO KILL A YOMA?
HUH?
NO... THIS TIME IT'S SOMETHING ELSE.
I CAN'T REALLY TALK ABOUT IT. IT'S A PROBLEM WITHIN OUR ORGANIZATION.
BUT ARE YOU SAYING...
...THAT THERE *IS* A YOMA HERE?
WE'RE NOT CERTAIN, BUT...
...WITHIN THE PAST FEW MONTHS, PEOPLE HAVE BEEN GOING MISSING ON A REGULAR BASIS.
ASSUMING IT'S THE WORK OF A YOMA, WE'VE INCREASED THE TOWN PATROLS.
AND NOW YOU TWO SHOW UP...

READ THIS WAY

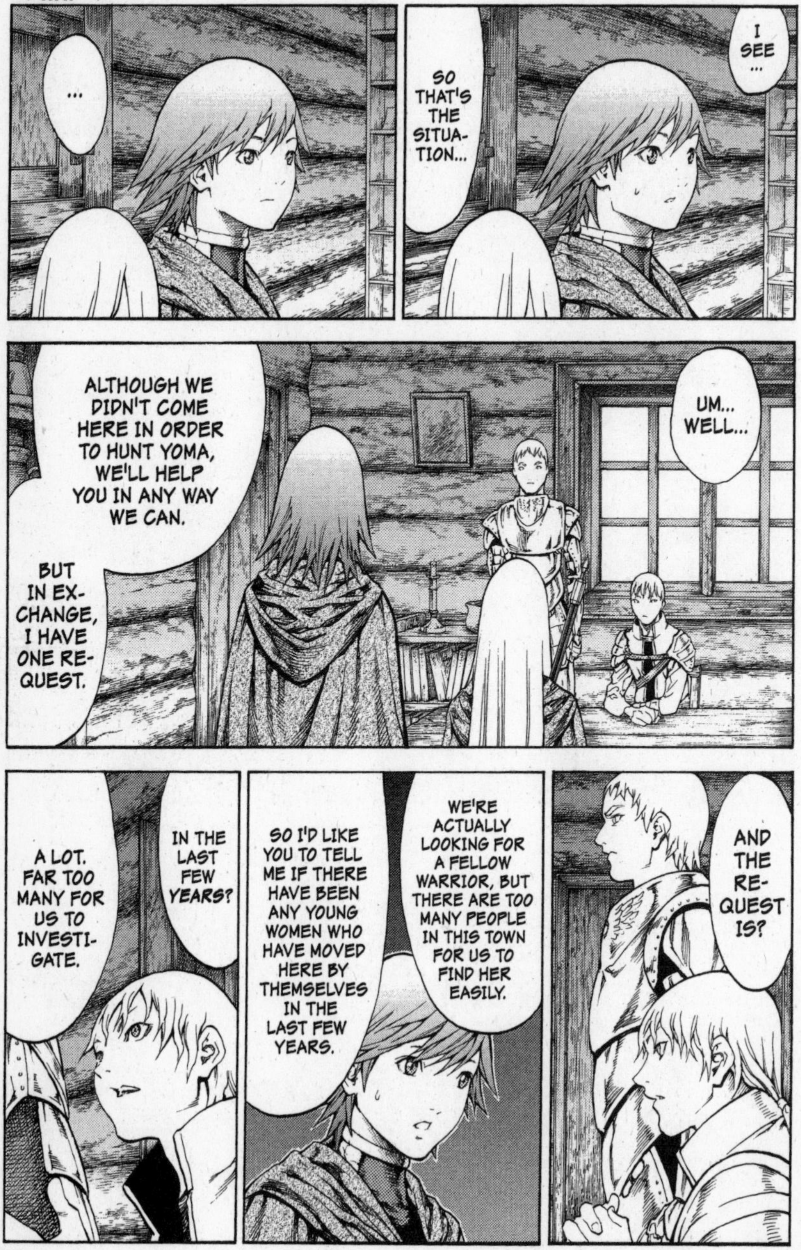
I SEE...
SO THAT'S THE SITUATION...
...
UM... WELL...
ALTHOUGH WE DIDN'T COME HERE IN ORDER TO HUNT YOMA, WE'LL HELP YOU IN ANY WAY WE CAN.
BUT IN EXCHANGE, I HAVE ONE REQUEST.
AND THE REQUEST IS?
WE'RE ACTUALLY LOOKING FOR A FELLOW WARRIOR, BUT THERE ARE TOO MANY PEOPLE IN THIS TOWN FOR US TO FIND HER EASILY.
SO I'D LIKE YOU TO TELL ME IF THERE HAVE BEEN ANY YOUNG WOMEN WHO HAVE MOVED HERE BY THEMSELVES IN THE LAST FEW YEARS.
IN THE LAST FEW YEARS?
A LOT. FAR TOO MANY FOR US TO INVESTIGATE.

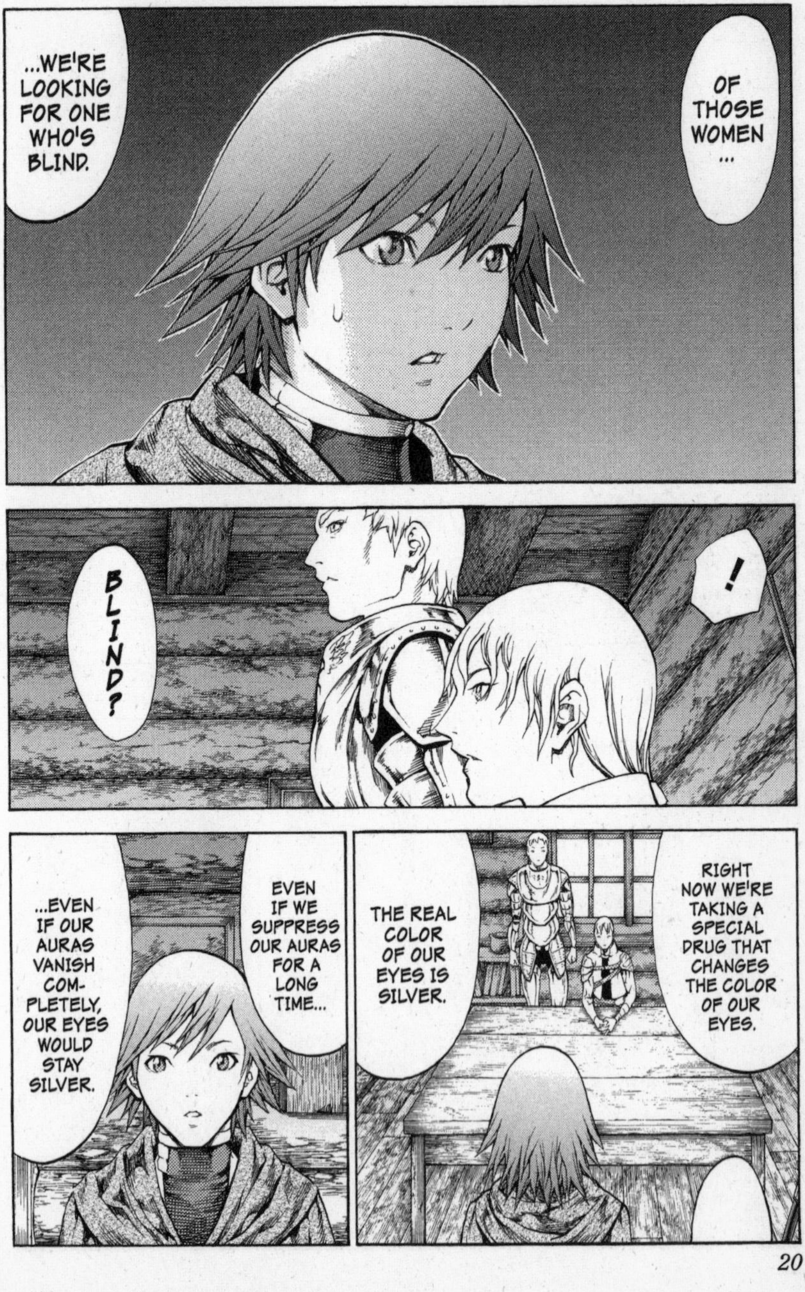

OF THOSE WOMEN...
...WE'RE LOOKING FOR ONE WHO'S BLIND.
!
BLIND?
RIGHT NOW WE'RE TAKING A SPECIAL DRUG THAT CHANGES THE COLOR OF OUR EYES.
THE REAL COLOR OF OUR EYES IS SILVER.
EVEN IF WE SUPPRESS OUR AURAS FOR A LONG TIME...
...EVEN IF OUR AURAS VANISH COM-PLETELY, OUR EYES WOULD STAY SILVER.

READ THIS WAY

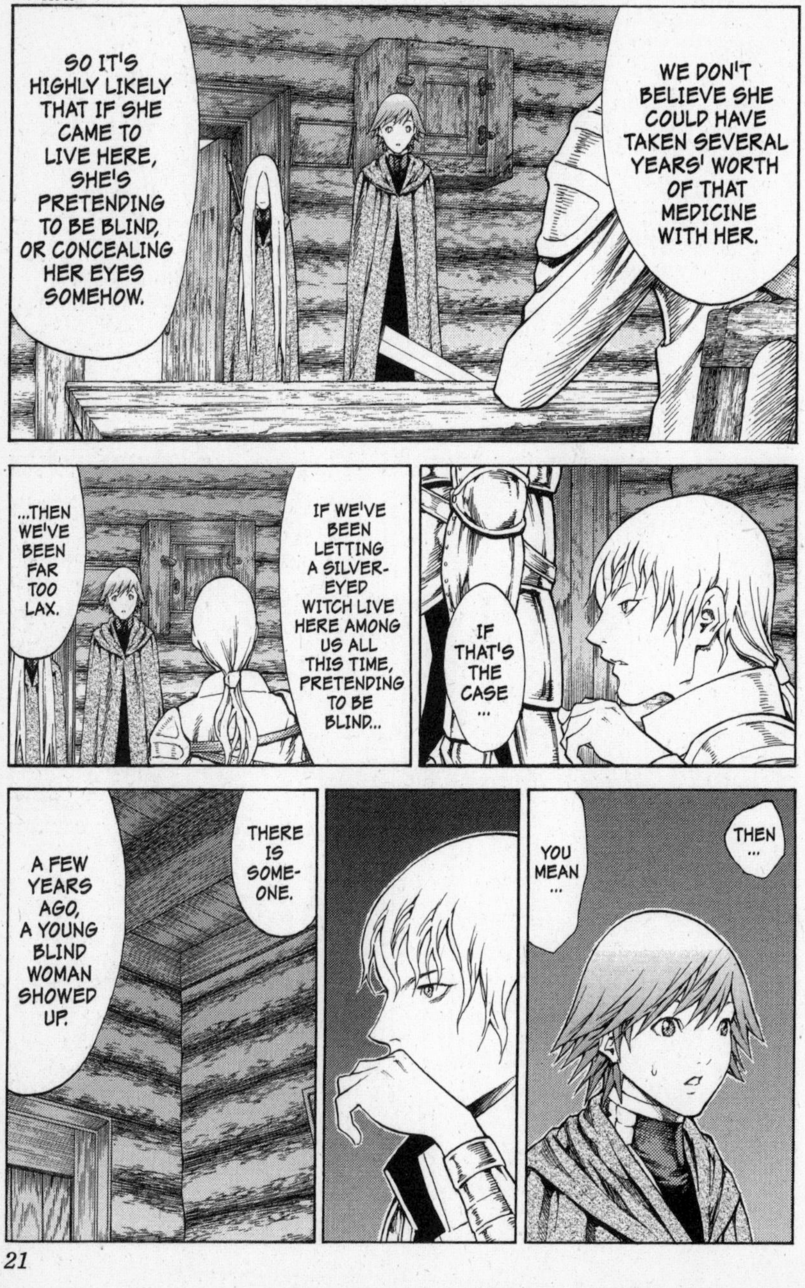
WE DON'T BELIEVE SHE COULD HAVE TAKEN SEVERAL YEARS' WORTH OF THAT MEDICINE WITH HER.
SO IT'S HIGHLY LIKELY THAT IF SHE CAME TO LIVE HERE, SHE'S PRETENDING TO BE BLIND, OR CONCEALING HER EYES SOMEHOW.
IF THAT'S THE CASE...
IF WE'VE BEEN LETTING A SILVER-EYED WITCH LIVE HERE AMONG US ALL THIS TIME, PRETENDING TO BE BLIND...
...THEN WE'VE BEEN FAR TOO LAX.
THEN...
YOU MEAN...
THERE IS SOME-ONE.
A FEW YEARS AGO, A YOUNG BLIND WOMAN SHOWED UP.

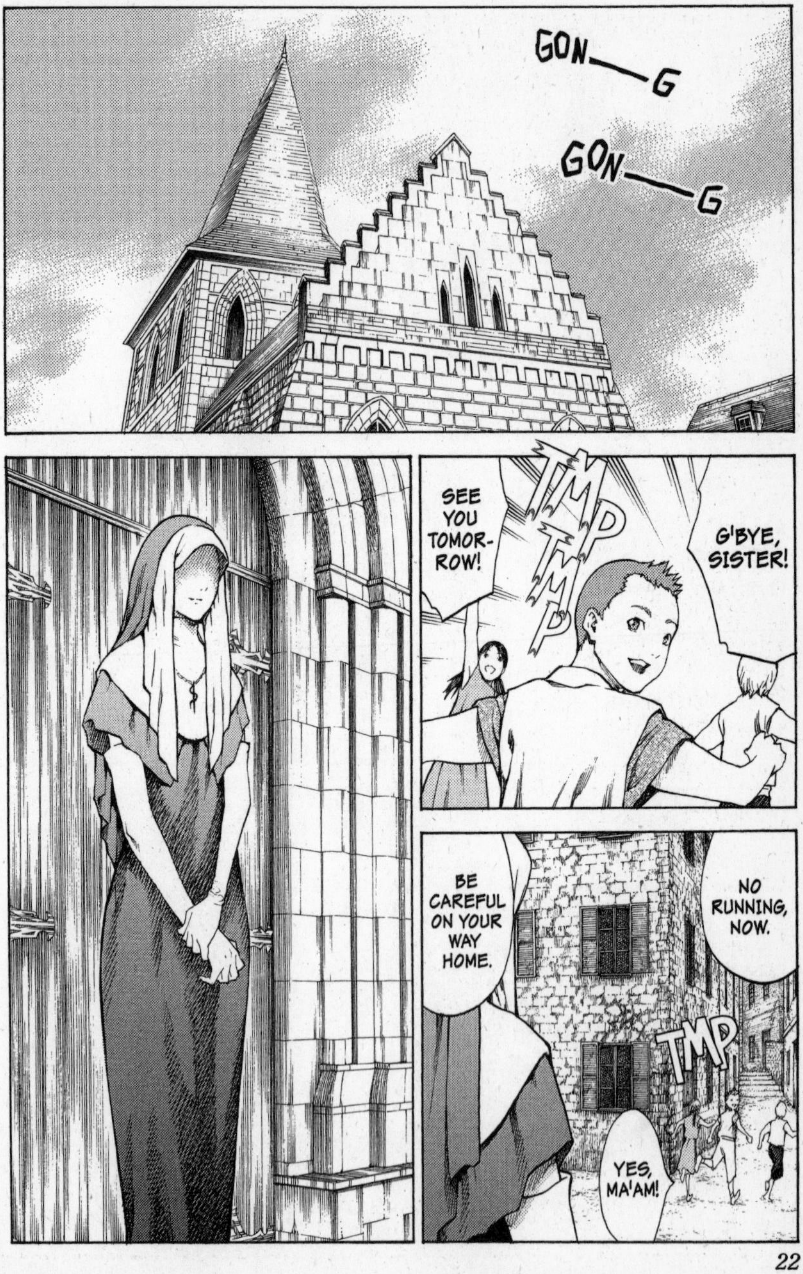
GON—G
GON—G
G'BYE, SISTER!
TMP TMP TMP
SEE YOU TOMORROW!
NO RUNNING, NOW.
BE CAREFUL ON YOUR WAY HOME.
TMP
YES, MA'AM!

READ THIS WAY

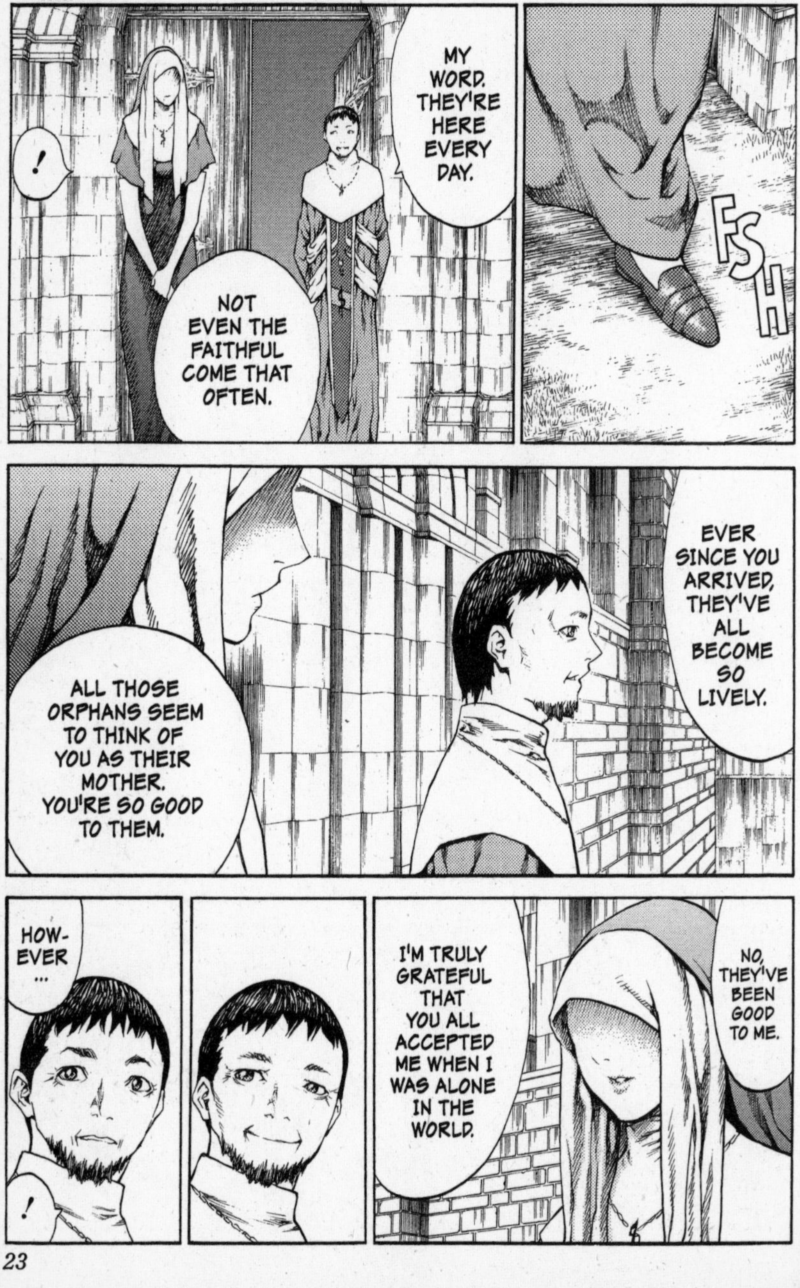
FSH
MY WORD. THEY'RE HERE EVERY DAY.
!
NOT EVEN THE FAITHFUL COME THAT OFTEN.
EVER SINCE YOU ARRIVED, THEY'VE ALL BECOME SO LIVELY.
ALL THOSE ORPHANS SEEM TO THINK OF YOU AS THEIR MOTHER. YOU'RE SO GOOD TO THEM.
NO, THEY'VE BEEN GOOD TO ME.
I'M TRULY GRATEFUL THAT YOU ALL ACCEPTED ME WHEN I WAS ALONE IN THE WORLD.
HOW-EVER ...
!

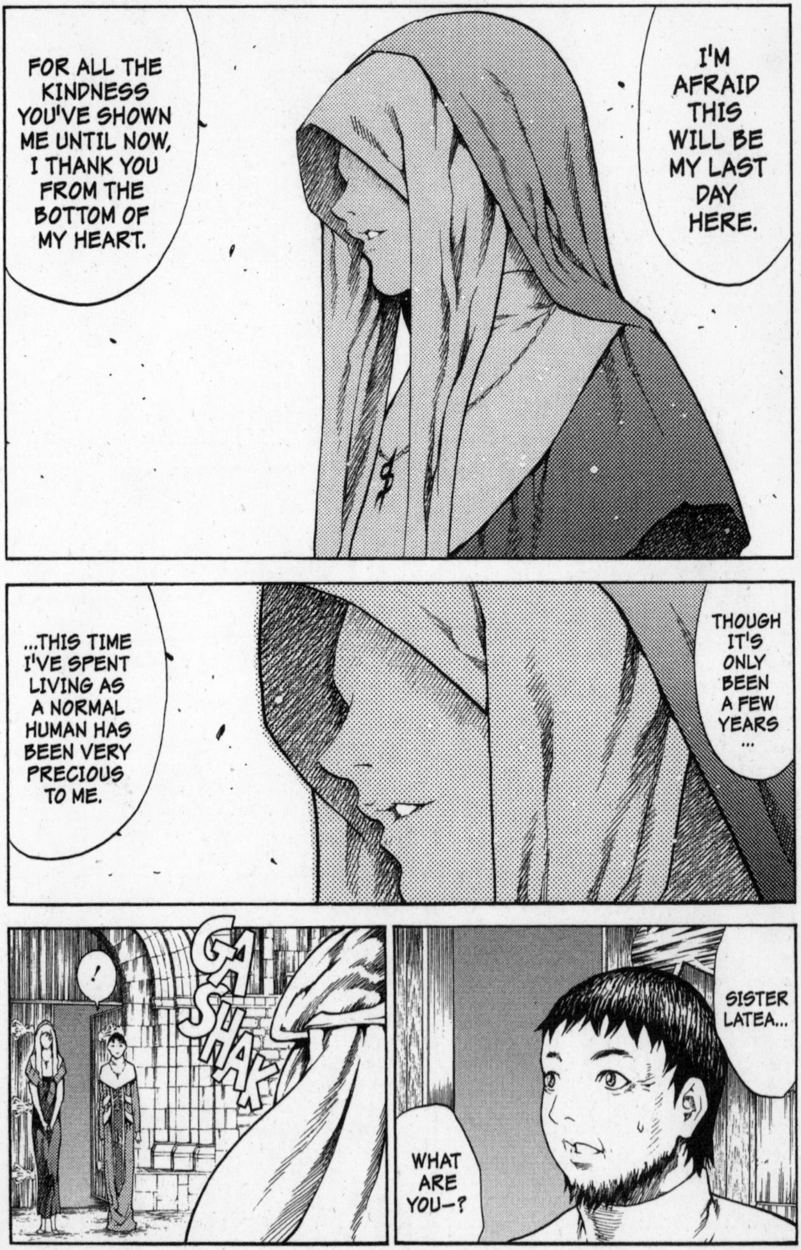
I'M AFRAID THIS WILL BE MY LAST DAY HERE.
FOR ALL THE KINDNESS YOU'VE SHOWN ME UNTIL NOW, I THANK YOU FROM THE BOTTOM OF MY HEART.
THOUGH IT'S ONLY BEEN A FEW YEARS ...
...THIS TIME I'VE SPENT LIVING AS A NORMAL HUMAN HAS BEEN VERY PRECIOUS TO ME.
SISTER LATEA...
WHAT ARE YOU-?
GASHAK
!

READ THIS WAY

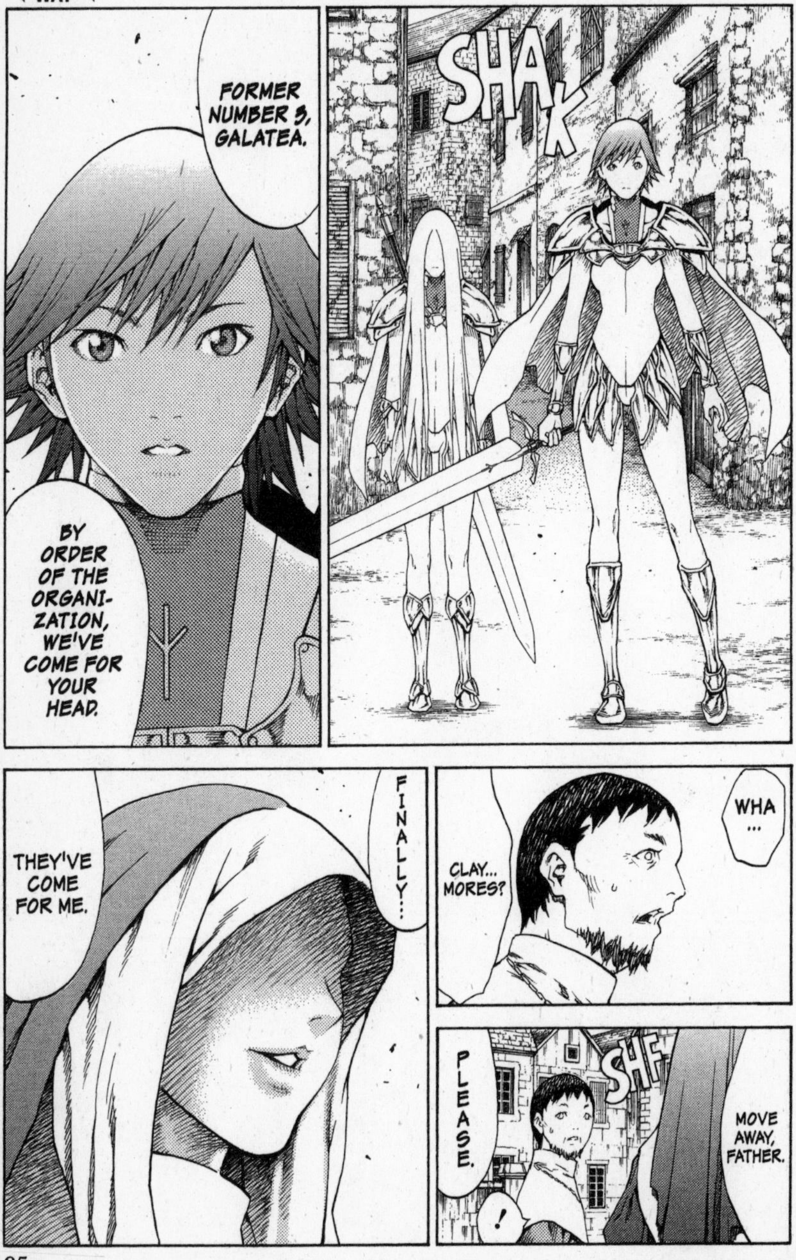
SHAK
FORMER NUMBER 3, GALATEA.
BY ORDER OF THE ORGANI-ZATION, WE'VE COME FOR YOUR HEAD.
WHA...
CLAY... MORES?
SHF
MOVE AWAY, FATHER.
PLEASE.
!
FINALLY...
THEY'VE COME FOR ME.

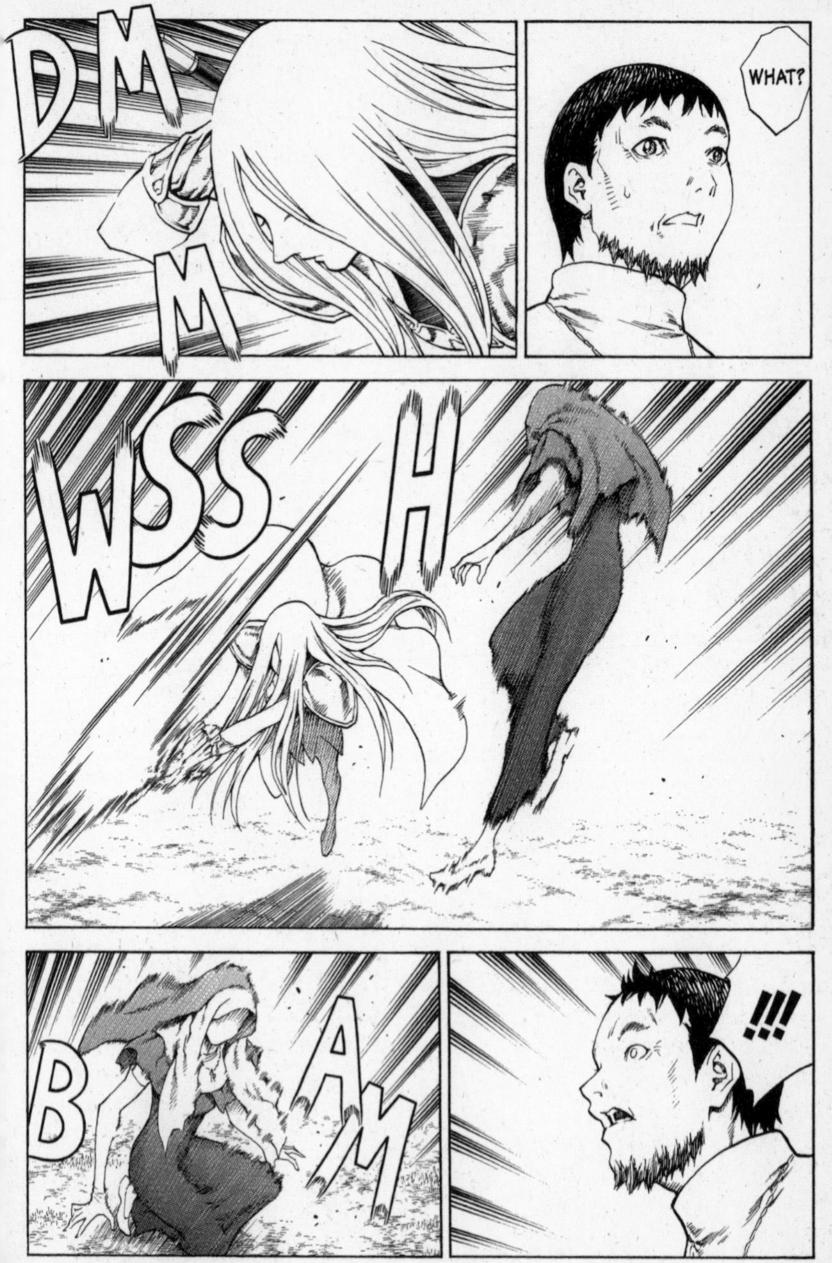
WHAT?
DMM
WSSH
!!!
BAM

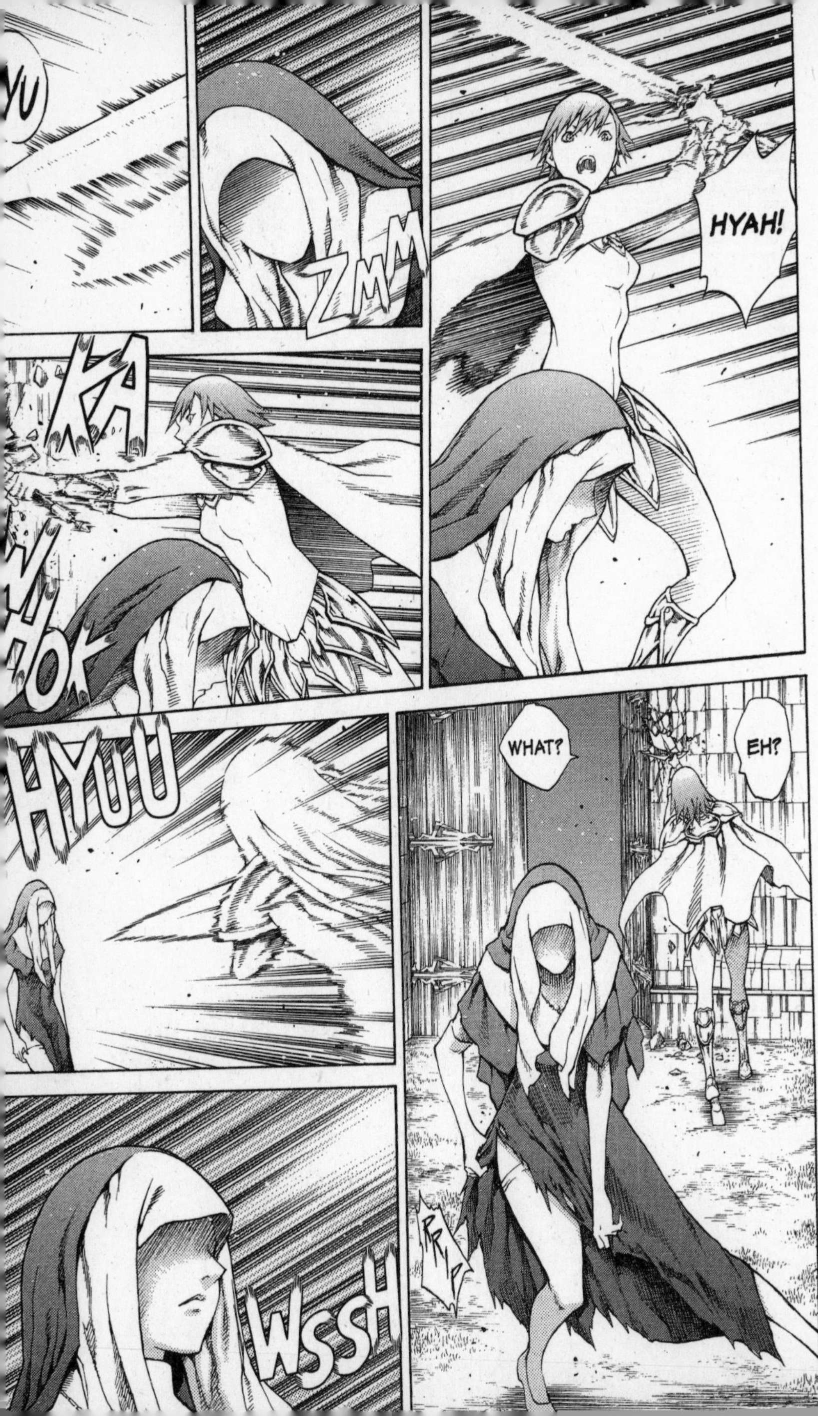
HYAH!
ZMM
YU
KA
EH?
WHAT?
RRRIP
HYUU
WSSH

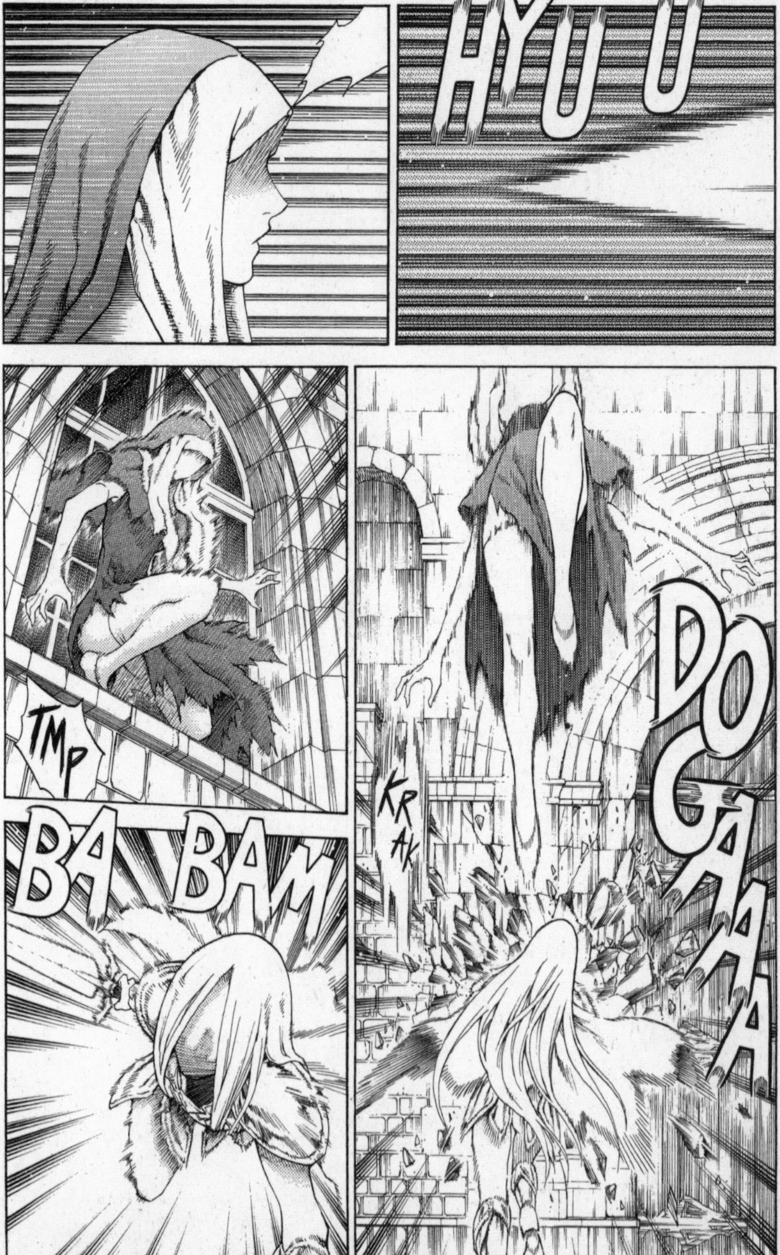
HYUU
DOGAAAA
KRAK
TMP
BA BAM

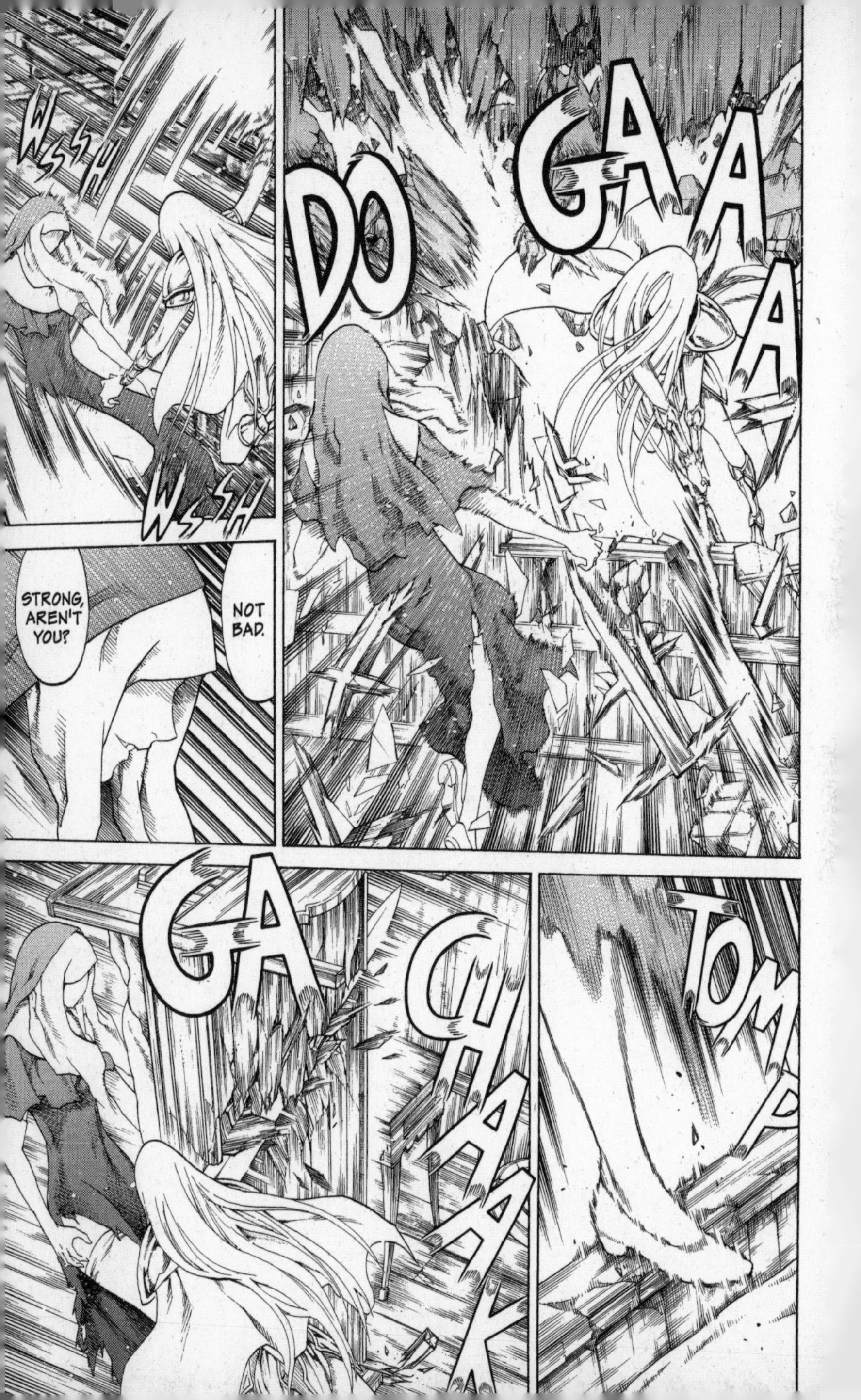
DOGAAA
WSSH
WSSH
NOT BAD.
STRONG, AREN'T YOU?
TOMP
GACHAAAK

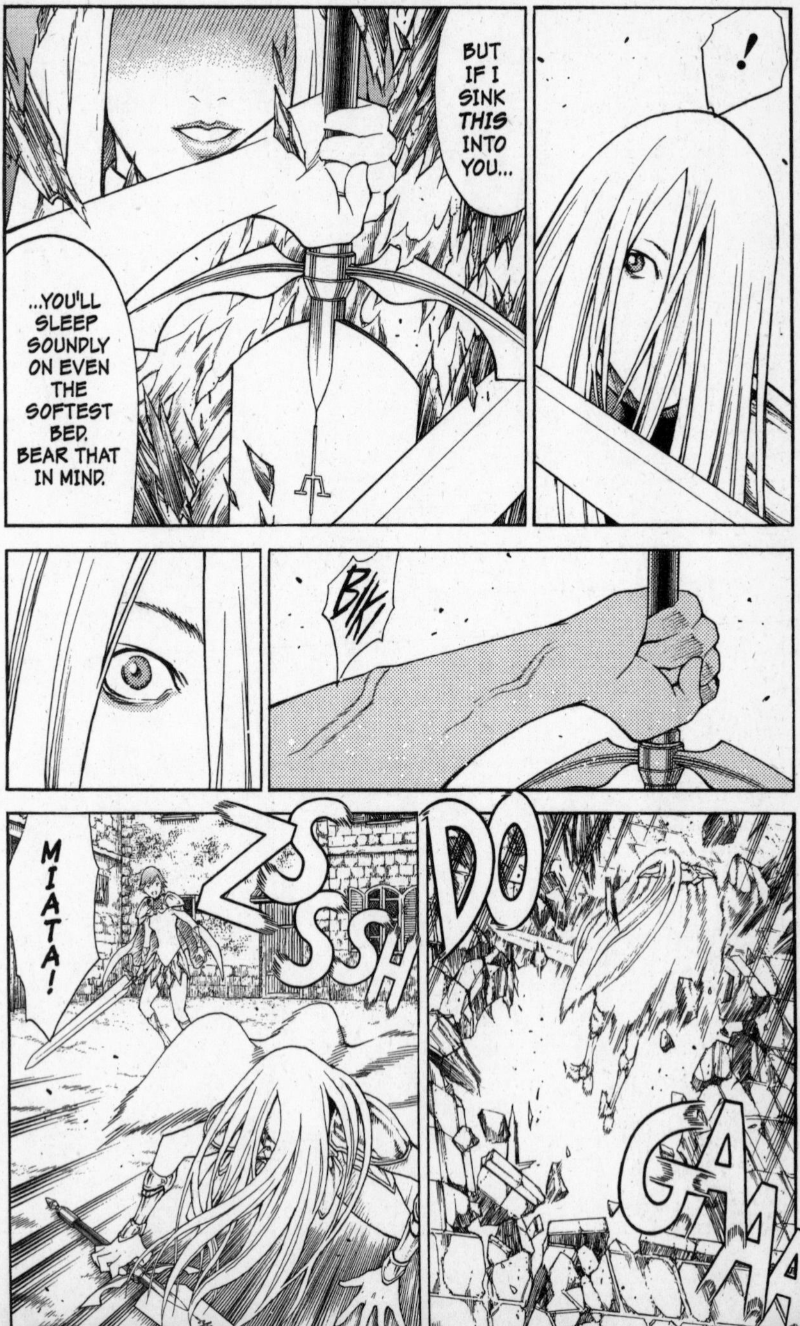
!
BUT IF I SINK THIS INTO YOU...
...YOU'LL SLEEP SOUNDLY ON EVEN THE SOFTEST BED. BEAR THAT IN MIND.
BIKI
DO
GAAAA
MIATA!
ZSSSH

READ THIS WAY

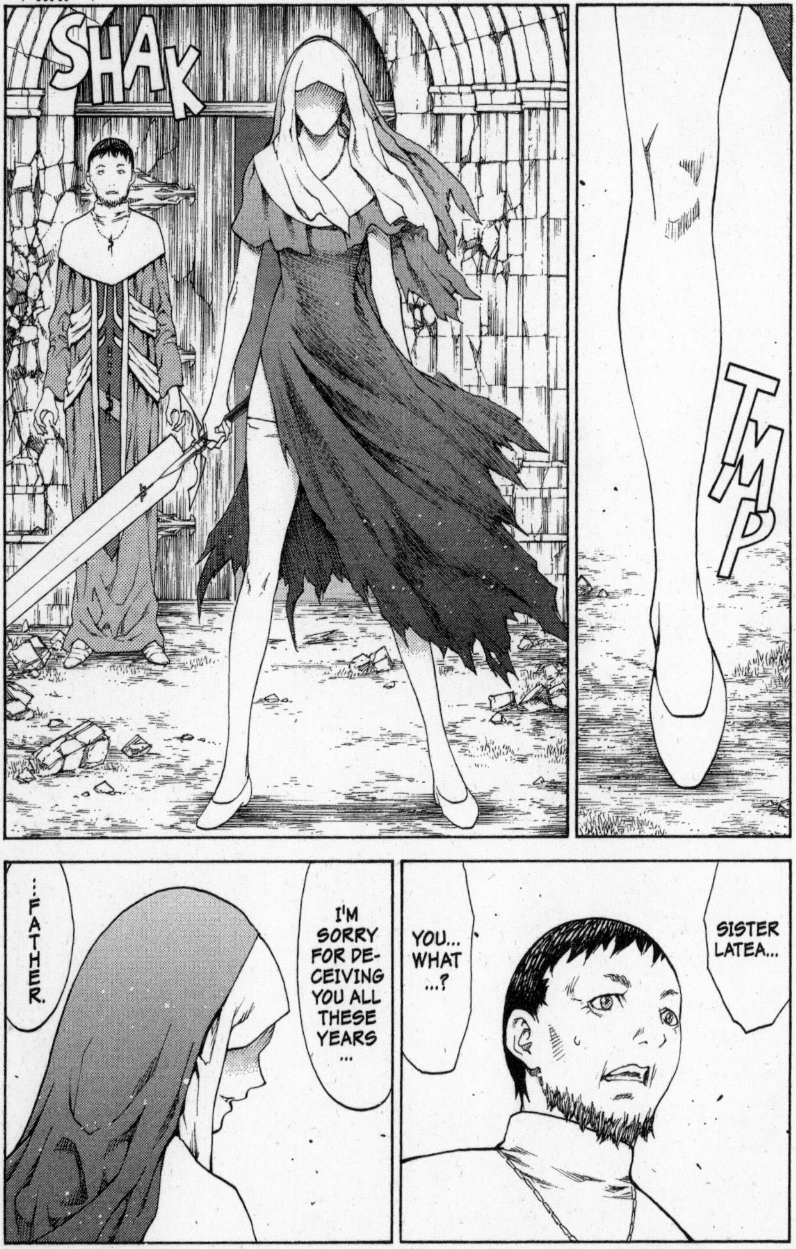
TMP
SHAK
SISTER LATEA...
YOU... WHAT ...?
I'M SORRY FOR DE-CEIVING YOU ALL THESE YEARS ...
...FATHER.

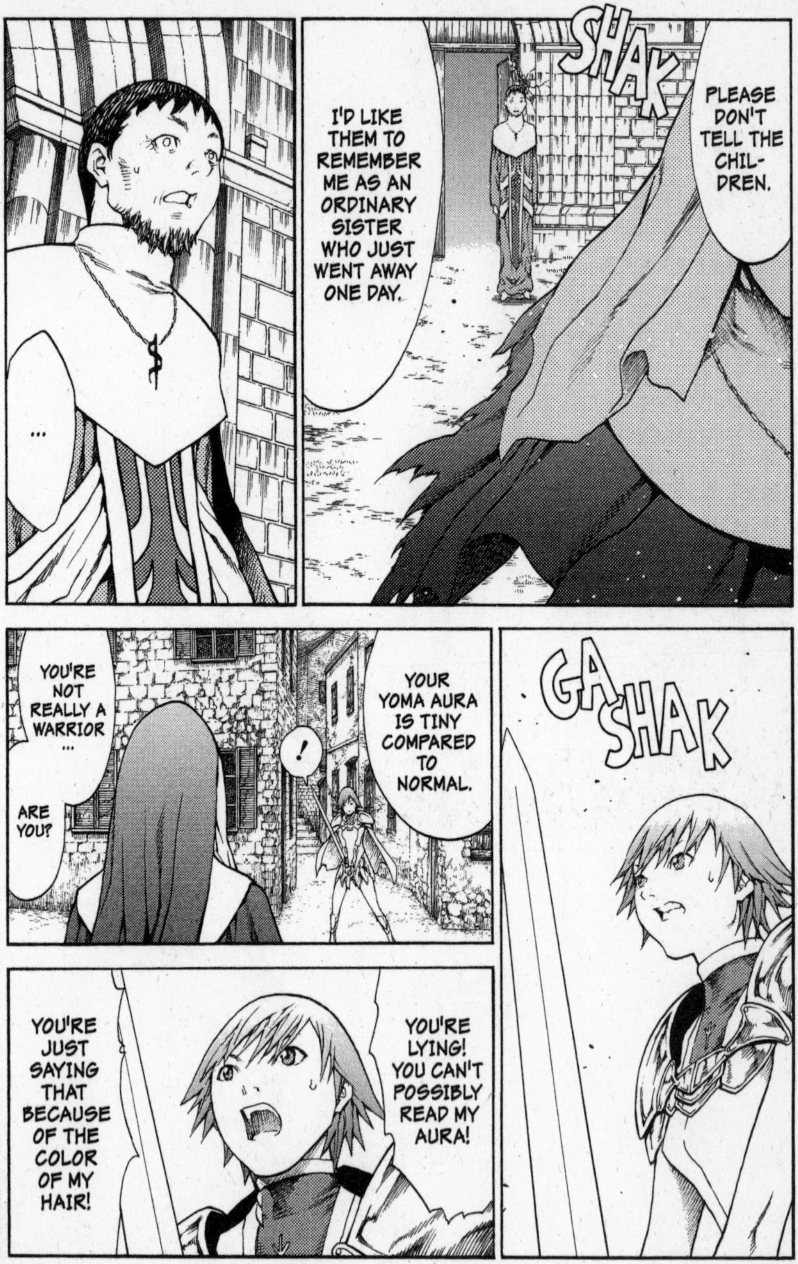

SHAK
PLEASE DON'T TELL THE CHIL-DREN.
I'D LIKE THEM TO REMEMBER ME AS AN ORDINARY SISTER WHO JUST WENT AWAY ONE DAY.
...
GA SHAK
YOUR YOMA AURA IS TINY COMPARED TO NORMAL.
!
YOU'RE NOT REALLY A WARRIOR ...
ARE YOU?
YOU'RE LYING! YOU CAN'T POSSIBLY READ MY AURA!
YOU'RE JUST SAYING THAT BECAUSE OF THE COLOR OF MY HAIR!

READ THIS WAY

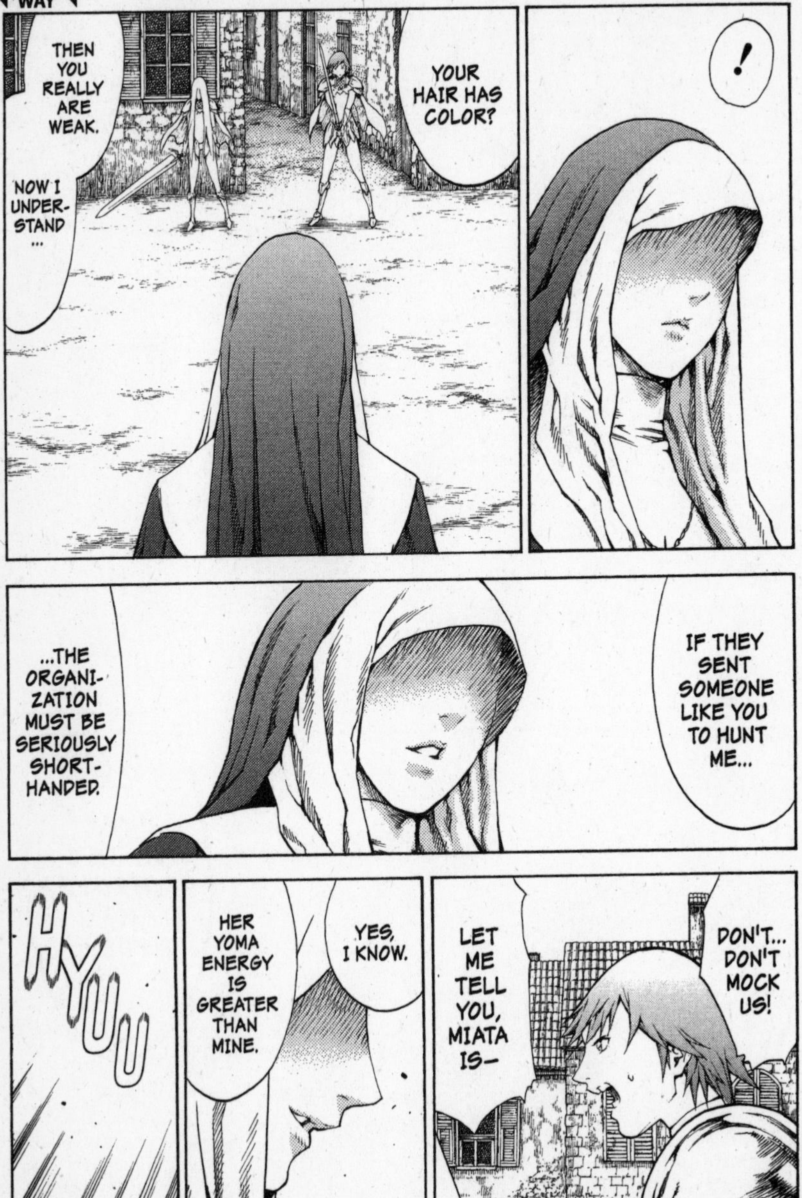
!
YOUR HAIR HAS COLOR?
THEN YOU REALLY ARE WEAK.
NOW I UNDERSTAND...
IF THEY SENT SOMEONE LIKE YOU TO HUNT ME...
...THE ORGANIZATION MUST BE SERIOUSLY SHORTHANDED.
DON'T... DON'T MOCK US!
LET ME TELL YOU, MIATA IS—
YES, I KNOW.
HER YOMA ENERGY IS GREATER THAN MINE.
HYUU

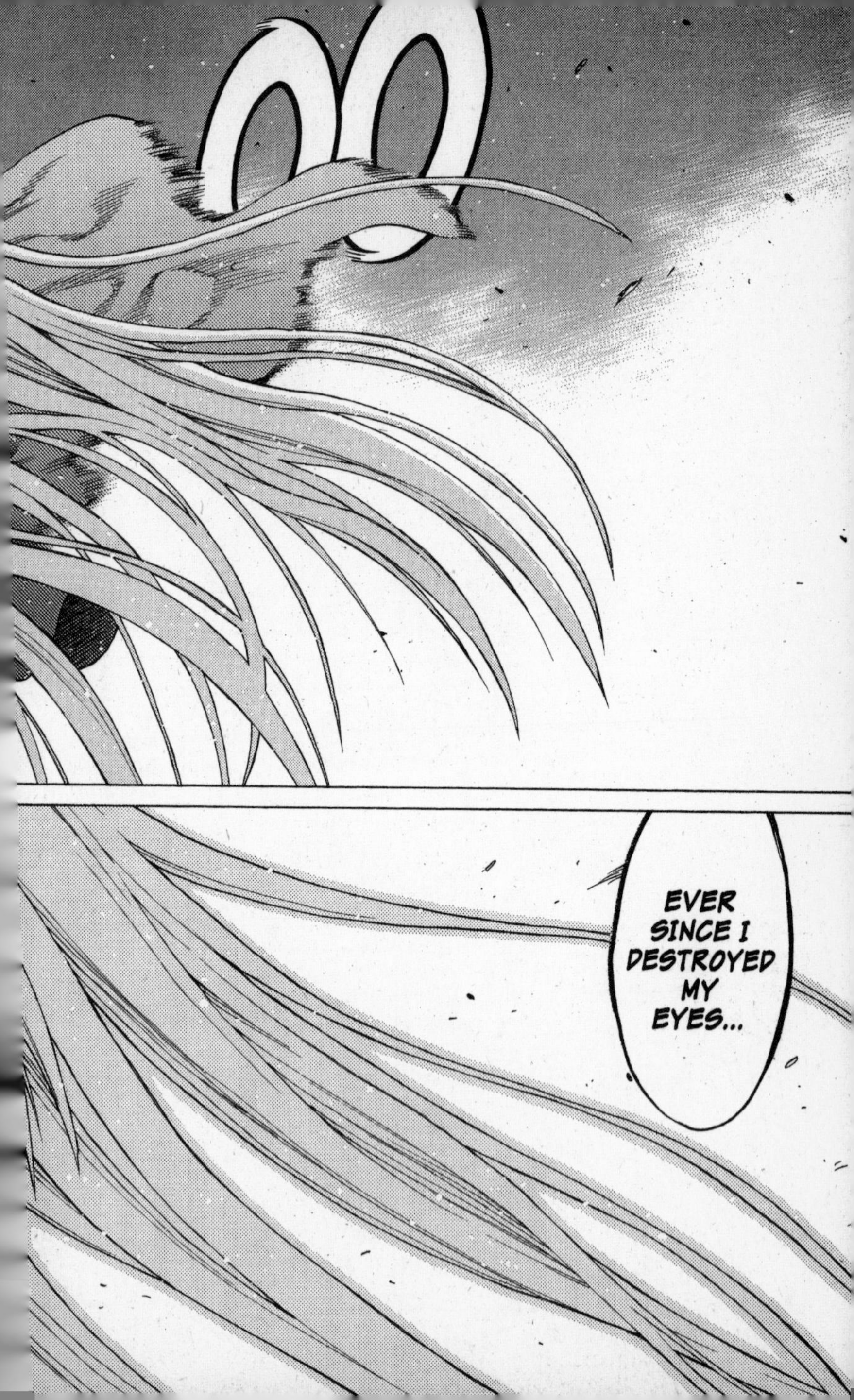
EVER SINCE I DESTROYED MY EYES...

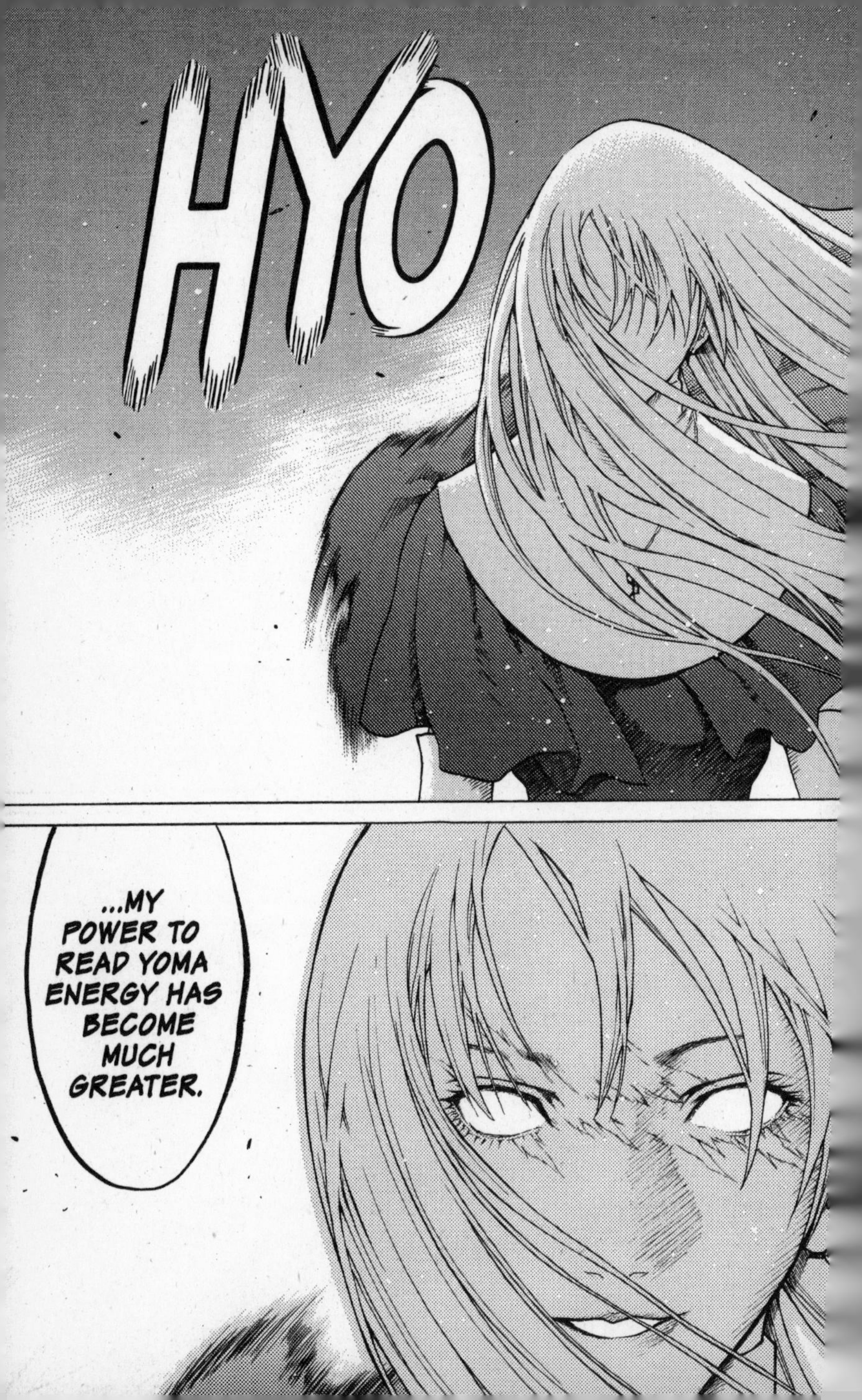
HYO
...MY POWER TO READ YOMA ENERGY HAS BECOME MUCH GREATER.

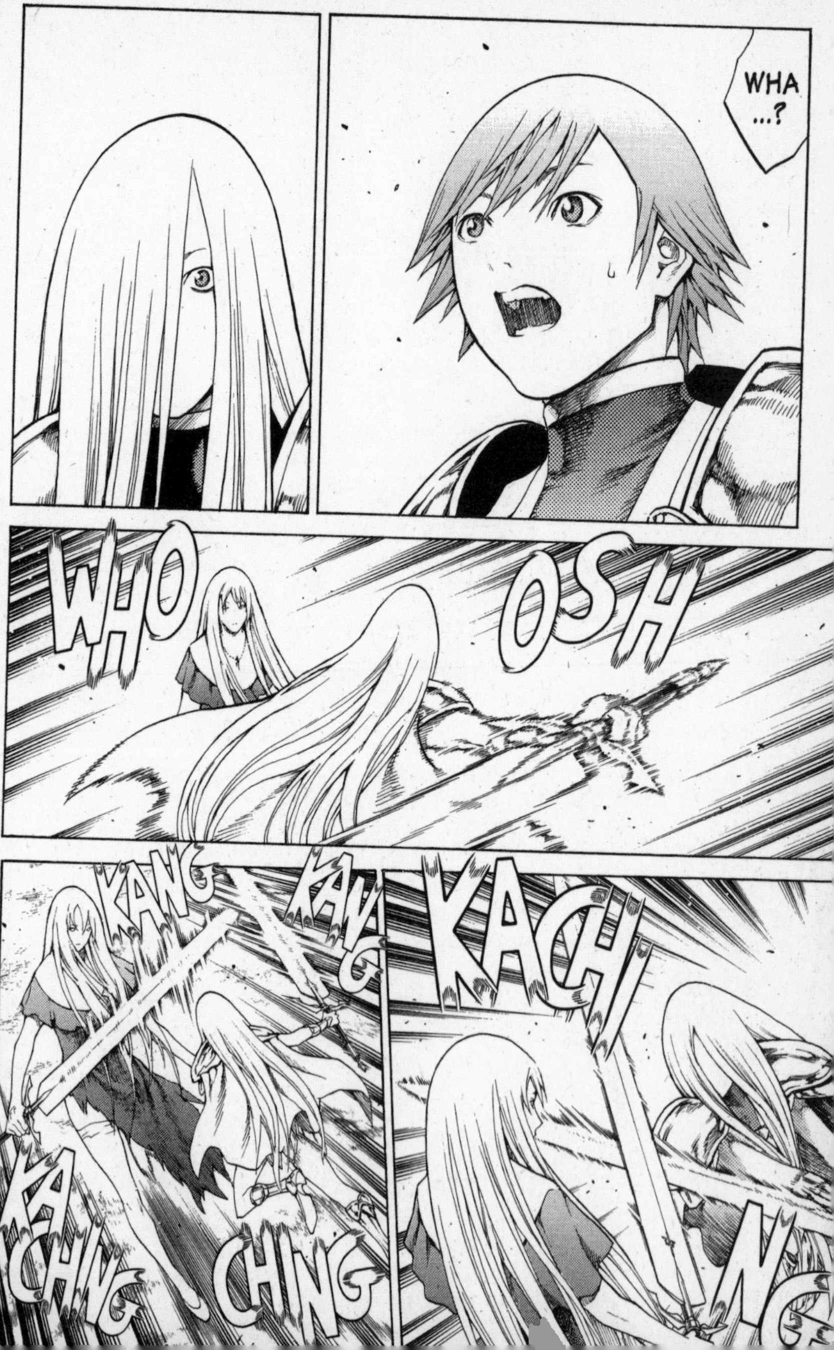
WHA ...?
WHOOSH
KACHI
NNG
KANG
KANG
KACHING
CHING

READ THIS WAY

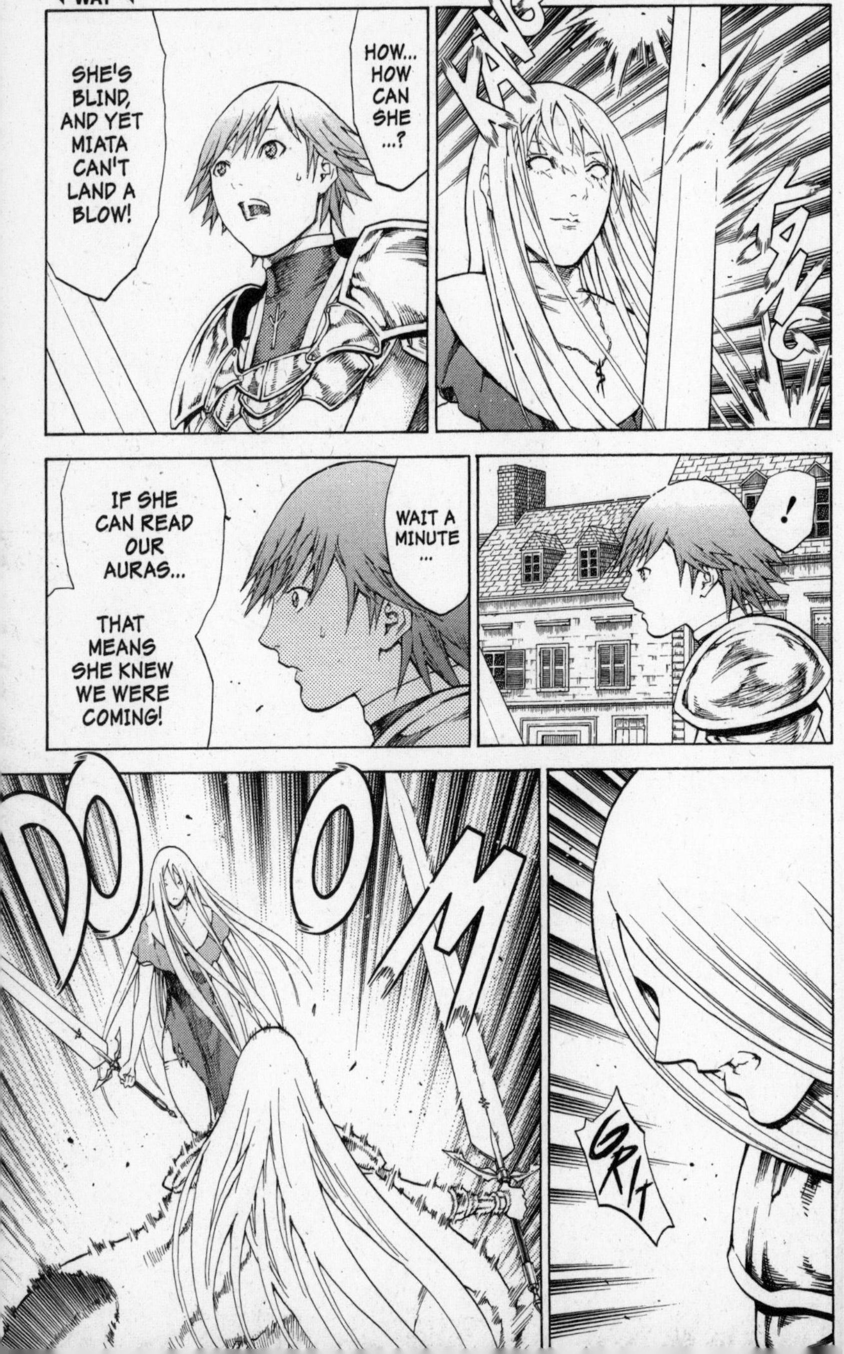
KANG
KANG
HOW... HOW CAN SHE ...?
SHE'S BLIND, AND YET MIATA CAN'T LAND A BLOW!
!
WAIT A MINUTE ...
IF SHE CAN READ OUR AURAS...
THAT MEANS SHE KNEW WE WERE COMING!
GRIT
DOOM

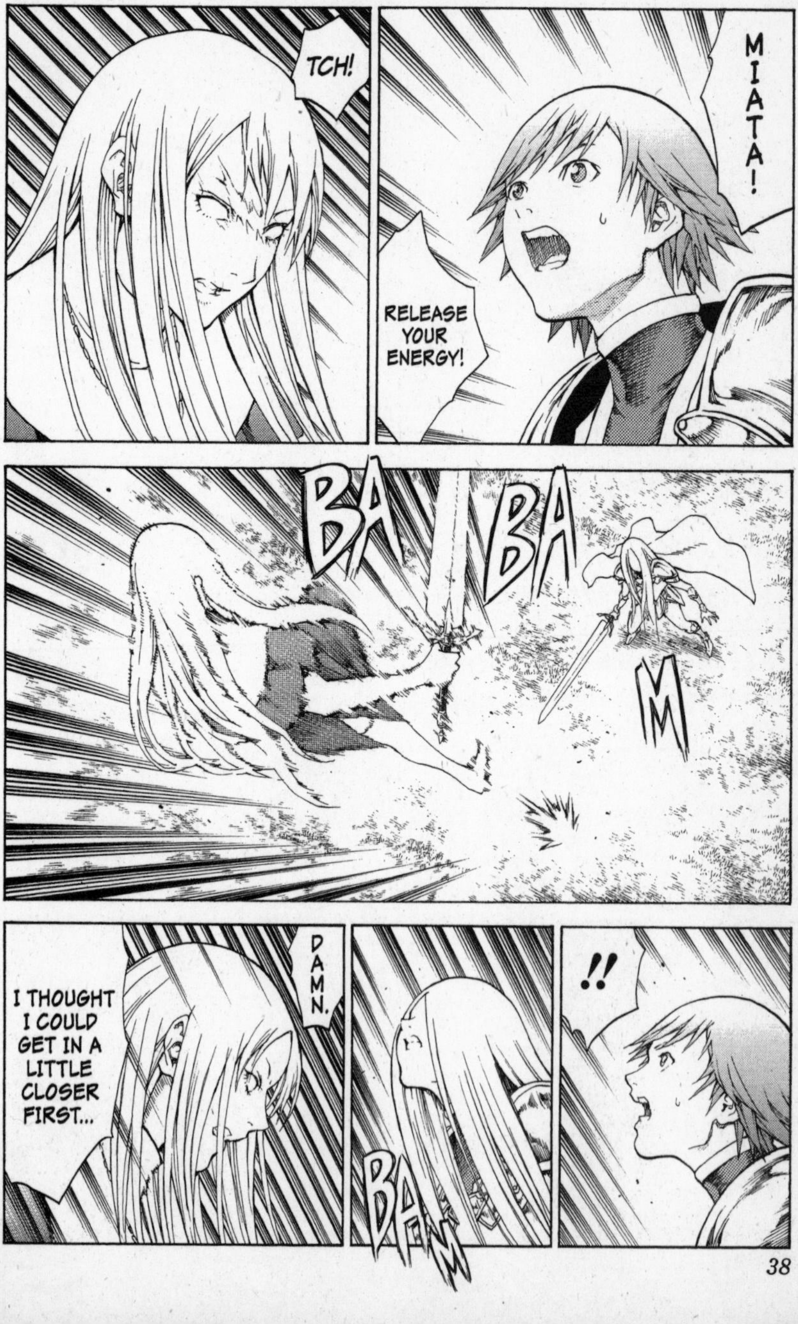
MIATA!
RELEASE YOUR ENERGY!
TCH!
BABABAMM
!!
BAM
DAMN.
I THOUGHT I COULD GET IN A LITTLE CLOSER FIRST...

READ THIS WAY

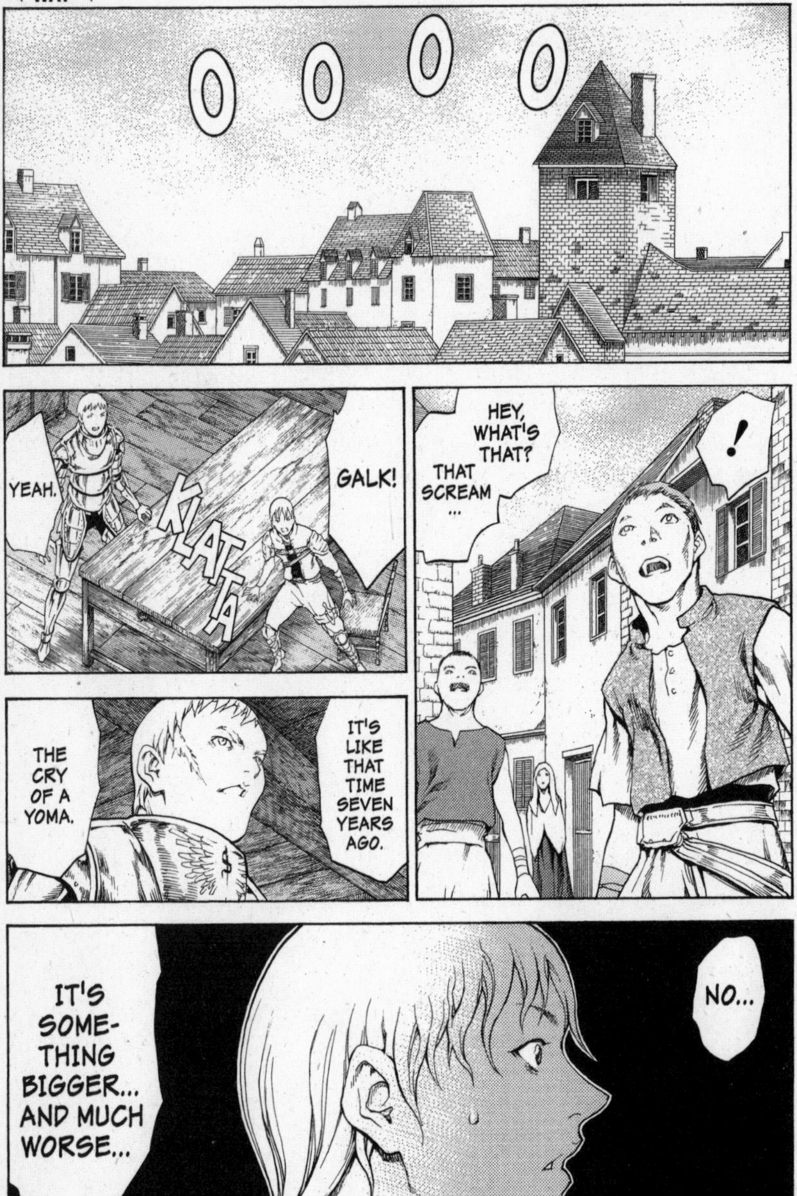
OOOO
!
HEY, WHAT'S THAT?
THAT SCREAM ...
GALK!
KLATATA
YEAH.
IT'S LIKE THAT TIME SEVEN YEARS AGO.
THE CRY OF A YOMA.
NO...
IT'S SOME-THING BIGGER... AND MUCH WORSE...

クレイモア
Claymore

Scene 75: A Child Weapon, Part 3

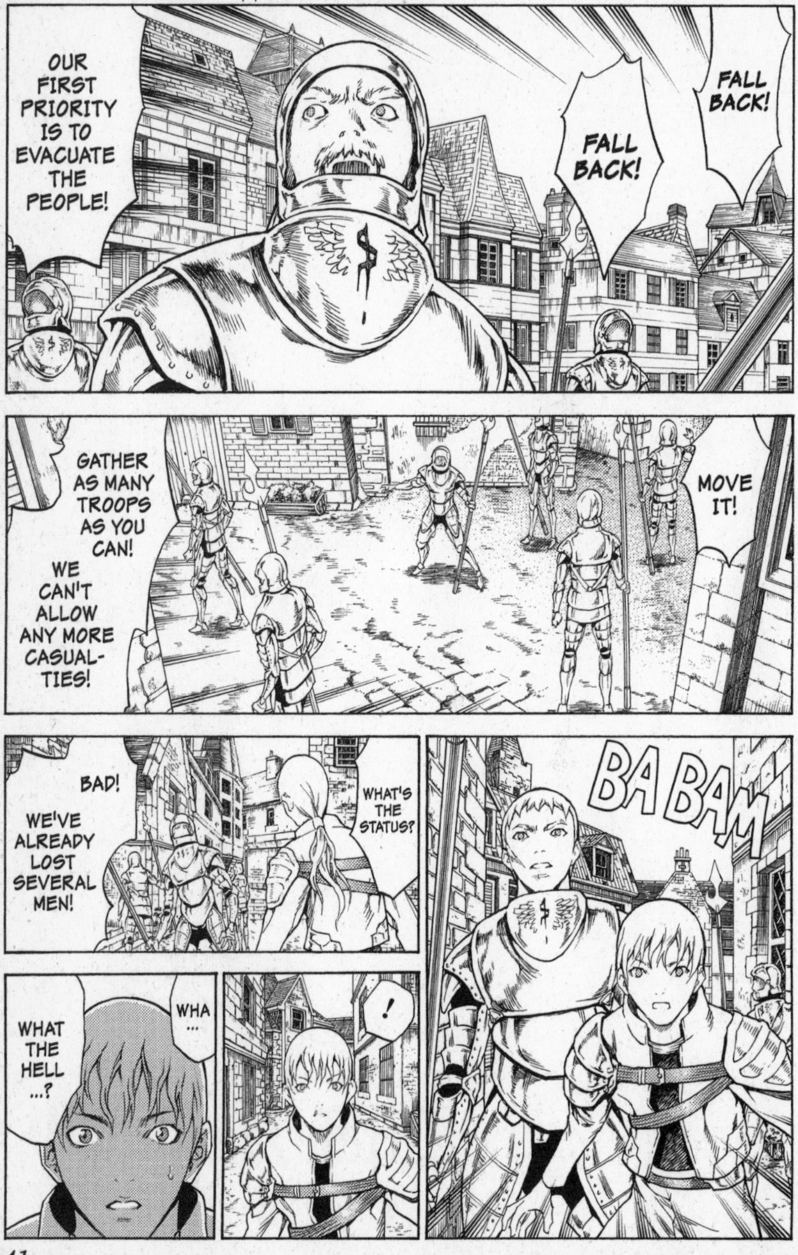
FALL BACK!
FALL BACK!
OUR FIRST PRIORITY IS TO EVACUATE THE PEOPLE!
MOVE IT!
GATHER AS MANY TROOPS AS YOU CAN!
WE CAN'T ALLOW ANY MORE CASUAL-TIES!
BA BAM
WHAT'S THE STATUS?
BAD!
WE'VE ALREADY LOST SEVERAL MEN!
!
WHA ...
WHAT THE HELL ...?

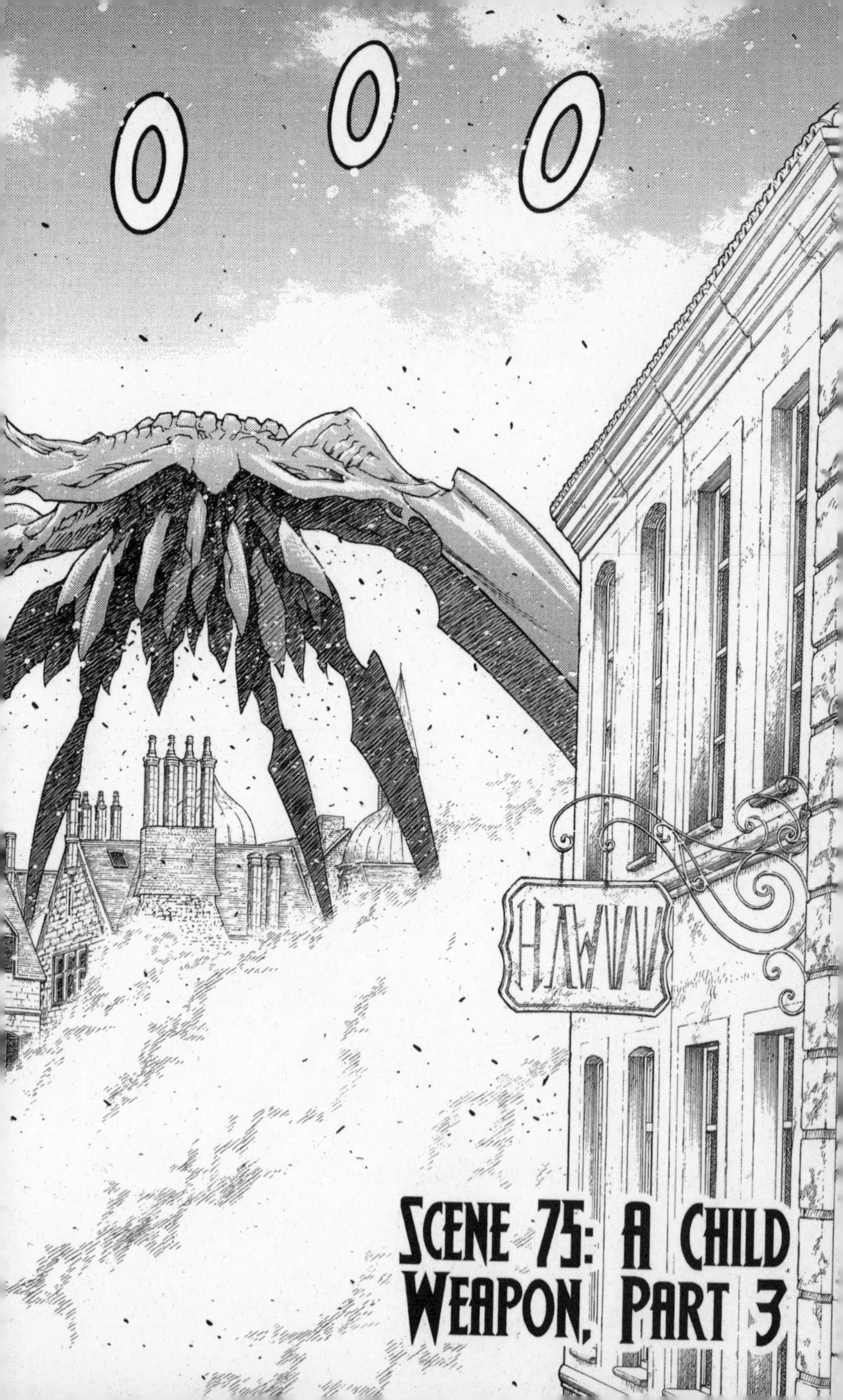
SCENE 75: A CHILD
WEAPON, PART 3

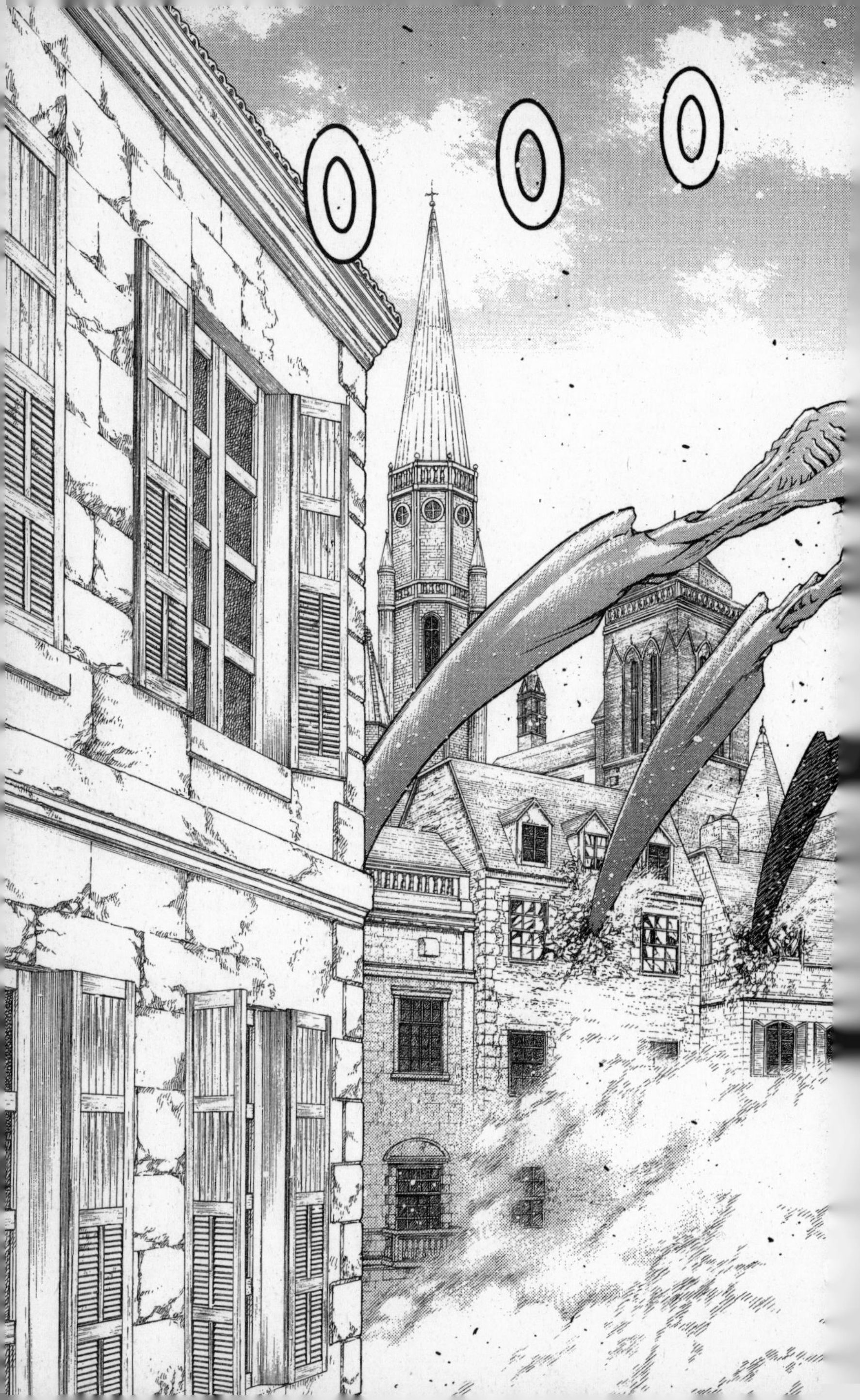
OOO

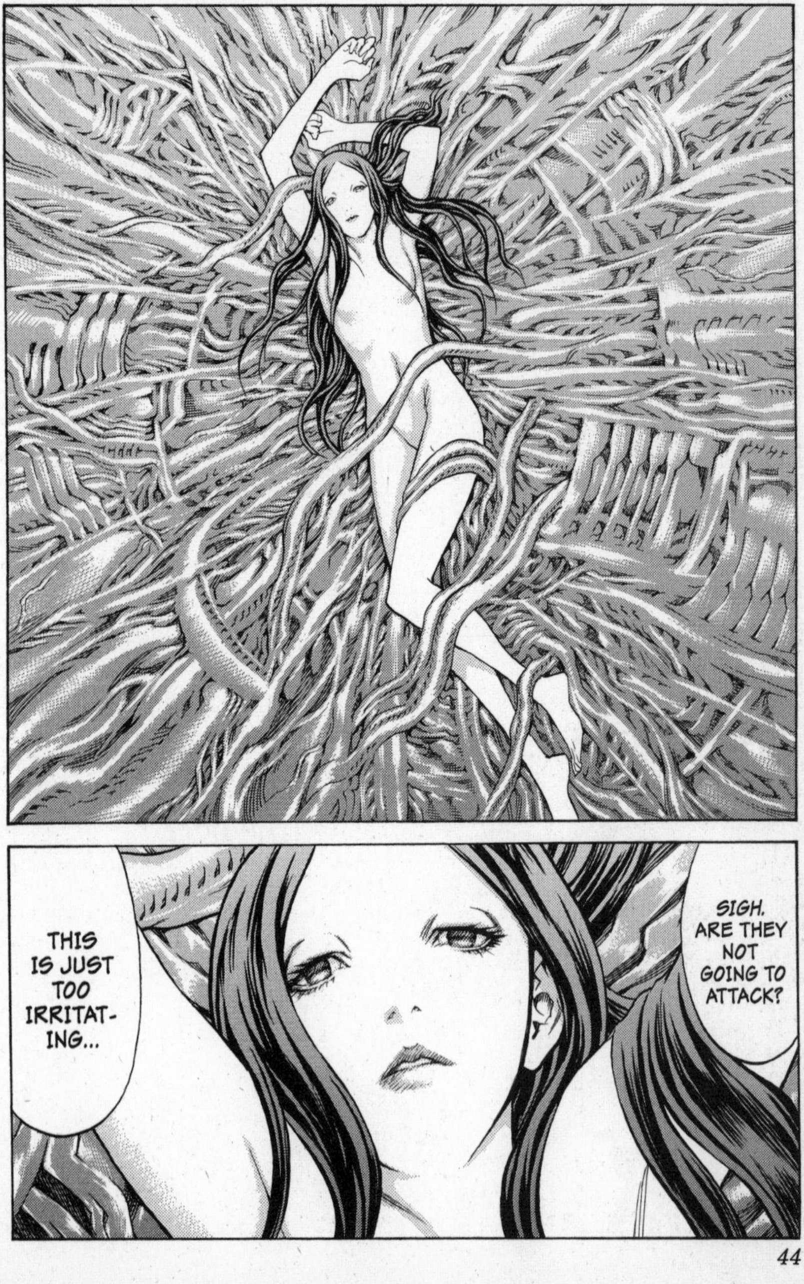
SIGH. ARE THEY NOT GOING TO ATTACK?
THIS IS JUST TOO IRRITAT-ING...

READ THIS WAY

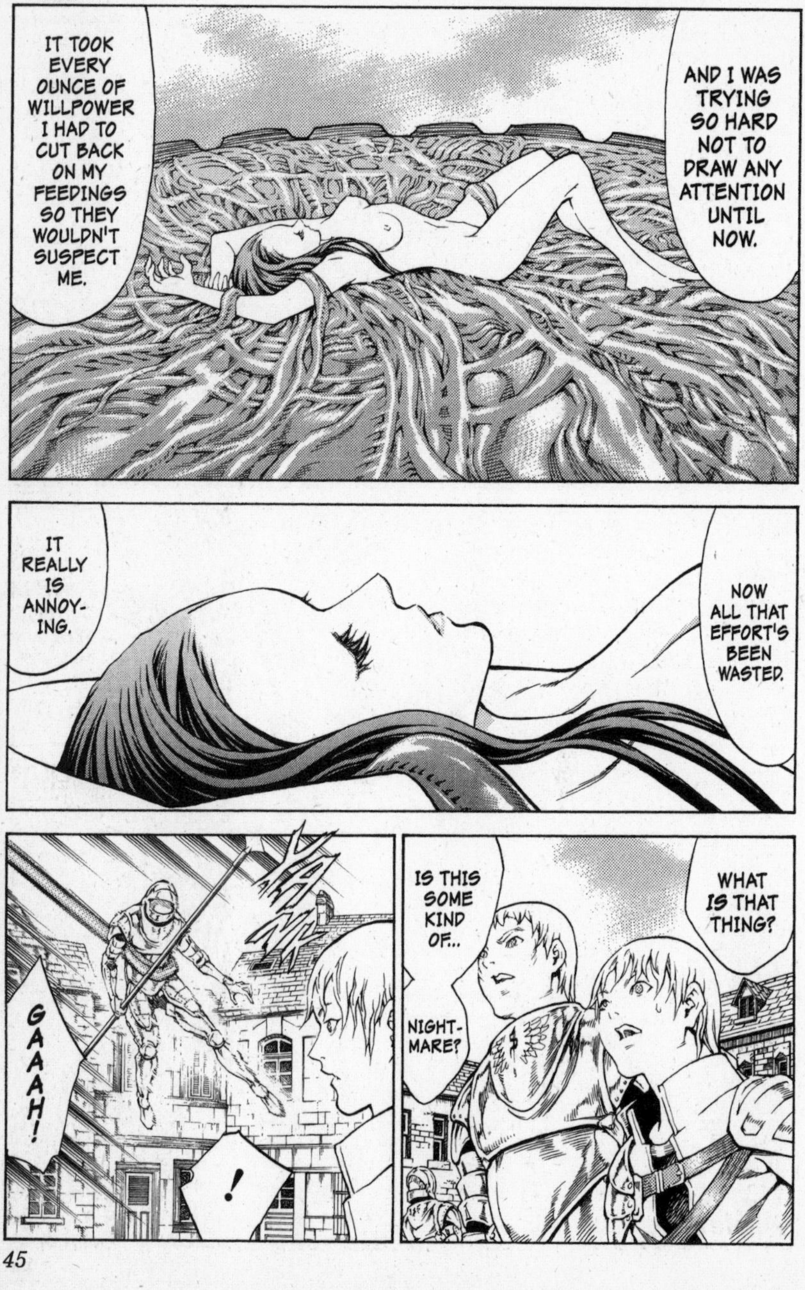
AND I WAS TRYING SO HARD NOT TO DRAW ANY ATTENTION UNTIL NOW.
IT TOOK EVERY OUNCE OF WILLPOWER I HAD TO CUT BACK ON MY FEEDINGS SO THEY WOULDN'T SUSPECT ME.
NOW ALL THAT EFFORT'S BEEN WASTED.
IT REALLY IS ANNOYING.
WHAT IS THAT THING?
IS THIS SOME KIND OF...
NIGHTMARE?
YANK
GAAAH!
!

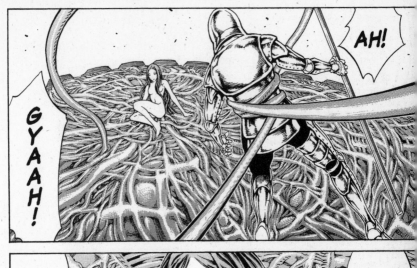

AH!

GYAAH!

I'LL BE GENTLE ...

DON'T BE AFRAID. IT'S ALL RIGHT.

AH...

GH...

AH...

AH...

SHAK

SHP

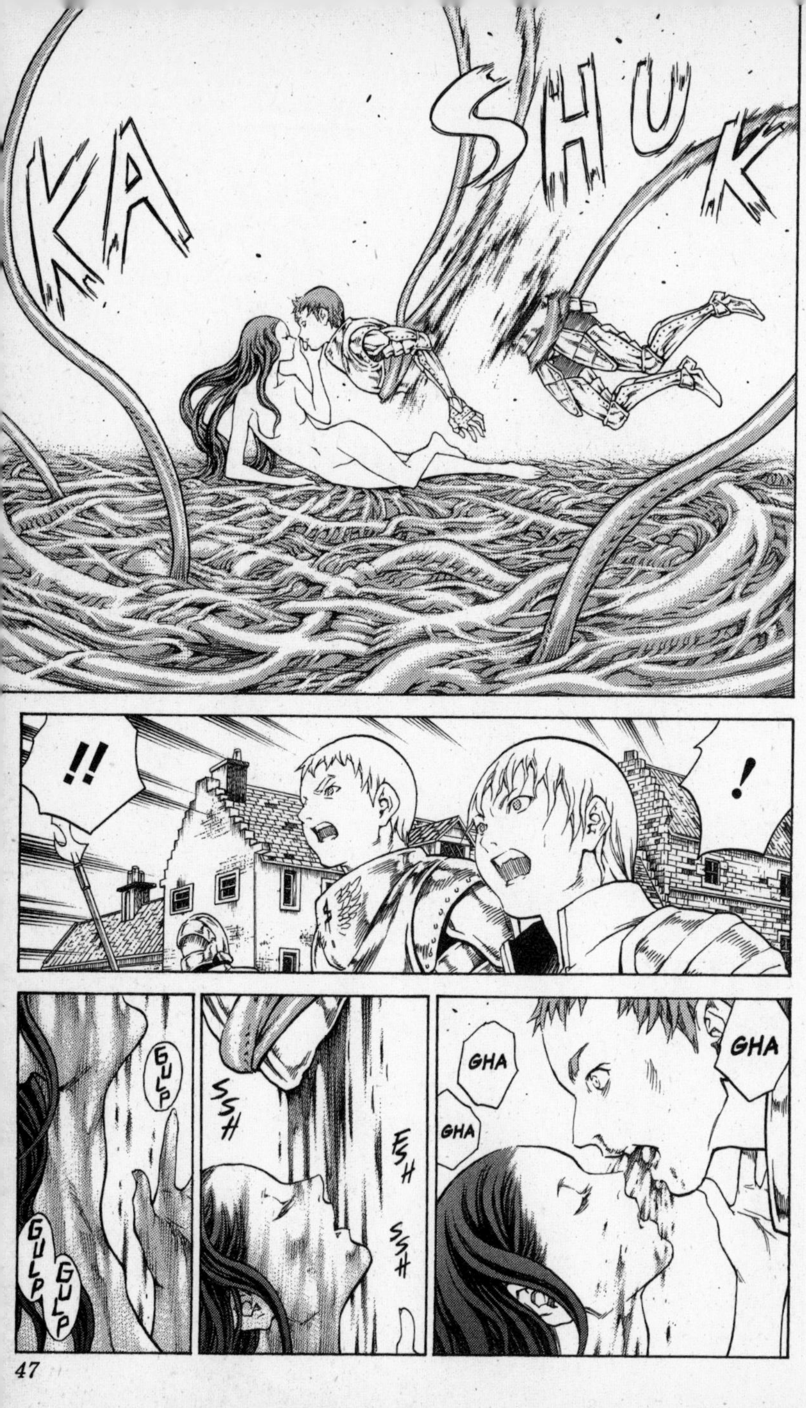

KA SHUK
!
!!
GHA
GHA
GHA
FSH
SSH
SSH
GULP
GULP
GULP

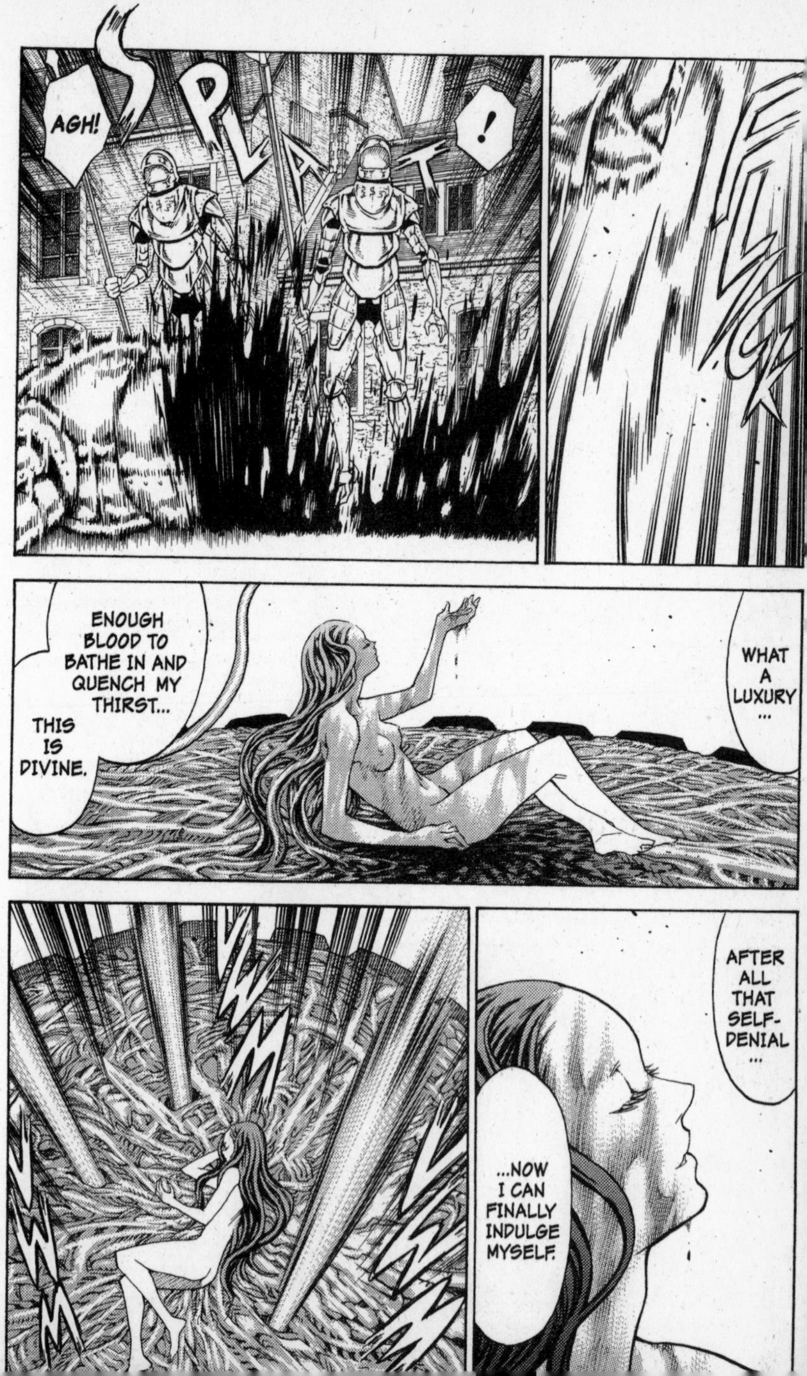

SPLAT
AGH!
!
WHAT A LUXURY...
ENOUGH BLOOD TO BATHE IN AND QUENCH MY THIRST...
THIS IS DIVINE.
AFTER ALL THAT SELF-DENIAL...
...NOW I CAN FINALLY INDULGE MYSELF.

READ THIS WAY

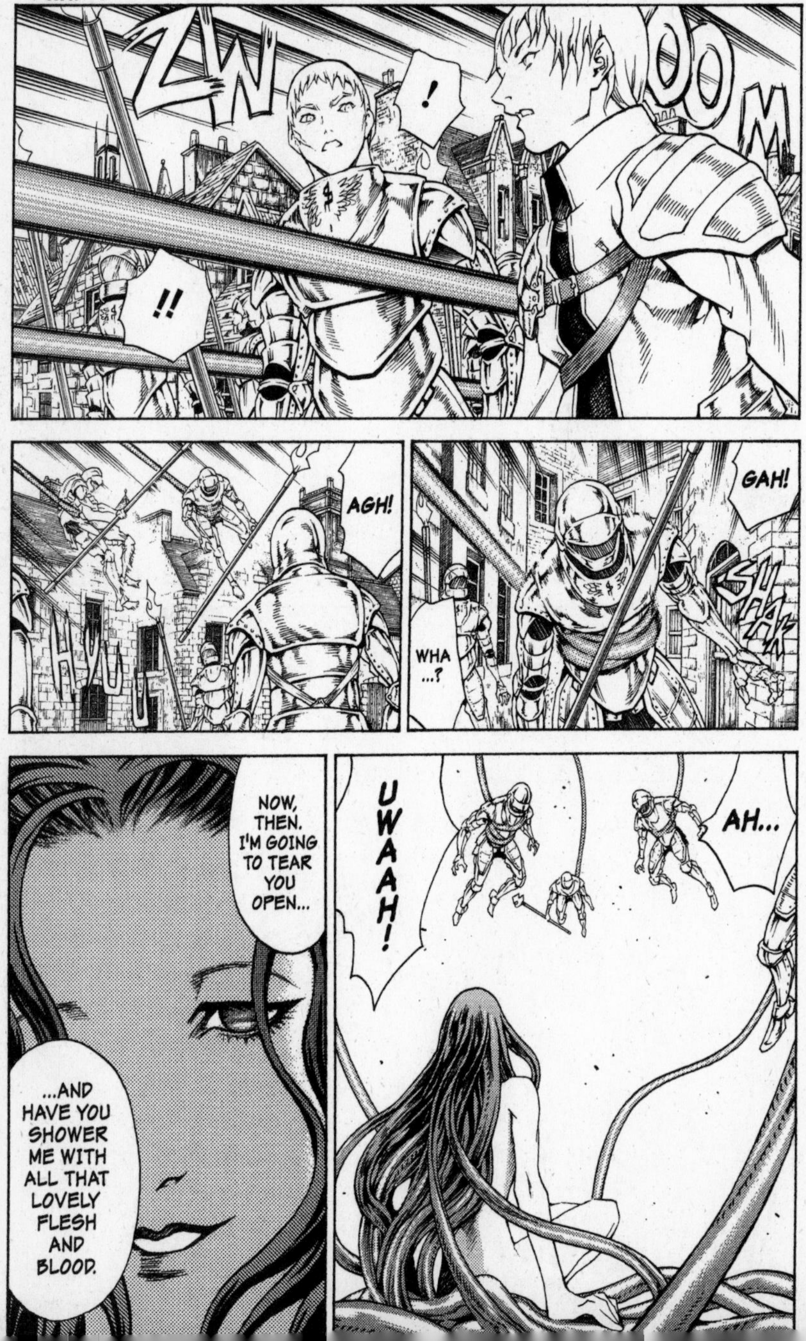

OOM
!
ZW
!!
GAH!
KSHAK
WHA ...?
AGH!
HYUU
AH...
UWAAAH!
NOW, THEN. I'M GOING TO TEAR YOU OPEN...
...AND HAVE YOU SHOWER ME WITH ALL THAT LOVELY FLESH AND BLOOD.

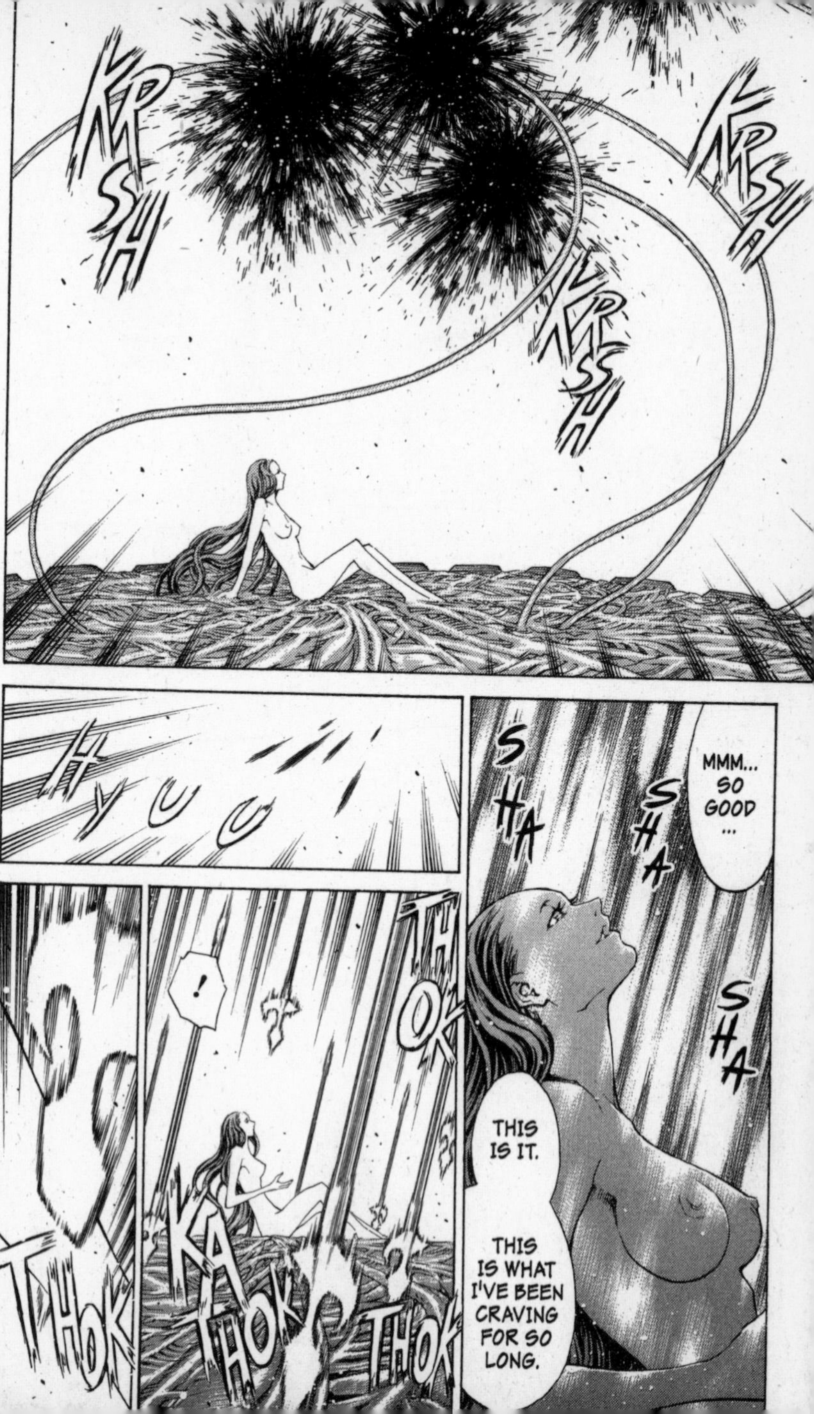
KRRSSH
KRRSSH
KRRSSH
SHA
SHA
MMM... SO GOOD ...
SHA
THIS IS IT.
THIS IS WHAT I'VE BEEN CRAVING FOR SO LONG.
HYUU
THOK
!
KA THOK
THOK
THOK

READ THIS WAY

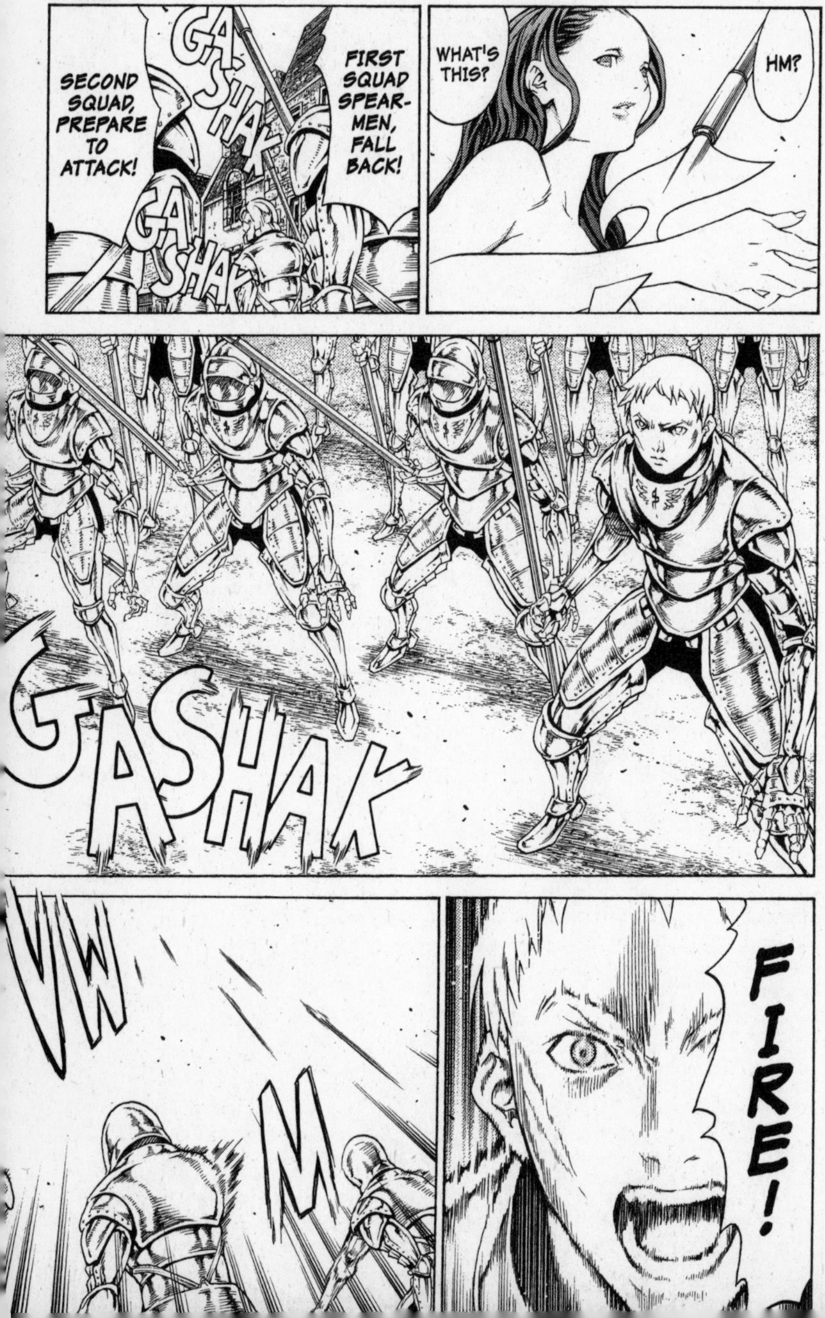
HM?
WHAT'S THIS?
FIRST SQUAD SPEARMEN, FALL BACK!
GASHAK
SECOND SQUAD, PREPARE TO ATTACK!
GASHAK
GASHAK
FIRE!
VWM

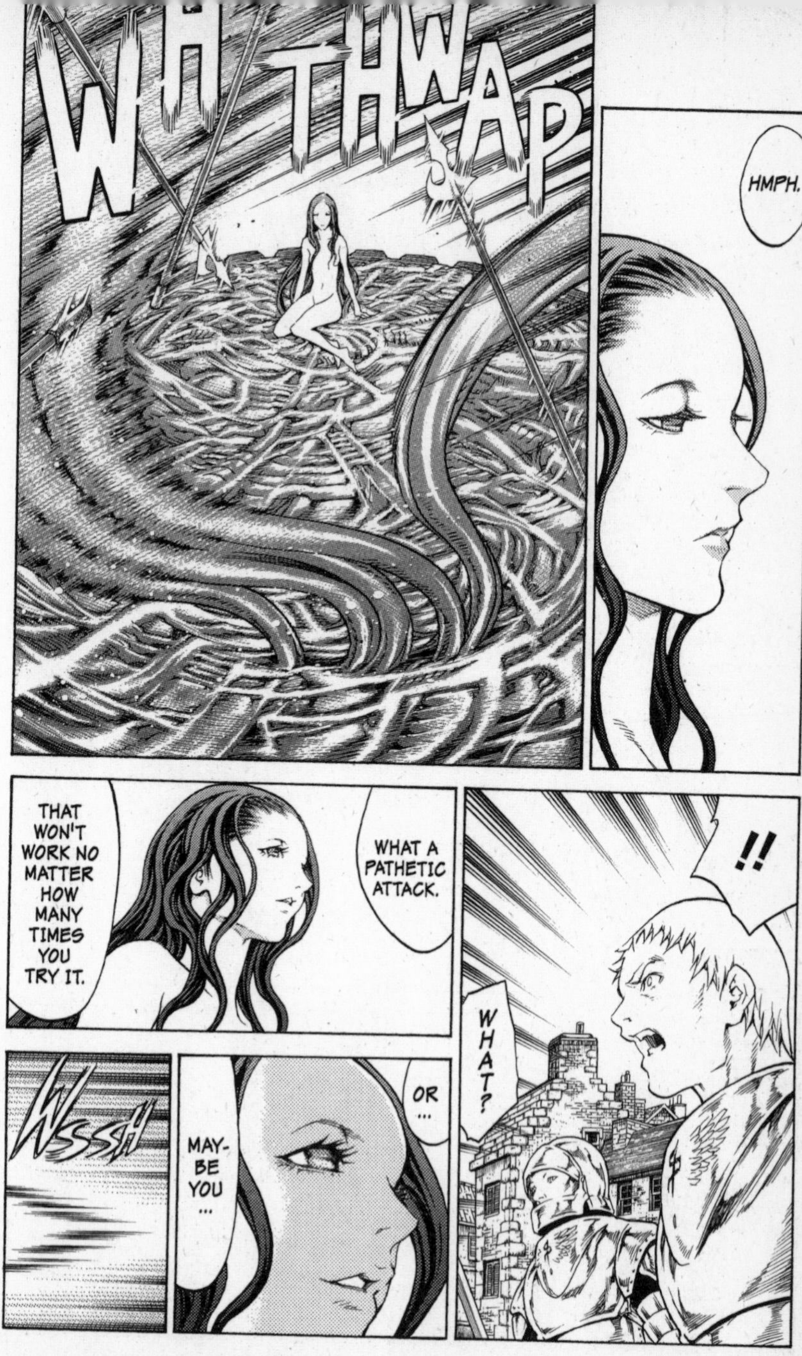
HMPH.
THWAP
WH
!!
WHAT?
WHAT A PATHETIC ATTACK.
THAT WON'T WORK NO MATTER HOW MANY TIMES YOU TRY IT.
OR ...
MAY-BE YOU ...
WSSSH

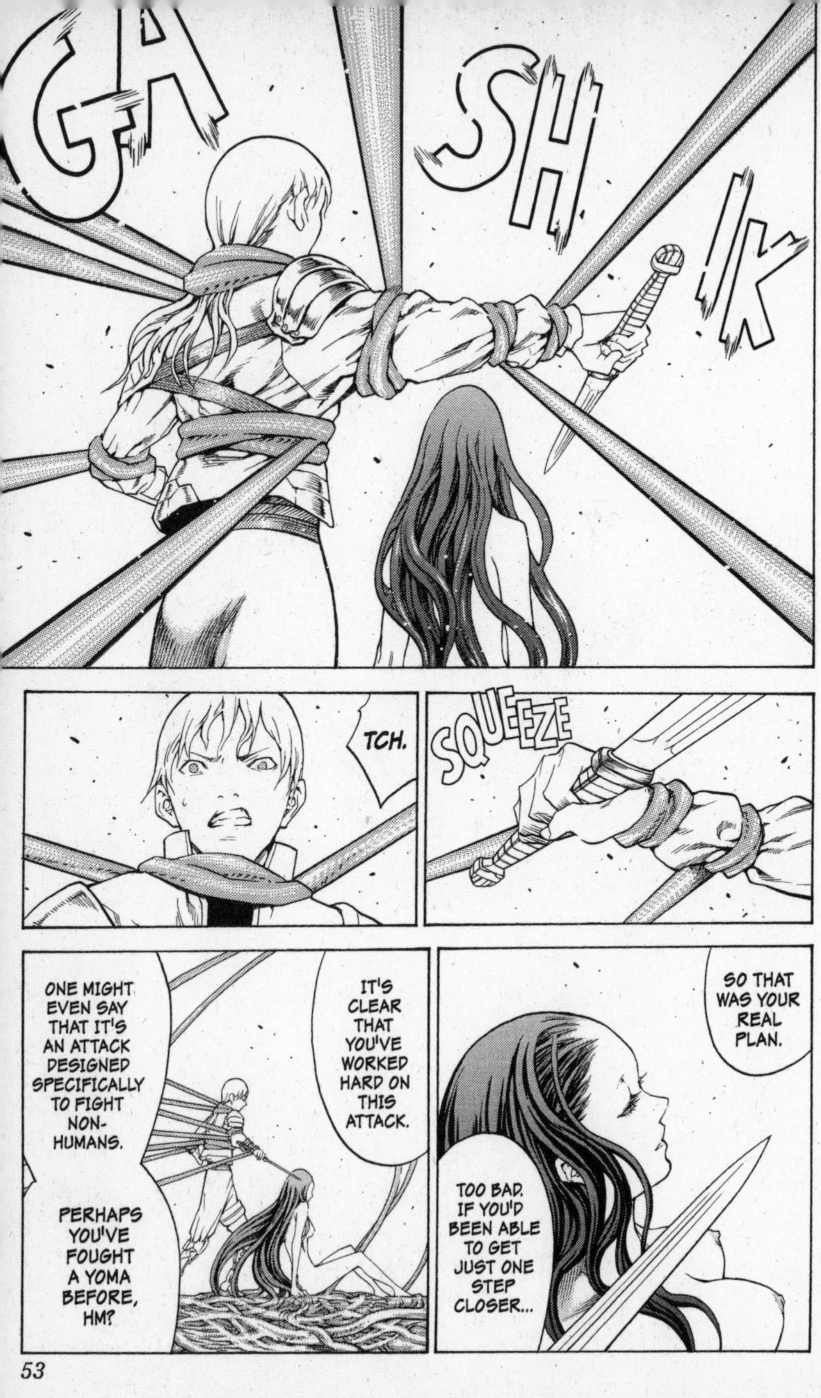
GASHIK
SQUEEZE
TCH.
SO THAT WAS YOUR REAL PLAN.
TOO BAD. IF YOU'D BEEN ABLE TO GET JUST ONE STEP CLOSER...
IT'S CLEAR THAT YOU'VE WORKED HARD ON THIS ATTACK.
ONE MIGHT EVEN SAY THAT IT'S AN ATTACK DESIGNED SPECIFICALLY TO FIGHT NON-HUMANS.
PERHAPS YOU'VE FOUGHT A YOMA BEFORE, HM?

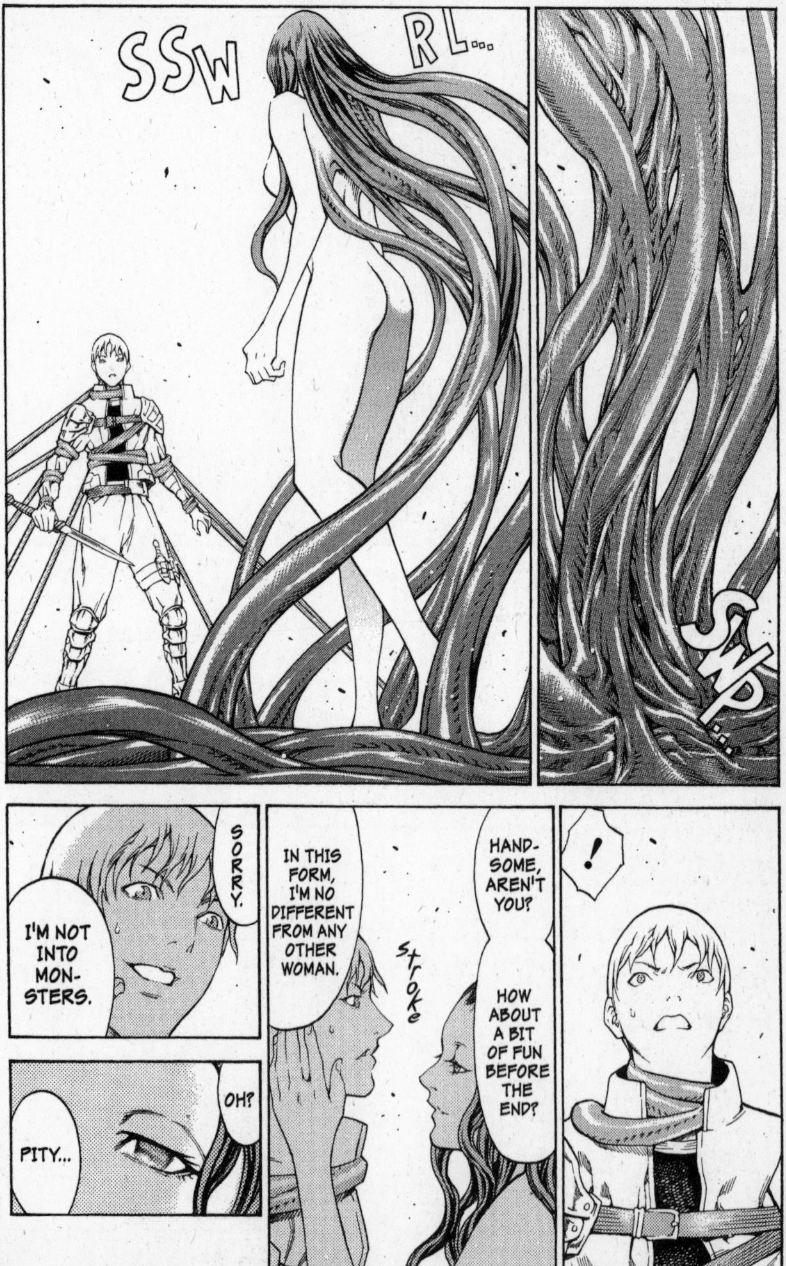
SWP...
SSWRL...
!
HANDSOME, AREN'T YOU?
HOW ABOUT A BIT OF FUN BEFORE THE END?
stroke
IN THIS FORM, I'M NO DIFFERENT FROM ANY OTHER WOMAN.
SORRY.
I'M NOT INTO MONSTERS.
OH?
PITY...

READ THIS WAY

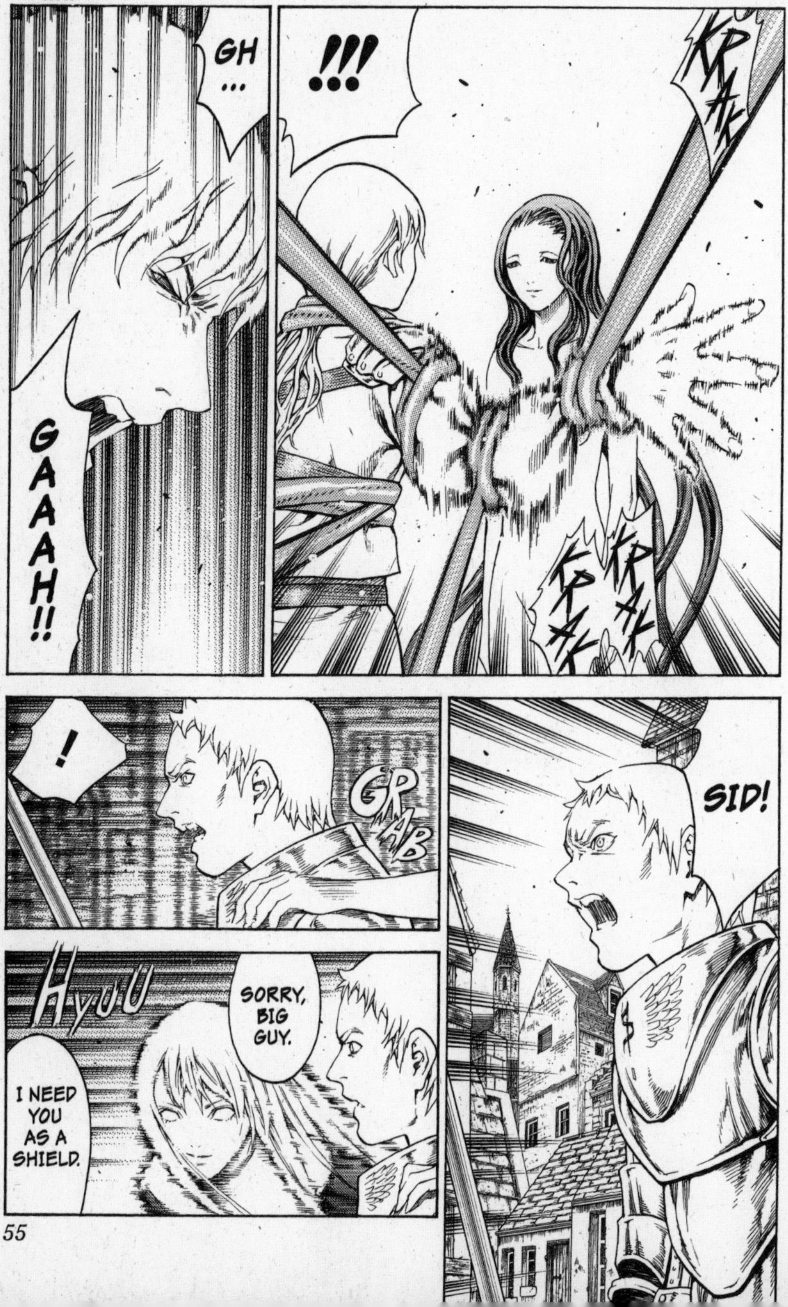
KRAK
!!!
KRAK
KRAK
GH...
GAAAAH!!
SID!
!
GRAB
SORRY, BIG GUY.
HYUU
I NEED YOU AS A SHIELD.

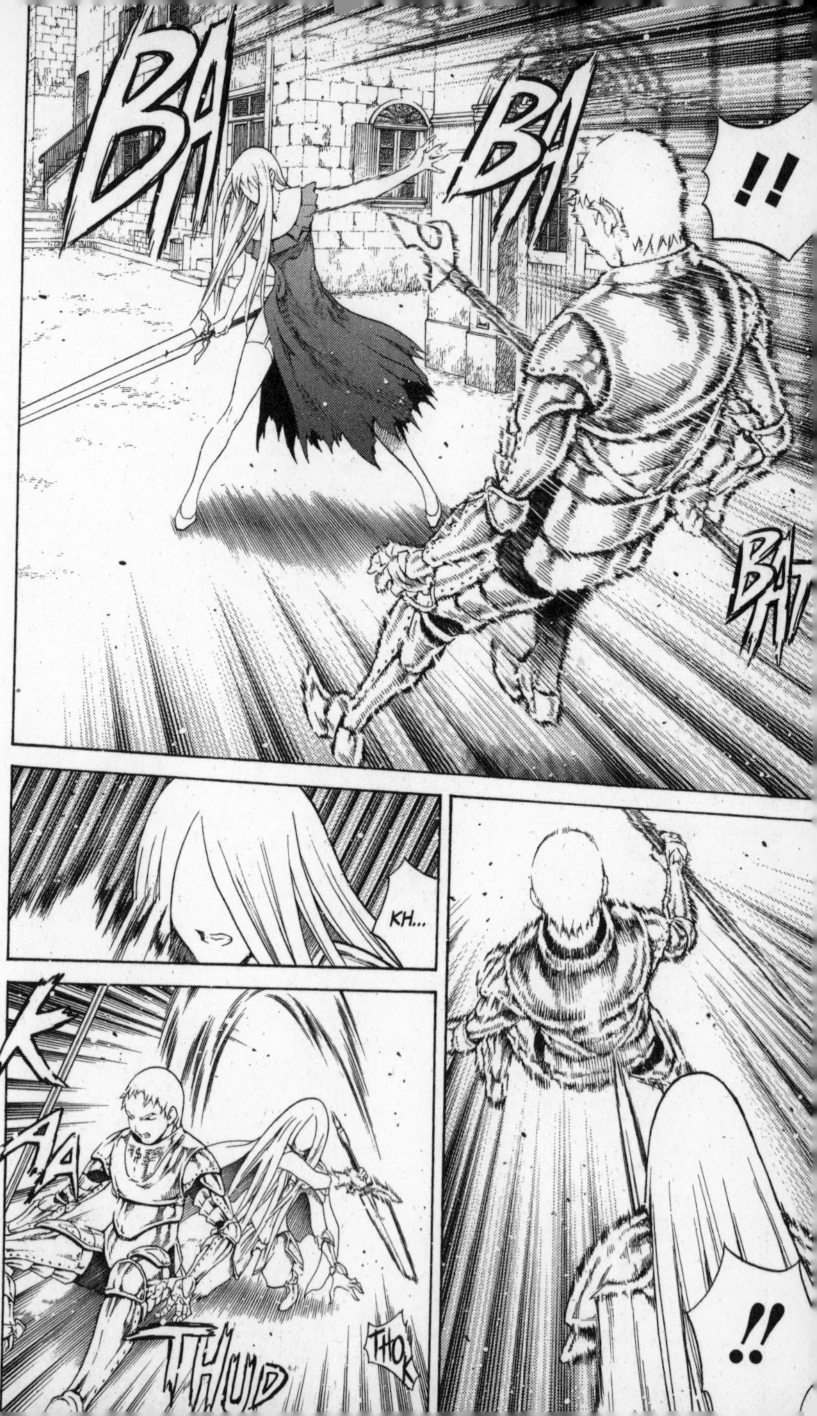
!!
BA
BA
BAT
KH...
!!
K
AA
THOK
THUD

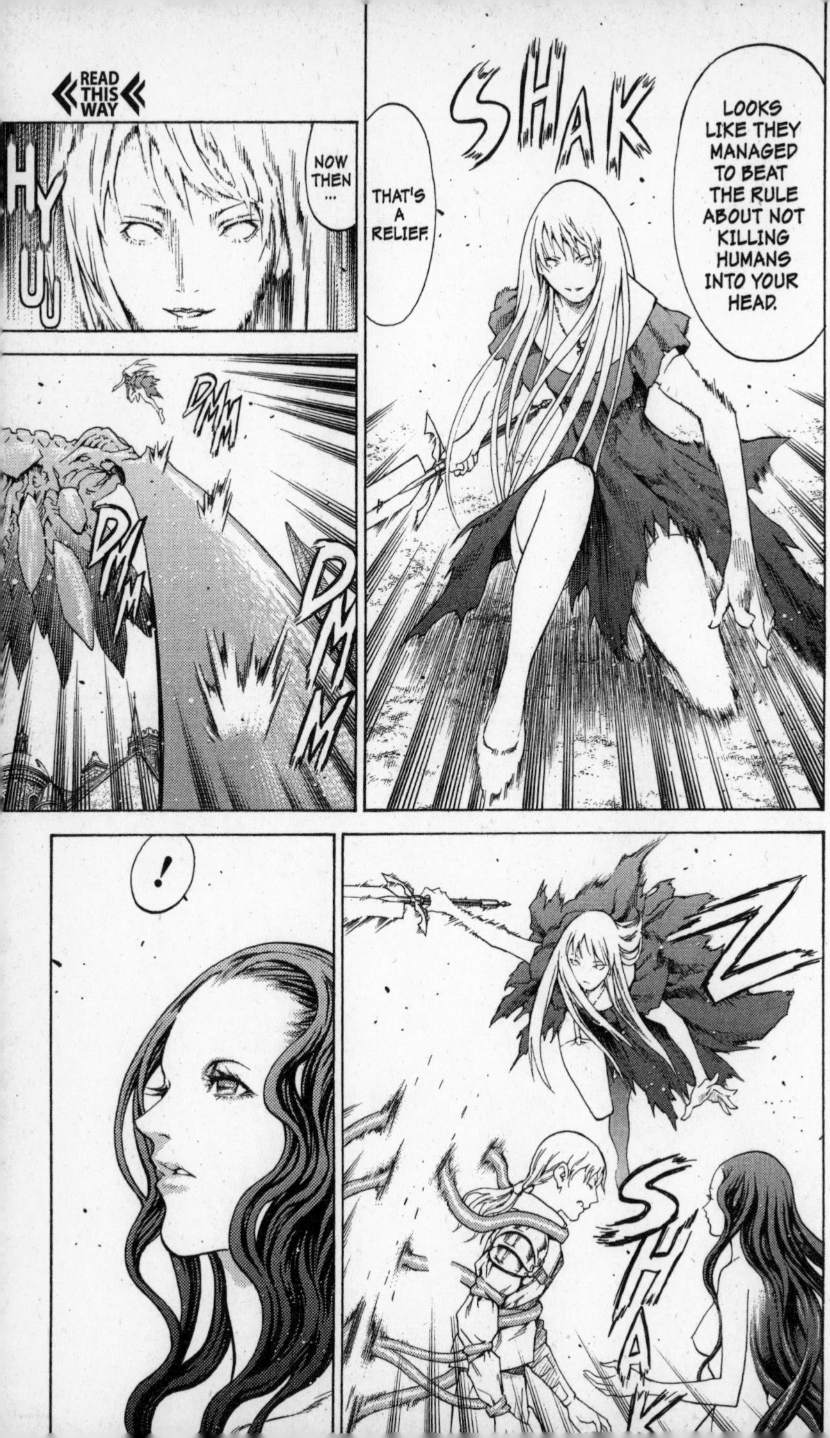
READ THIS WAY
SHAK
LOOKS LIKE THEY MANAGED TO BEAT THE RULE ABOUT NOT KILLING HUMANS INTO YOUR HEAD.
THAT'S A RELIEF.
NOW THEN ...
HYUU
DMM
DMM
DMMM
ZN
SHA
!

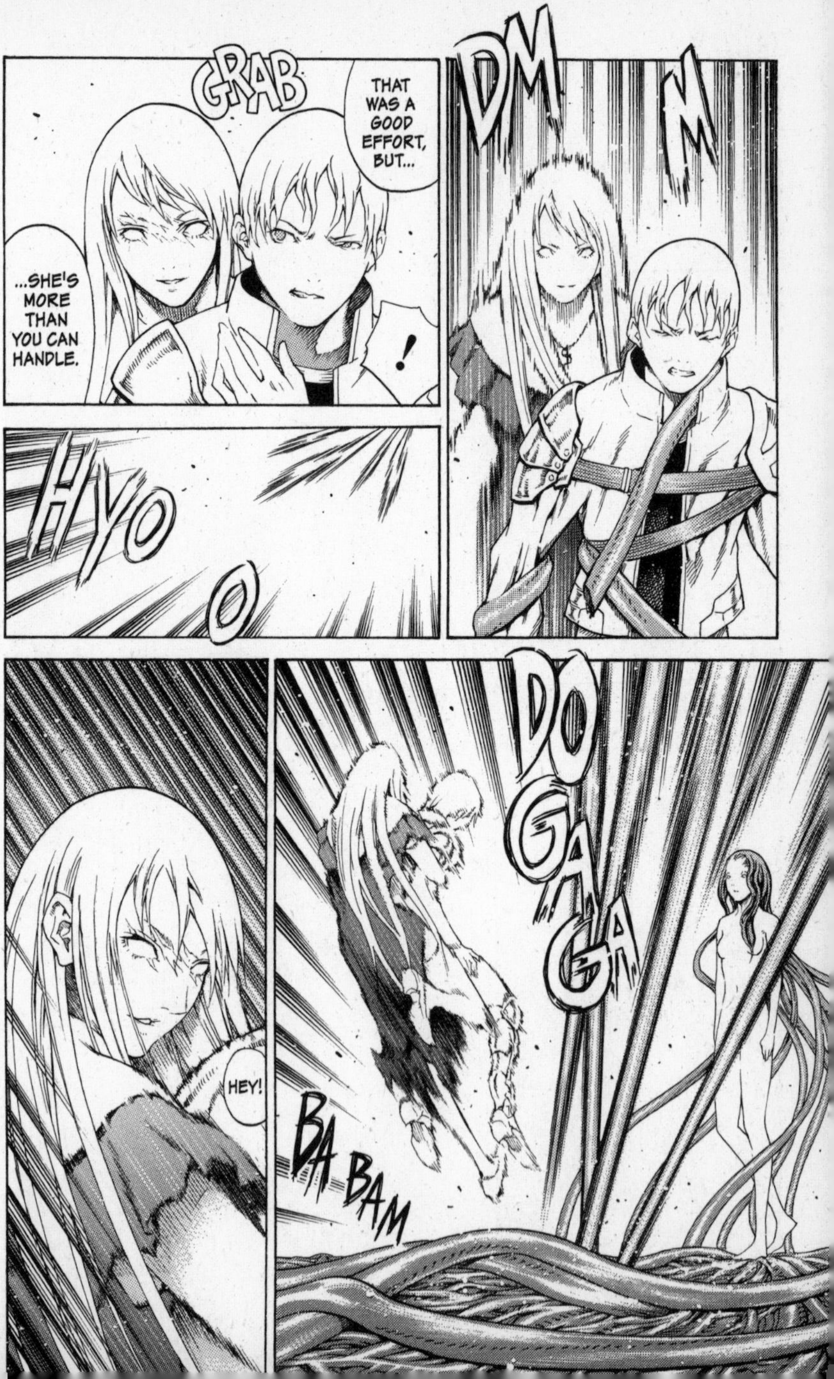
DM
M
THAT WAS A GOOD EFFORT, BUT...
GRAB
!
...SHE'S MORE THAN YOU CAN HANDLE.
HYO
O
DO
GA
GA
BA BAM
HEY!

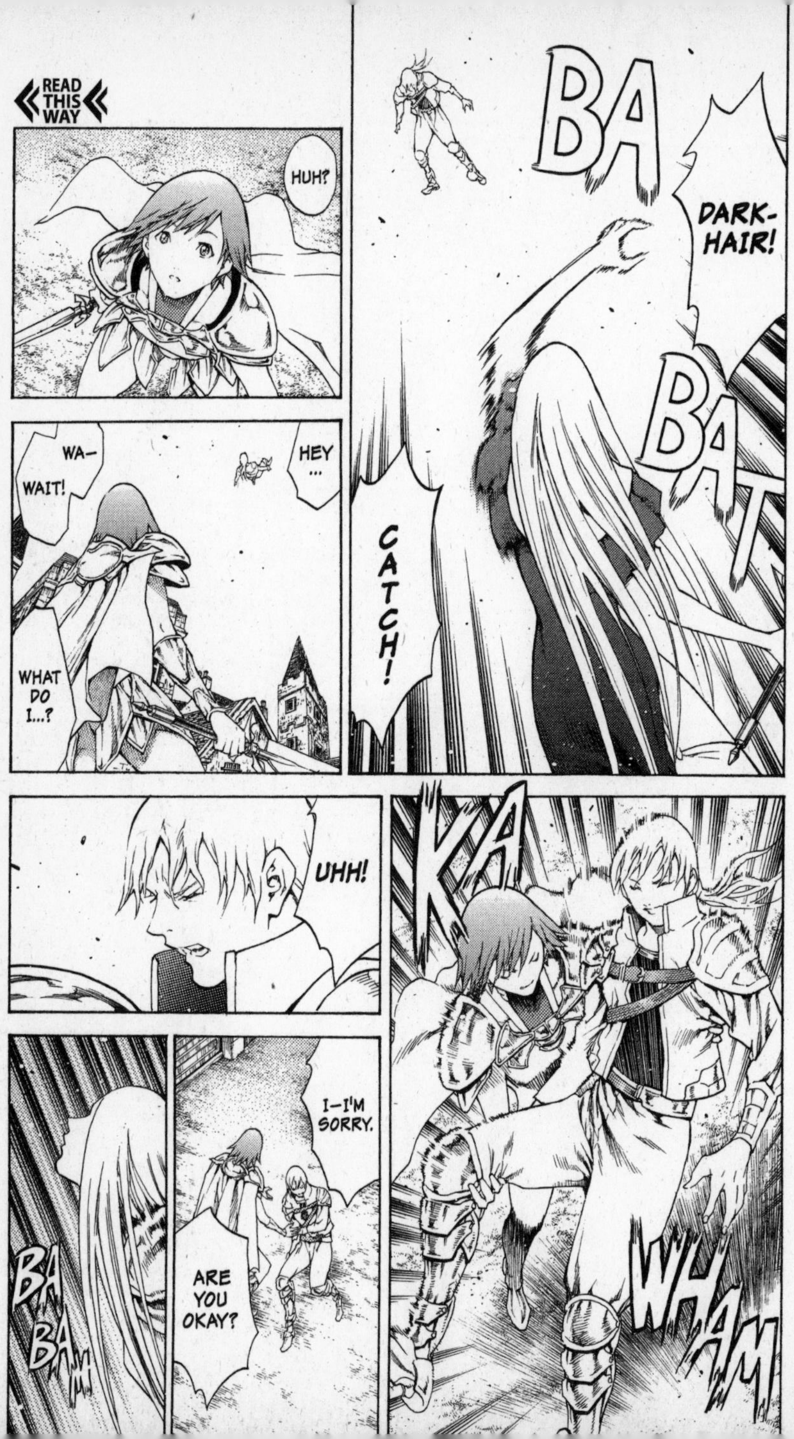
READ THIS WAY
BA
DARK-HAIR!
BAT
CATCH!
HUH?
HEY ...
WA-WAIT!
WHAT DO I...?
KA
WHAM
UHH!
I-I'M SORRY.
ARE YOU OKAY?
BABAM

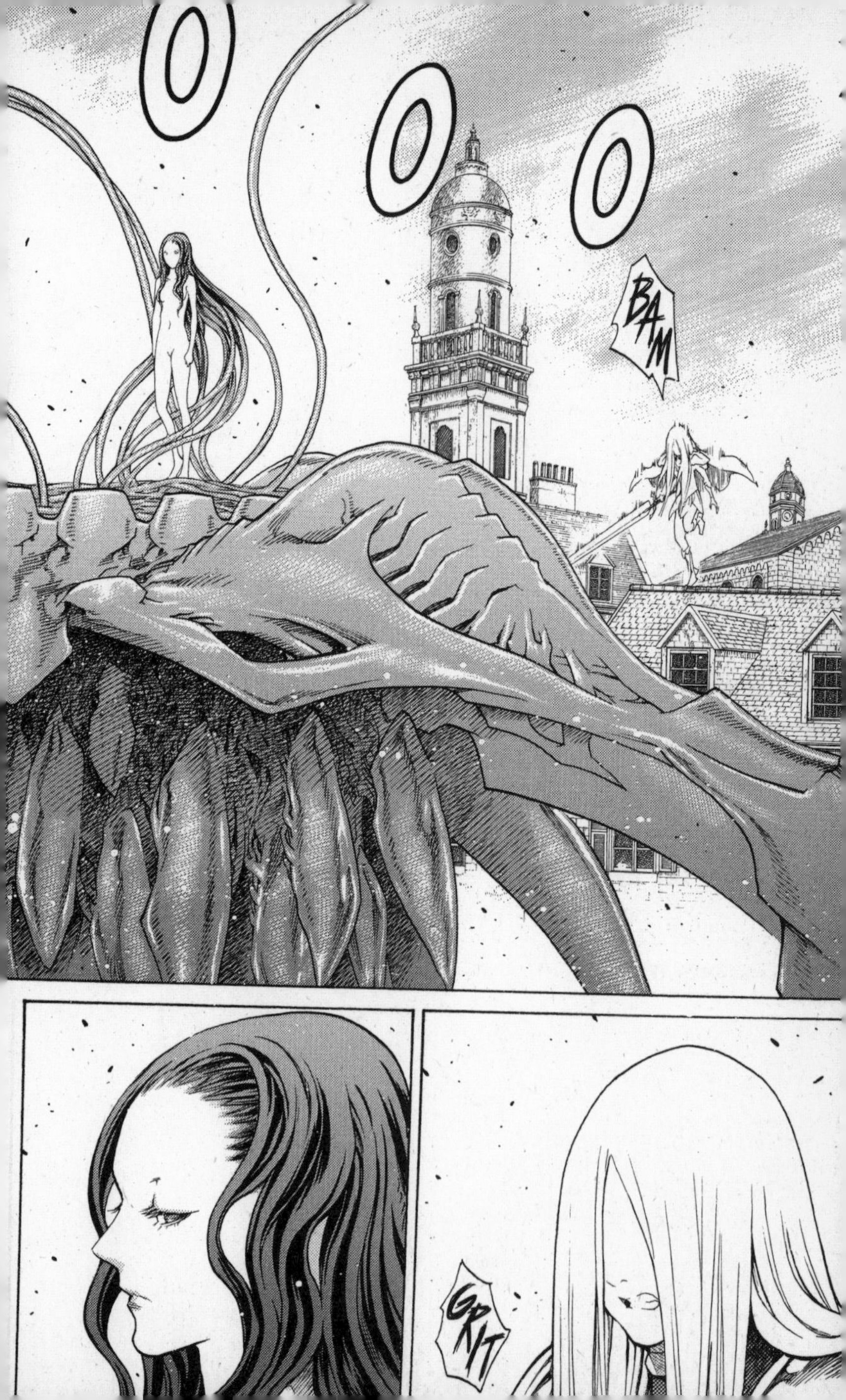
OOOO
BAM
GRIT

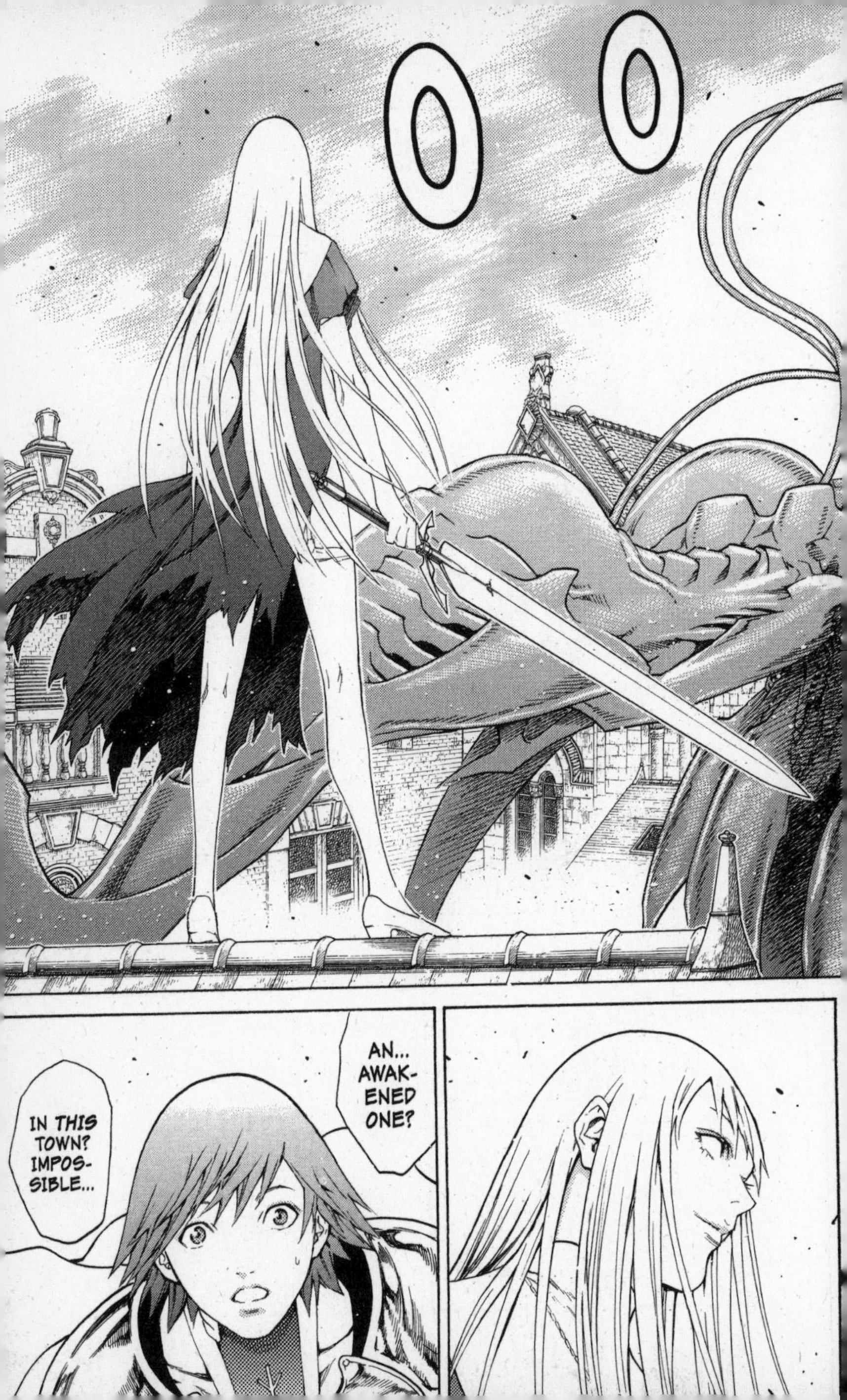
O O
AN... AWAK- ENED ONE?
IN THIS TOWN? IMPOS- SIBLE...

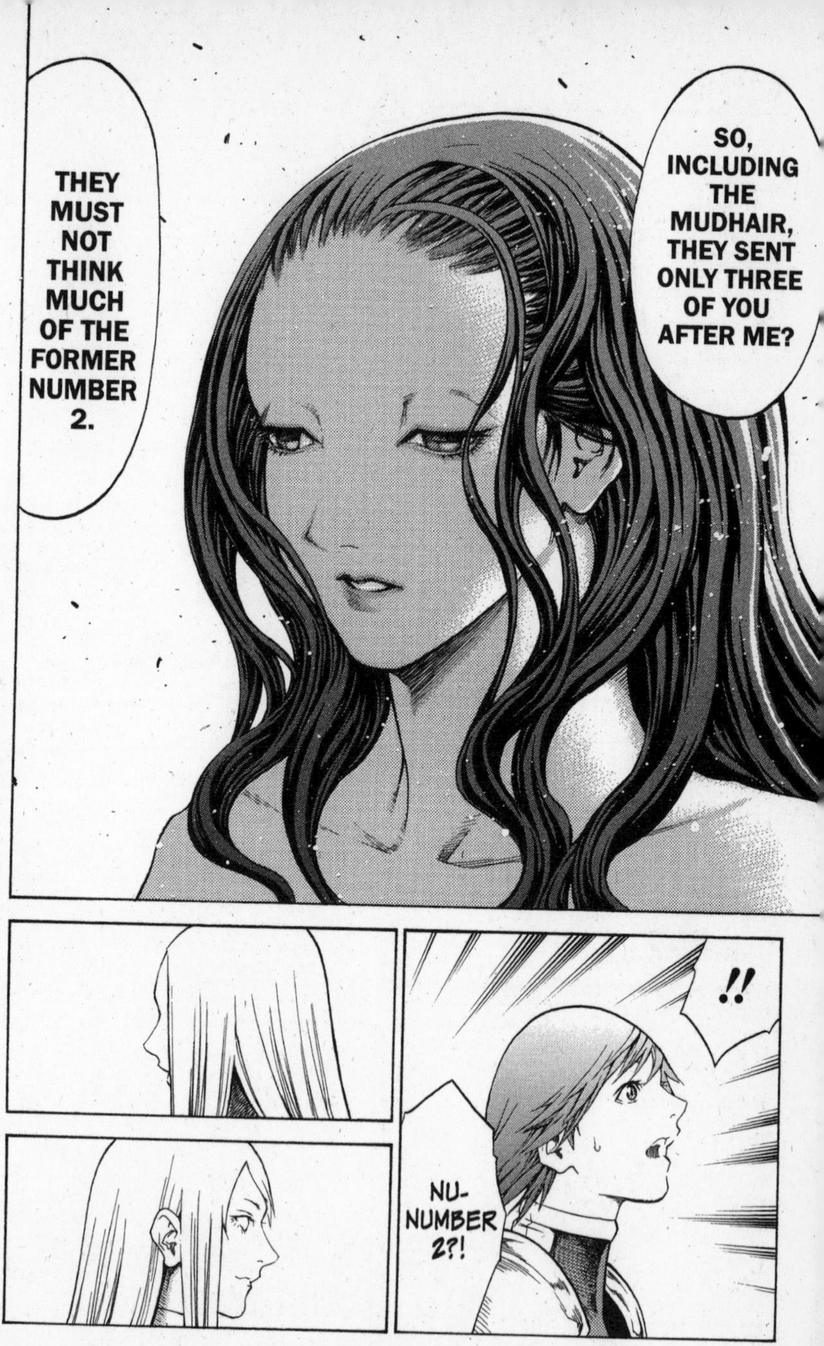
SO, INCLUDING THE MUDHAIR, THEY SENT ONLY THREE OF YOU AFTER ME?
THEY MUST NOT THINK MUCH OF THE FORMER NUMBER 2.
!!
NU-NUMBER 2?!

READ THIS WAY

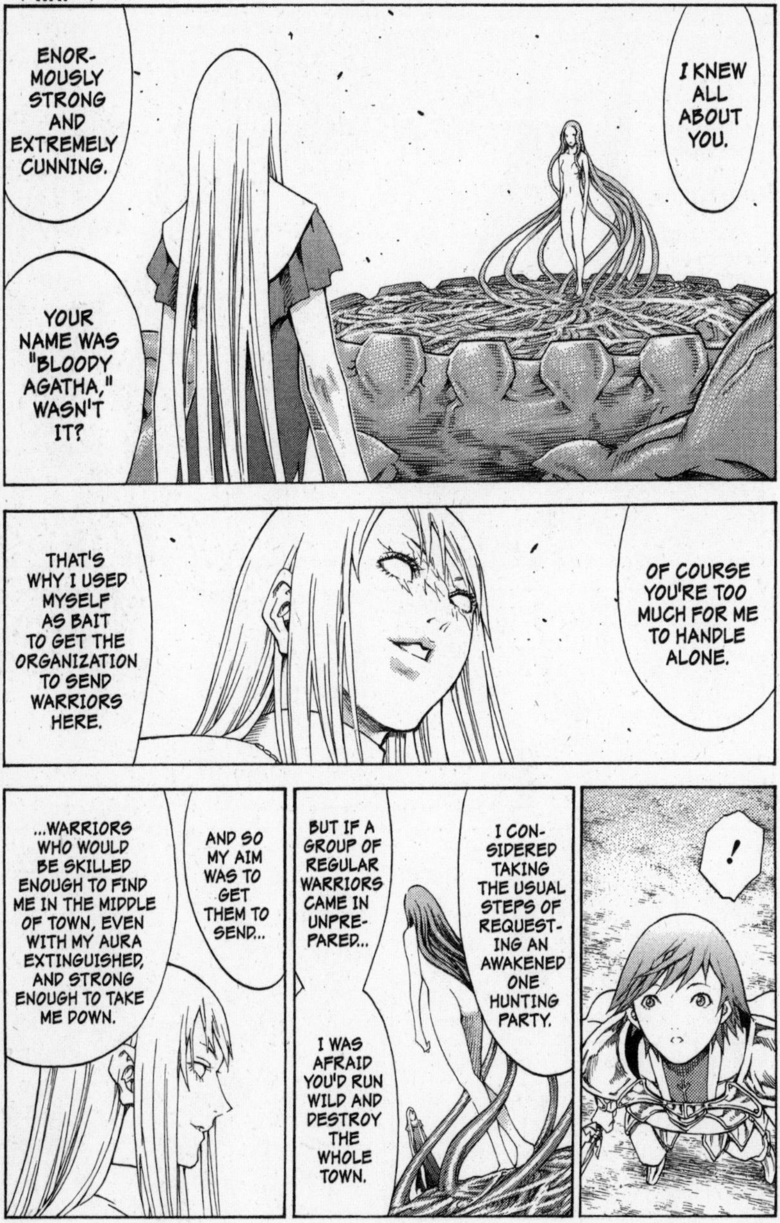
I KNEW ALL ABOUT YOU.
ENOR-MOUSLY STRONG AND EXTREMELY CUNNING.
YOUR NAME WAS "BLOODY AGATHA," WASN'T IT?
OF COURSE YOU'RE TOO MUCH FOR ME TO HANDLE ALONE.
THAT'S WHY I USED MYSELF AS BAIT TO GET THE ORGANIZATION TO SEND WARRIORS HERE.
!
I CON-SIDERED TAKING THE USUAL STEPS OF REQUEST-ING AN AWAKENED ONE HUNTING PARTY.
BUT IF A GROUP OF REGULAR WARRIORS CAME IN UNPRE-PARED...
I WAS AFRAID YOU'D RUN WILD AND DESTROY THE WHOLE TOWN.
AND SO MY AIM WAS TO GET THEM TO SEND...
...WARRIORS WHO WOULD BE SKILLED ENOUGH TO FIND ME IN THE MIDDLE OF TOWN, EVEN WITH MY AURA EXTINGUISHED, AND STRONG ENOUGH TO TAKE ME DOWN.

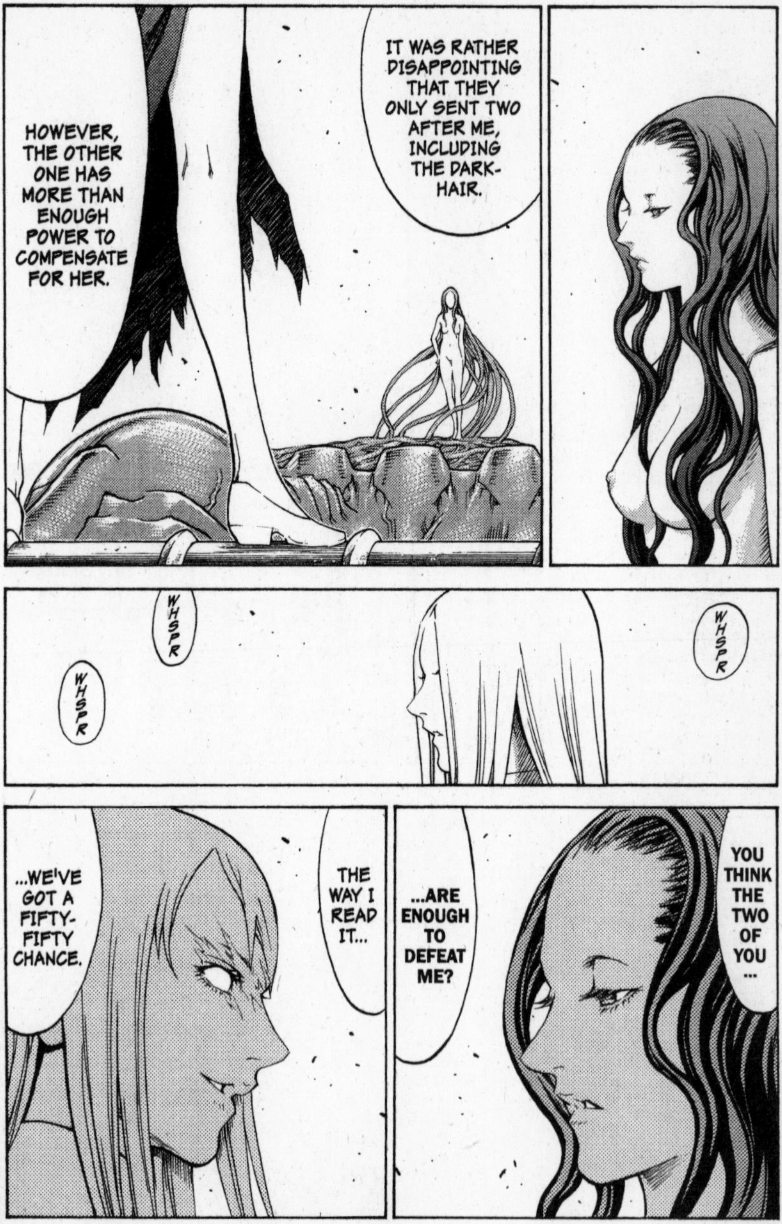
IT WAS RATHER DISAPPOINTING THAT THEY ONLY SENT TWO AFTER ME, INCLUDING THE DARK-HAIR.
HOWEVER, THE OTHER ONE HAS MORE THAN ENOUGH POWER TO COMPENSATE FOR HER.
WHSPR
WHSPR
WHSPR
YOU THINK THE TWO OF YOU ...
...ARE ENOUGH TO DEFEAT ME?
THE WAY I READ IT...
...WE'VE GOT A FIFTY-FIFTY CHANCE.

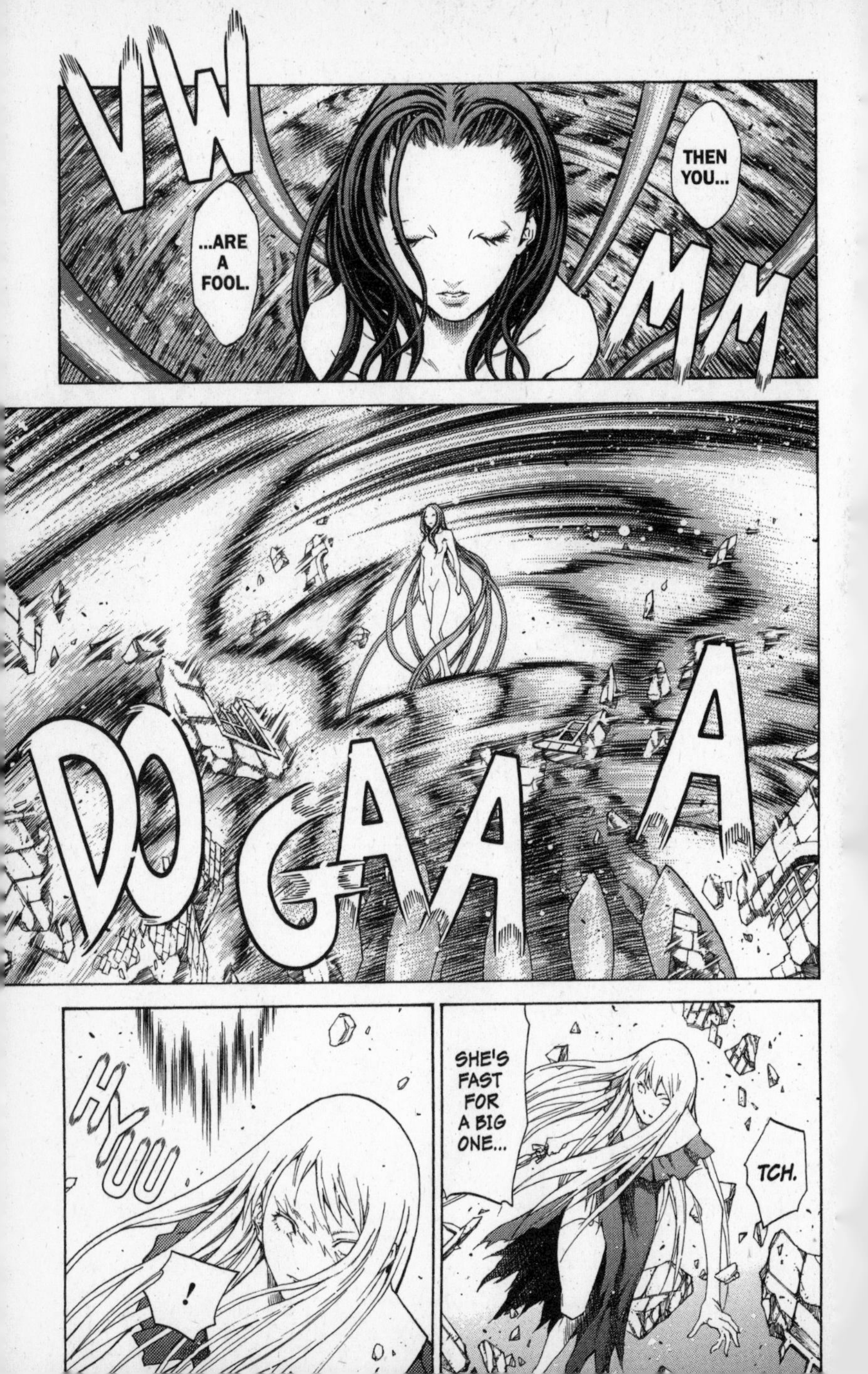
THEN YOU...
VWMM
...ARE A FOOL.
DOGAAA
SHE'S FAST FOR A BIG ONE...
TCH.
HYUU
!

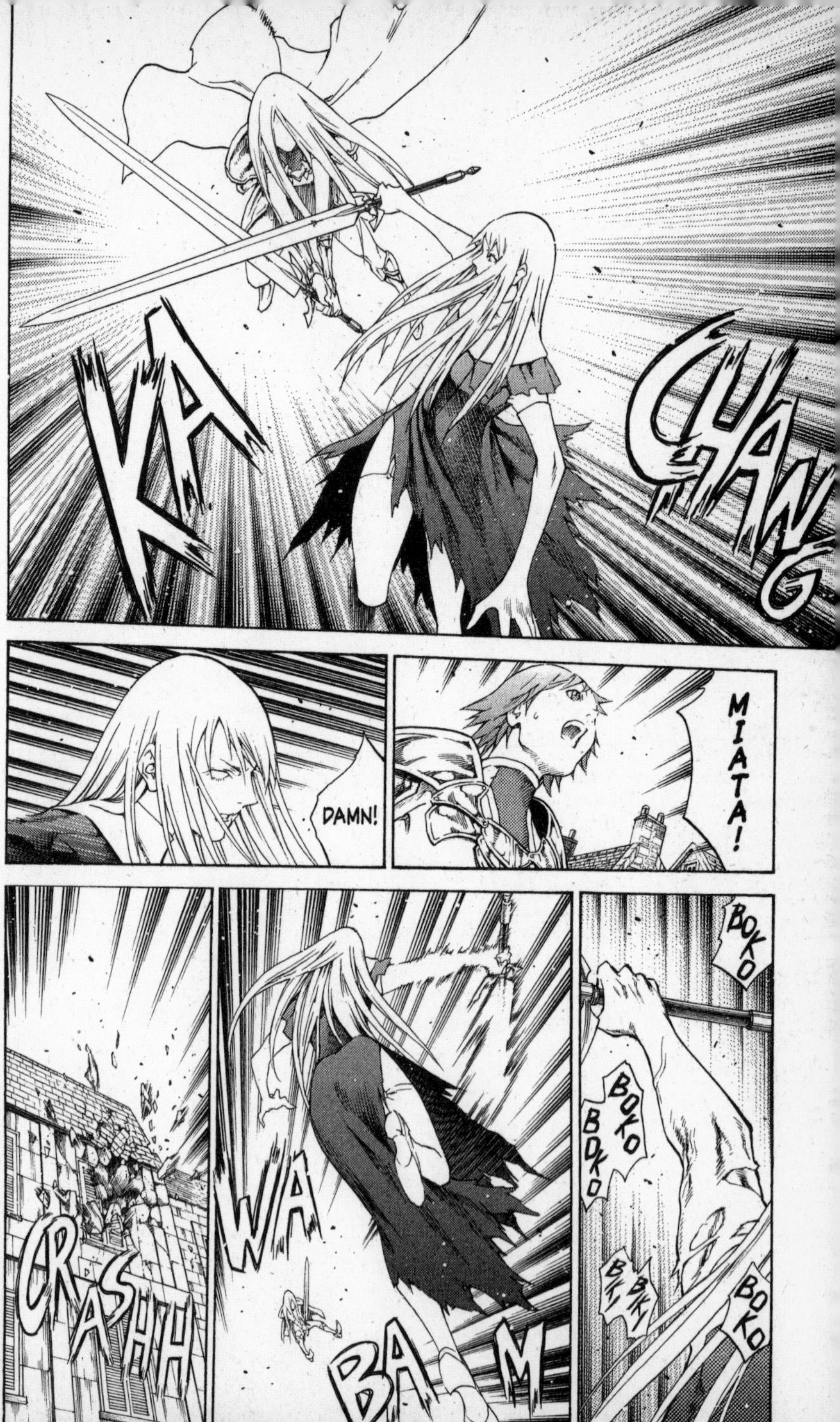
CHANG
KA
MIATA!
DAMN!
BOKO
BOKO
BOKO
BKI
BKI
BOKO
WA
BAM
CRASHH

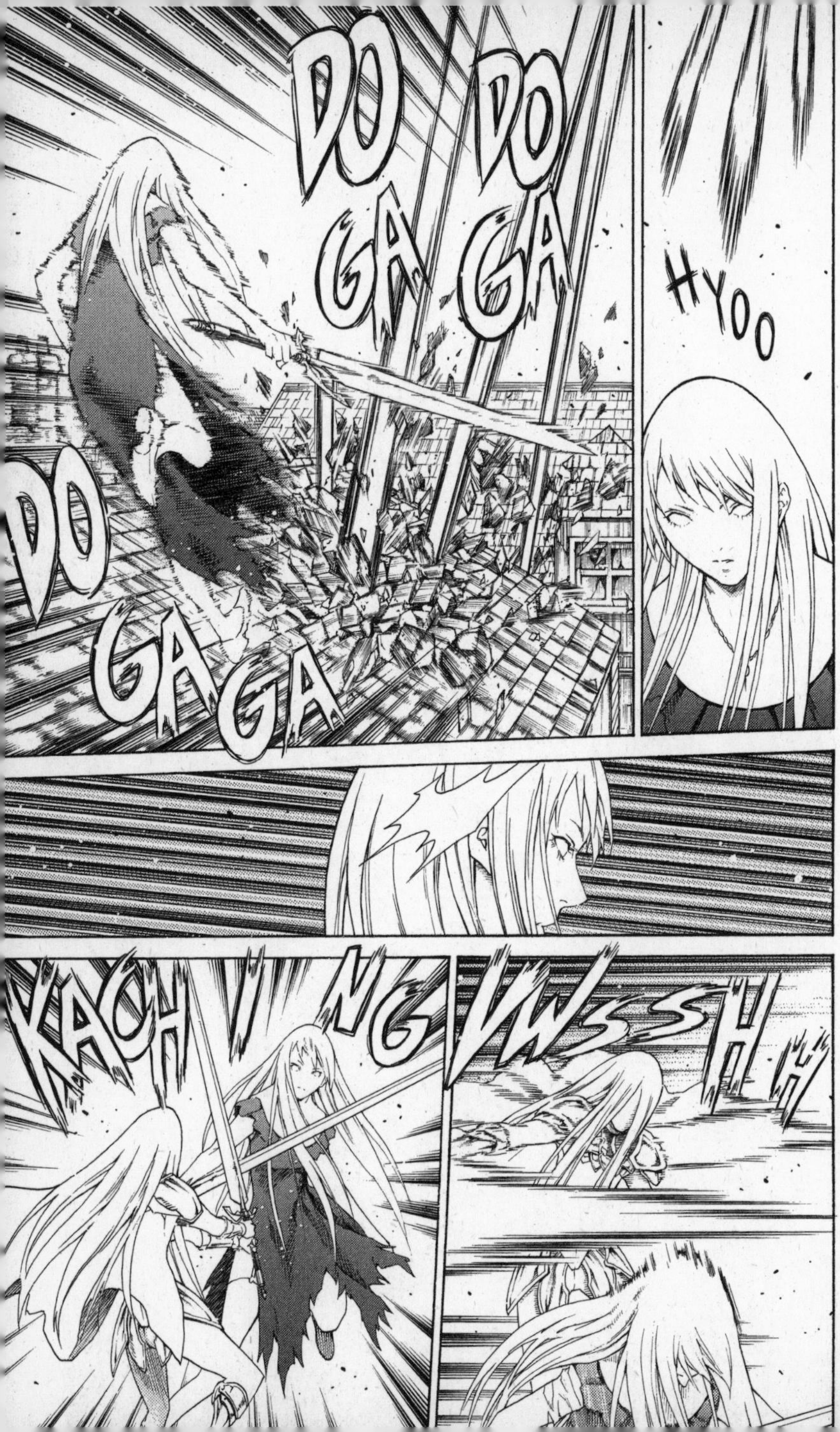
HYOO
DO GA
DO GA
DO GA
VWSSSHH
KACHIING

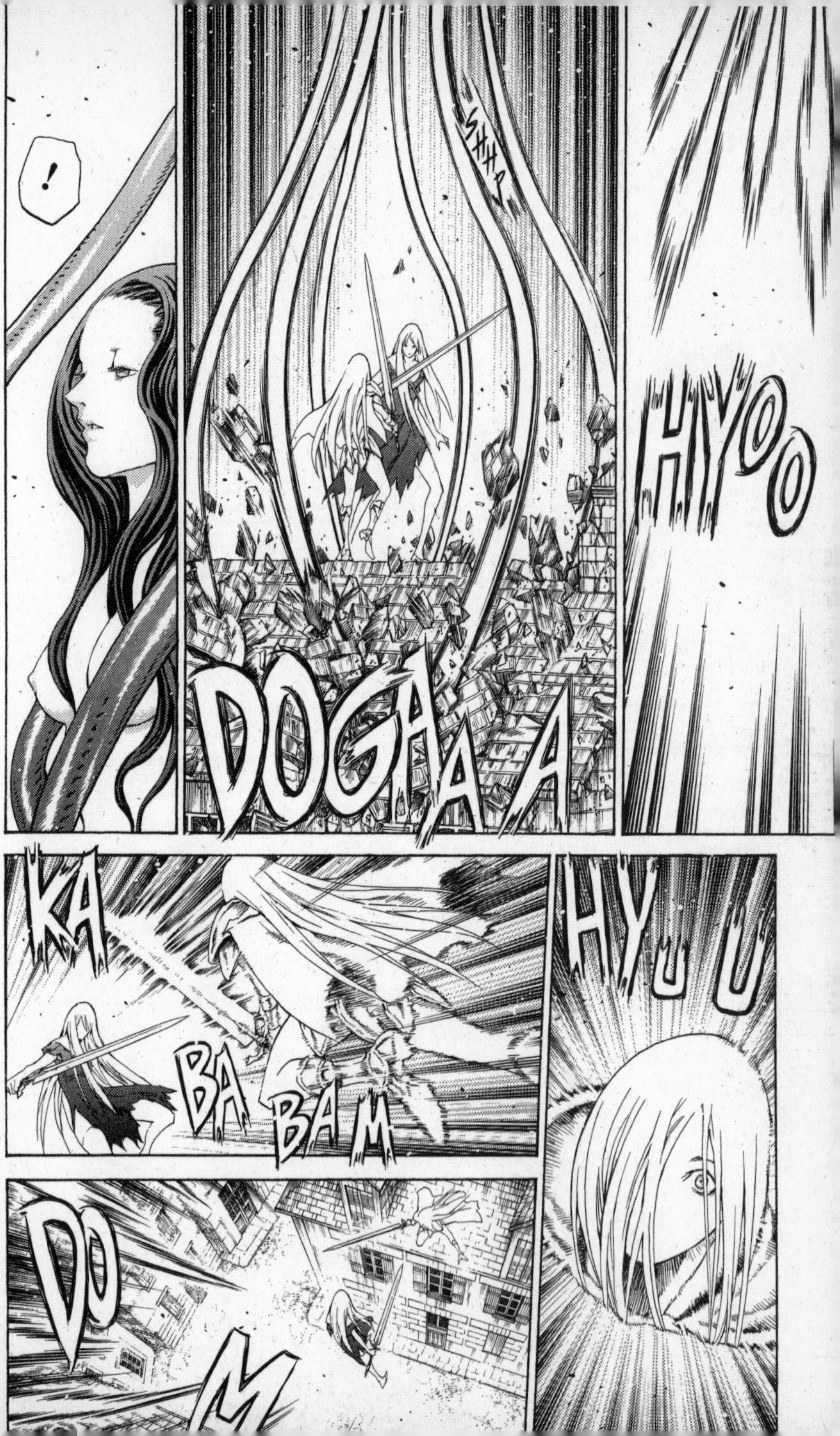
HYOO
SHHP
DOGAAA
!
HYUU
KA
BA BA BAM
DOM

READ THIS WAY

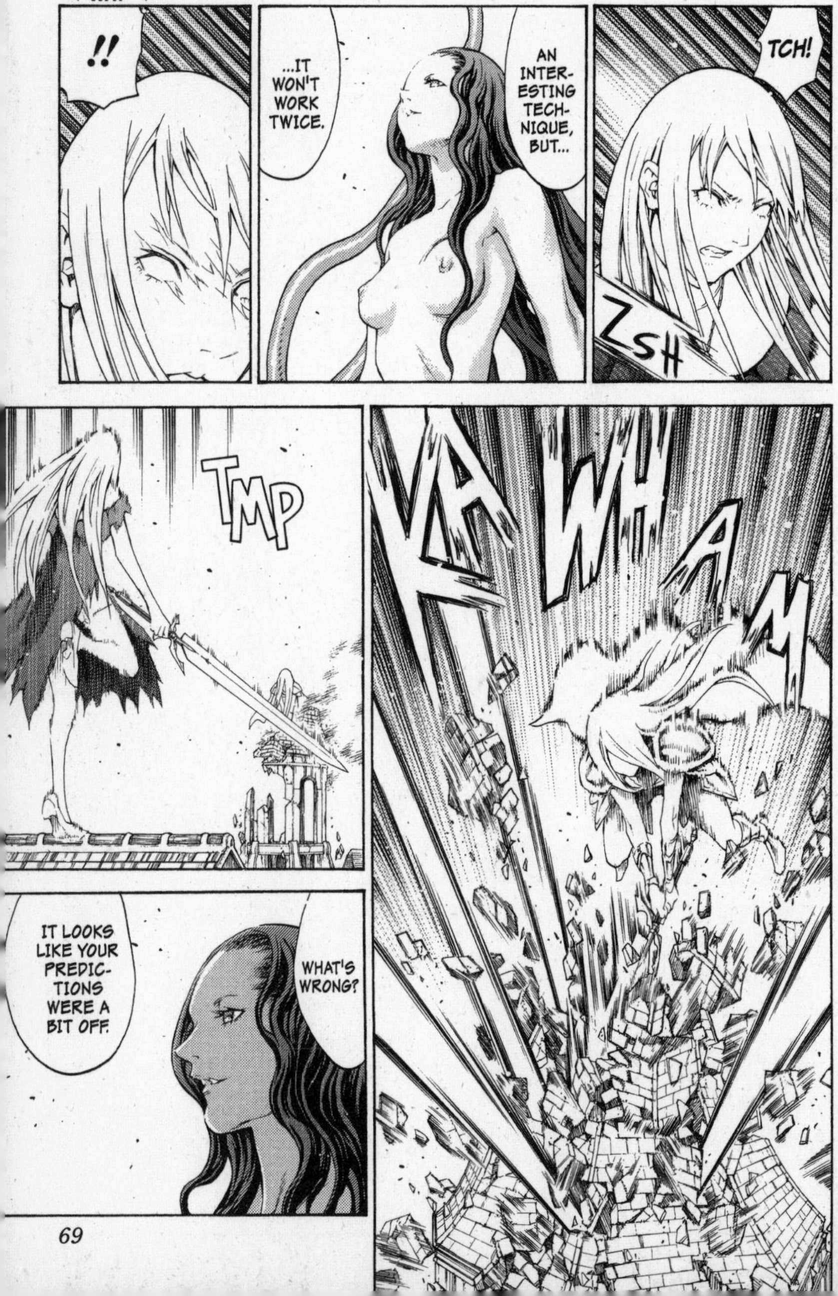

TCH!
ZSH
AN INTER-ESTING TECH-NIQUE, BUT...
...IT WON'T WORK TWICE.
!!
WHAM
TMP
WHAT'S WRONG?
IT LOOKS LIKE YOUR PREDIC-TIONS WERE A BIT OFF.

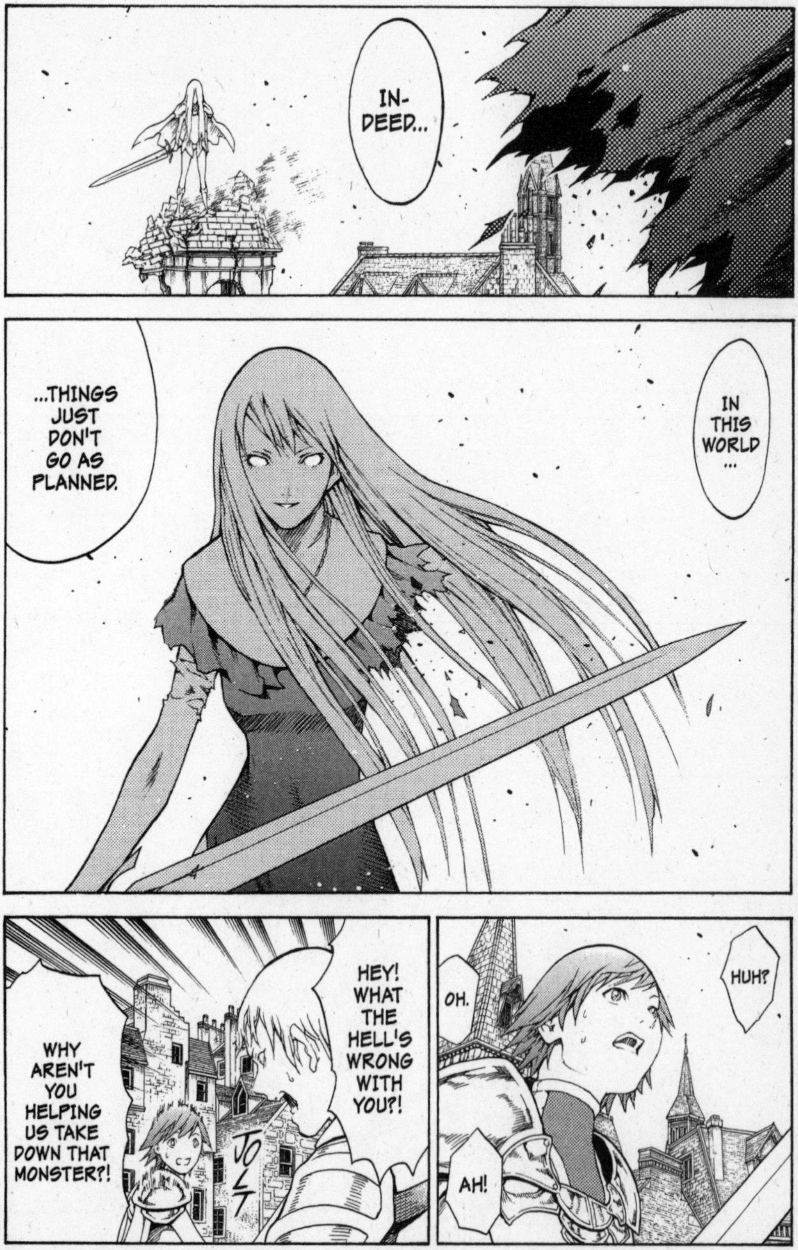
IN-DEED...
IN THIS WORLD ...
...THINGS JUST DON'T GO AS PLANNED.
HUH?
OH.
AH!
HEY! WHAT THE HELL'S WRONG WITH YOU?!
WHY AREN'T YOU HELPING US TAKE DOWN THAT MONSTER?!
JOLT

READ THIS WAY

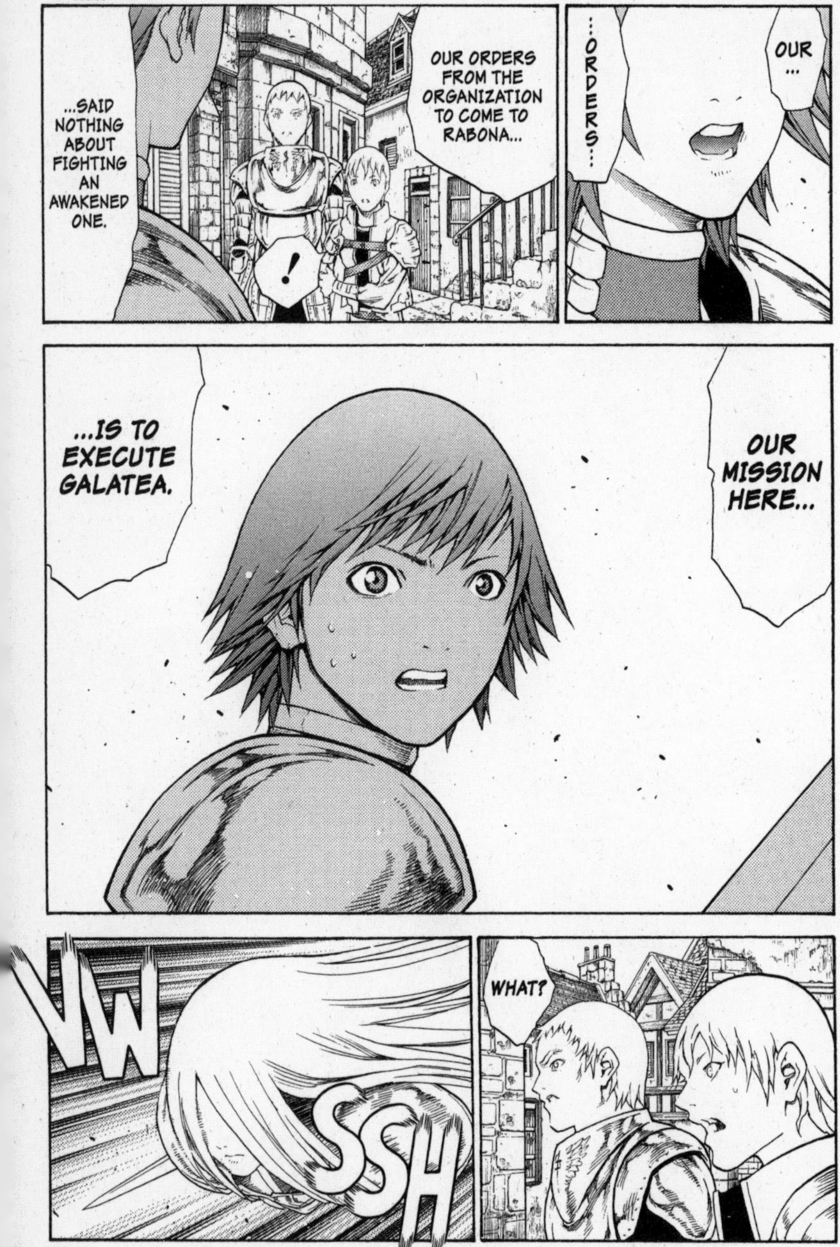

OUR ...
...ORDERS...
OUR ORDERS FROM THE ORGANIZATION TO COME TO RABONA...
...SAID NOTHING ABOUT FIGHTING AN AWAKENED ONE.
!
OUR MISSION HERE...
...IS TO EXECUTE GALATEA.
WHAT?
VW
SSH

Scene 76: A Child Weapon, Part 4

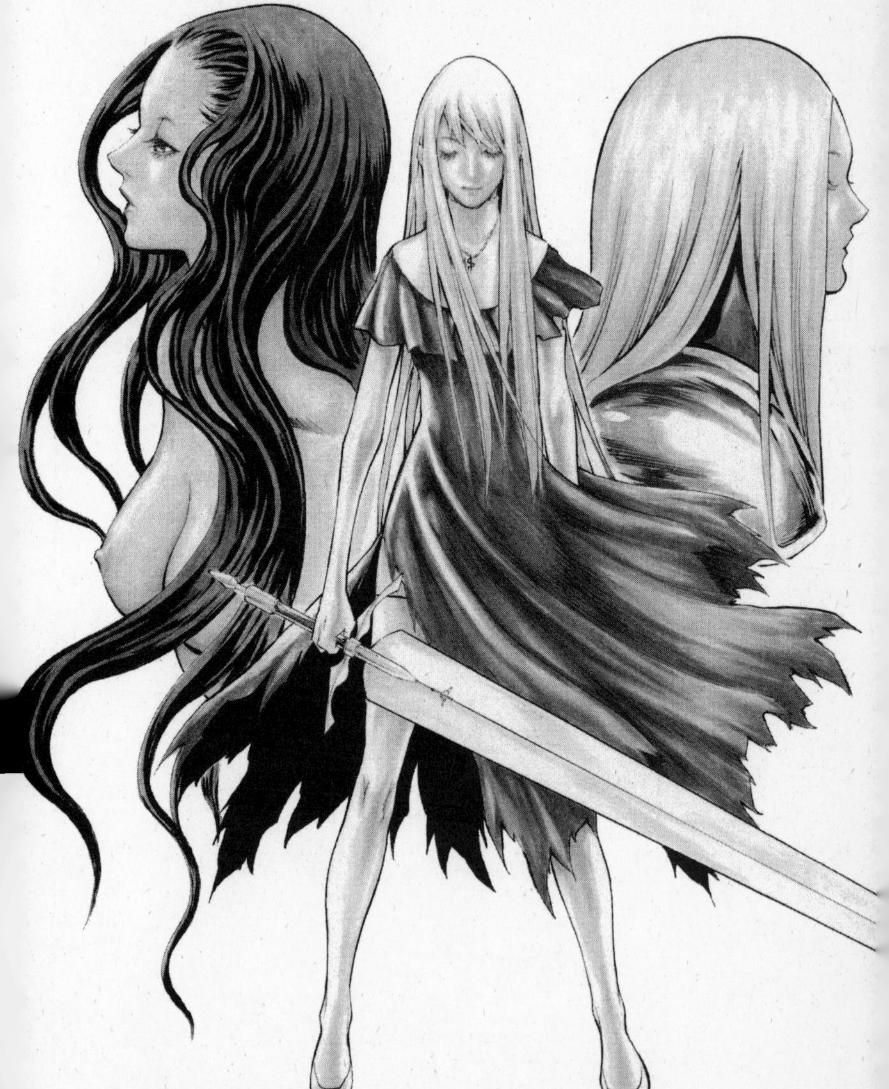

READ THIS WAY

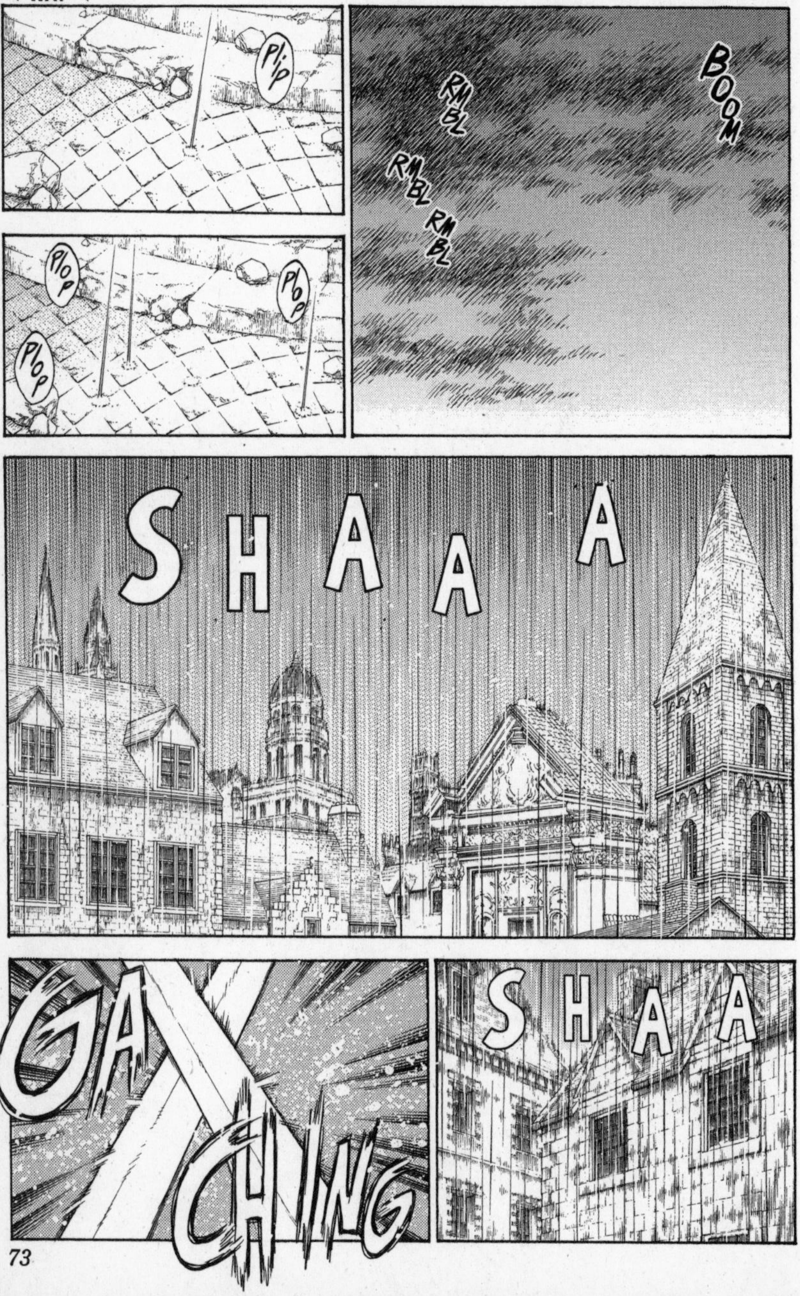
BOOM
RMBL
RMBL
RMBL
Plip
Plop
Plop
Plop
SHAAA
SHAA
GACHING

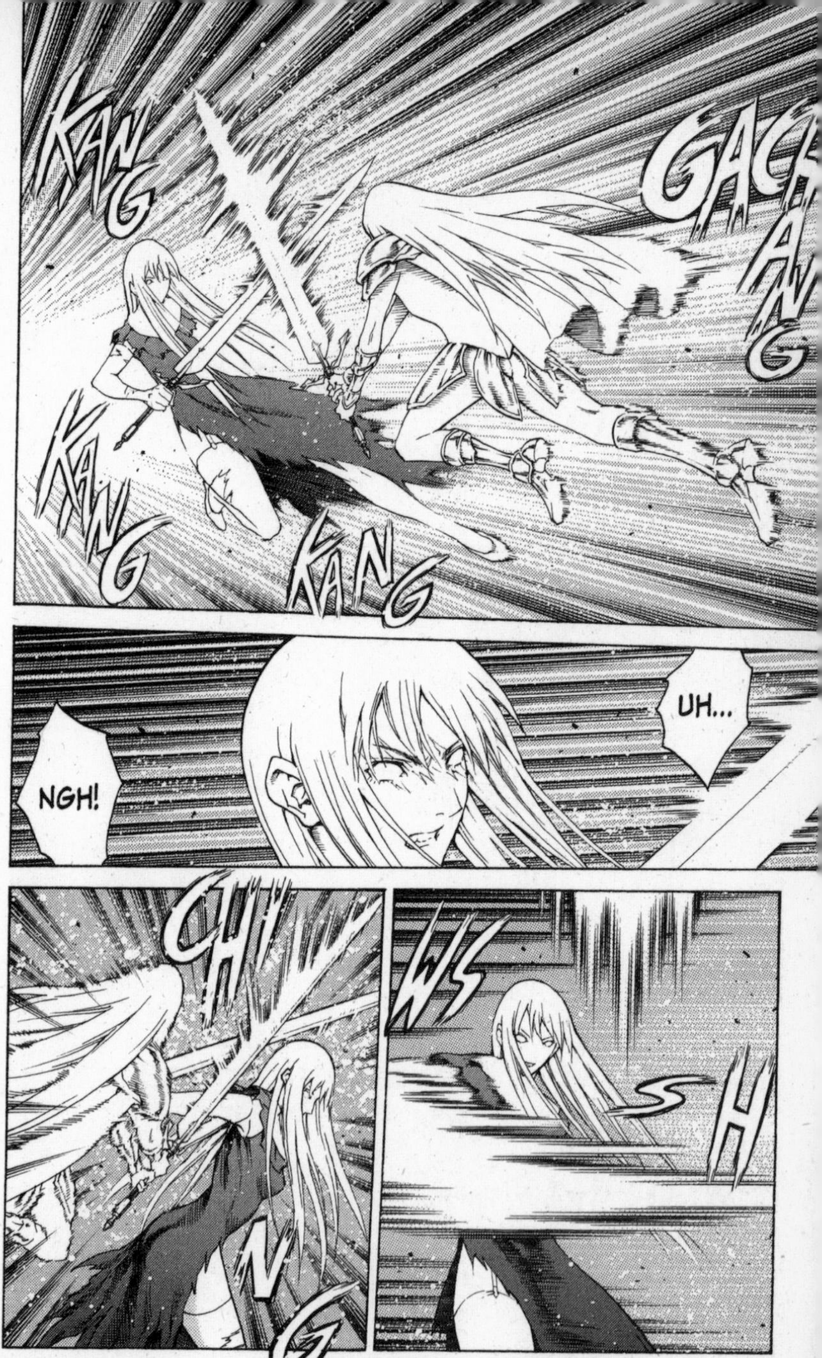
GACHANG
KANG
KANG
KANG
UH...
NGH!
WSSH
CHING

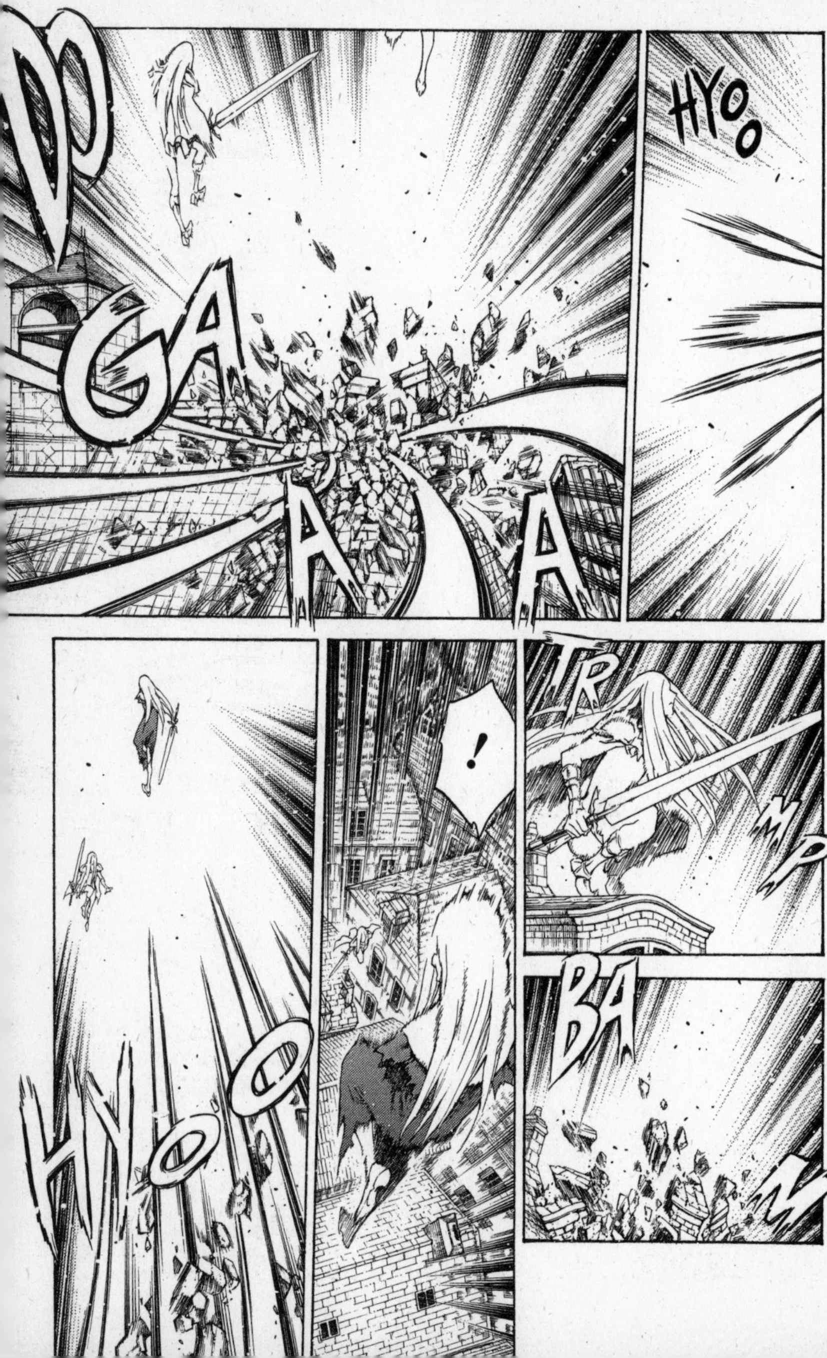
HYOOO
DOGAAA
TRMP
BAN
!
HYOOO

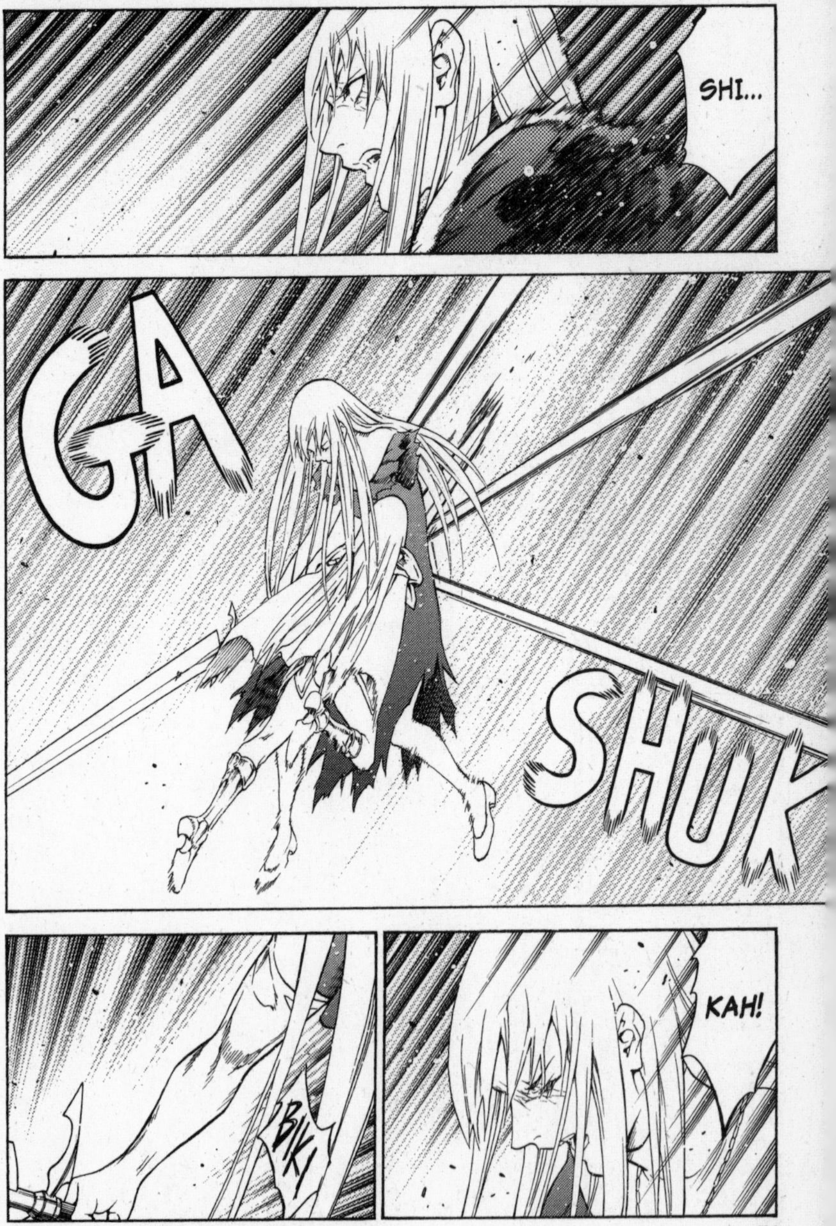
SHI...
GA
SHUK
KAH!
BIKI

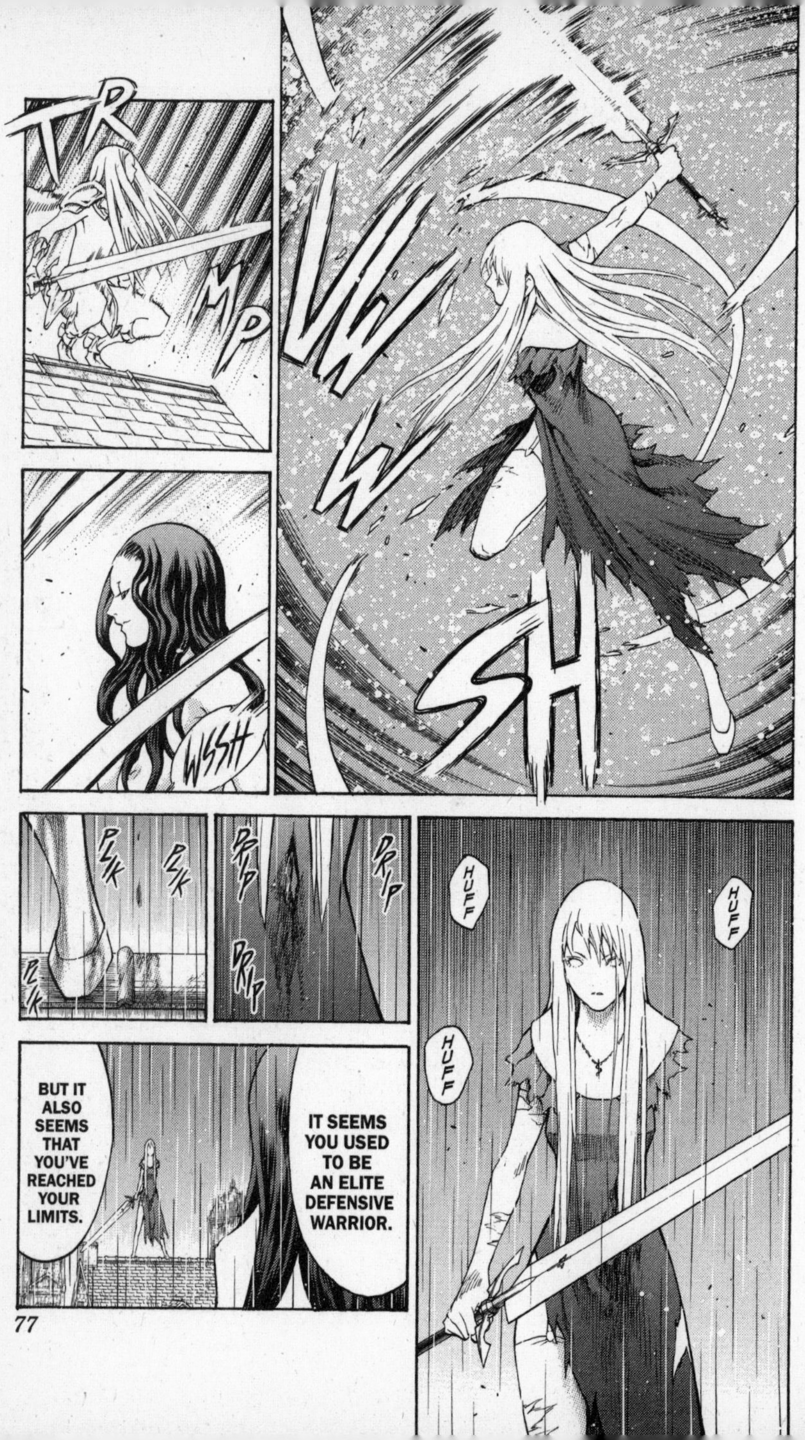
VWWSH
TRMP
WSSH
HUFF
HUFF
HUFF
DRIP
DRIP
DRIP
PLIK
PLIK
PLIK
IT SEEMS YOU USED TO BE AN ELITE DEFENSIVE WARRIOR.
BUT IT ALSO SEEMS THAT YOU'VE REACHED YOUR LIMITS.

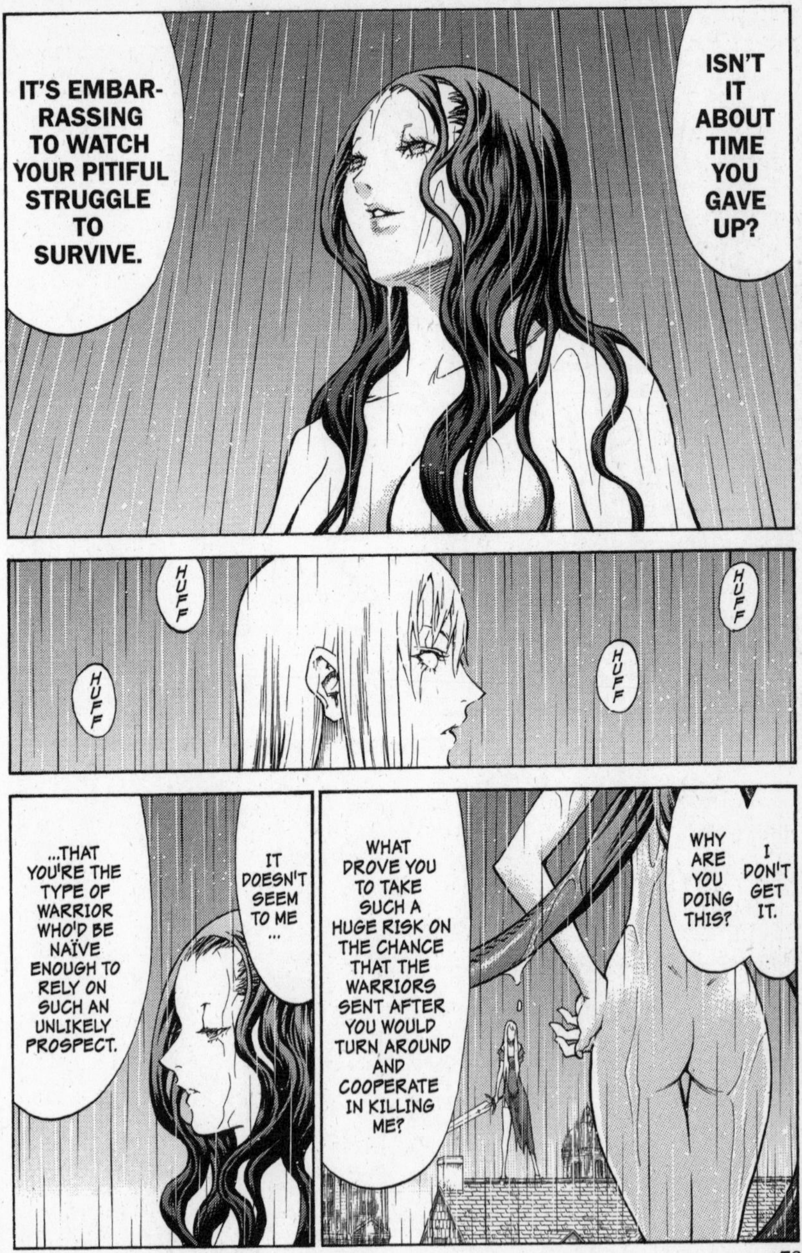
ISN'T IT ABOUT TIME YOU GAVE UP?
IT'S EMBARRASSING TO WATCH YOUR PITIFUL STRUGGLE TO SURVIVE.
HUFF
HUFF
HUFF
HUFF
I DON'T GET IT.
WHY ARE YOU DOING THIS?
WHAT DROVE YOU TO TAKE SUCH A HUGE RISK ON THE CHANCE THAT THE WARRIORS SENT AFTER YOU WOULD TURN AROUND AND COOPERATE IN KILLING ME?
IT DOESN'T SEEM TO ME ...
...THAT YOU'RE THE TYPE OF WARRIOR WHO'D BE NAÏVE ENOUGH TO RELY ON SUCH AN UNLIKELY PROSPECT.

READ THIS WAY

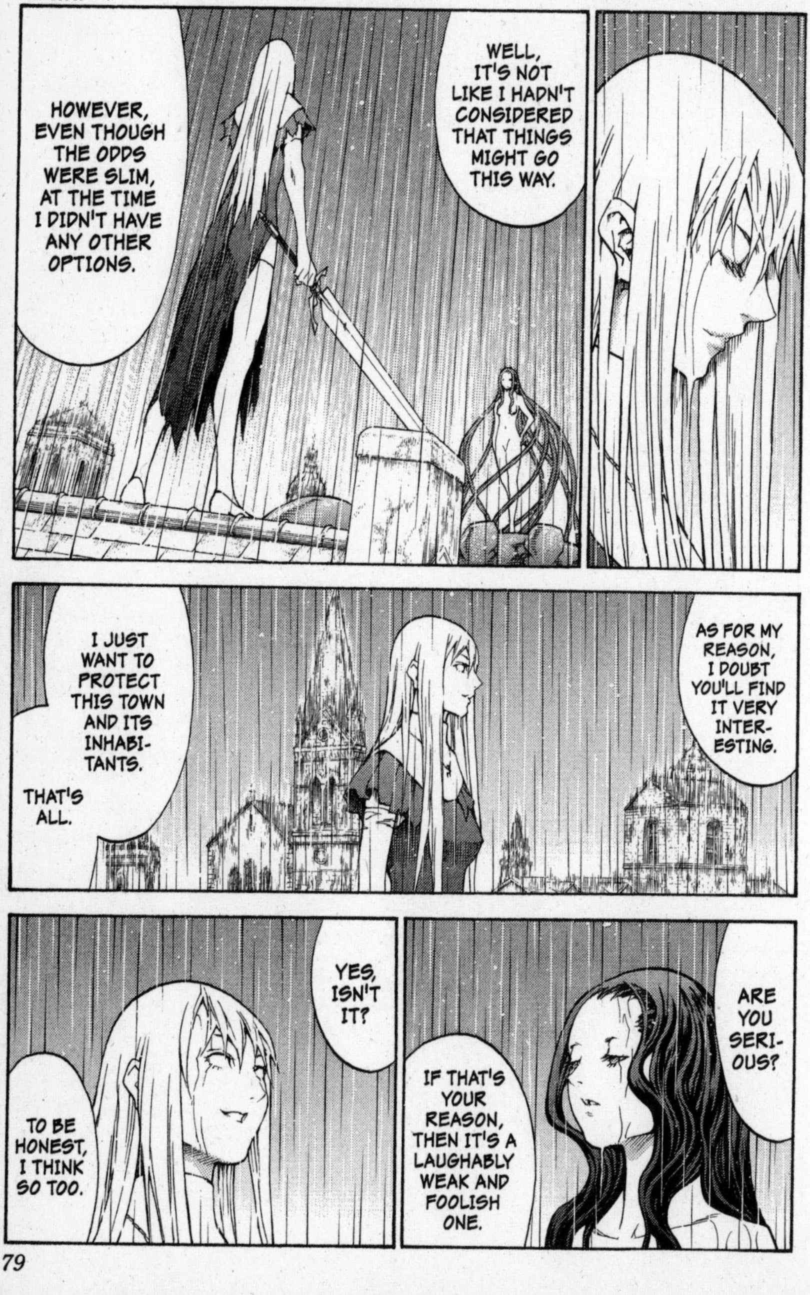
WELL, IT'S NOT LIKE I HADN'T CONSIDERED THAT THINGS MIGHT GO THIS WAY.
HOWEVER, EVEN THOUGH THE ODDS WERE SLIM, AT THE TIME I DIDN'T HAVE ANY OTHER OPTIONS.
AS FOR MY REASON, I DOUBT YOU'LL FIND IT VERY INTER-ESTING.
I JUST WANT TO PROTECT THIS TOWN AND ITS INHABI-TANTS.
THAT'S ALL.
ARE YOU SERI-OUS?
IF THAT'S YOUR REASON, THEN IT'S A LAUGHABLY WEAK AND FOOLISH ONE.
YES, ISN'T IT?
TO BE HONEST, I THINK SO TOO.

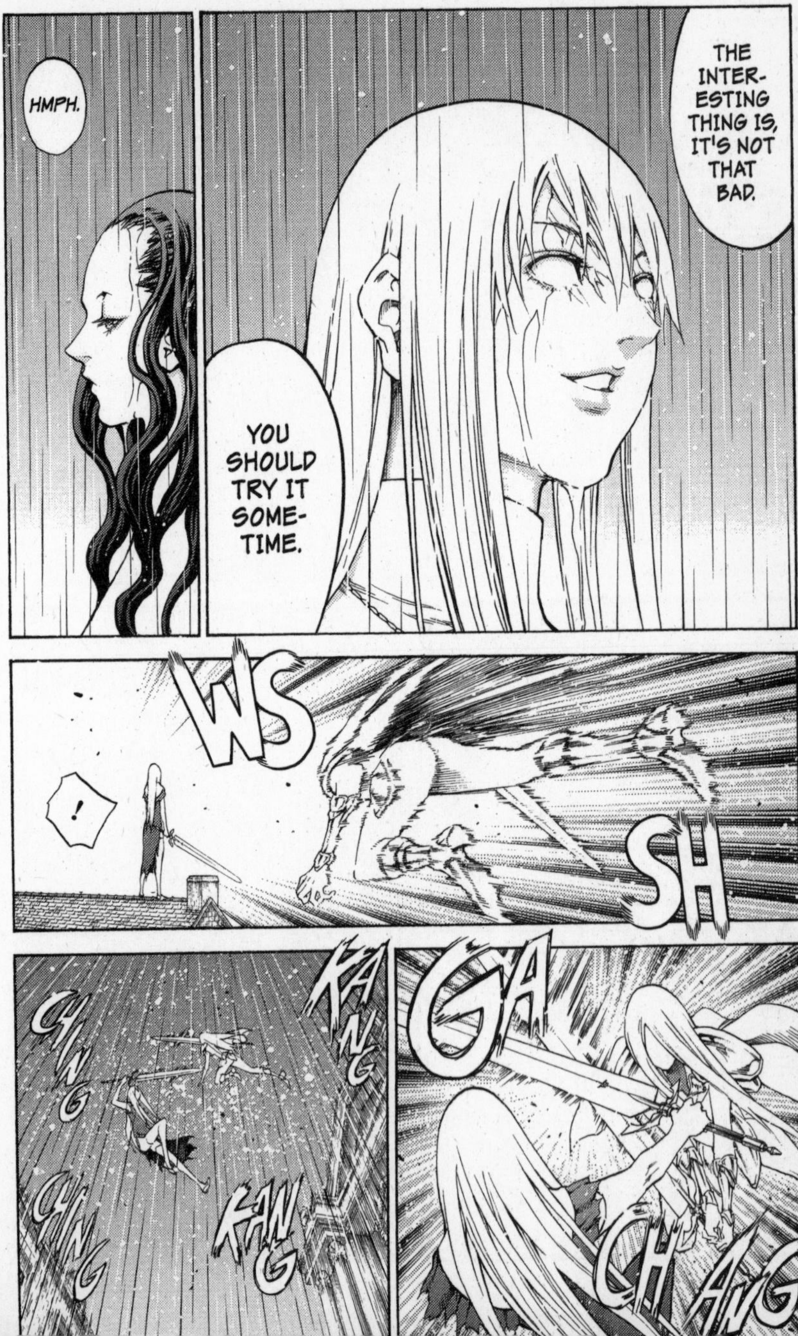
THE INTER-ESTING THING IS, IT'S NOT THAT BAD.
YOU SHOULD TRY IT SOME-TIME.
HMPH.
WSSH
!
GA
CHANG
KANG
KANG
CHING
CHING

READ THIS WAY

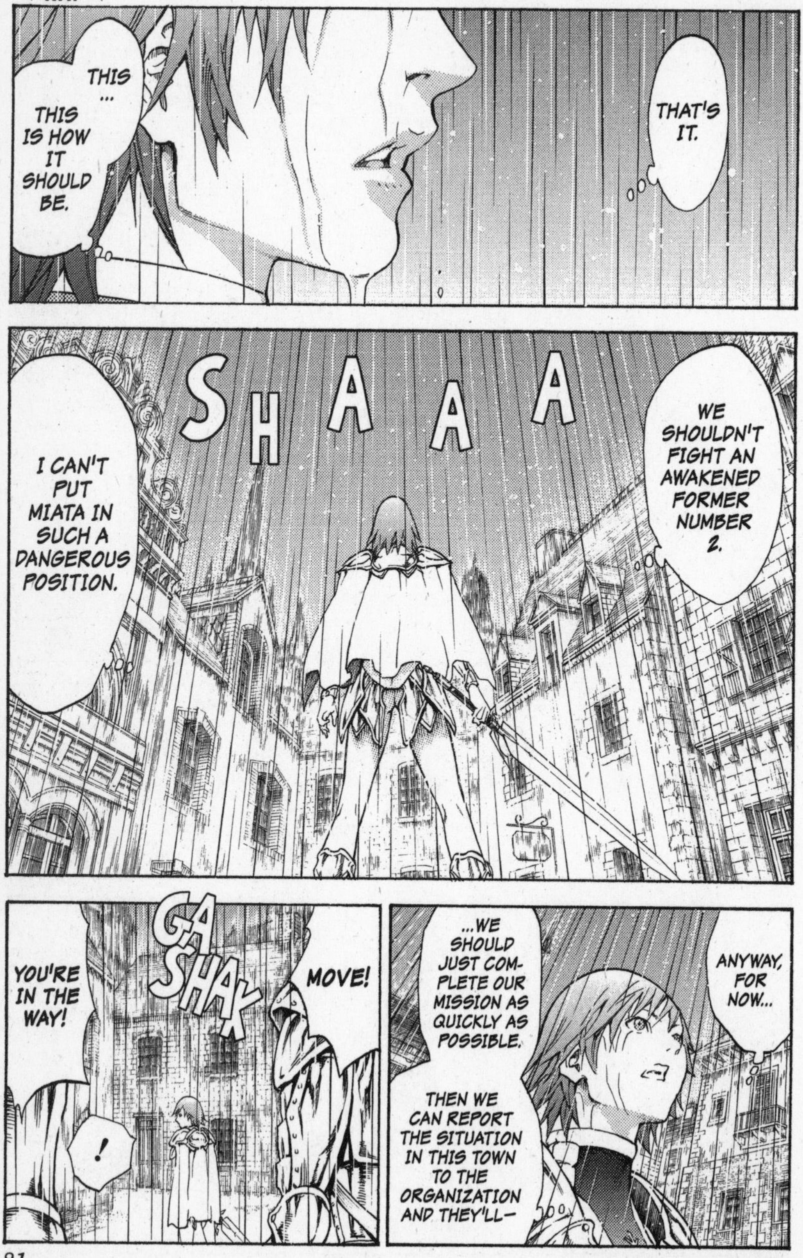

THAT'S IT.
THIS... THIS IS HOW IT SHOULD BE.
WE SHOULDN'T FIGHT AN AWAKENED FORMER NUMBER 2.
SHAAA
I CAN'T PUT MIATA IN SUCH A DANGEROUS POSITION.
ANYWAY, FOR NOW...
...WE SHOULD JUST COMPLETE OUR MISSION AS QUICKLY AS POSSIBLE.
THEN WE CAN REPORT THE SITUATION IN THIS TOWN TO THE ORGANIZATION AND THEY'LL—
MOVE!
GASHAK
YOU'RE IN THE WAY!
!

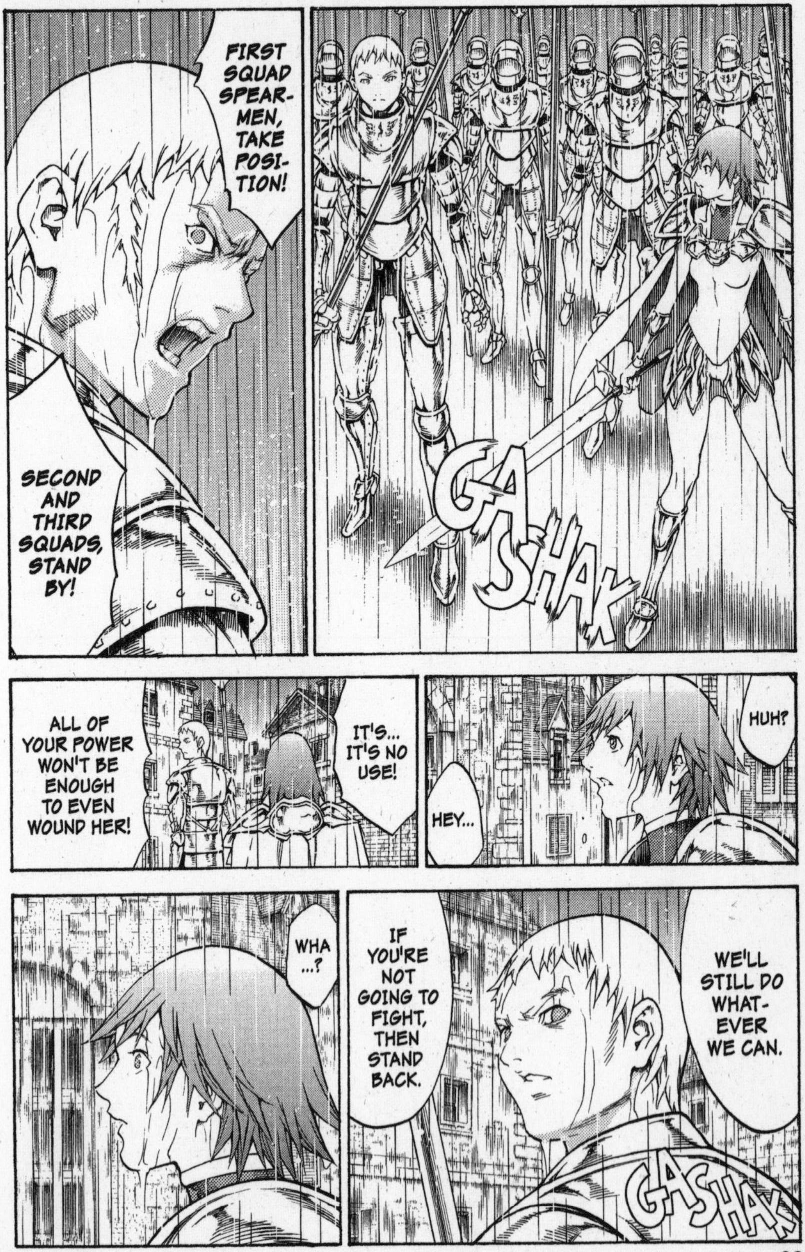
GASHAK
FIRST SQUAD SPEAR-MEN, TAKE POSI-TION!
SECOND AND THIRD SQUADS, STAND BY!
HUH?
HEY...
IT'S... IT'S NO USE!
ALL OF YOUR POWER WON'T BE ENOUGH TO EVEN WOUND HER!
WE'LL STILL DO WHAT-EVER WE CAN.
IF YOU'RE NOT GOING TO FIGHT, THEN STAND BACK.
GASHAK
WHA ...?

READ THIS WAY

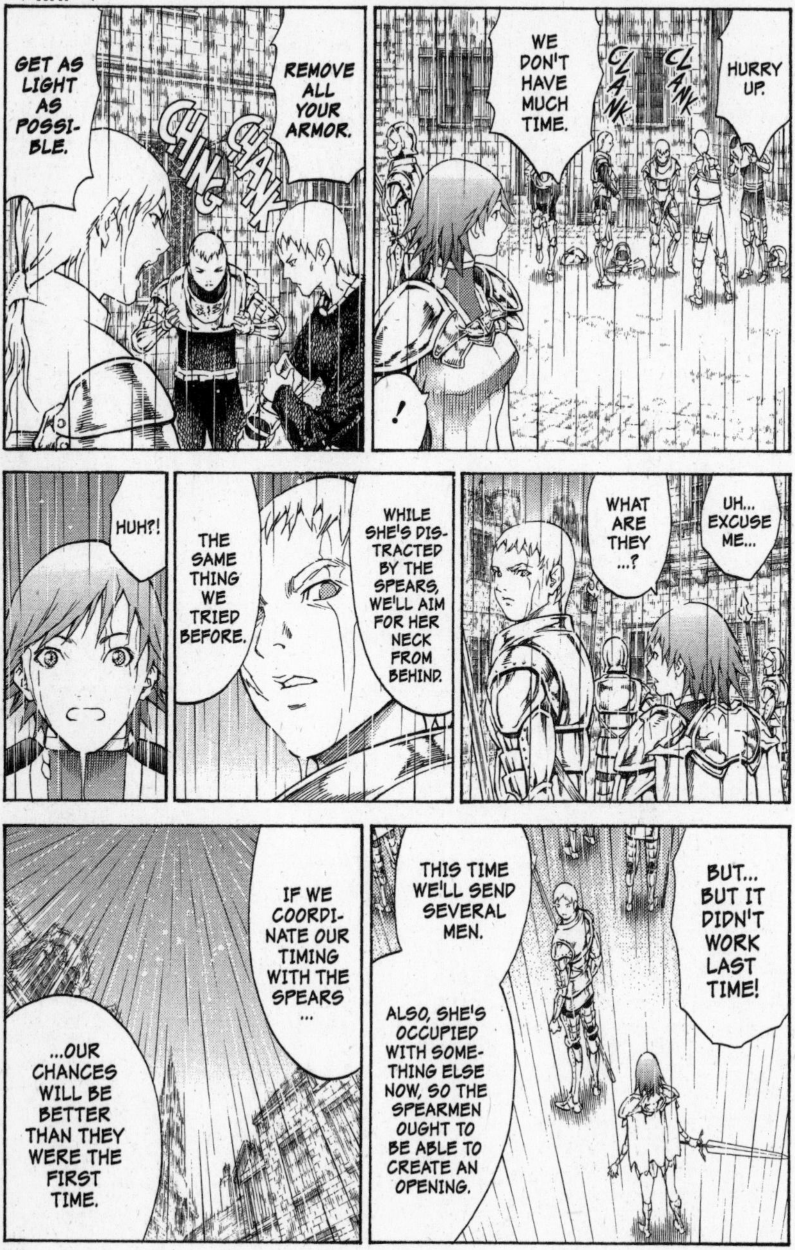

HURRY UP.
CLANK
CLANK
WE DON'T HAVE MUCH TIME.
!
REMOVE ALL YOUR ARMOR.
CHANK
CHING
GET AS LIGHT AS POSSIBLE.
UH... EXCUSE ME...
WHAT ARE THEY ...?
WHILE SHE'S DISTRACTED BY THE SPEARS, WE'LL AIM FOR HER NECK FROM BEHIND.
THE SAME THING WE TRIED BEFORE.
HUH?!
BUT... BUT IT DIDN'T WORK LAST TIME!
THIS TIME WE'LL SEND SEVERAL MEN.
ALSO, SHE'S OCCUPIED WITH SOMETHING ELSE NOW, SO THE SPEARMEN OUGHT TO BE ABLE TO CREATE AN OPENING.
IF WE COORDINATE OUR TIMING WITH THE SPEARS ...
...OUR CHANCES WILL BE BETTER THAN THEY WERE THE FIRST TIME.

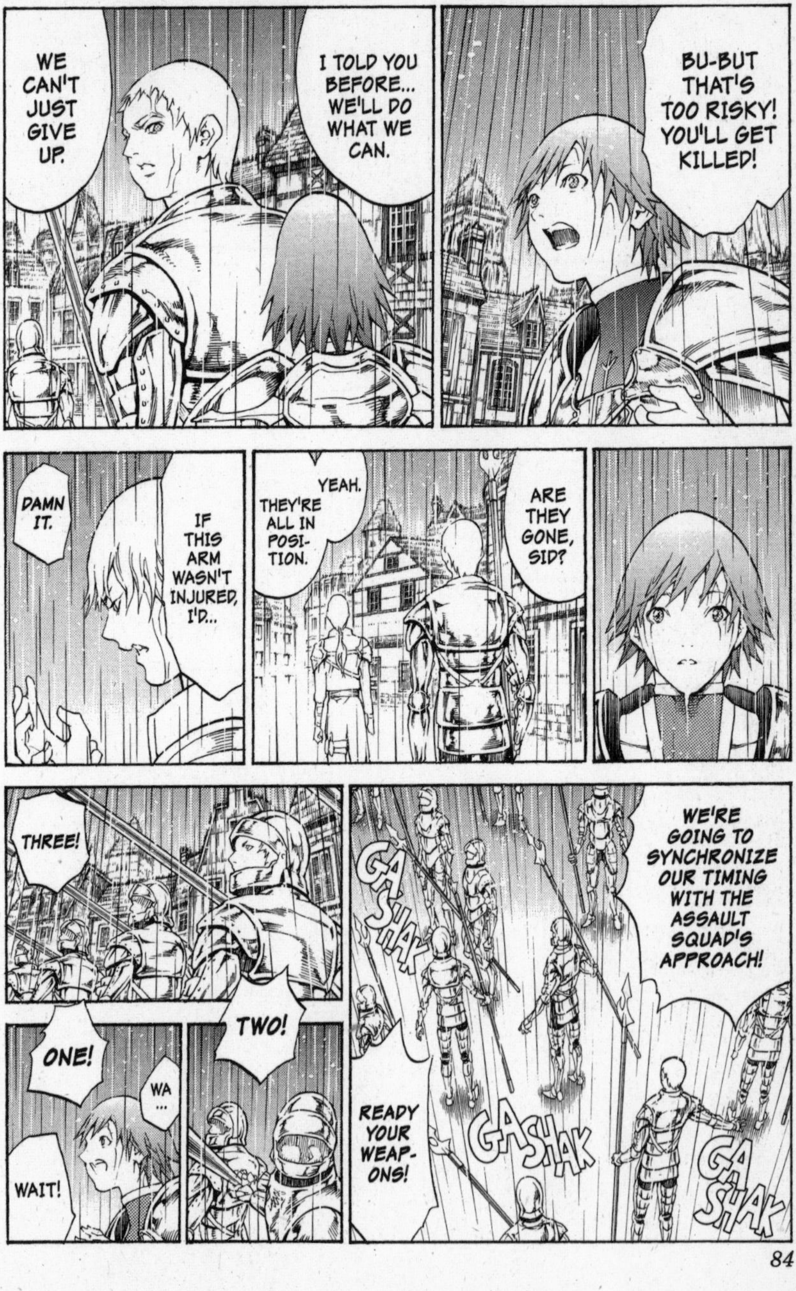
BU-BUT THAT'S TOO RISKY! YOU'LL GET KILLED!
I TOLD YOU BEFORE... WE'LL DO WHAT WE CAN.
WE CAN'T JUST GIVE UP.
ARE THEY GONE, SID?
YEAH.
THEY'RE ALL IN POSITION.
IF THIS ARM WASN'T INJURED, I'D...
DAMN IT.
WE'RE GOING TO SYNCHRONIZE OUR TIMING WITH THE ASSAULT SQUAD'S APPROACH!
GASHAK
READY YOUR WEAPONS!
GASHAK
GASHAK
THREE!
TWO!
ONE!
WA...
WAIT!

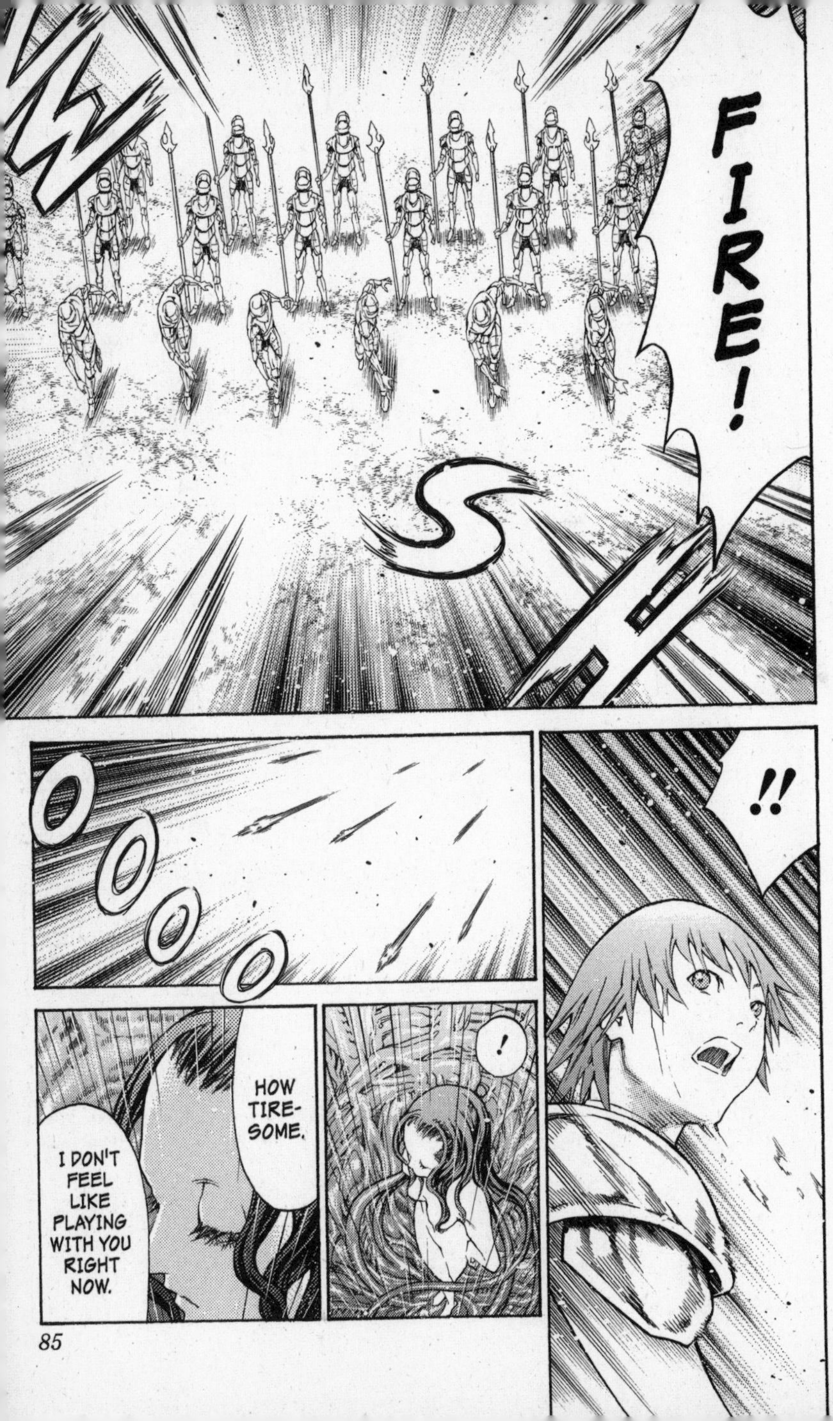
FIRE!
!!
!
HOW TIRE-SOME.
I DON'T FEEL LIKE PLAYING WITH YOU RIGHT NOW.

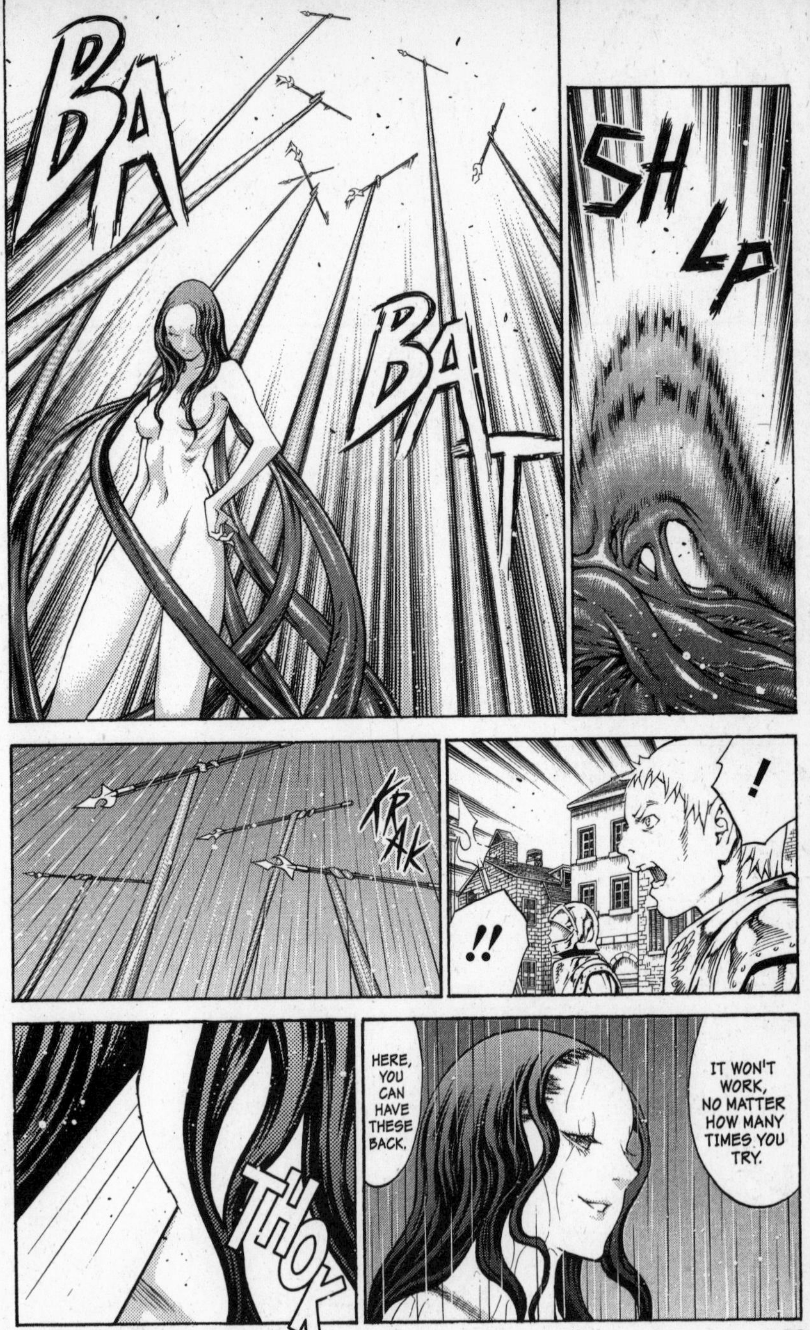
SHLP
BA
BAT
!
!!
KRAK
IT WON'T WORK, NO MATTER HOW MANY TIMES YOU TRY.
HERE, YOU CAN HAVE THESE BACK.
THOK

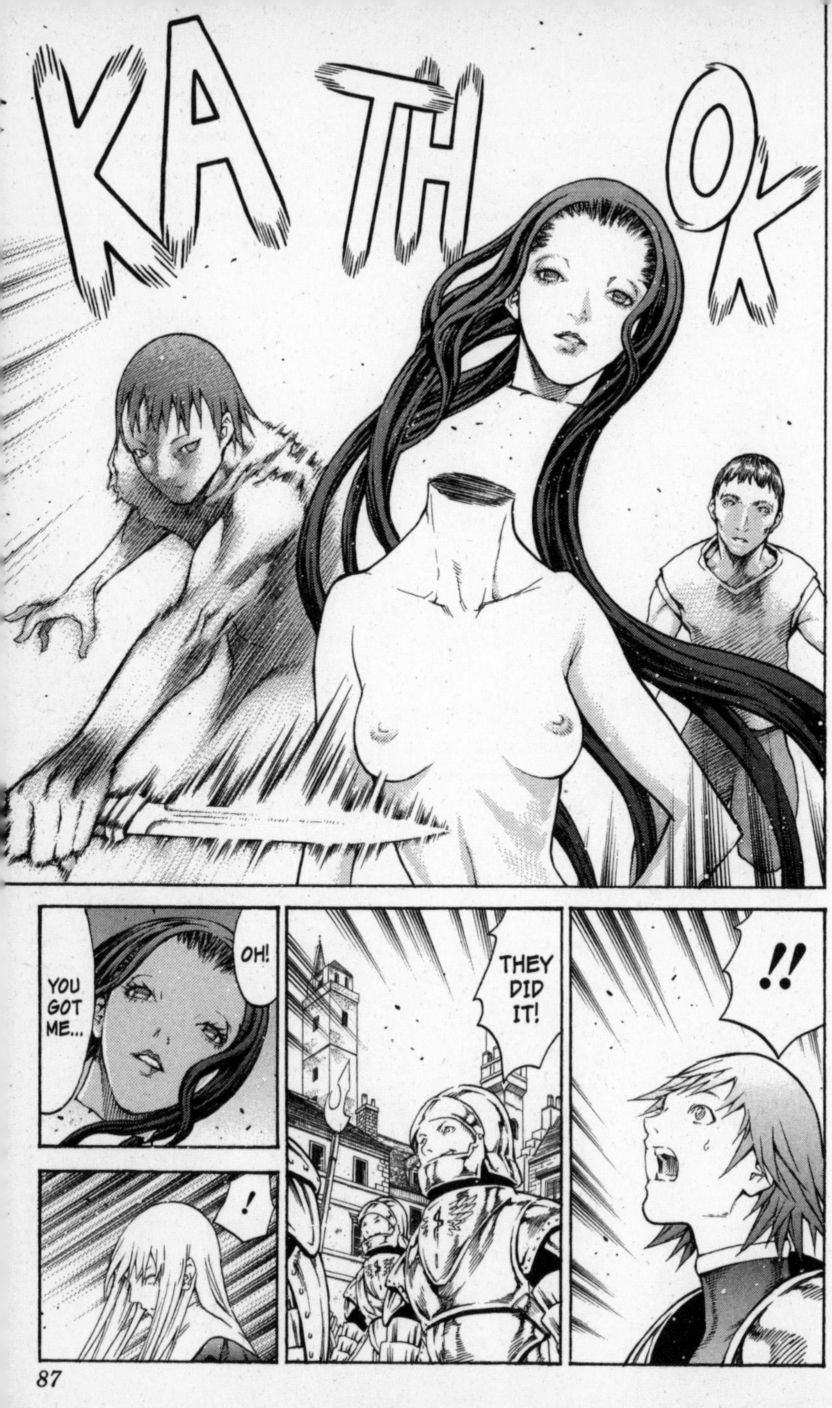
KATHOK
!!
THEY DID IT!
OH!
YOU GOT ME...
!

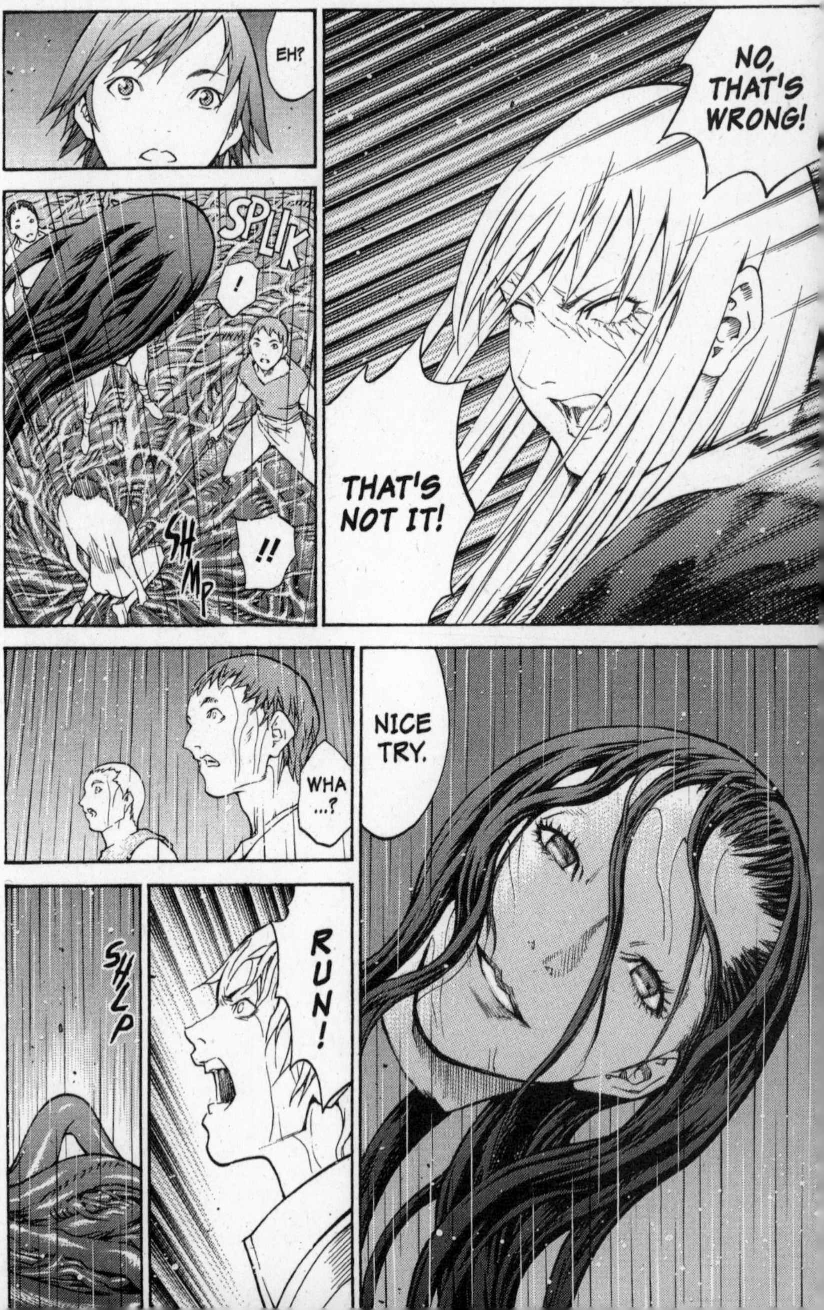
NO, THAT'S WRONG!
THAT'S NOT IT!
EH?
SPLIK
!
SHMP
!!
NICE TRY.
WHA ...?
RUN!
SHLP

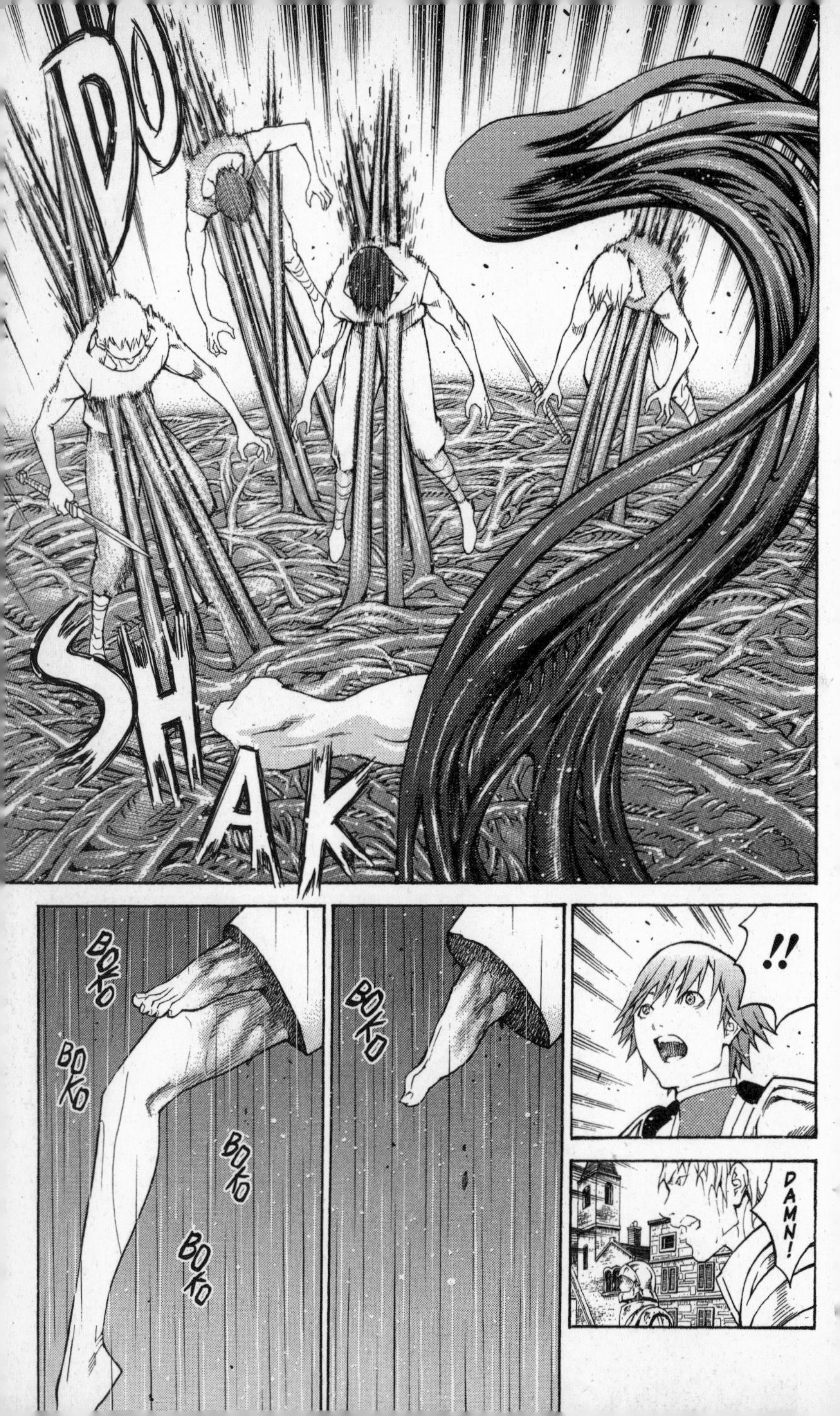
DO
SHAK
!!
DAMN!
BOKO
BOKO
BOKO
BOKO
BOKO

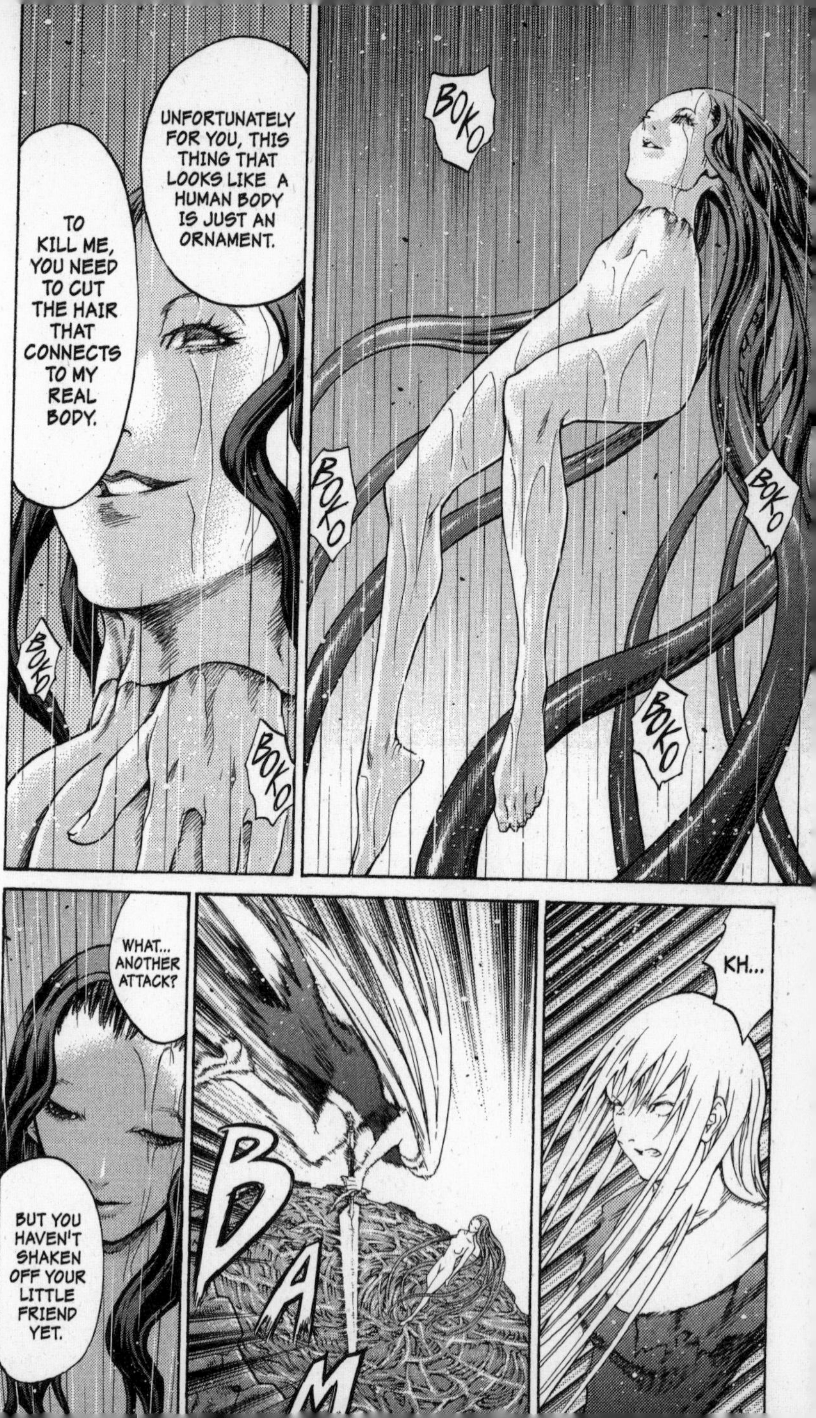
BOKO
BOKO
BOKO
BOKO
UNFORTUNATELY FOR YOU, THIS THING THAT LOOKS LIKE A HUMAN BODY IS JUST AN ORNAMENT.
TO KILL ME, YOU NEED TO CUT THE HAIR THAT CONNECTS TO MY REAL BODY.
BOKO
BOKO
KH...
BADAM
WHAT... ANOTHER ATTACK?
BUT YOU HAVEN'T SHAKEN OFF YOUR LITTLE FRIEND YET.

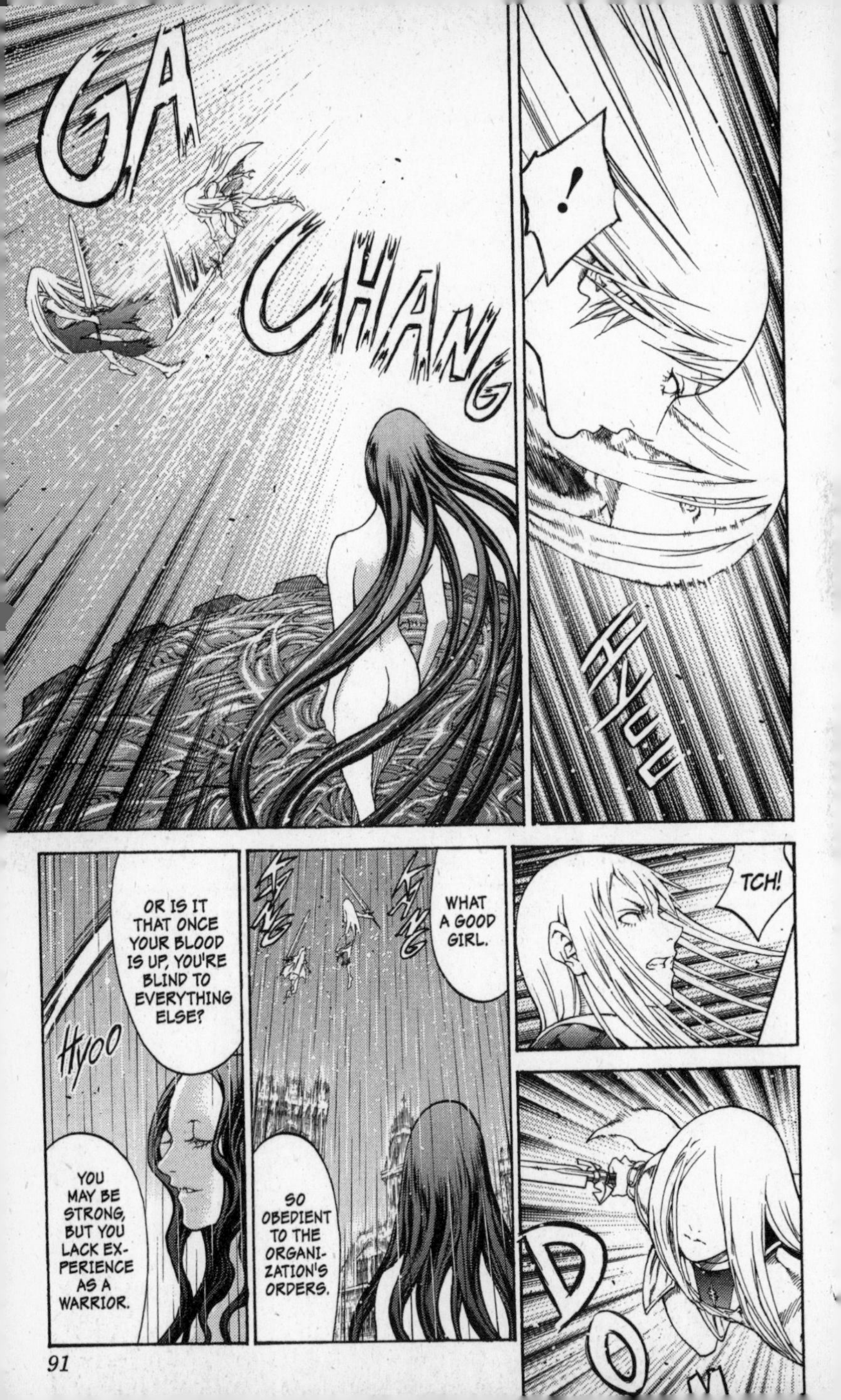
!
HYUU
GA CHANG
TCH!
DO
WHAT A GOOD GIRL.
SO OBEDIENT TO THE ORGANIZATION'S ORDERS.
OR IS IT THAT ONCE YOUR BLOOD IS UP, YOU'RE BLIND TO EVERYTHING ELSE?
HYOO
YOU MAY BE STRONG, BUT YOU LACK EXPERIENCE AS A WARRIOR.

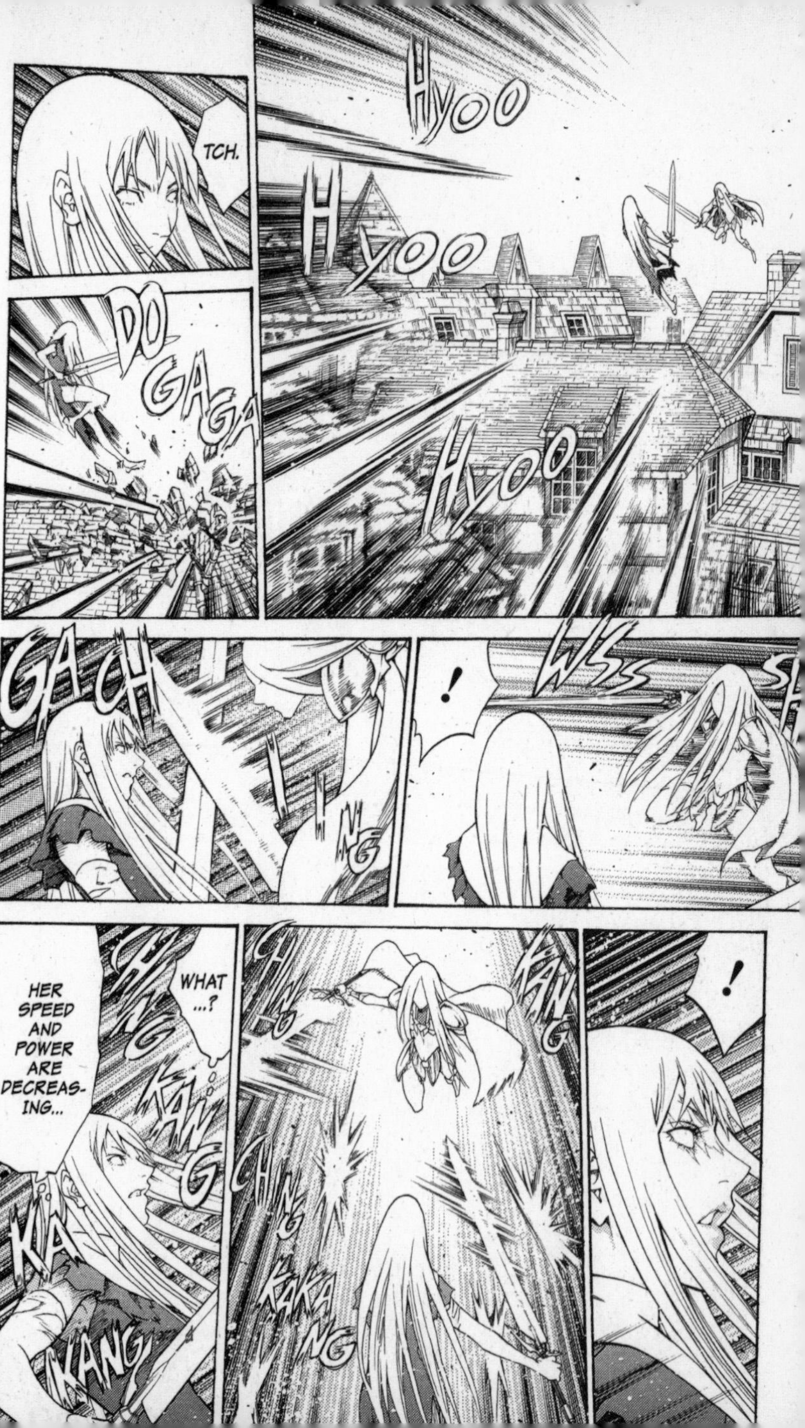
Hyoo
H yoo
Hyoo
TCH.
DO GA GA
!
WSS
GACCH
KANG
!
CHING
CHING
KAKANG
WHAT ...?
HER SPEED AND POWER ARE DECREAS-ING...
CHING
KANG
KA KANG

READ THIS WAY

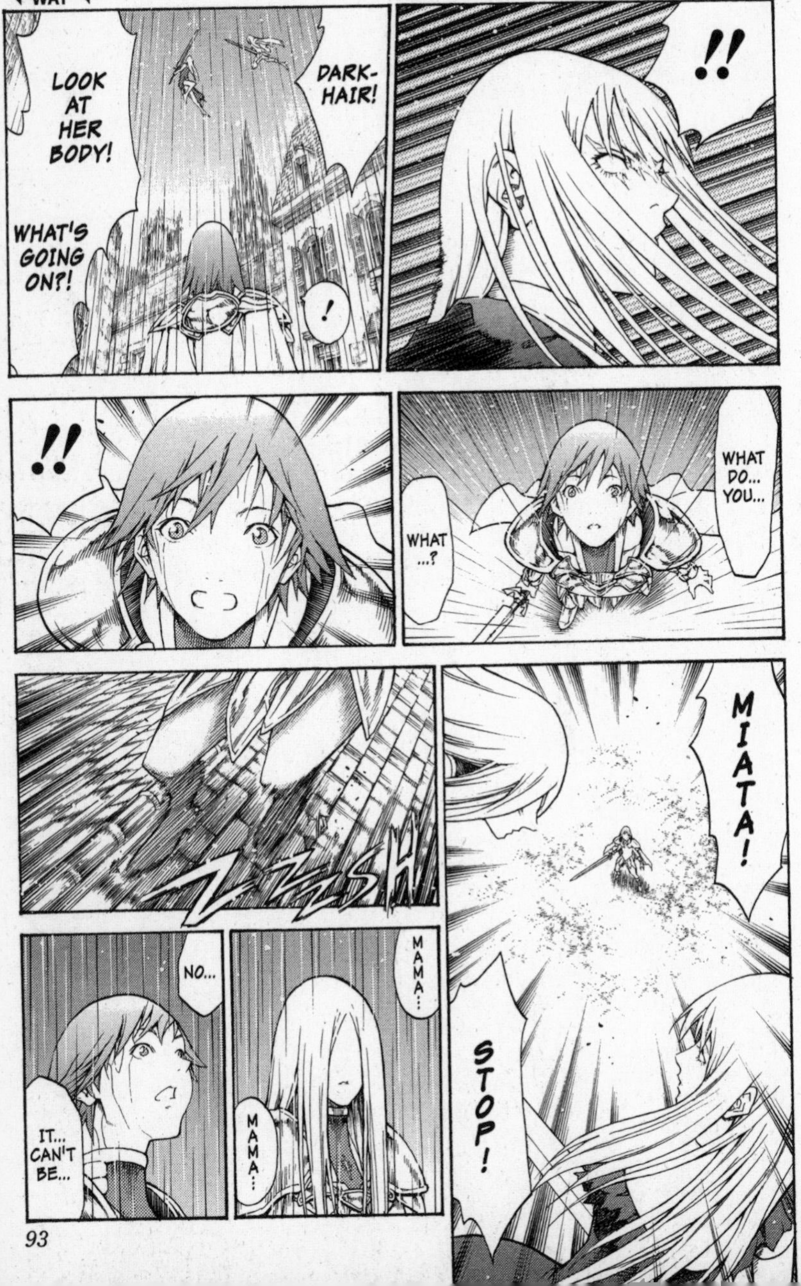
!!
DARK-HAIR!
LOOK AT HER BODY!
WHAT'S GOING ON?!
!
WHAT DO... YOU...
WHAT ...?
!!
MIATA!
STOP!
ZZZSH
MAMA...
MAMA...
NO...
IT... CAN'T BE...

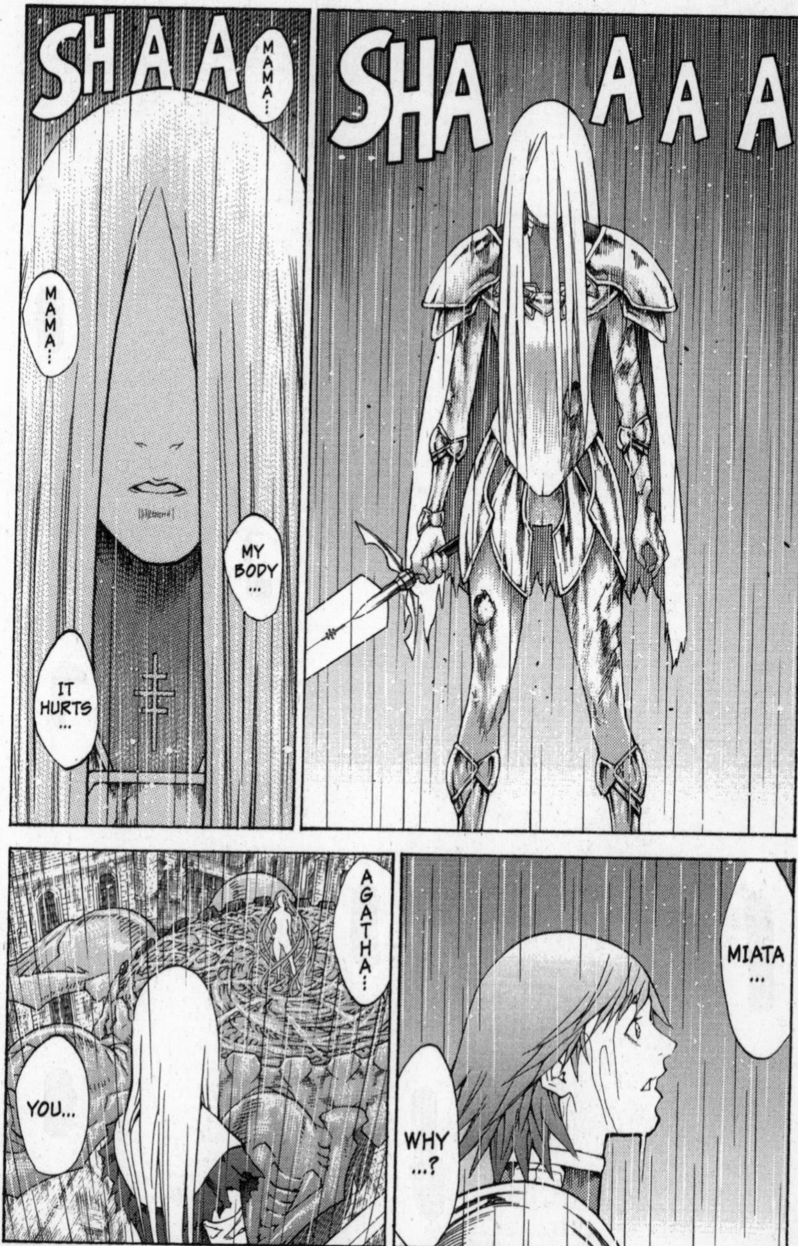
SHA AAA
SHAA
MAMA...
MAMA...
MY BODY...
IT HURTS...
MIATA...
WHY...?
AGATHA...
YOU...

READ THIS WAY

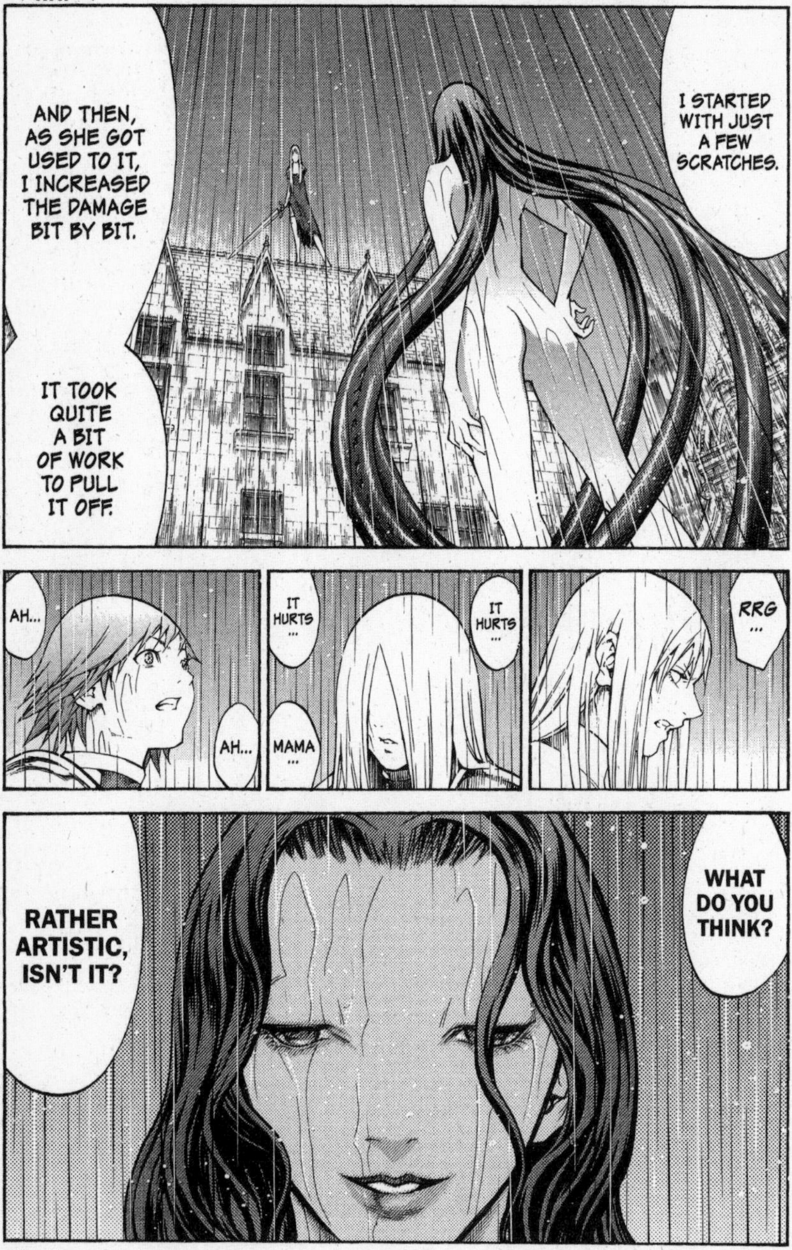

I STARTED WITH JUST A FEW SCRATCHES.
AND THEN, AS SHE GOT USED TO IT, I INCREASED THE DAMAGE BIT BY BIT.
IT TOOK QUITE A BIT OF WORK TO PULL IT OFF.
RRG...
IT HURTS...
IT HURTS...
MAMA...
AH...
AH...
WHAT DO YOU THINK?
RATHER ARTISTIC, ISN'T IT?

クレイモア
Claymore

Scene 77: A Child Weapon, Part 5

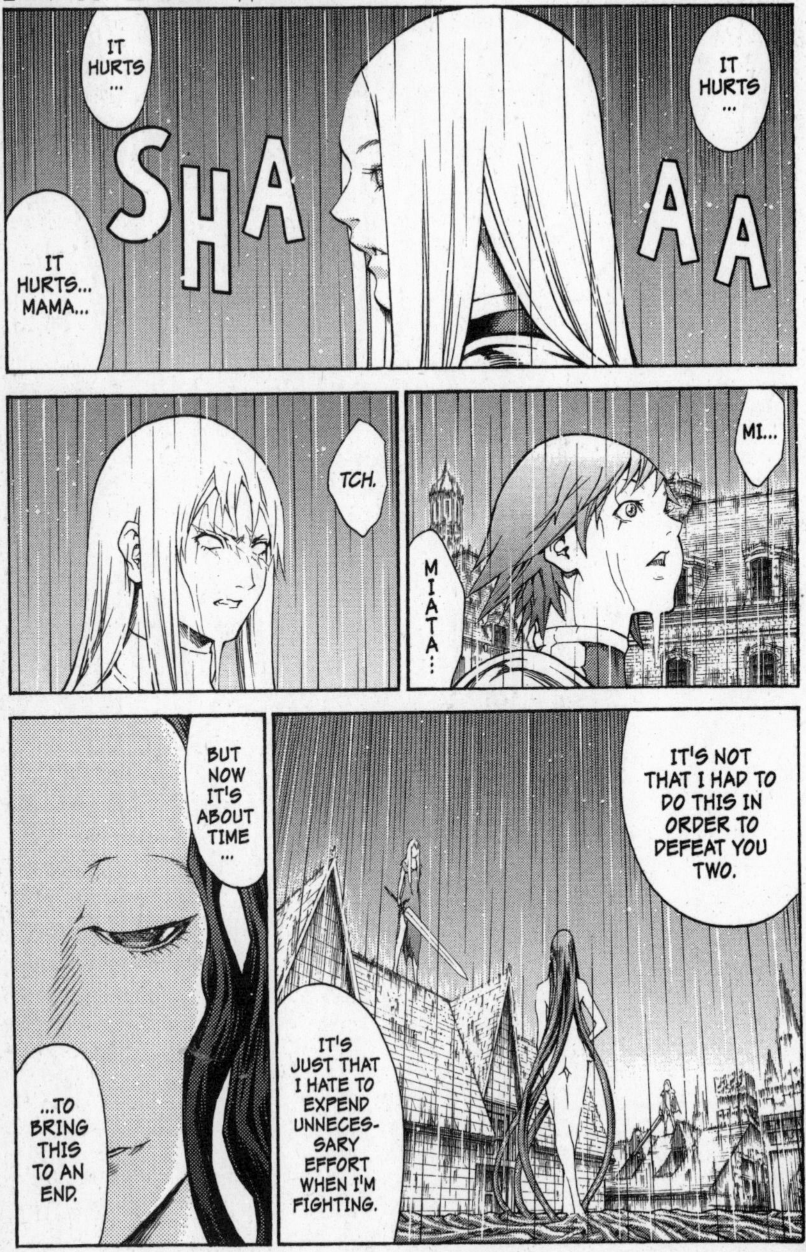
IT HURTS ...
IT HURTS ...
SHAAAA
IT HURTS... MAMA...
MI...
MIATA...
TCH.
IT'S NOT THAT I HAD TO DO THIS IN ORDER TO DEFEAT YOU TWO.
IT'S JUST THAT I HATE TO EXPEND UNNECES-SARY EFFORT WHEN I'M FIGHTING.
BUT NOW IT'S ABOUT TIME ...
...TO BRING THIS TO AN END.

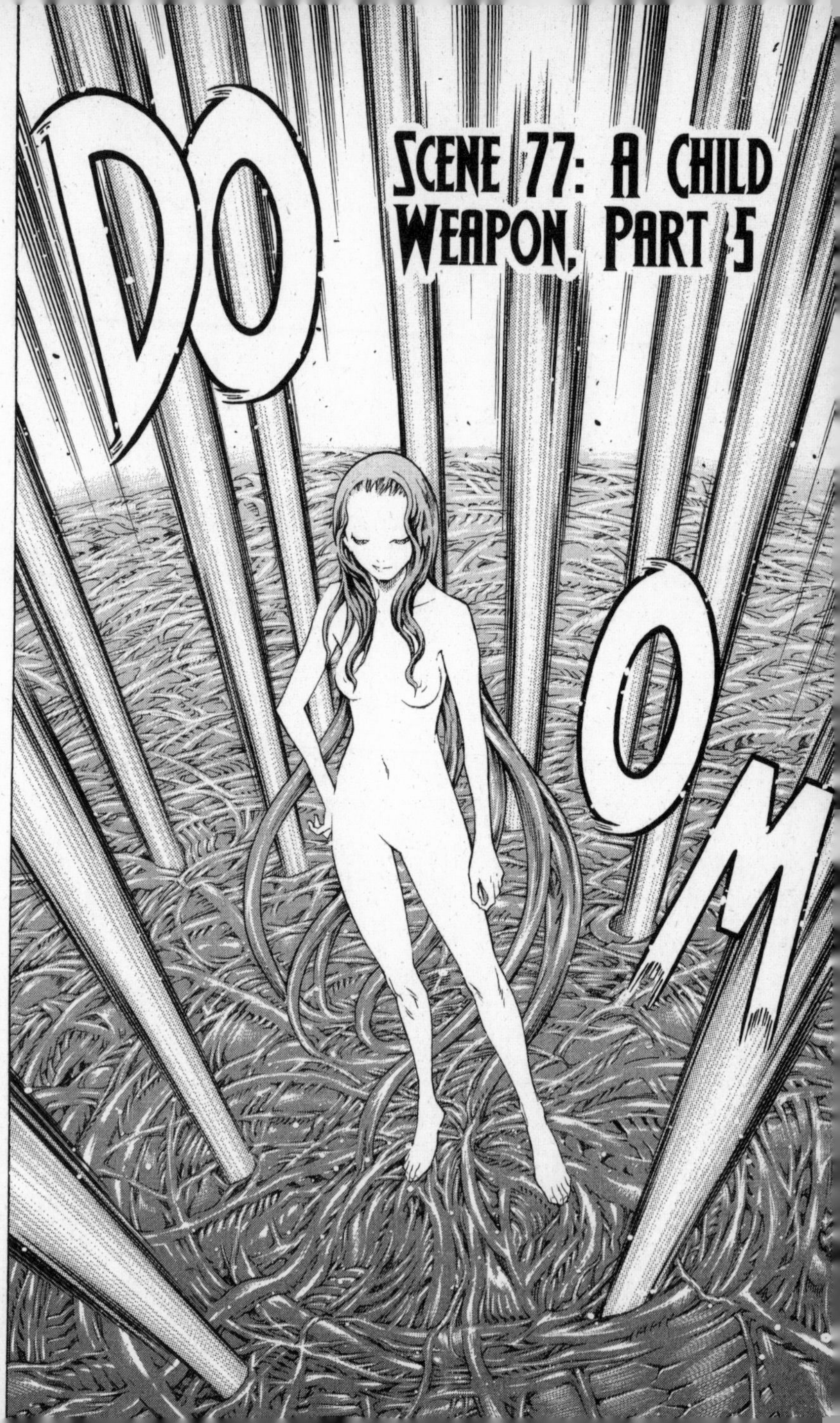
DO
SCENE 77: A CHILD WEAPON, PART 5
OM

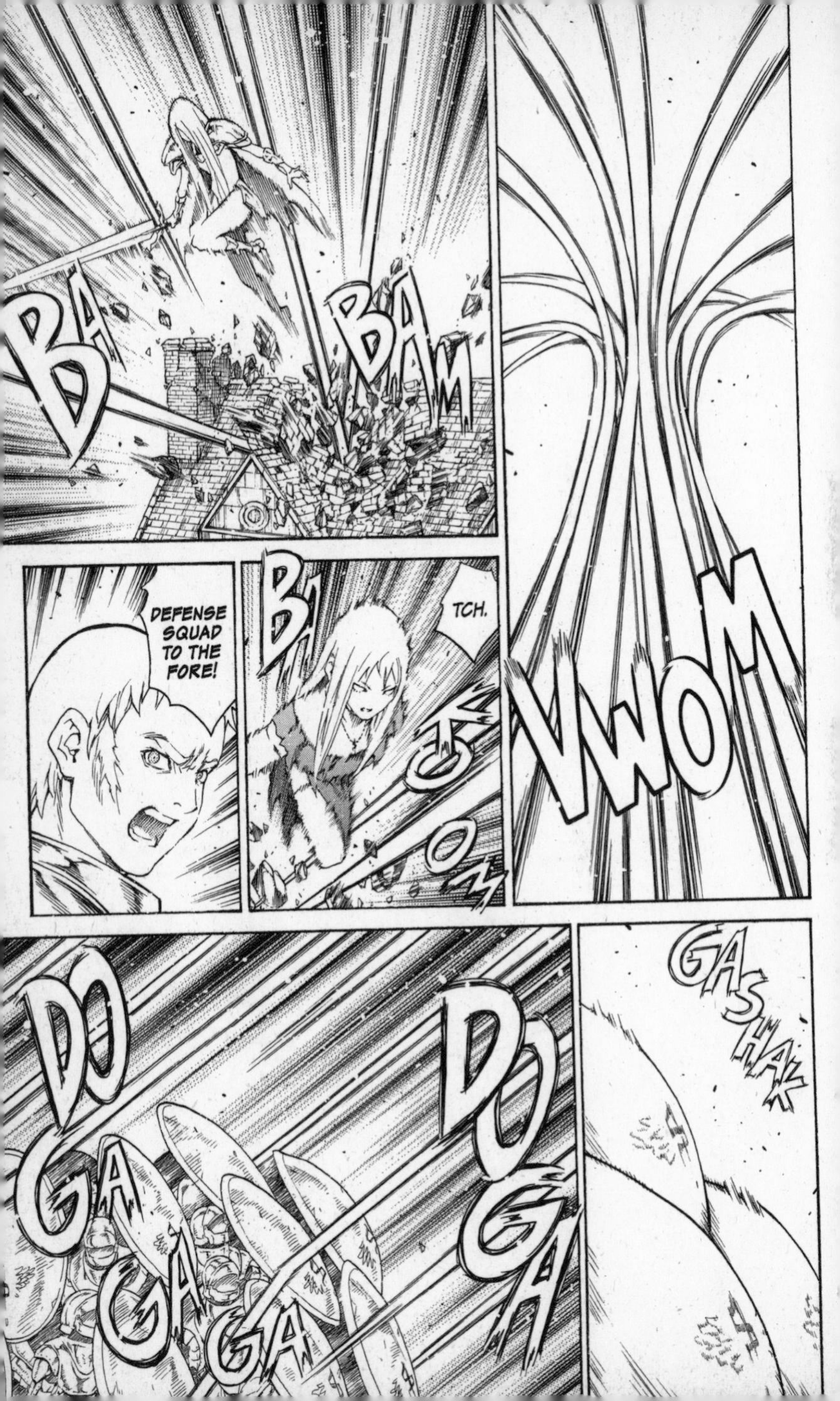
VWOM
BAM
BA
TCH.
DEFENSE SQUAD TO THE FORE!
GASHAK
DOGA
DO
GA
GA
GA

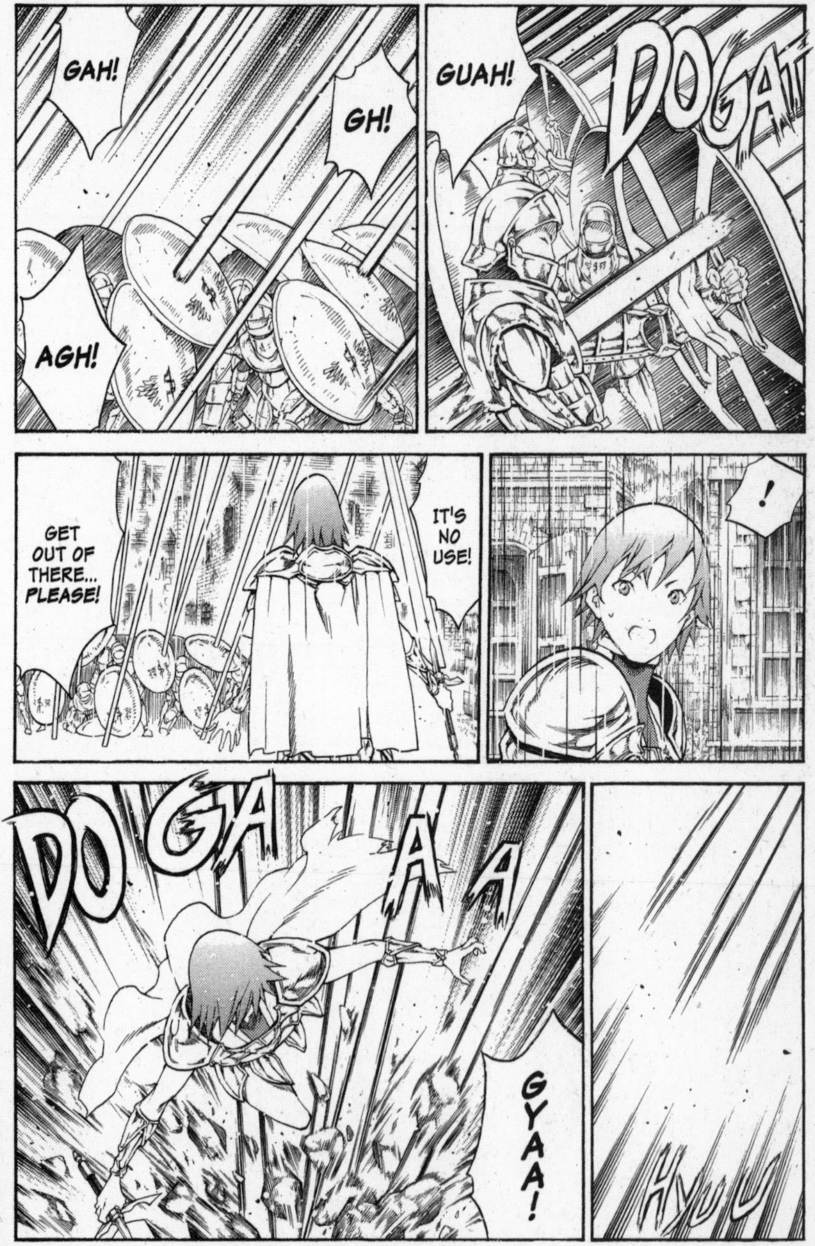
GUAH!
DOGAT
GH!
GAH!
AGH!
!
IT'S NO USE!
GET OUT OF THERE... PLEASE!
HYUU
DOGAAA
GYAAA!

READ THIS WAY

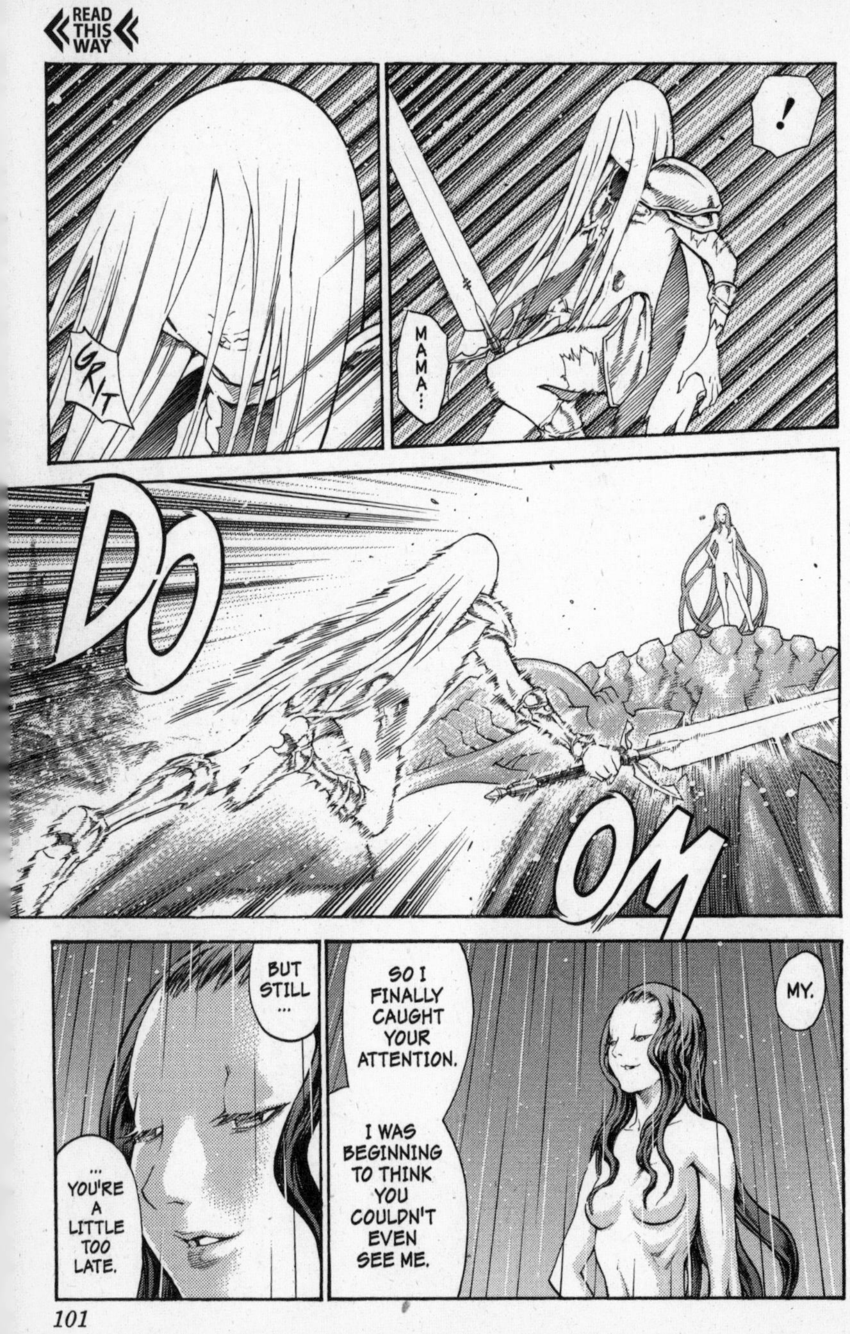
!
MAMA...
GRIT
DO
OM
MY.
SO I FINALLY CAUGHT YOUR ATTENTION.
I WAS BEGINNING TO THINK YOU COULDN'T EVEN SEE ME.
BUT STILL ...
... YOU'RE A LITTLE TOO LATE.

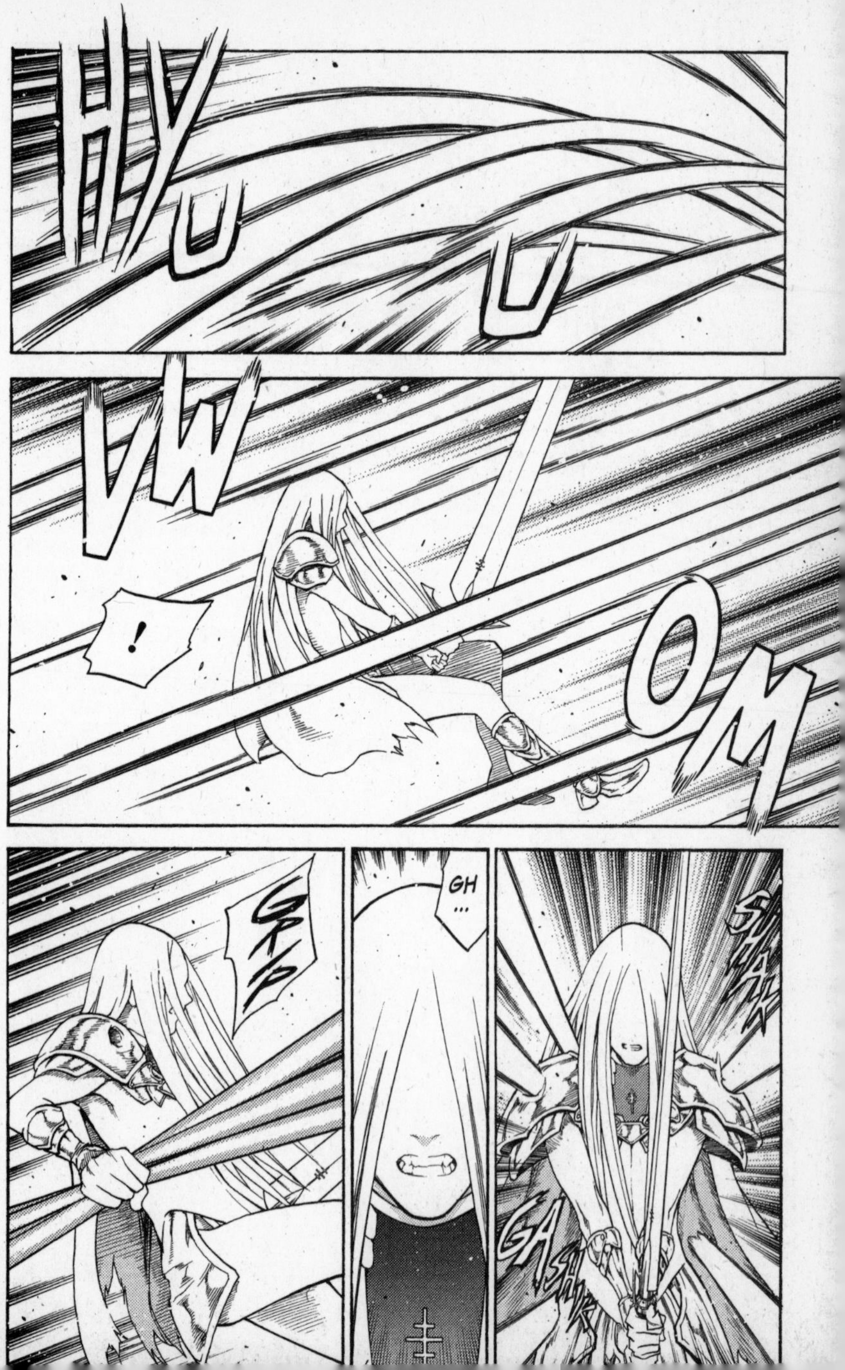
HYUUU
VWOM
!
SHAK
GASHK
GH...
GRIP

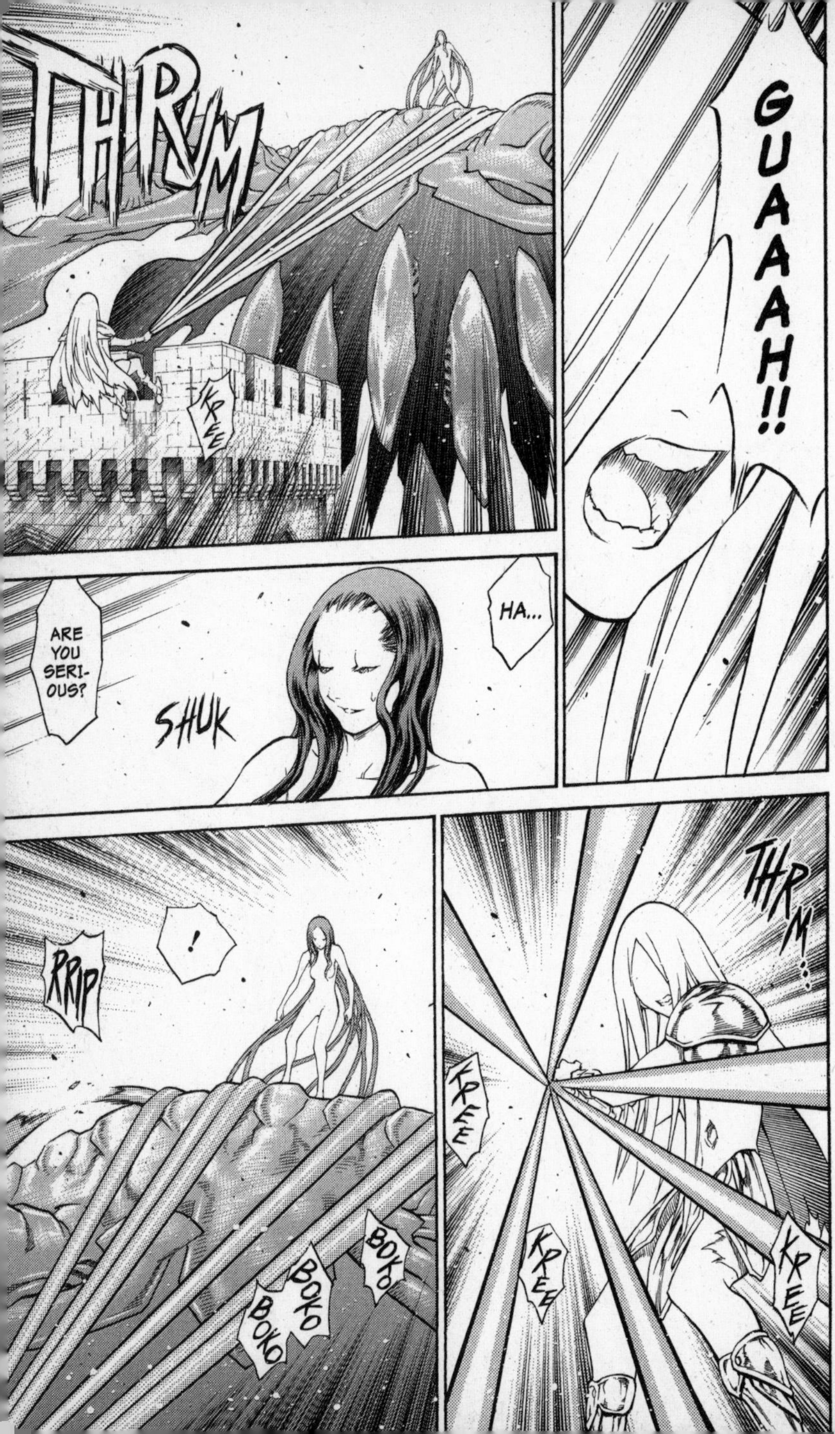
GUAAAAH!!
THRUM
KREE
HA...
ARE YOU SERI-OUS?
SHUK
THRM...
KREE
KREE
KREE
!
RRIP
BOKO
BOKO
BOKO

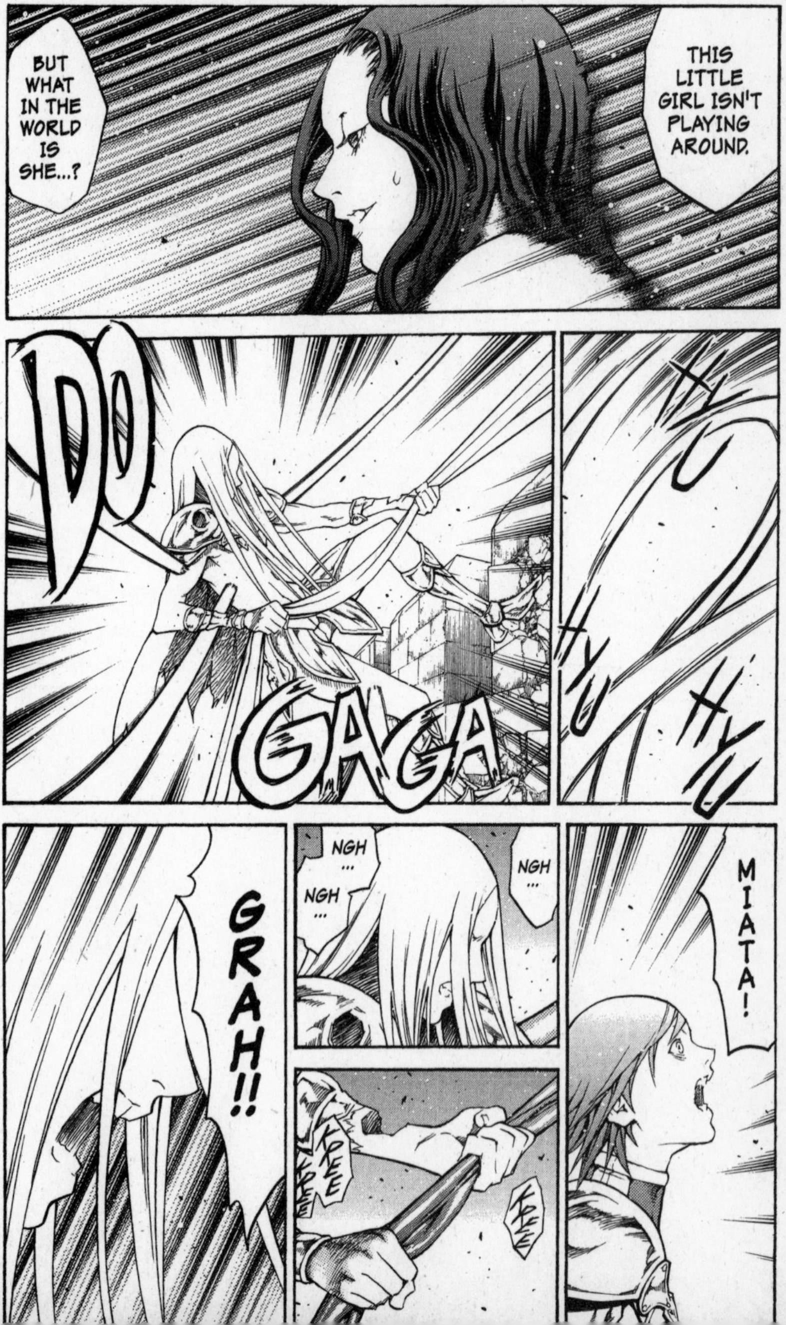
THIS LITTLE GIRL ISN'T PLAYING AROUND.
BUT WHAT IN THE WORLD IS SHE...?
HYU
HYU
HYU
DO
GAGA
MIATA!
NGH ...
NGH ...
NGH ...
GRAH!!
KREE
KREE
KREE

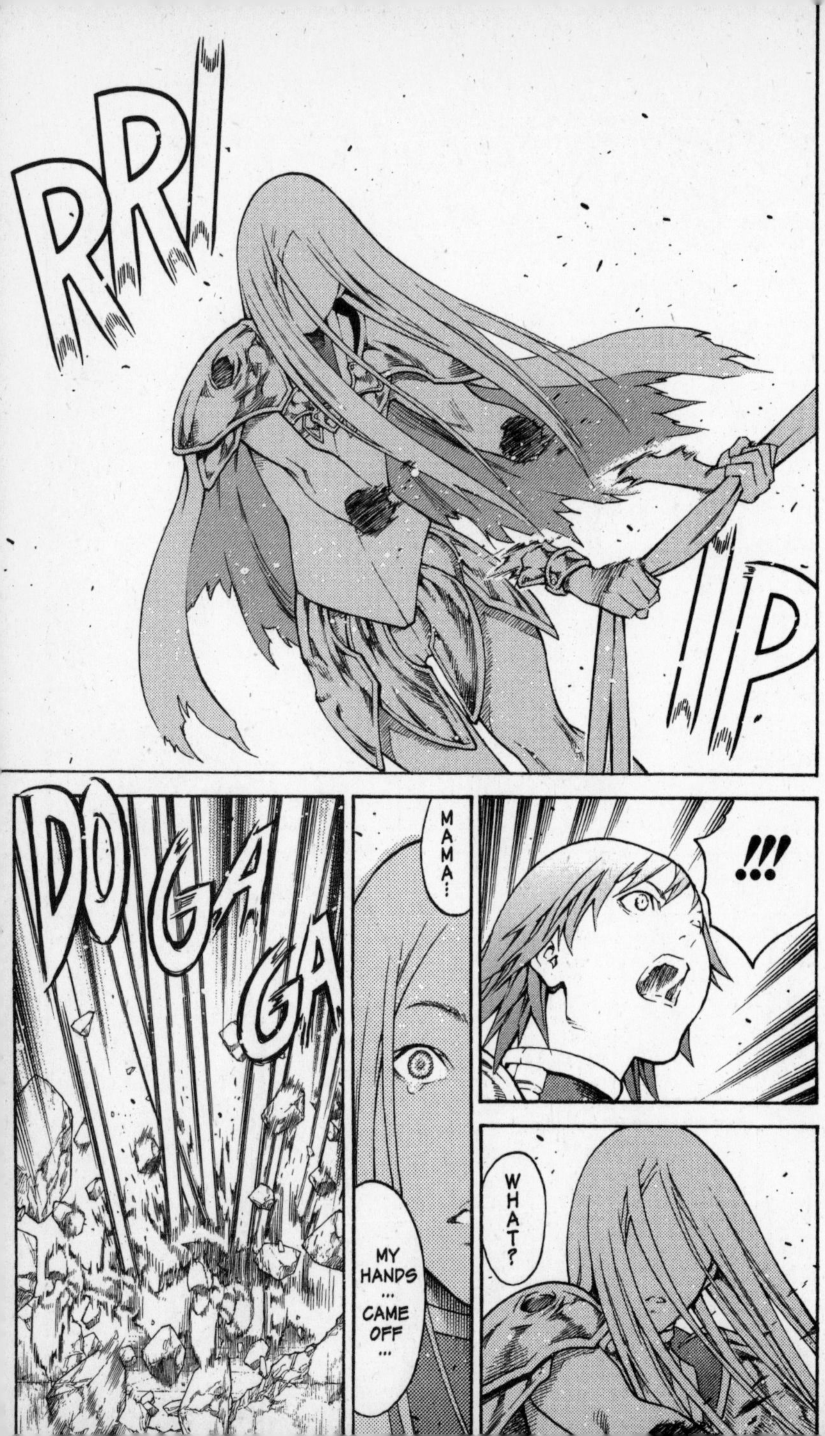
RRIP
!!!
WHAT?
MAMA!?
MY HANDS... CAME OFF...
DOGAGA

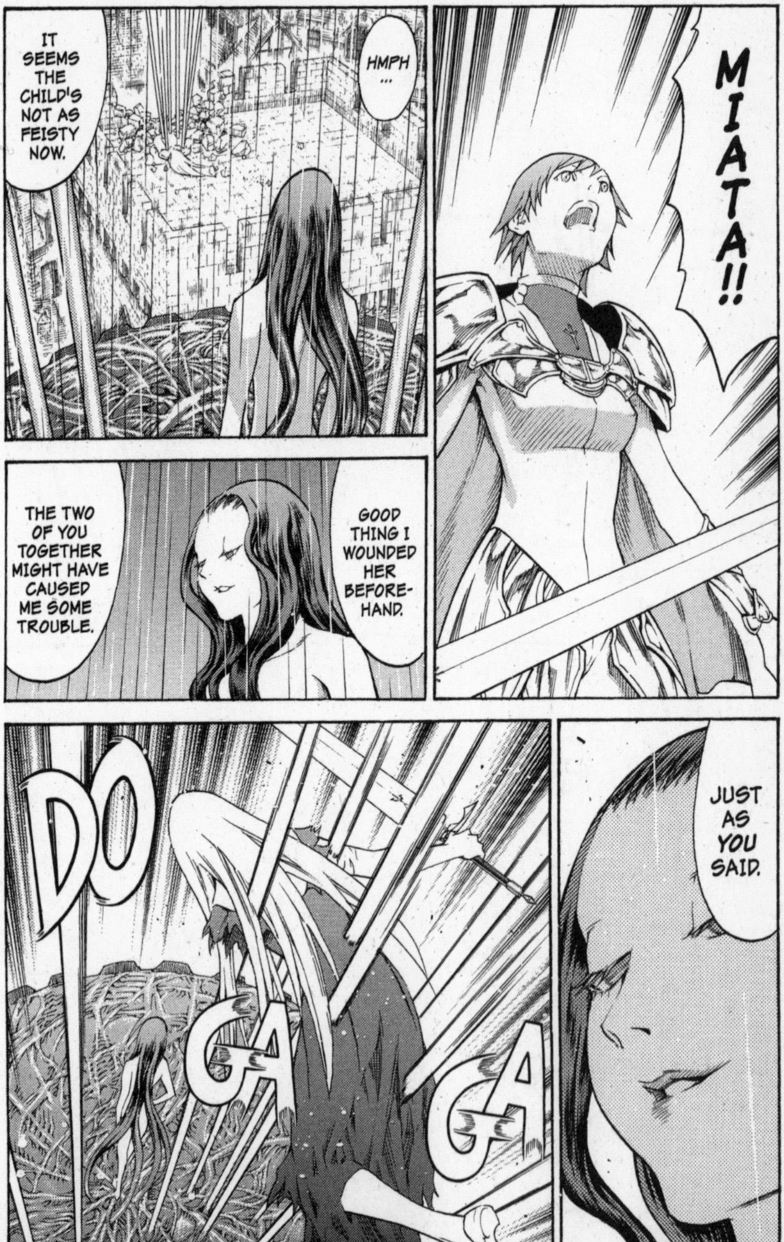
MIATA!!
HMPH...
IT SEEMS THE CHILD'S NOT AS FEISTY NOW.
GOOD THING I WOUNDED HER BEFORE-HAND.
THE TWO OF YOU TOGETHER MIGHT HAVE CAUSED ME SOME TROUBLE.
JUST AS YOU SAID.
DO
GA
GA

READ THIS WAY

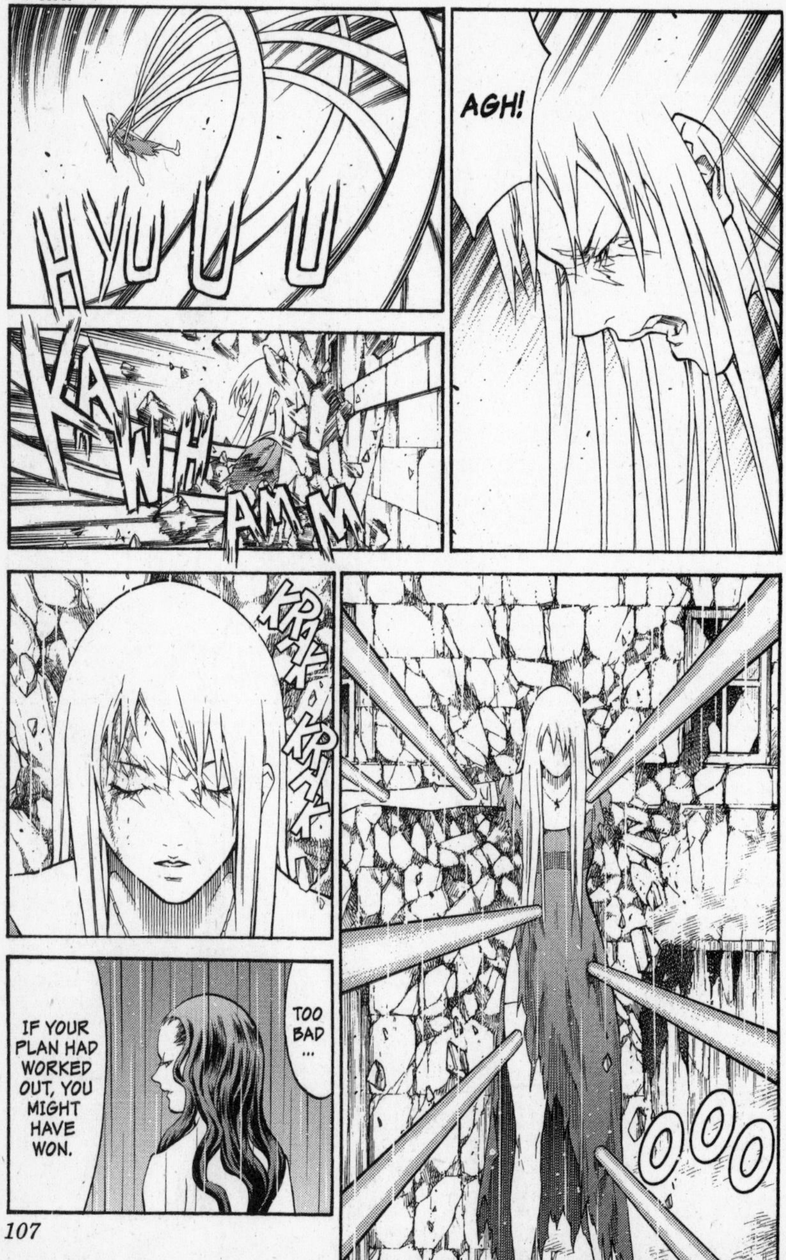
AGH!
HYUUUU
KAWHAMM
OOO
KRAK KRAK KRAK
TOO BAD ...
IF YOUR PLAN HAD WORKED OUT, YOU MIGHT HAVE WON.

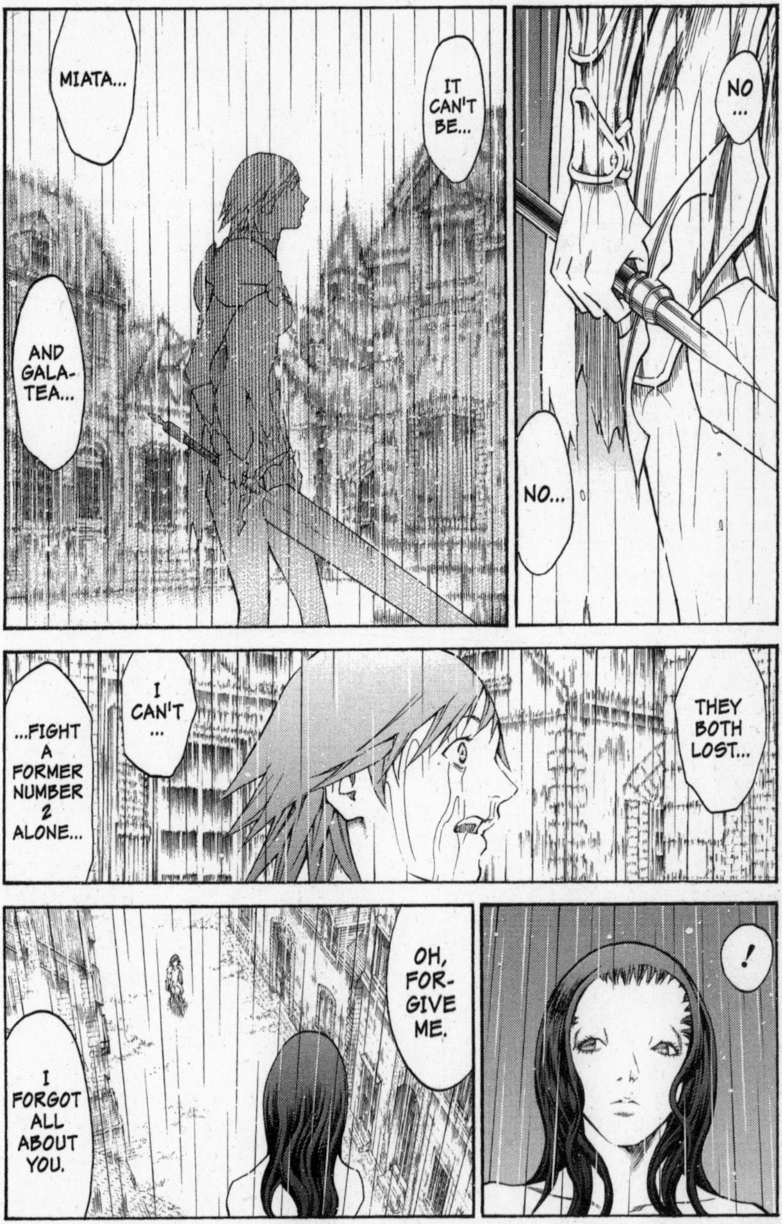
NO ...
NO...
IT CAN'T BE...
MIATA...
AND GALA-TEA...
THEY BOTH LOST...
I CAN'T ...
...FIGHT A FORMER NUMBER 2 ALONE...
!
OH, FOR-GIVE ME.
I FORGOT ALL ABOUT YOU.

READ THIS WAY

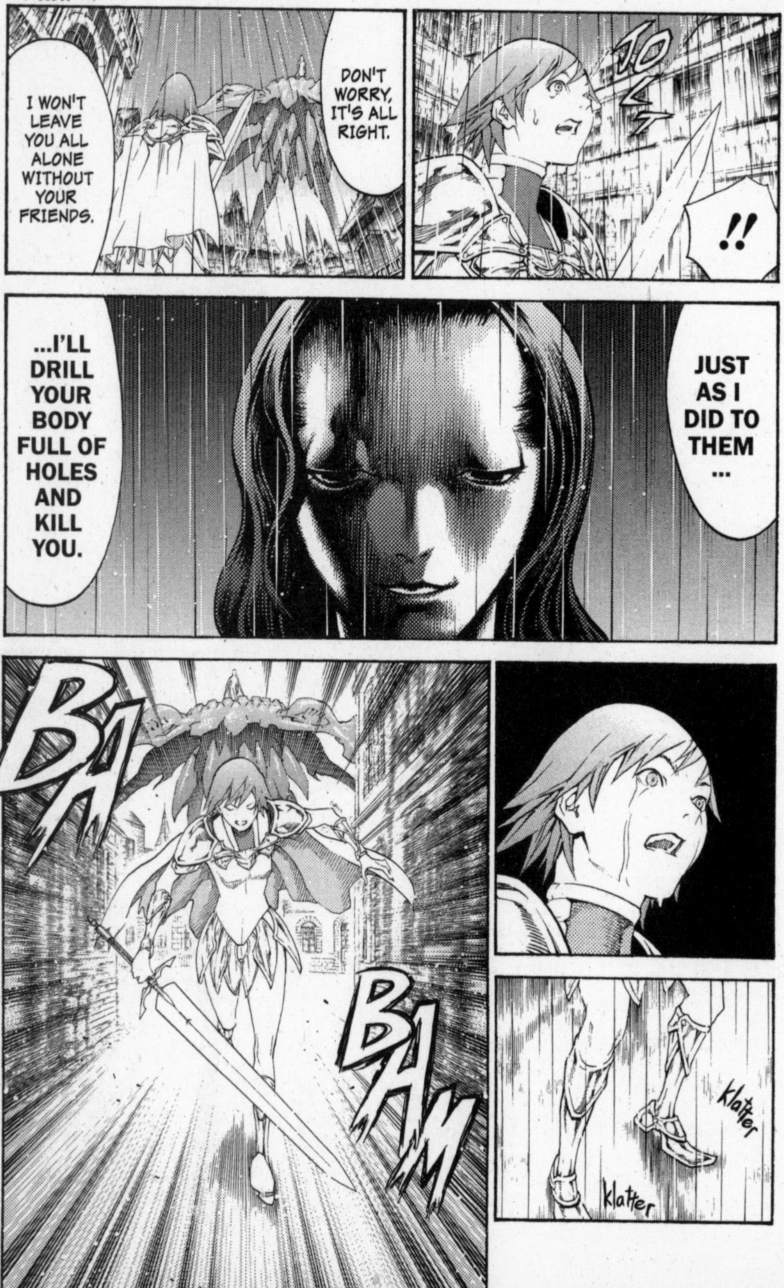
JOLT
!!
DON'T WORRY, IT'S ALL RIGHT.
I WON'T LEAVE YOU ALL ALONE WITHOUT YOUR FRIENDS.
JUST AS I DID TO THEM ...
...I'LL DRILL YOUR BODY FULL OF HOLES AND KILL YOU.
klatter
klatter
BA
BAM

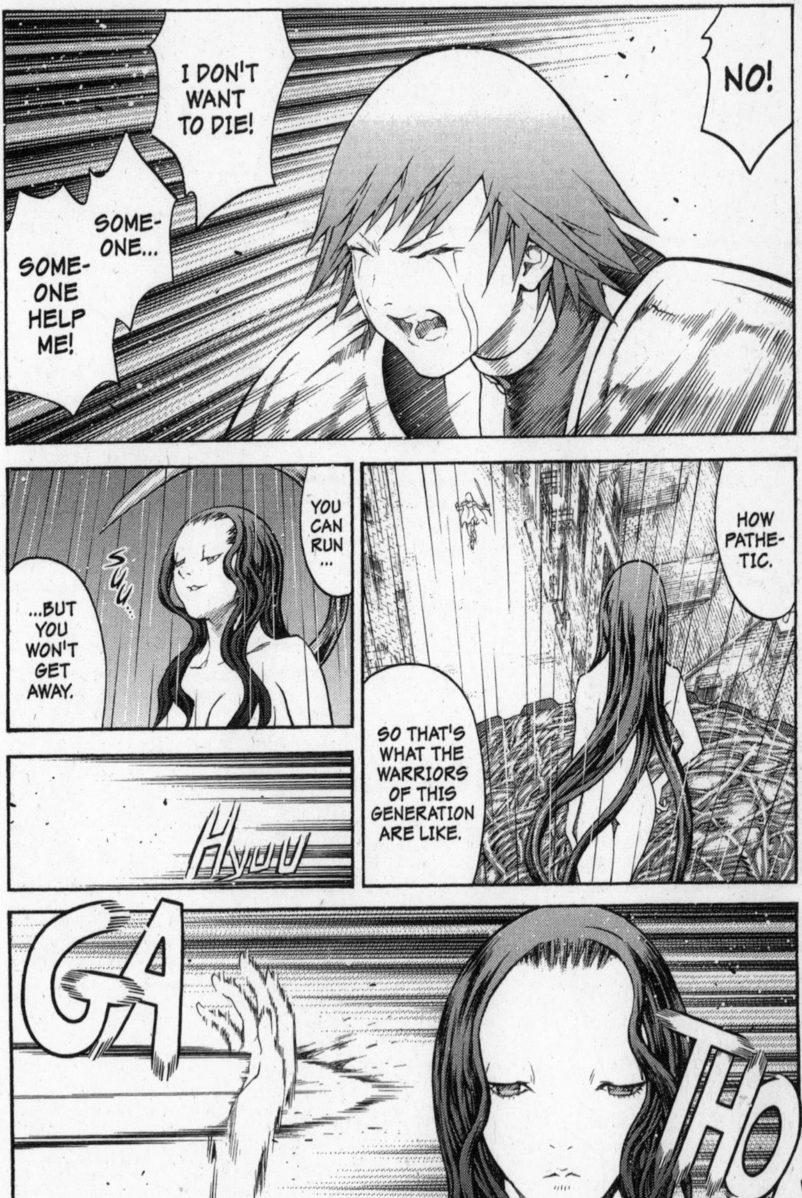
NO!
I DON'T WANT TO DIE!
SOME-ONE...
SOME-ONE HELP ME!
HOW PATHE-TIC.
SO THAT'S WHAT THE WARRIORS OF THIS GENERATION ARE LIKE.
YOU CAN RUN ...
SUU...
...BUT YOU WON'T GET AWAY.
Hyuu
GA
THOK

...DID YOU THROW THIS FROM THERE?

HOW ON EARTH...

!

MAMA...!

MAMA...!

MAMA...!

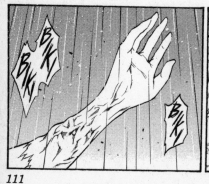

BIKI

BIKI

BIKI

BIKI

BIKI

BIKI

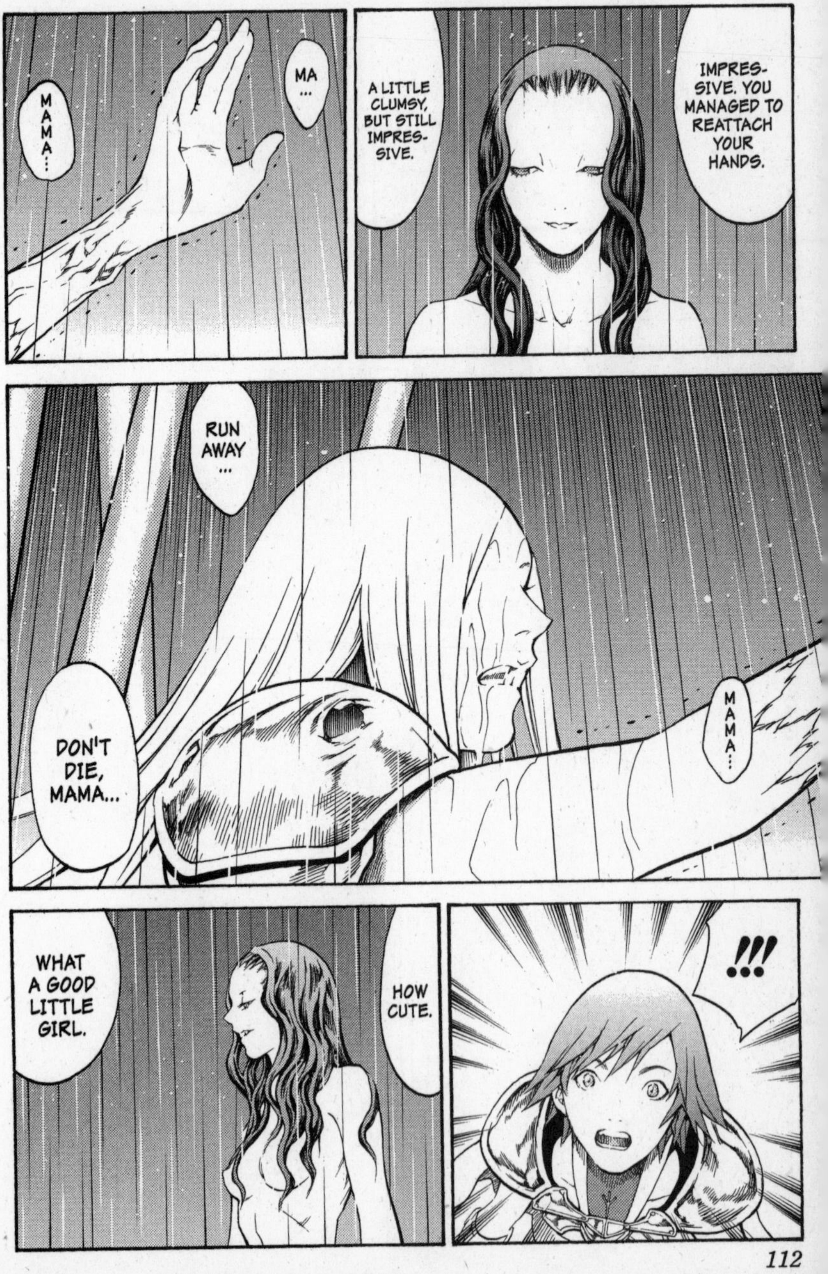

IMPRES-SIVE. YOU MANAGED TO REATTACH YOUR HANDS.
A LITTLE CLUMSY, BUT STILL IMPRES-SIVE.
MA ...
MAMA...
MAMA...
RUN AWAY ...
DON'T DIE, MAMA...
!!!
HOW CUTE.
WHAT A GOOD LITTLE GIRL.

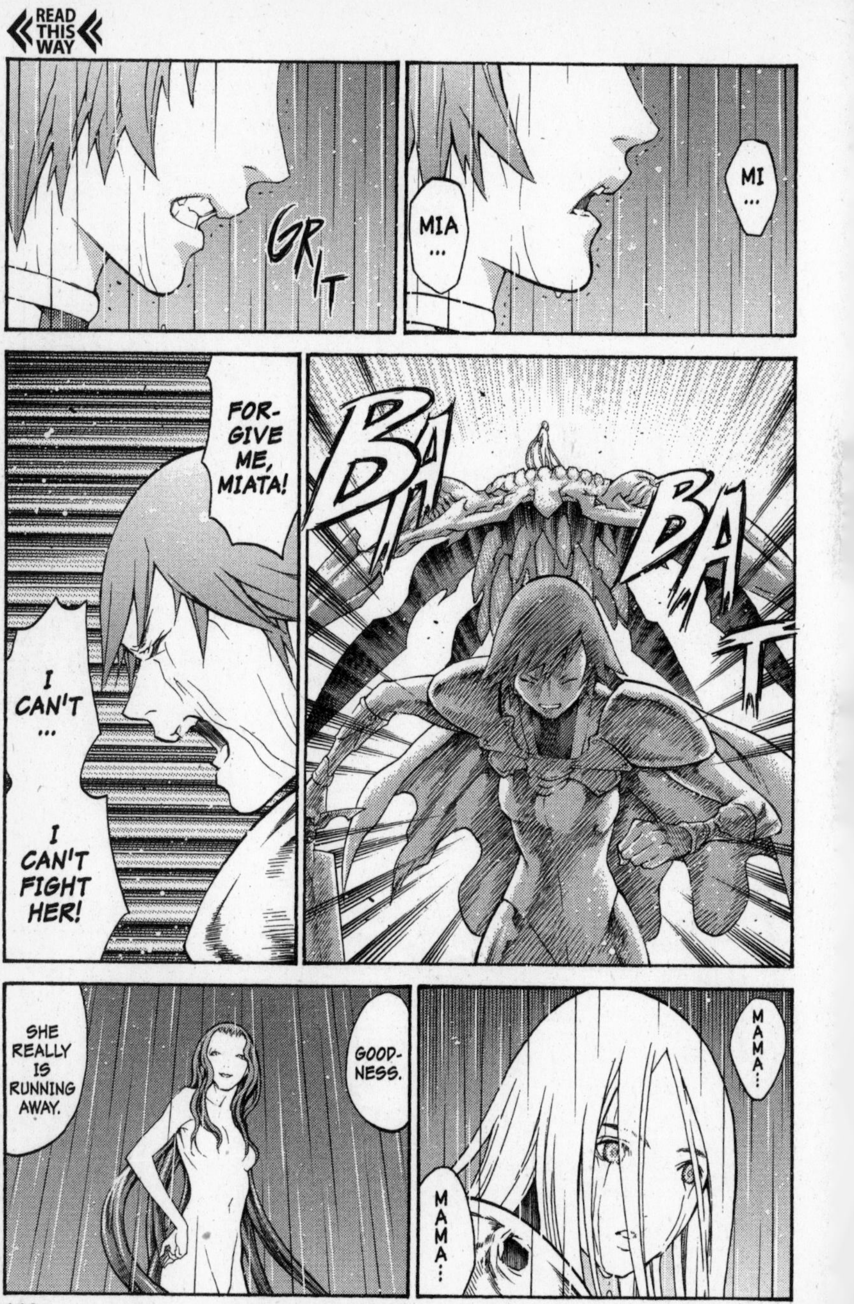
READ THIS WAY
MI...
MIA...
GRIT
BADA
BADAT
FOR-GIVE ME, MIATA!
I CAN'T...
I CAN'T FIGHT HER!
MAMA...
MAMA...
GOOD-NESS.
SHE REALLY IS RUNNING AWAY.

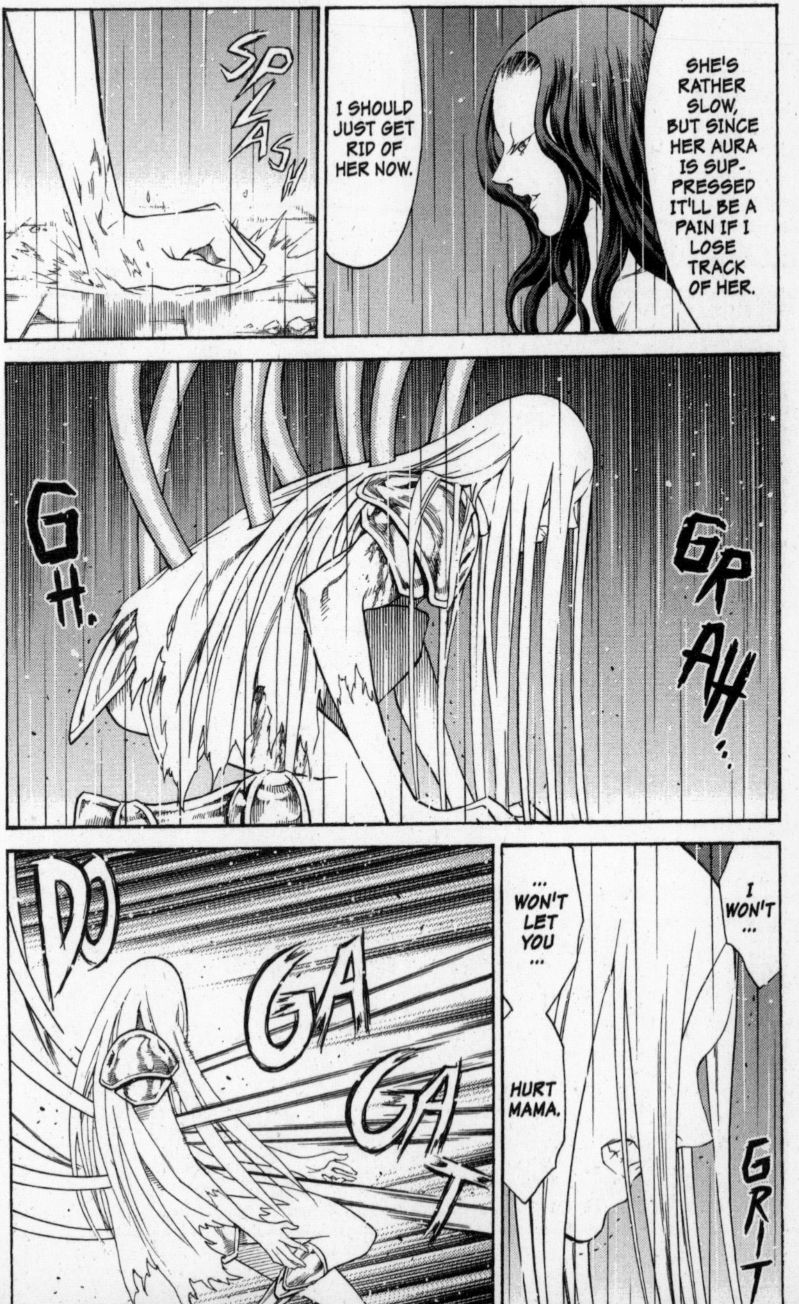

SHE'S RATHER SLOW, BUT SINCE HER AURA IS SUPPRESSED IT'LL BE A PAIN IF I LOSE TRACK OF HER.
I SHOULD JUST GET RID OF HER NOW.
SPLASH
GRAAH...
GH.
I WON'T ...
... WON'T LET YOU ...
HURT MAMA.
GRIT
DOGAGAT

READ THIS WAY

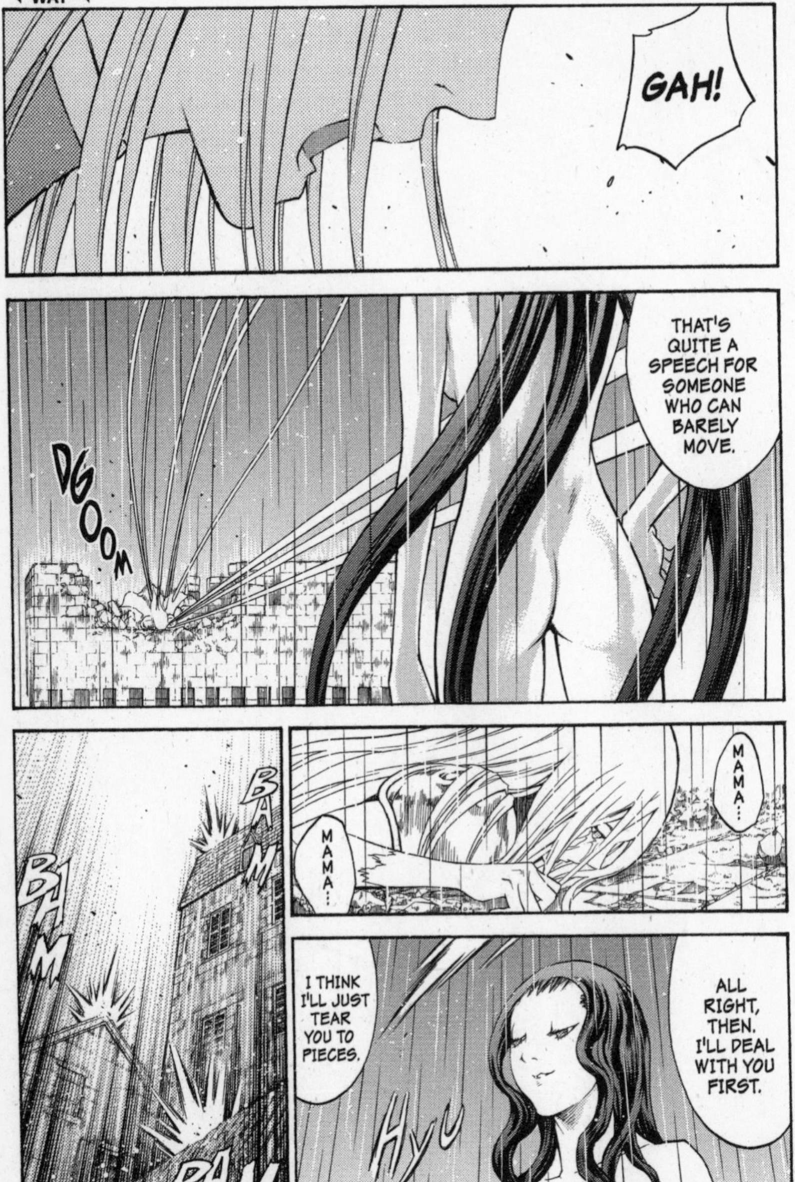
GAH!
THAT'S QUITE A SPEECH FOR SOMEONE WHO CAN BARELY MOVE.
DGOOOM
MAMA...
MAMA...
ALL RIGHT, THEN. I'LL DEAL WITH YOU FIRST.
I THINK I'LL JUST TEAR YOU TO PIECES.
HYU
BAM
BAHM
BAM

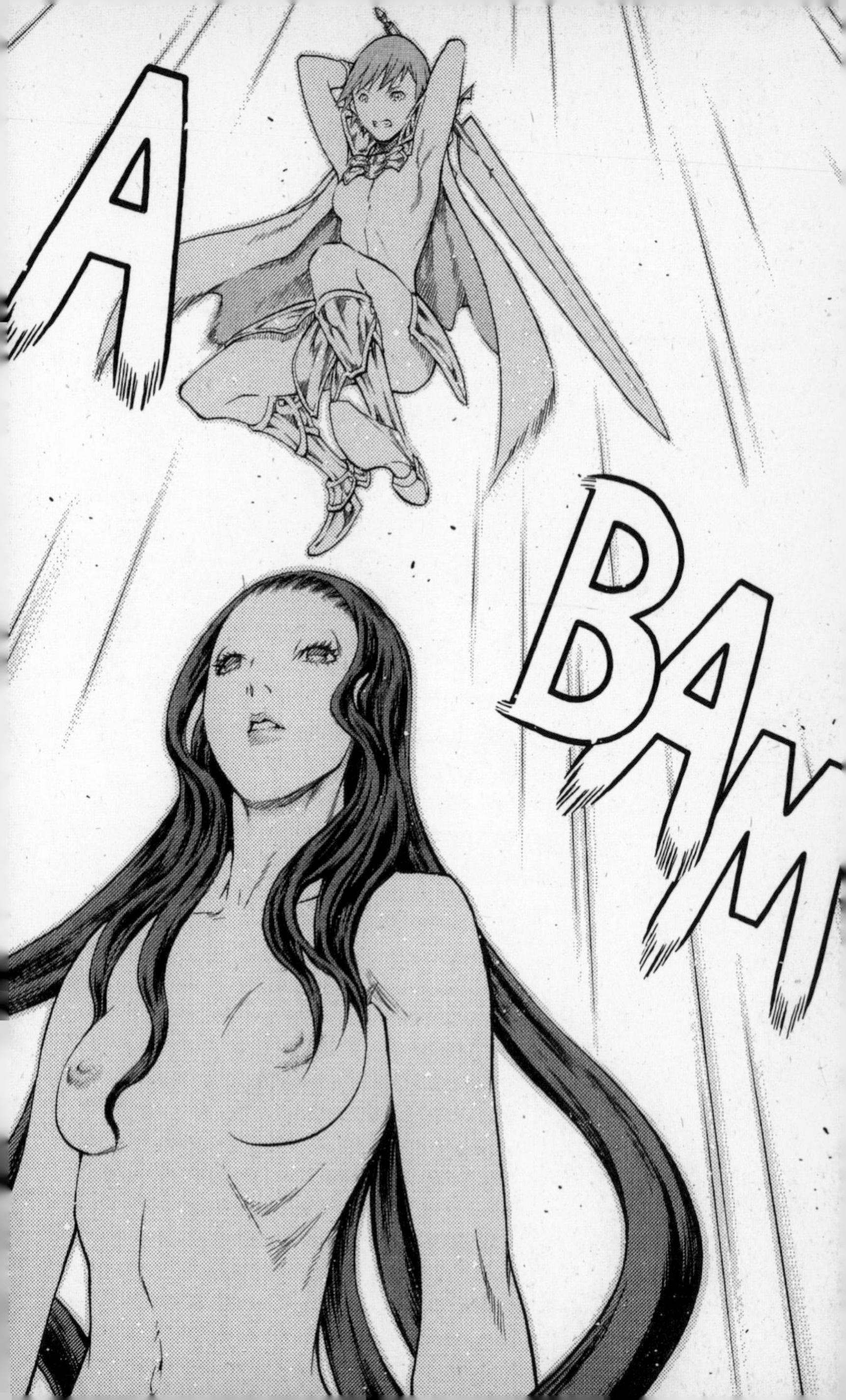
A
BAM

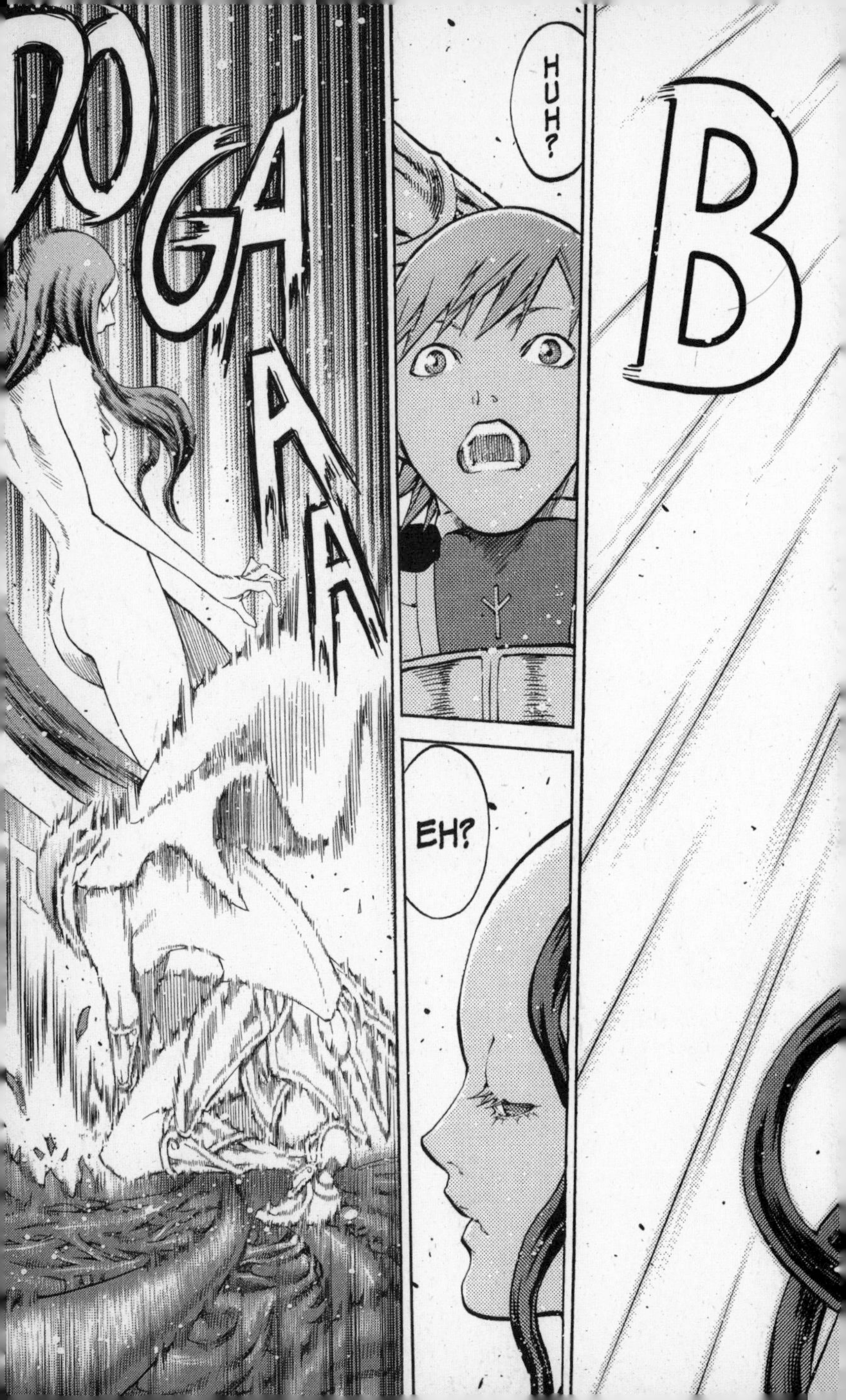
B
HUH?
EH?
DOGAAA

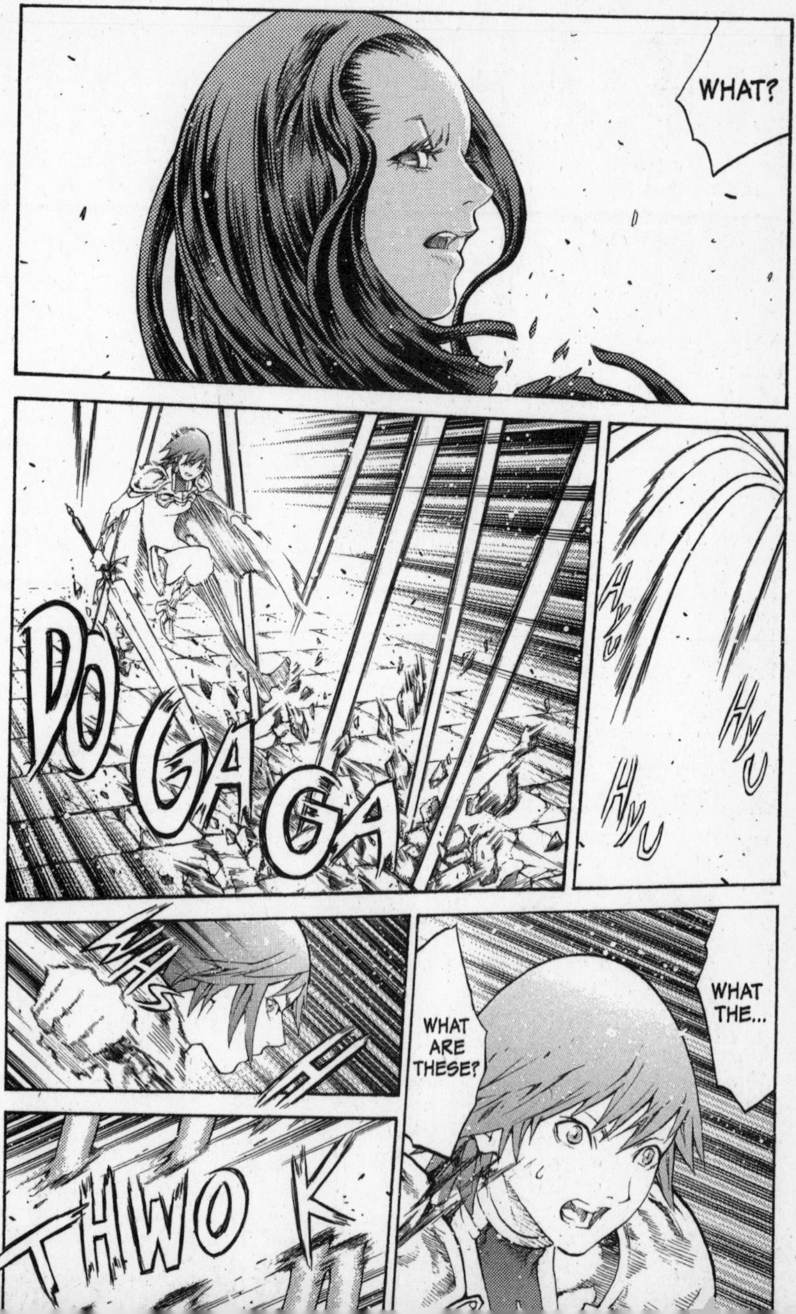
WHAT?
HYU HYU
HYU HYU
DO GAGA
WHAT THE...
WHAT ARE THESE?
WHSH
THWO K

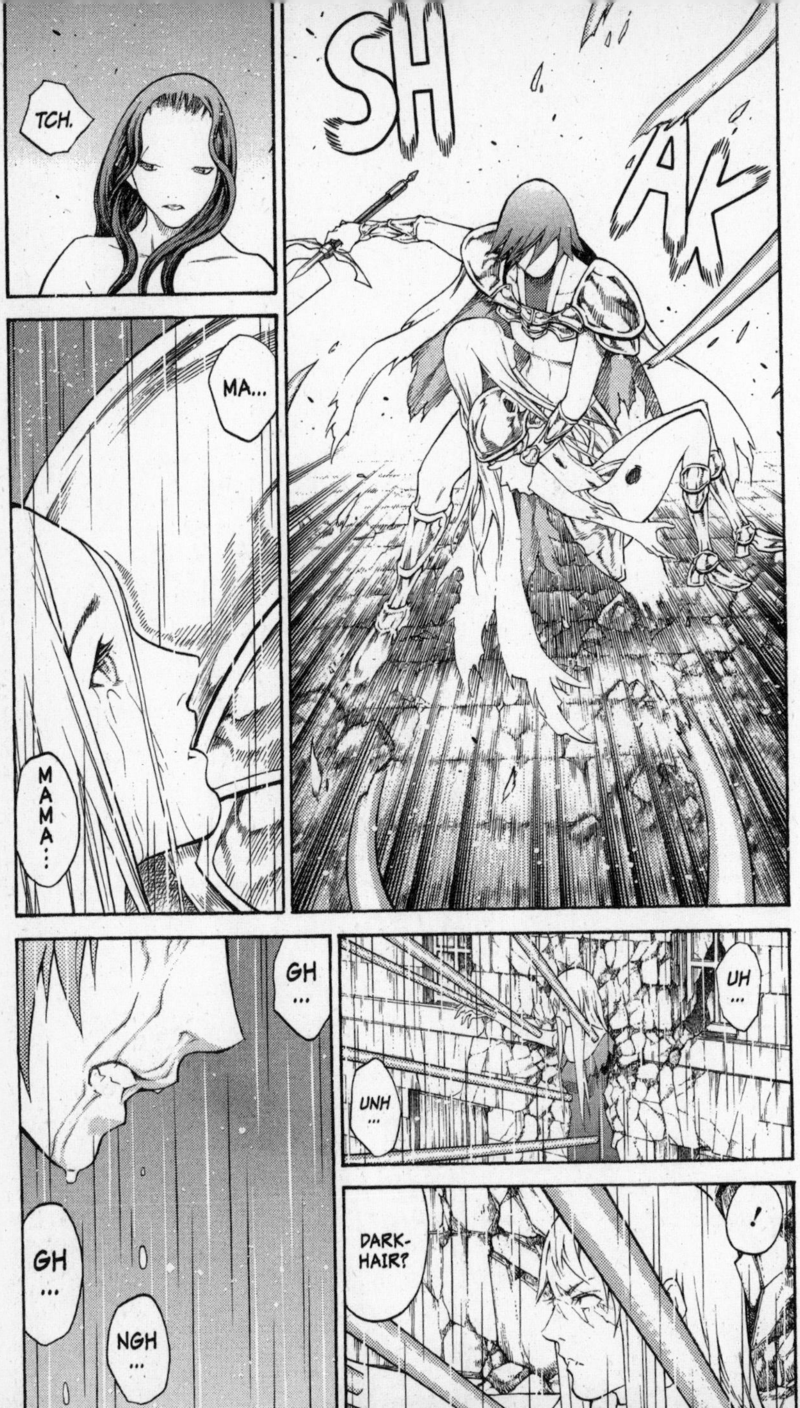
SHAK
TCH.
MA...
MAMA...
UH...
UNH...
!
DARK-HAIR?
GH...
GH...
NGH...

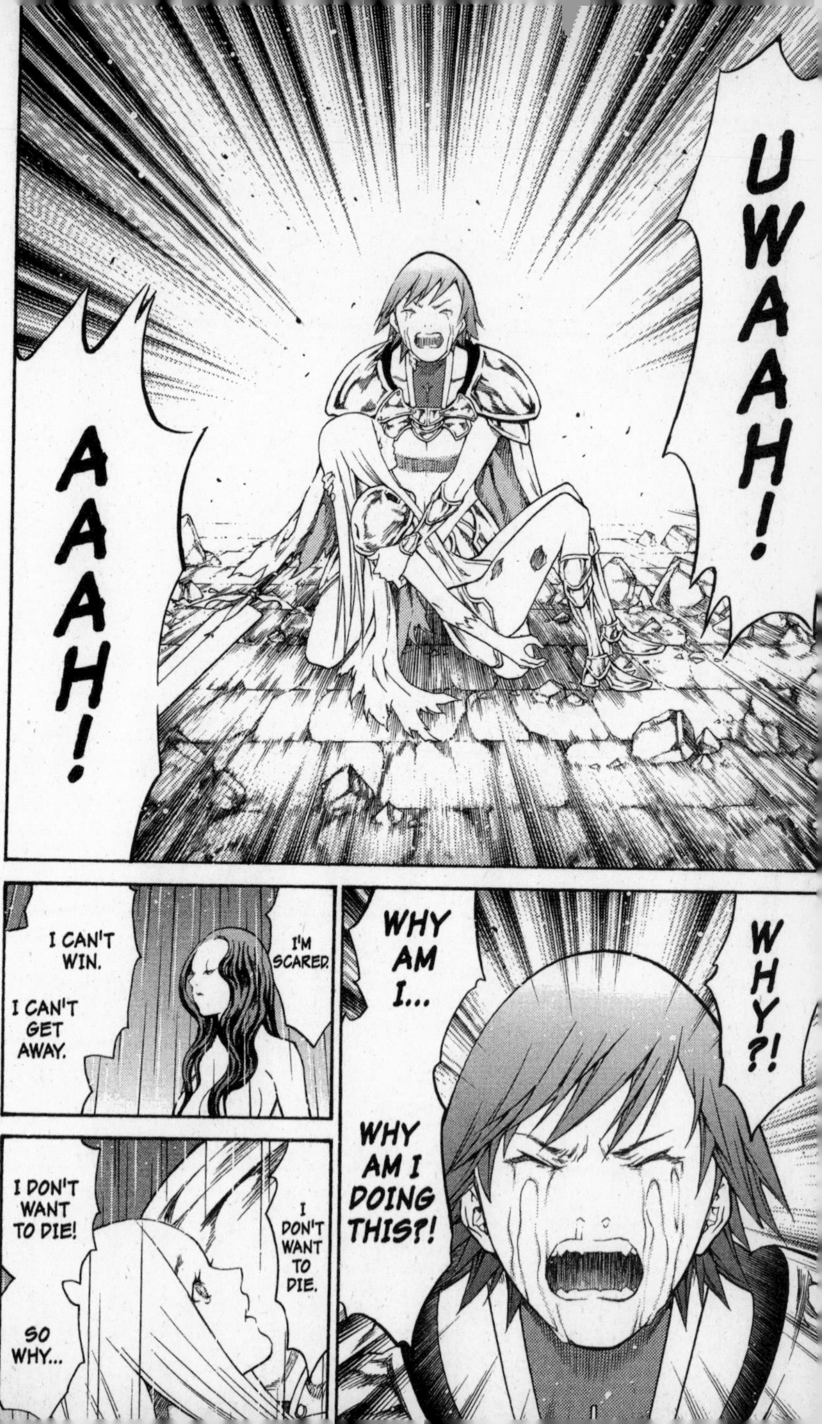
UWAAAH!
AAAH!
WHY?!
WHY AM I...
WHY AM I DOING THIS?!
I'M SCARED.
I CAN'T WIN.
I CAN'T GET AWAY.
I DON'T WANT TO DIE.
I DON'T WANT TO DIE!
SO WHY...

READ THIS WAY

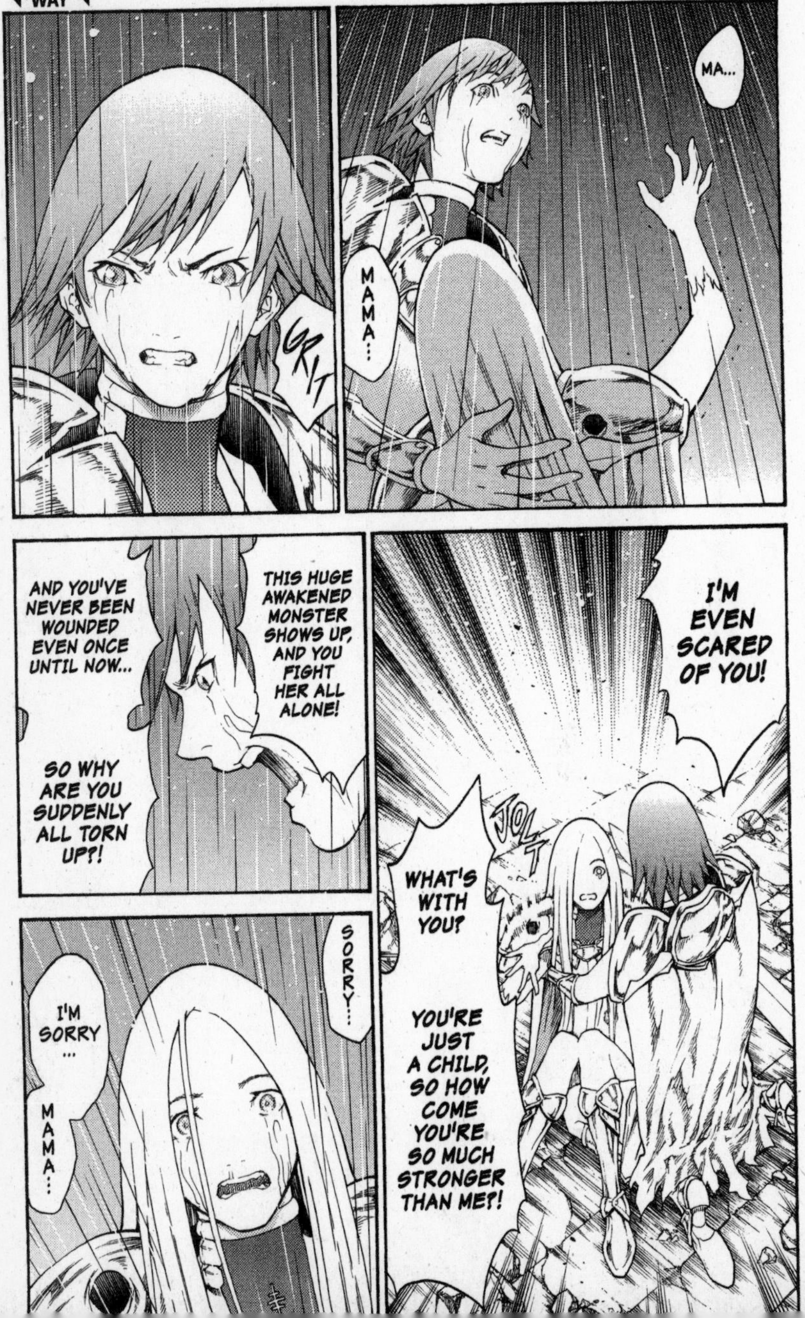
MA...
MAMA...
GRIT
I'M EVEN SCARED OF YOU!
JOLT
WHAT'S WITH YOU?
YOU'RE JUST A CHILD, SO HOW COME YOU'RE SO MUCH STRONGER THAN ME?!
THIS HUGE AWAKENED MONSTER SHOWS UP, AND YOU FIGHT HER ALL ALONE!
AND YOU'VE NEVER BEEN WOUNDED EVEN ONCE UNTIL NOW...
SO WHY ARE YOU SUDDENLY ALL TORN UP?!
SORRY...
I'M SORRY...
MAMA...

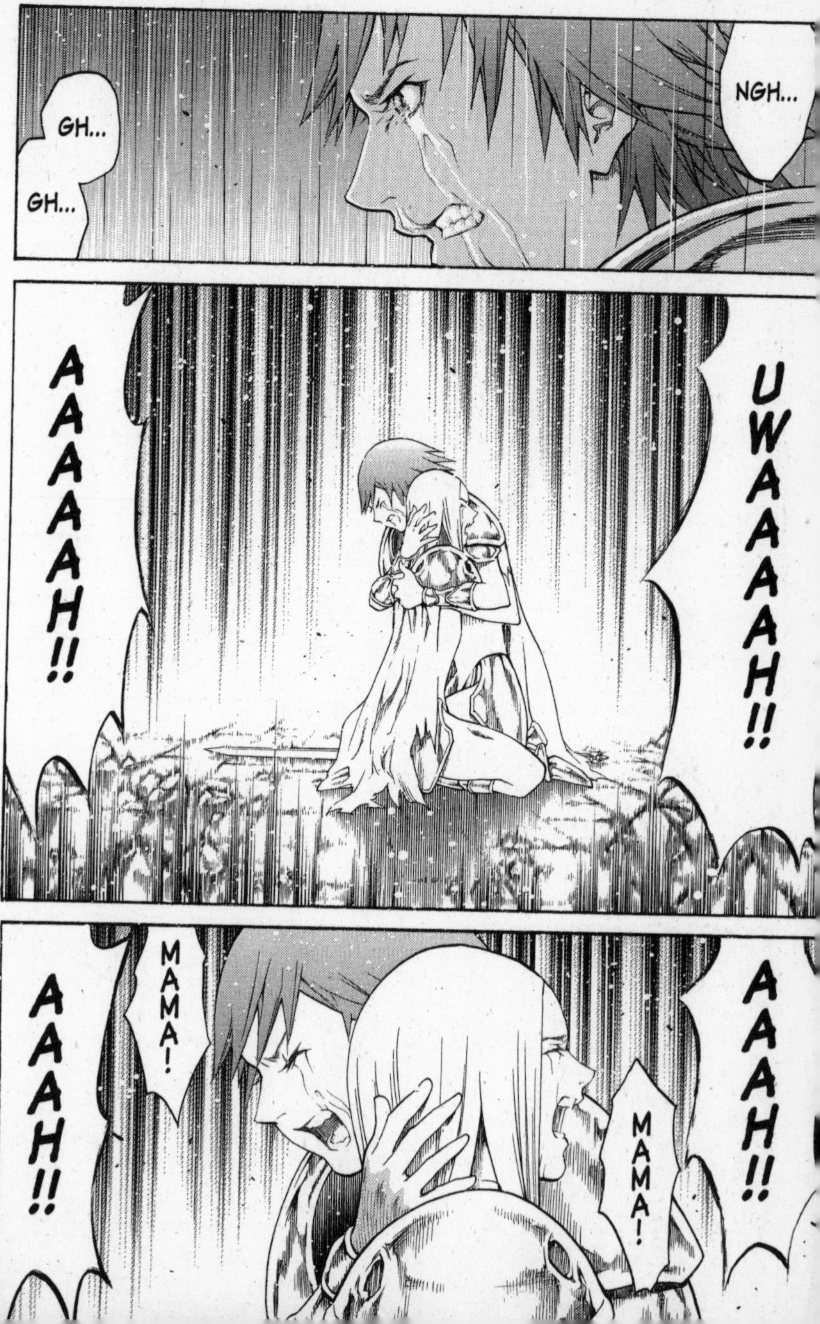
NGH...
GH...
GH...
UWAAAAH!!
AAAAAH!!
AAAH!!
MAMA!
MAMA!
AAAH!!

READ THIS WAY

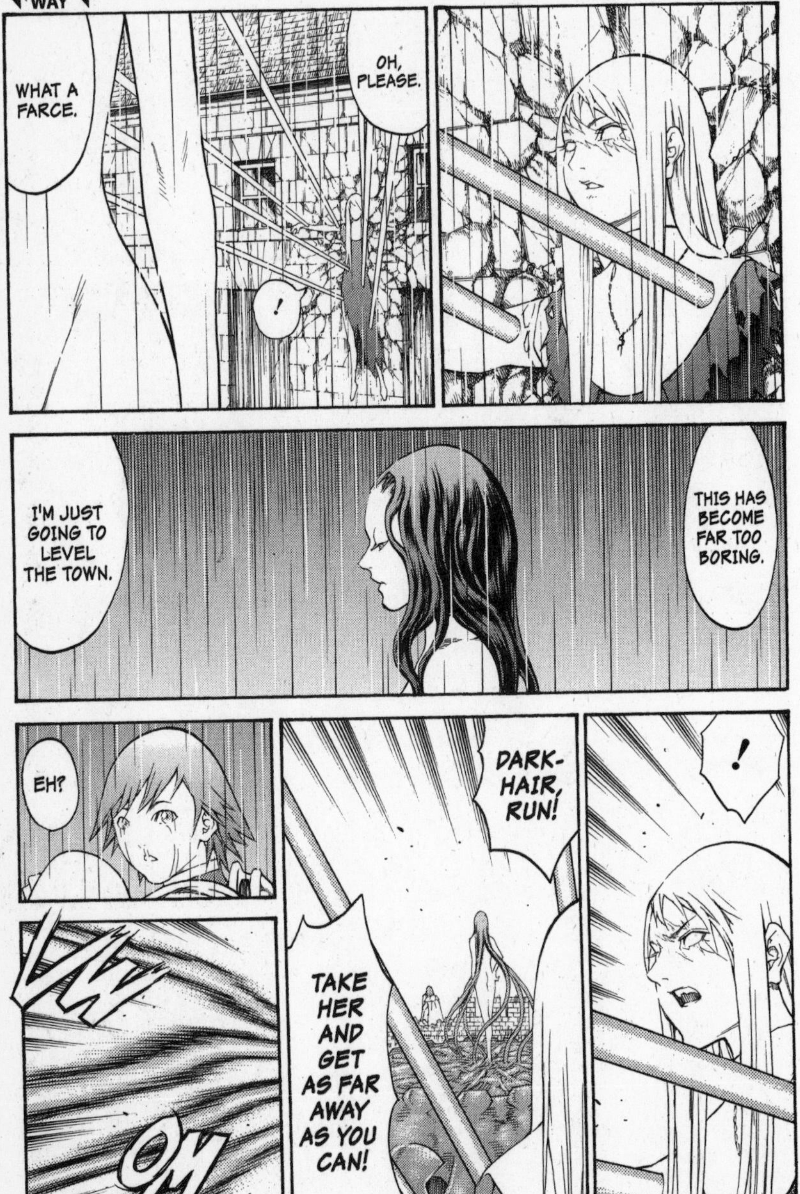
OH, PLEASE.
WHAT A FARCE.
!
THIS HAS BECOME FAR TOO BORING.
I'M JUST GOING TO LEVEL THE TOWN.
!
DARK-HAIR, RUN!
TAKE HER AND GET AS FAR AWAY AS YOU CAN!
EH?
VWOM

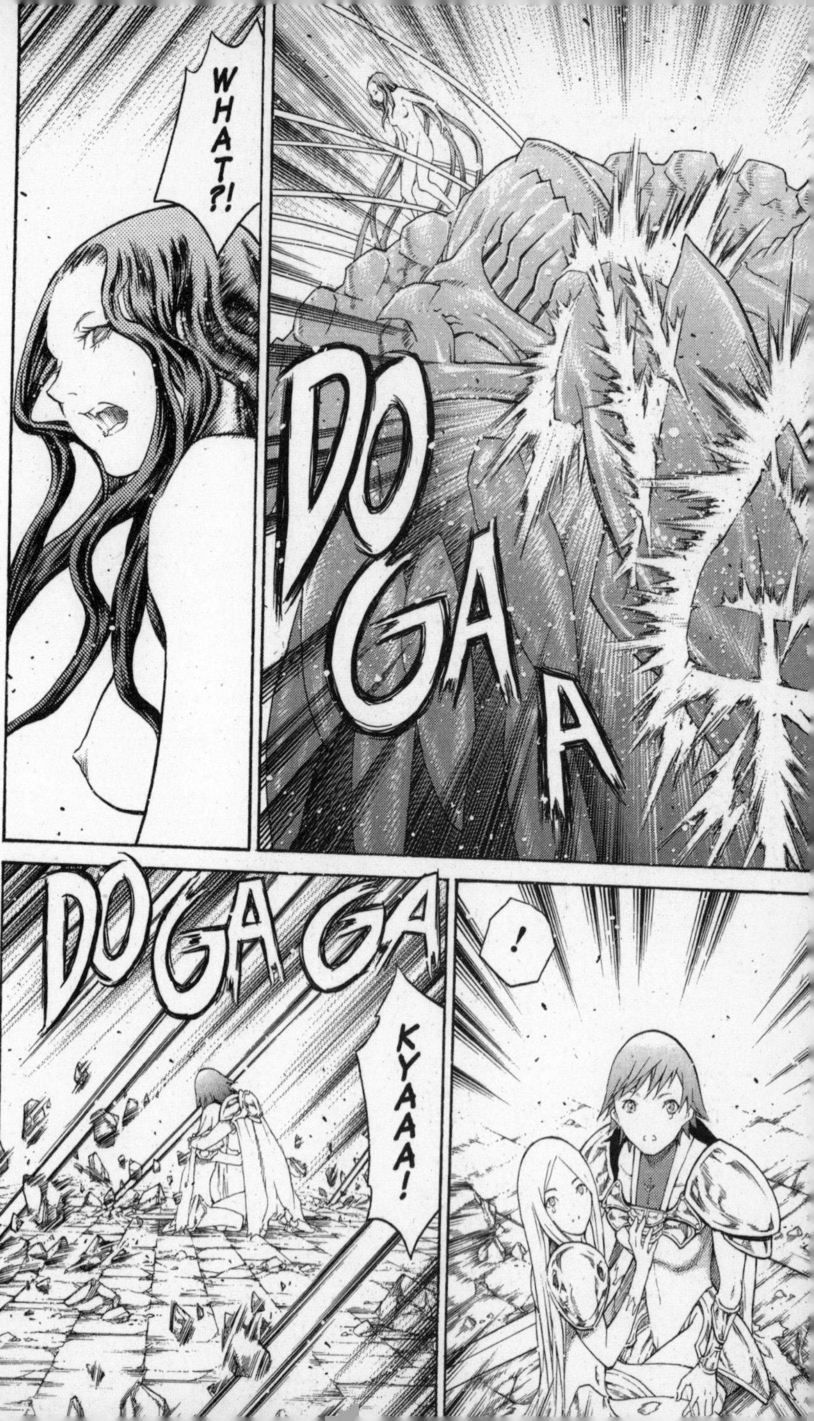
DOGAA
WHAT?!
!
DOGAGA
KYAAA!

READ THIS WAY

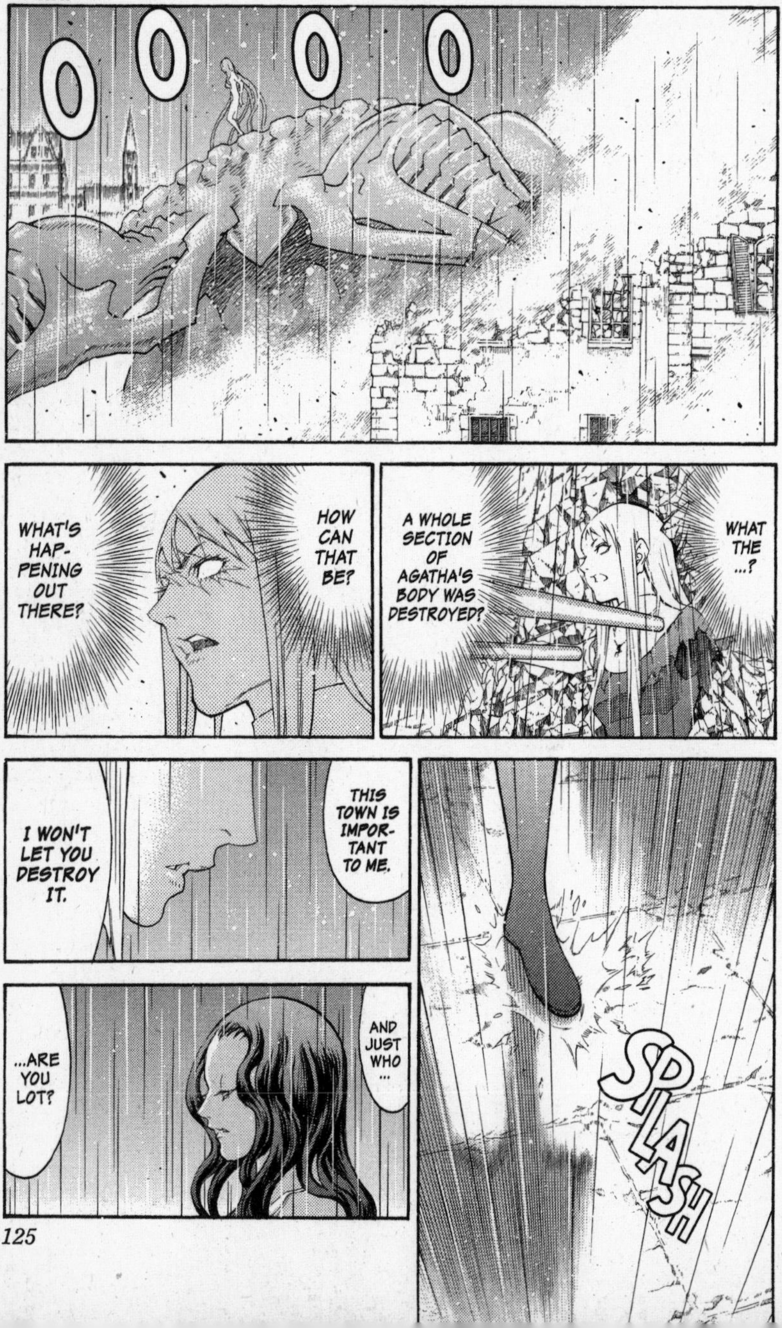
O O O O
WHAT THE ...?
A WHOLE SECTION OF AGATHA'S BODY WAS DESTROYED?
HOW CAN THAT BE?
WHAT'S HAP-PENING OUT THERE?
SPLASH
THIS TOWN IS IMPOR-TANT TO ME.
I WON'T LET YOU DESTROY IT.
AND JUST WHO ...
...ARE YOU LOT?

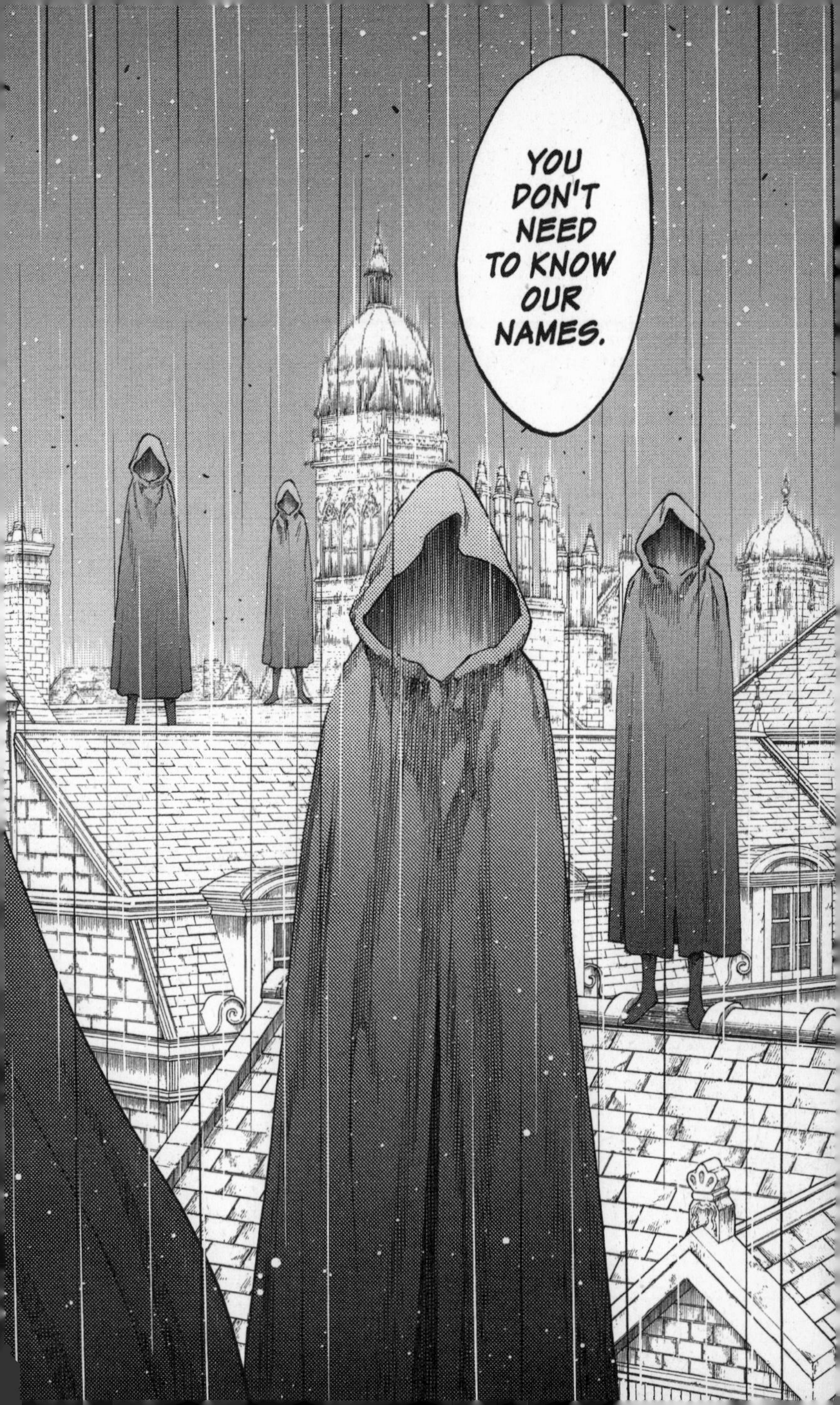
YOU DON'T NEED TO KNOW OUR NAMES.

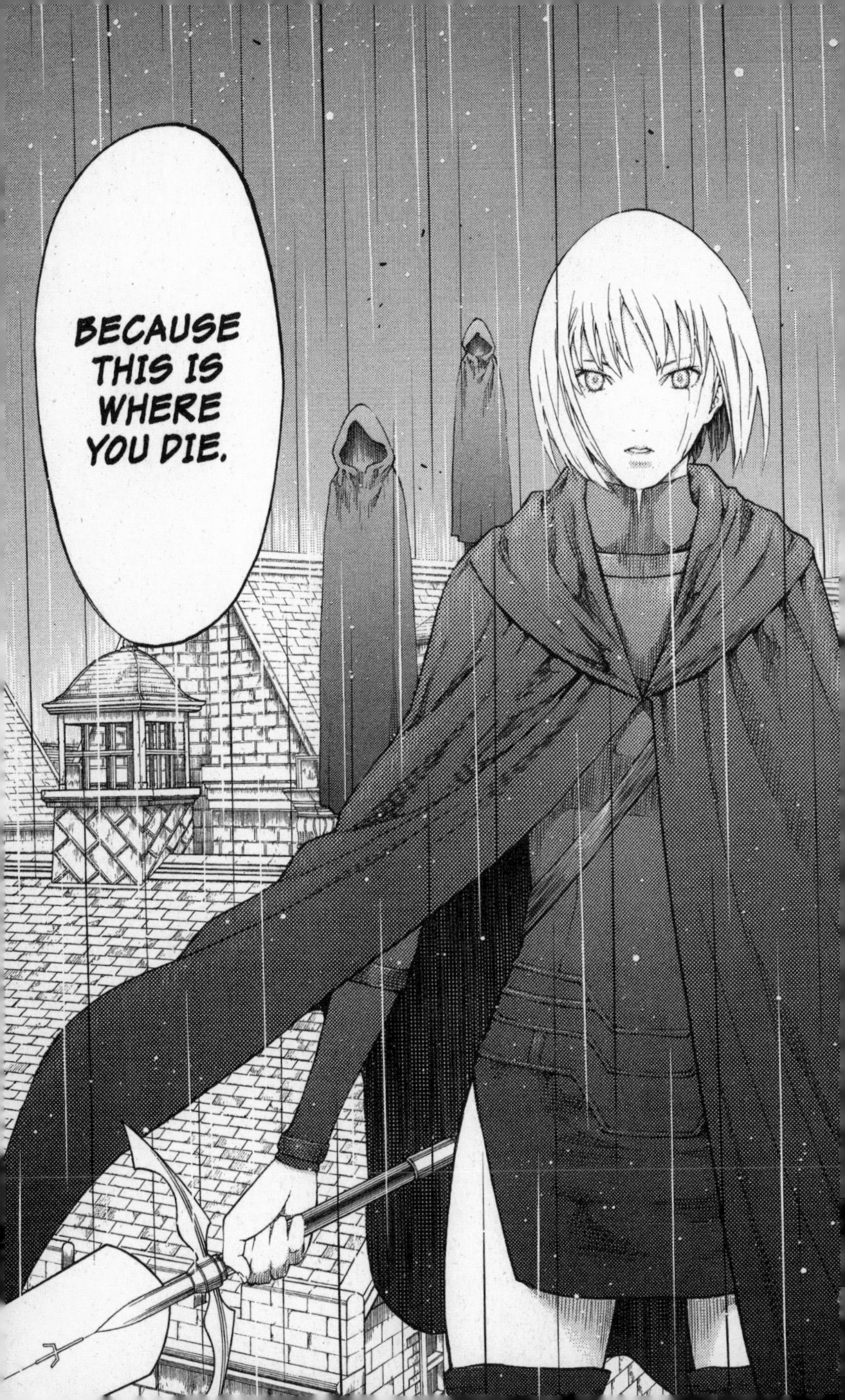
BECAUSE THIS IS WHERE YOU DIE.

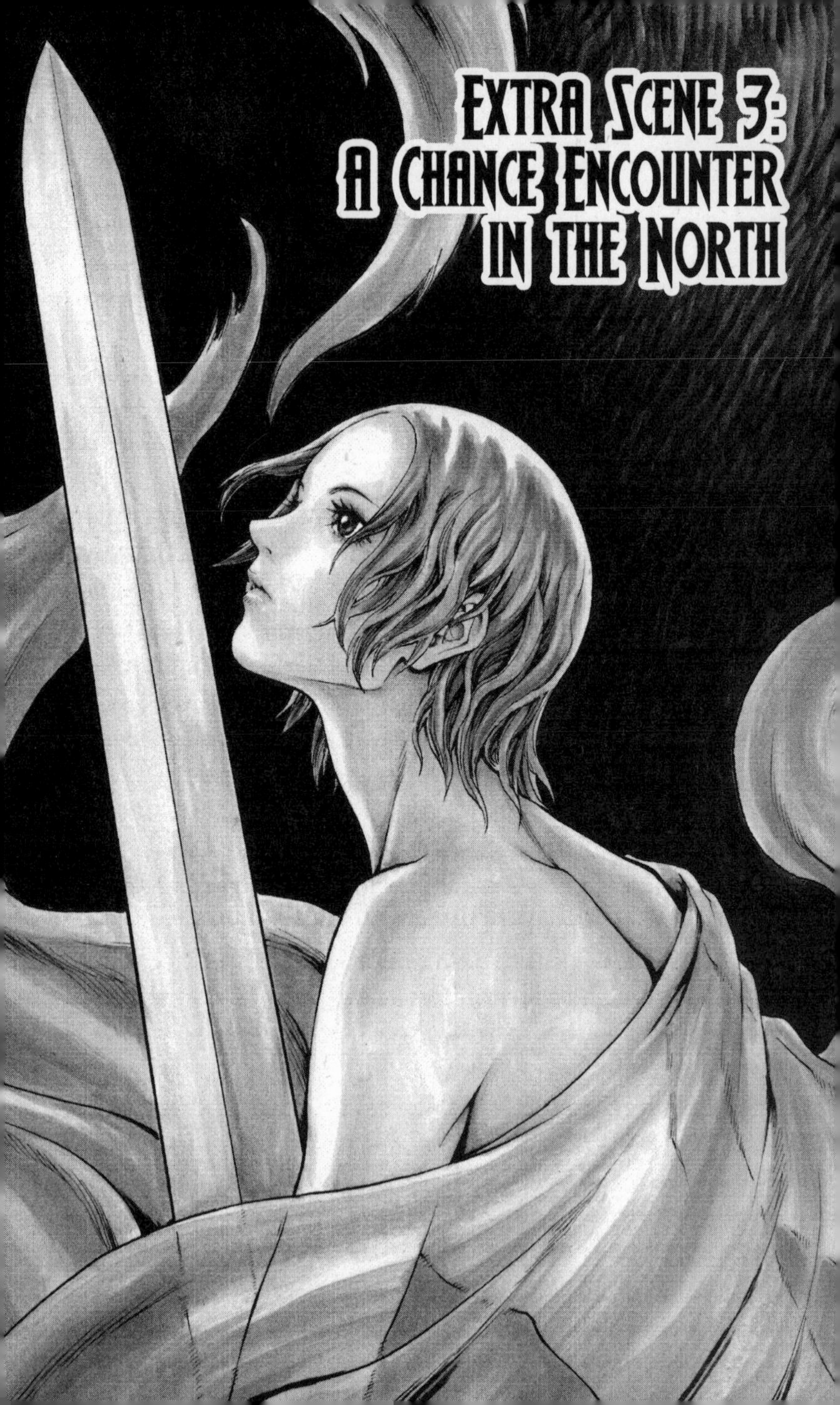
EXTRA SCENE 3:
A CHANCE ENCOUNTER
IN THE NORTH

READ THIS WAY

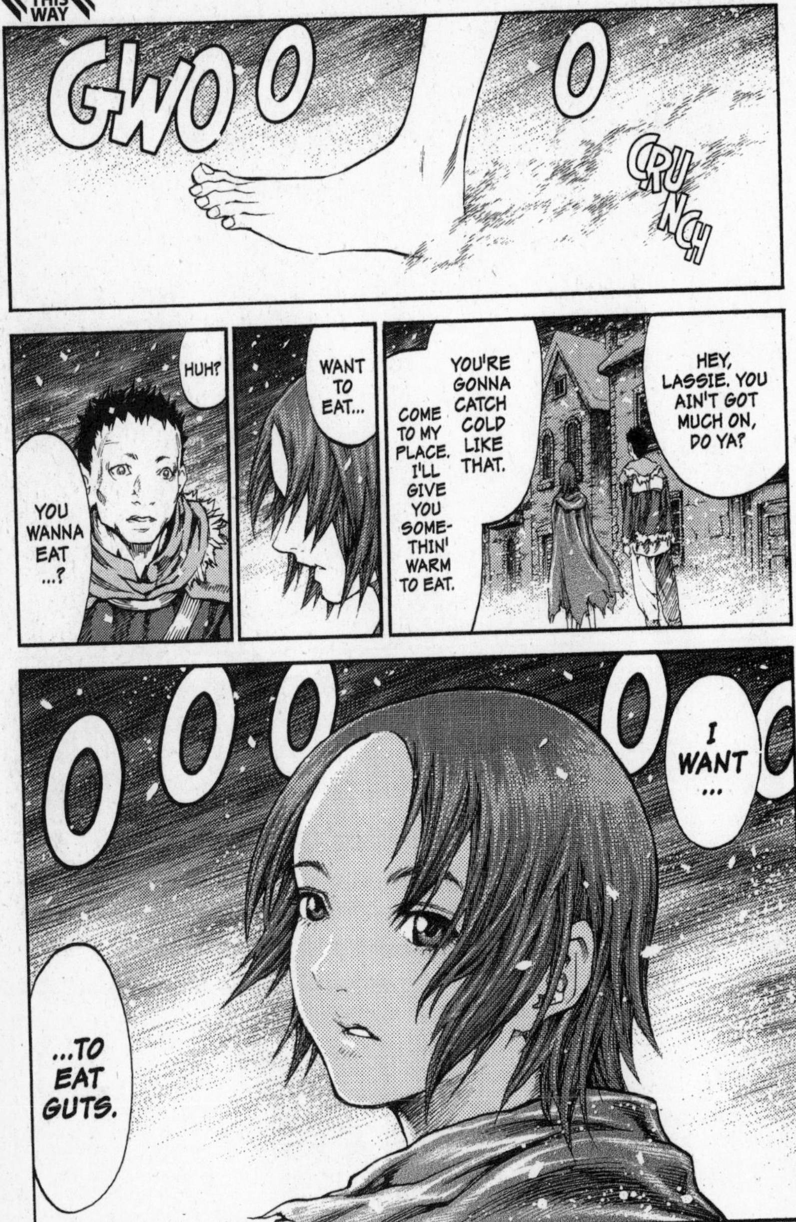

GWOOOO
CRUNCH
HEY, LASSIE. YOU AIN'T GOT MUCH ON, DO YA?
YOU'RE GONNA CATCH COLD LIKE THAT.
COME TO MY PLACE. I'LL GIVE YOU SOME-THIN' WARM TO EAT.
WANT TO EAT...
HUH?
YOU WANNA EAT ...?
OOOOOO
I WANT ...
...TO EAT GUTS.

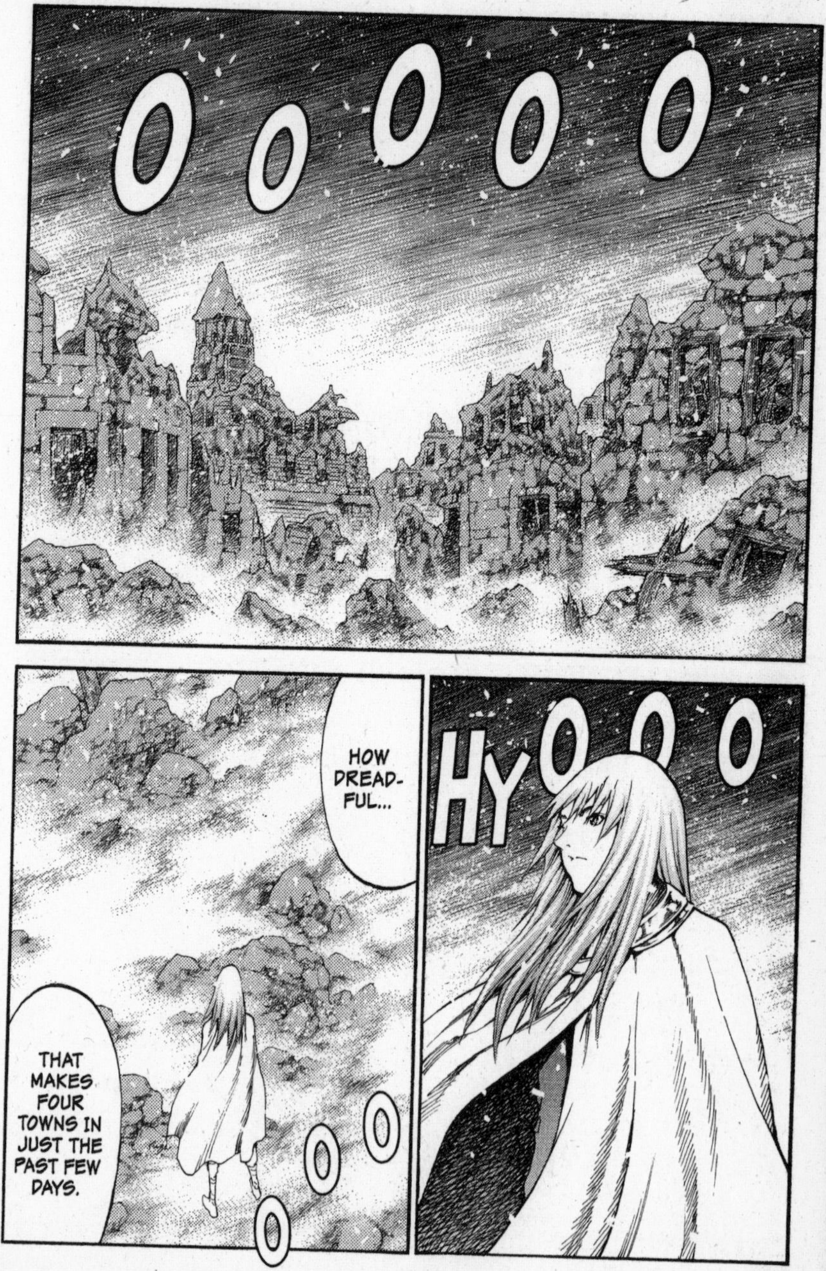
OOOOOO
HYOOO
HOW DREAD-FUL...
THAT MAKES FOUR TOWNS IN JUST THE PAST FEW DAYS.
OOOO

READ THIS WAY

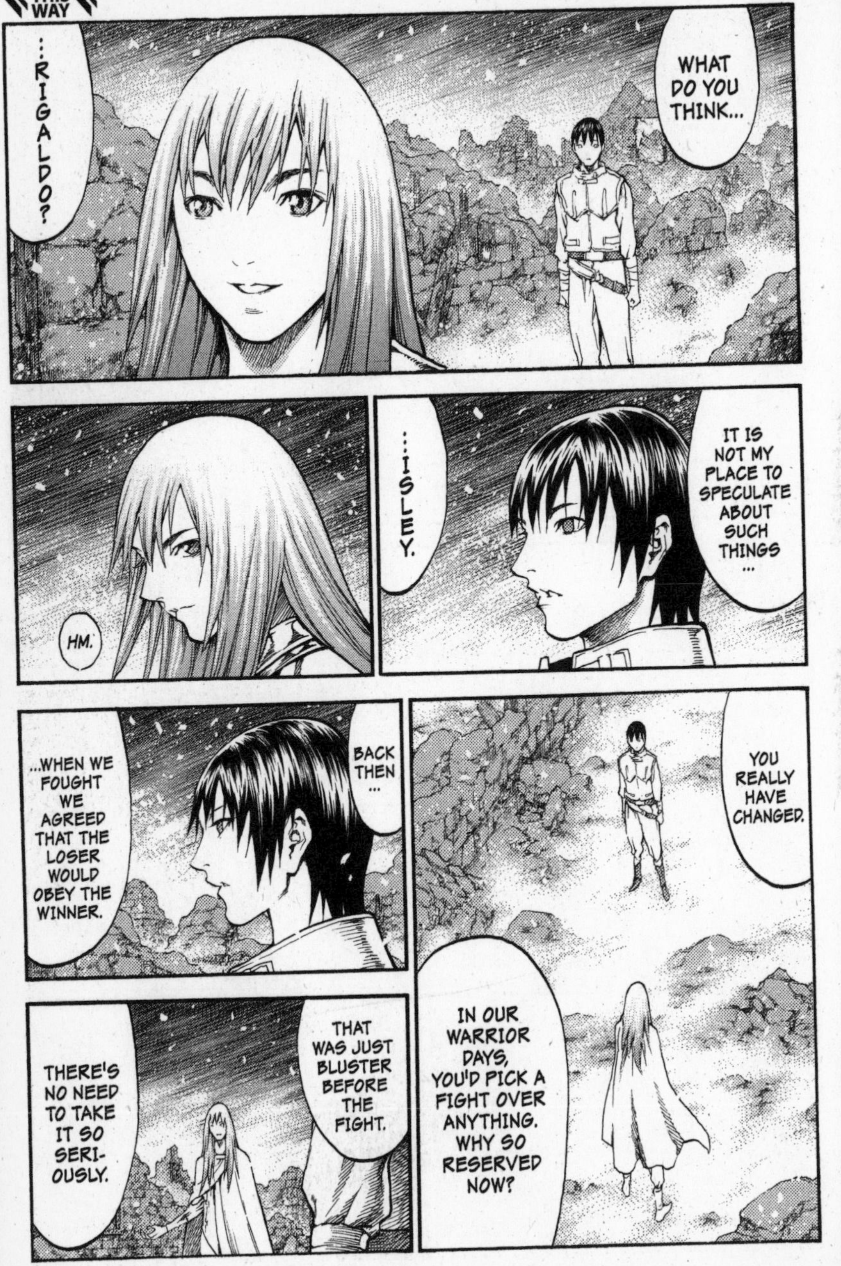

WHAT DO YOU THINK...
...RIGALDO?
IT IS NOT MY PLACE TO SPECULATE ABOUT SUCH THINGS...
...ISLEY.
HM.
YOU REALLY HAVE CHANGED.
IN OUR WARRIOR DAYS, YOU'D PICK A FIGHT OVER ANYTHING. WHY SO RESERVED NOW?
BACK THEN...
...WHEN WE FOUGHT WE AGREED THAT THE LOSER WOULD OBEY THE WINNER.
THAT WAS JUST BLUSTER BEFORE THE FIGHT.
THERE'S NO NEED TO TAKE IT SO SERI-OUSLY.

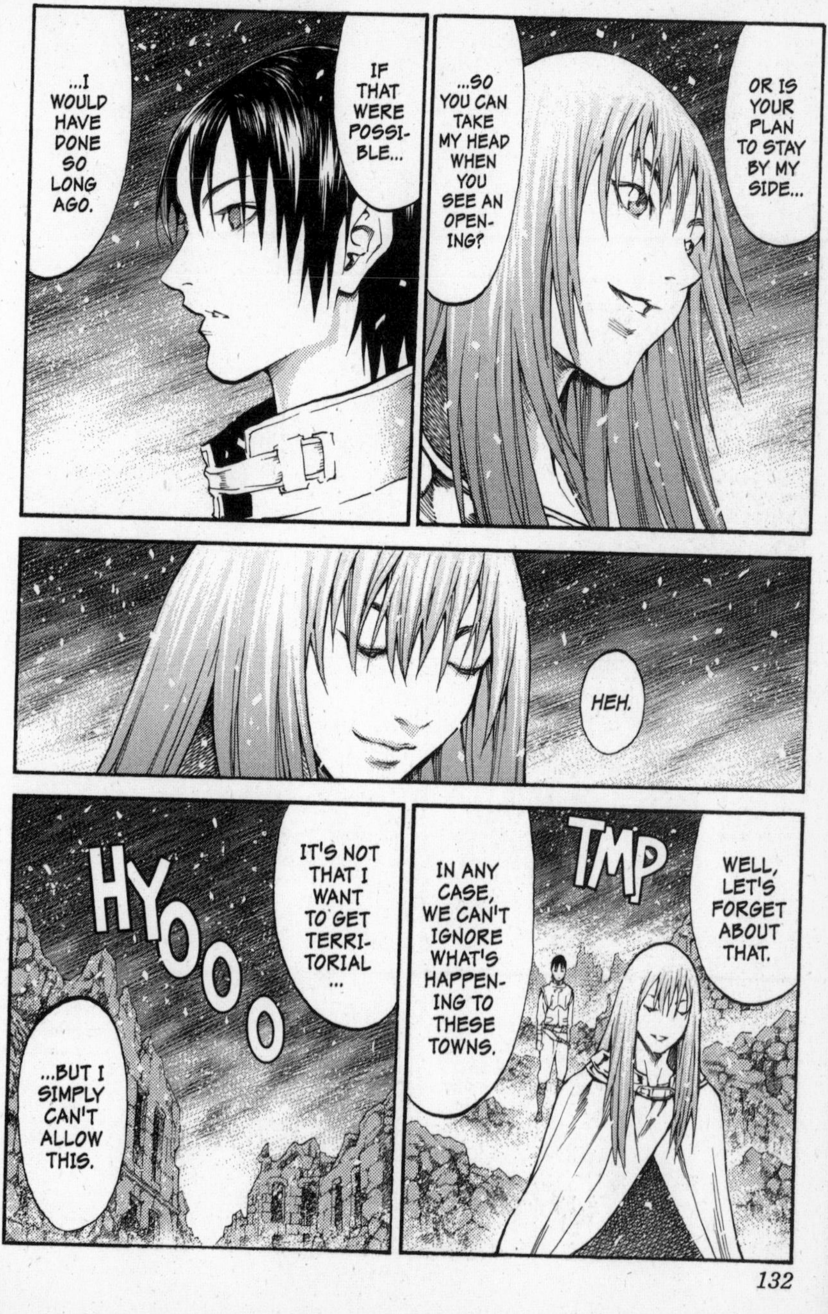
OR IS YOUR PLAN TO STAY BY MY SIDE...
...SO YOU CAN TAKE MY HEAD WHEN YOU SEE AN OPENING?
IF THAT WERE POSSIBLE...
...I WOULD HAVE DONE SO LONG AGO.
HEH.
TMP
WELL, LET'S FORGET ABOUT THAT.
IN ANY CASE, WE CAN'T IGNORE WHAT'S HAPPENING TO THESE TOWNS.
HYOOOO
IT'S NOT THAT I WANT TO GET TERRITORIAL...
...BUT I SIMPLY CAN'T ALLOW THIS.

READ THIS WAY

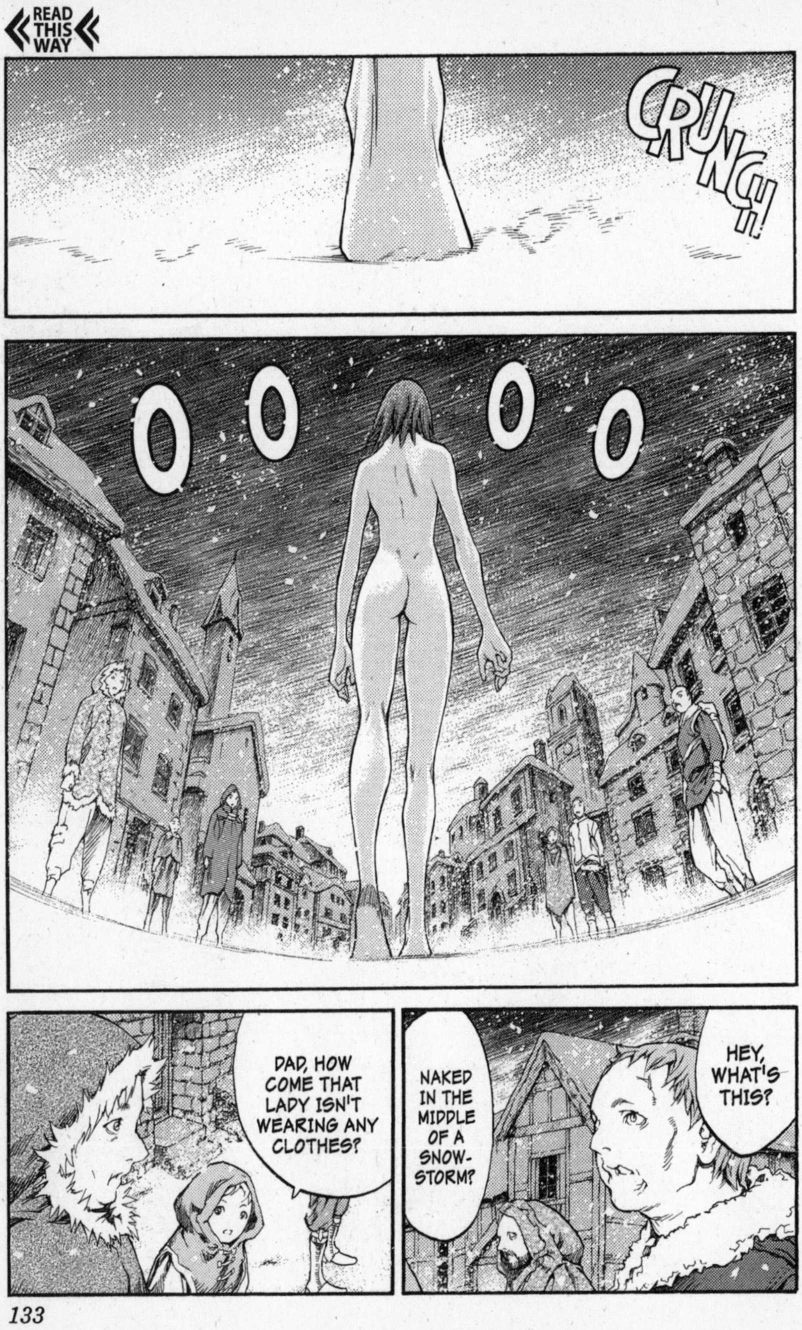
CRUNCH
OOOO
HEY, WHAT'S THIS?
NAKED IN THE MIDDLE OF A SNOW-STORM?
DAD, HOW COME THAT LADY ISN'T WEARING ANY CLOTHES?

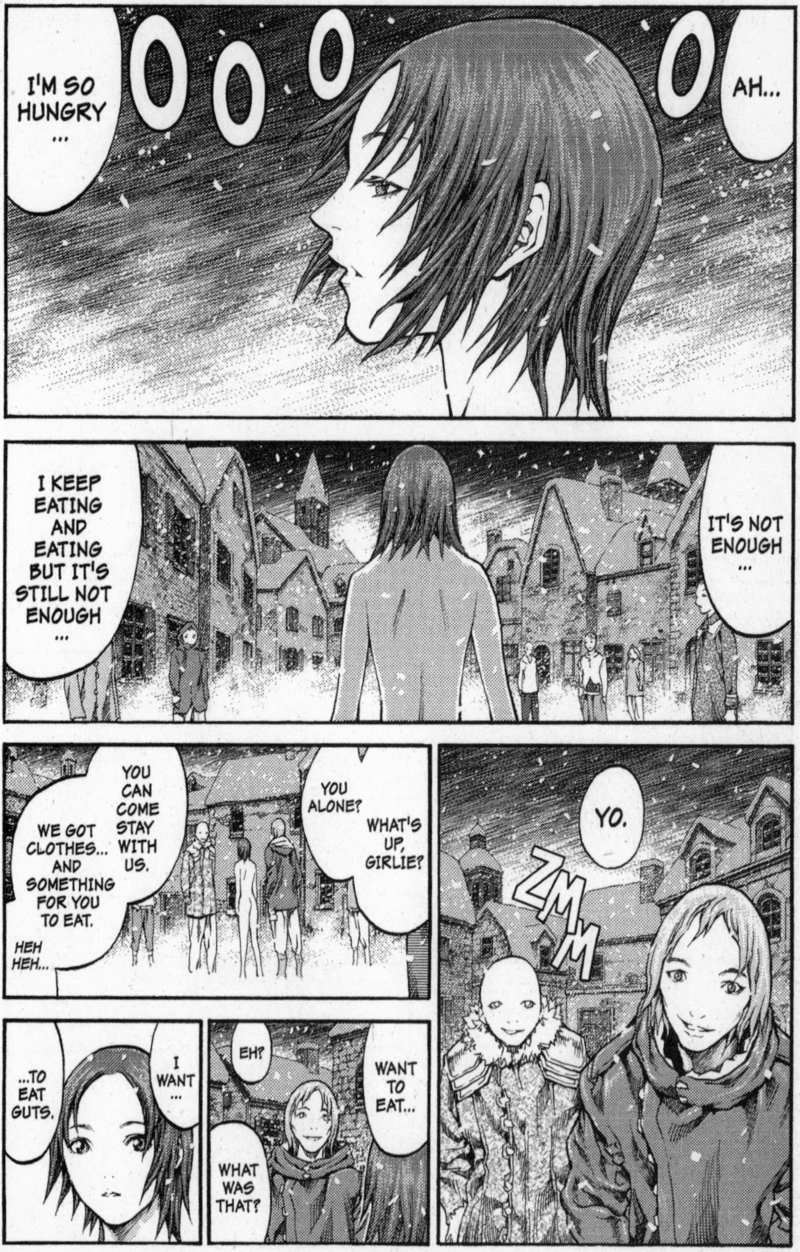

AH...
OOOO
I'M SO HUNGRY ...
IT'S NOT ENOUGH ...
I KEEP EATING AND EATING BUT IT'S STILL NOT ENOUGH ...
YO.
ZMM
WHAT'S UP, GIRLIE?
YOU ALONE?
YOU CAN COME STAY WITH US.
WE GOT CLOTHES... AND SOMETHING FOR YOU TO EAT.
HEH HEH...
WANT TO EAT...
EH?
WHAT WAS THAT?
I WANT ...
...TO EAT GUTS.

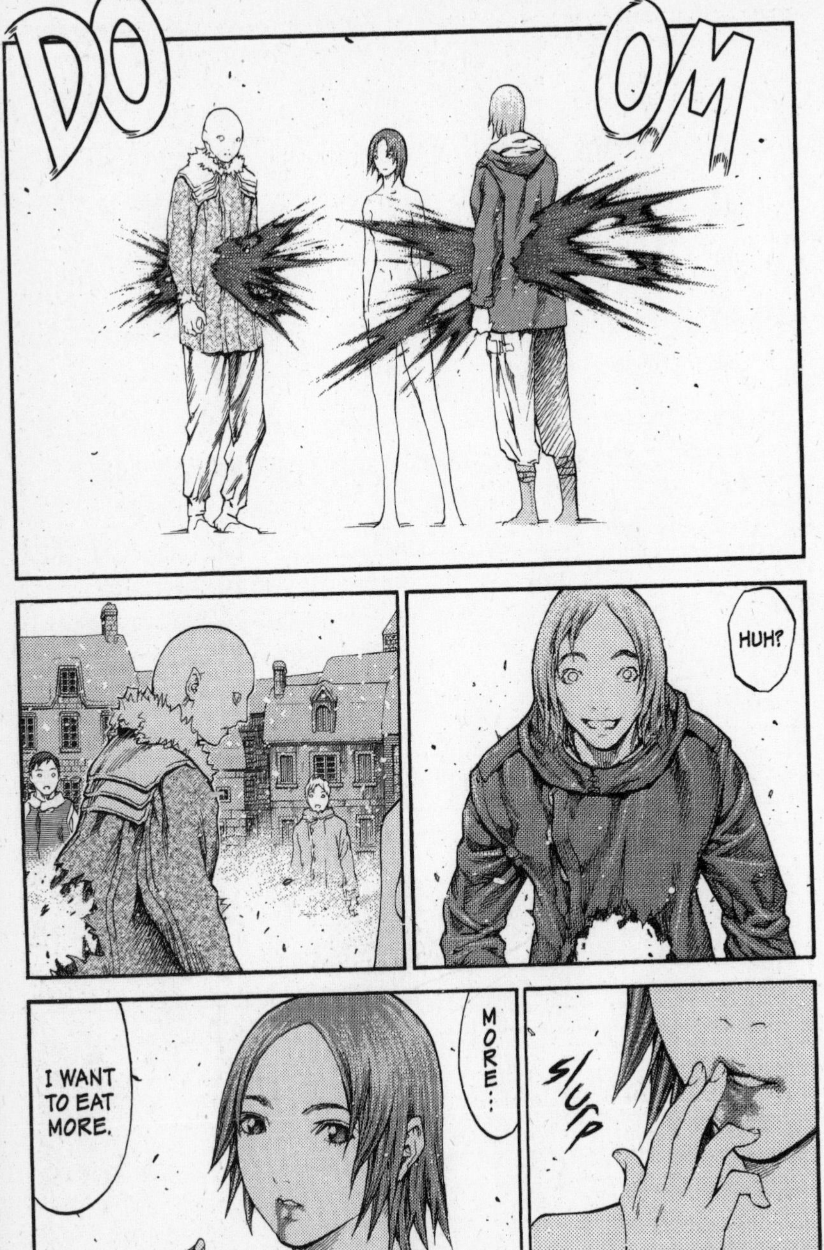
DO
OM
HUH?
SLURP
MORE...
I WANT TO EAT MORE.

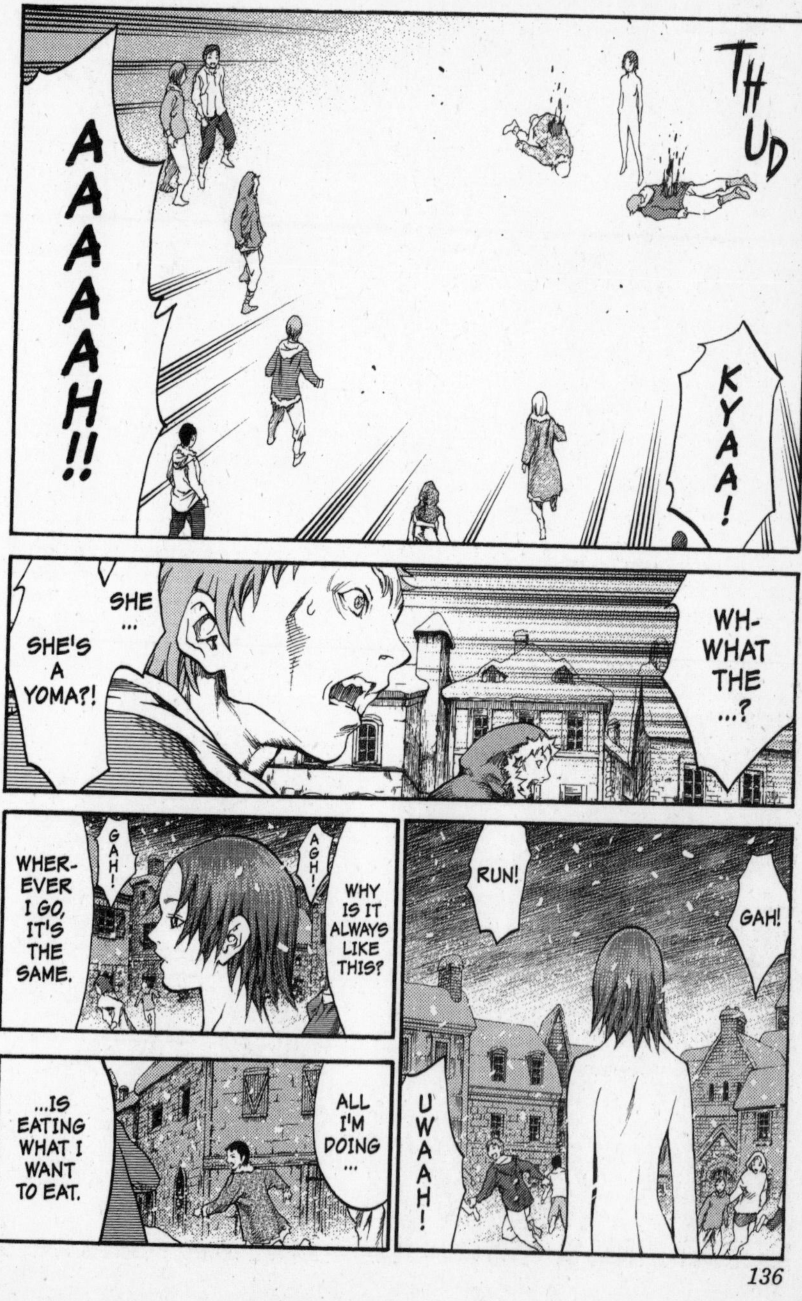
THUD
KYAA!
AAAAAAH!!
WH-WHAT THE...?
SHE...
SHE'S A YOMA?!
GAH!
RUN!
UWAAH!
WHY IS IT ALWAYS LIKE THIS?
AGH!
GAH!
WHEREVER I GO, IT'S THE SAME.
ALL I'M DOING...
...IS EATING WHAT I WANT TO EAT.

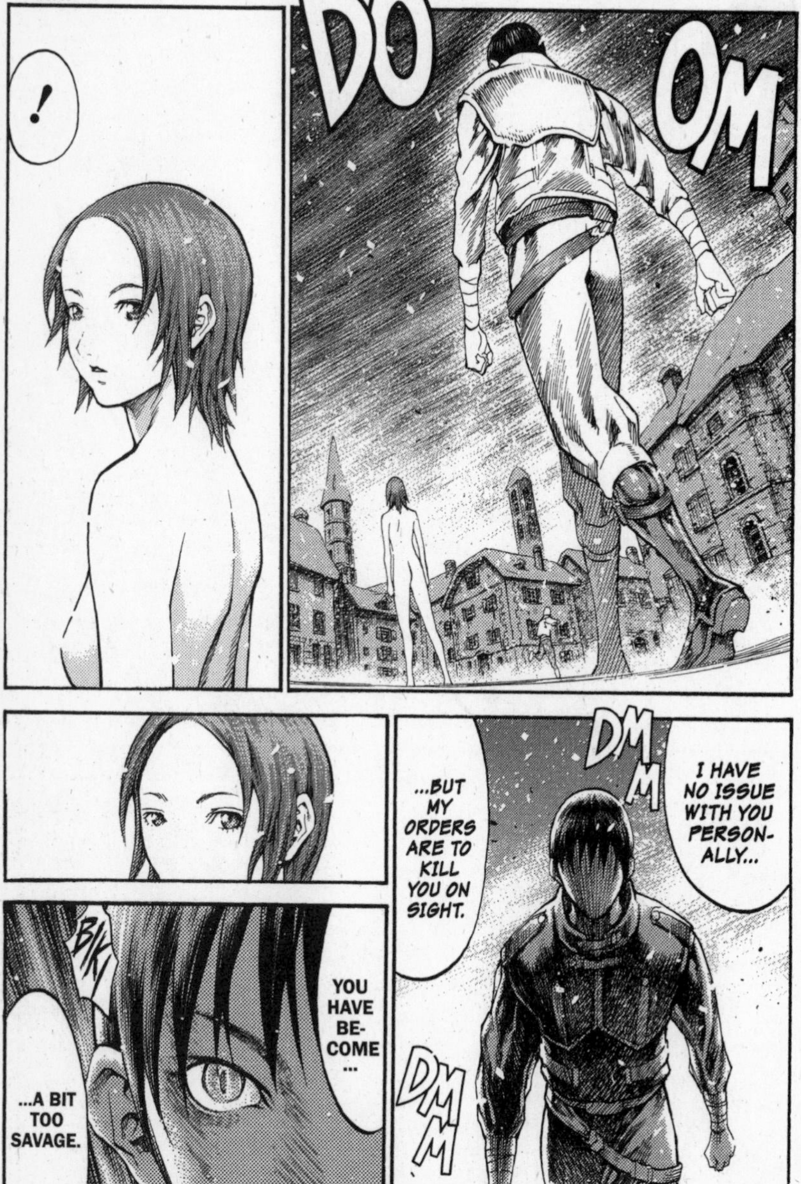
DOOM
!
DMM
I HAVE NO ISSUE WITH YOU PERSONALLY...
...BUT MY ORDERS ARE TO KILL YOU ON SIGHT.
DMM
BIKI
YOU HAVE BECOME ...
...A BIT TOO SAVAGE.

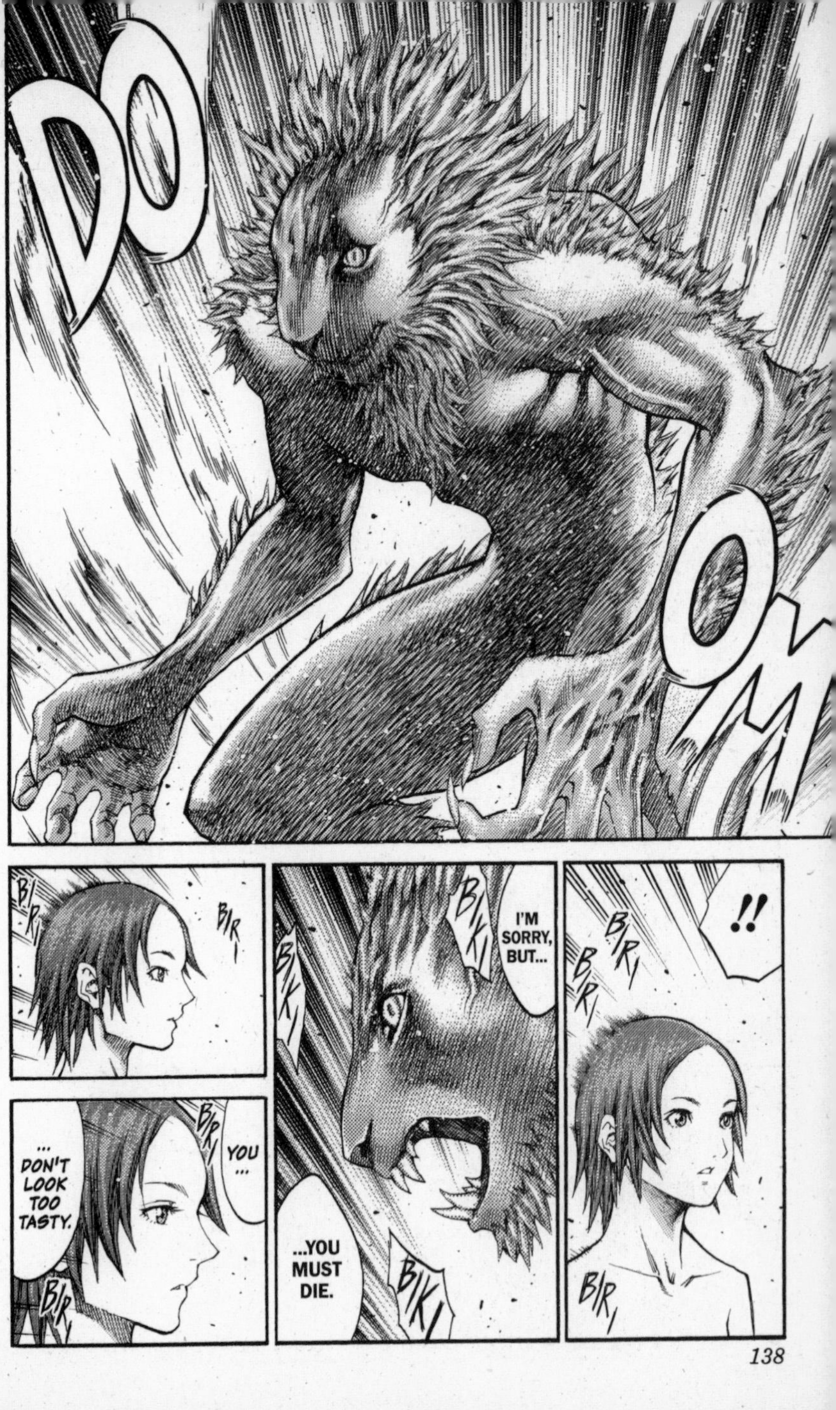
DOOM
!!
BIRI
BIRI
BIRI
I'M SORRY, BUT...
BIKI
BIKI
...YOU MUST DIE.
BIKI
BIRI
BIRI
YOU...
BIRI
...DON'T LOOK TOO TASTY.
BIRI

READ THIS WAY

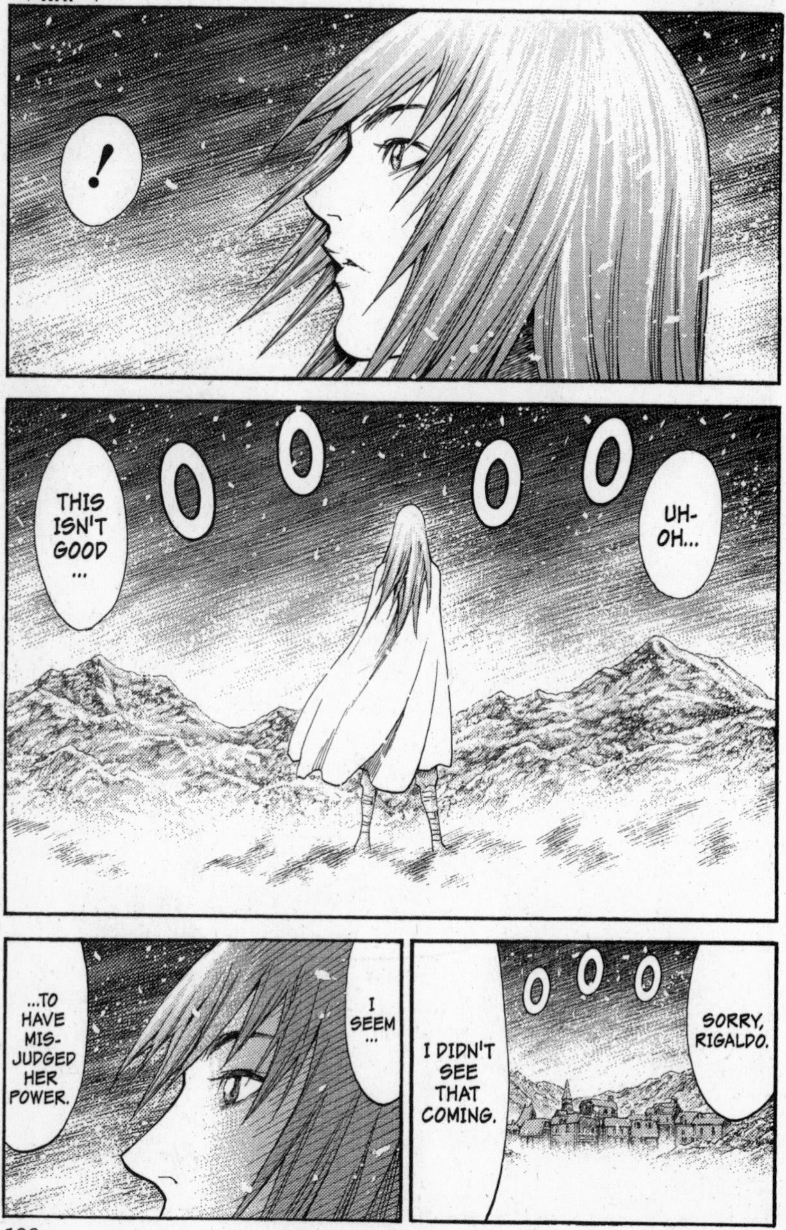
!
UH-OH...
THIS ISN'T GOOD ...
SORRY, RIGALDO.
I DIDN'T SEE THAT COMING.
I SEEM ...
...TO HAVE MIS-JUDGED HER POWER.

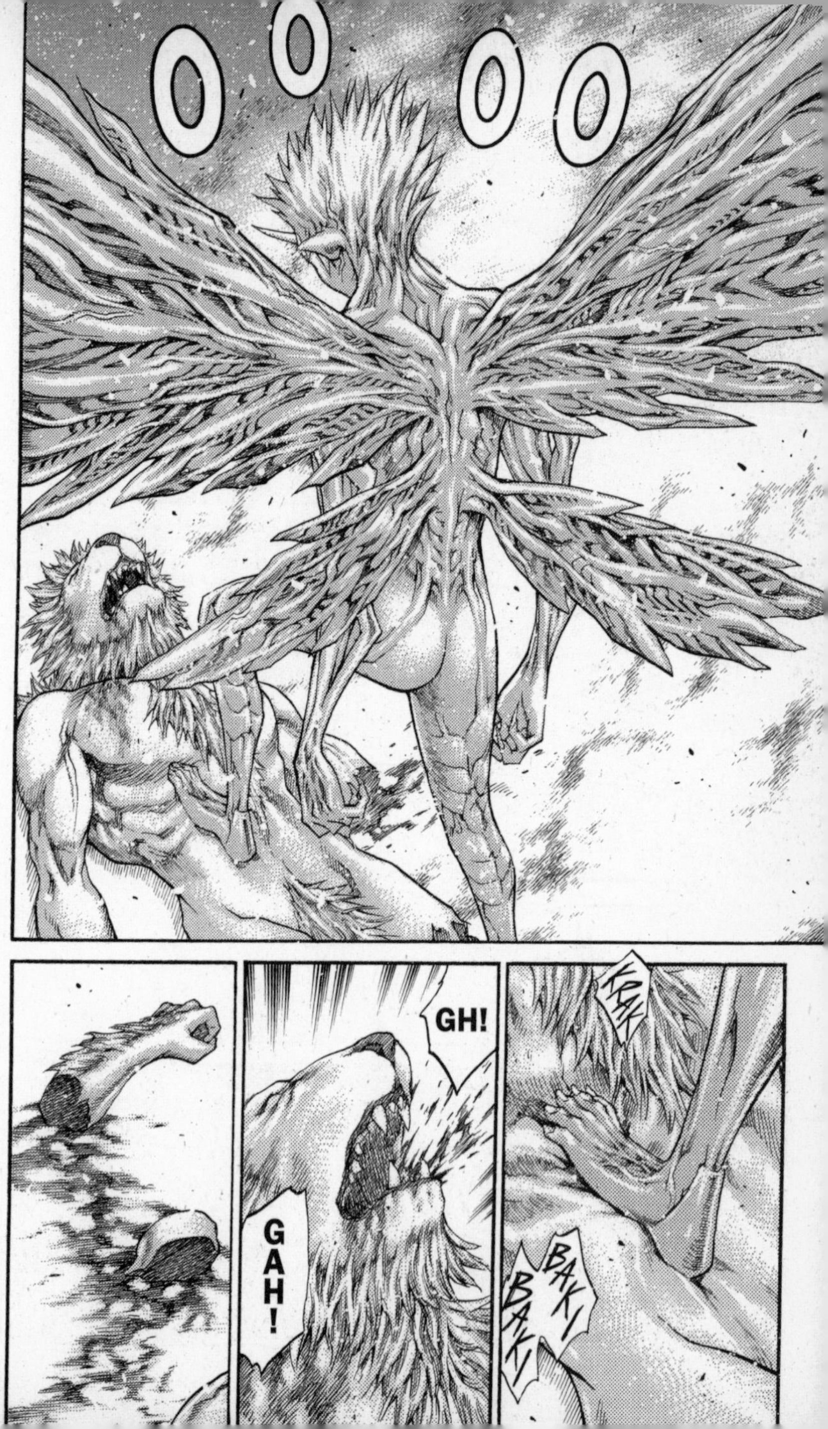

OOOO
KRAK
BAKI
BAKI
GH!
GAH!

I DON'T WANT...

...TO EAT YOU.

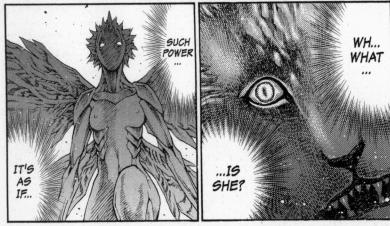

SUCH POWER...

IT'S AS IF...

WH... WHAT...

...IS SHE?

141

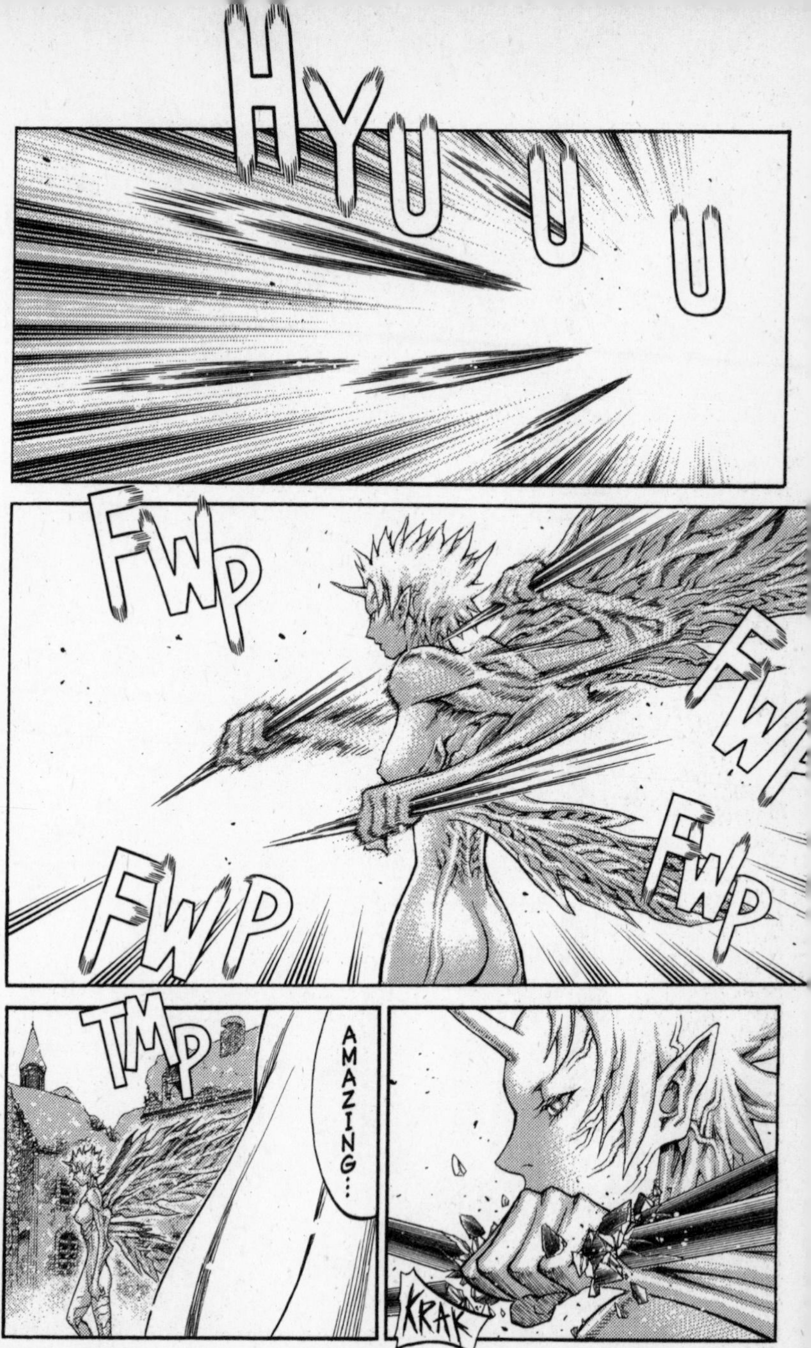
HYUUUU
FWP
FWP
FWP
FWP
KRAK
TMP
AMAZING...

READ THIS WAY

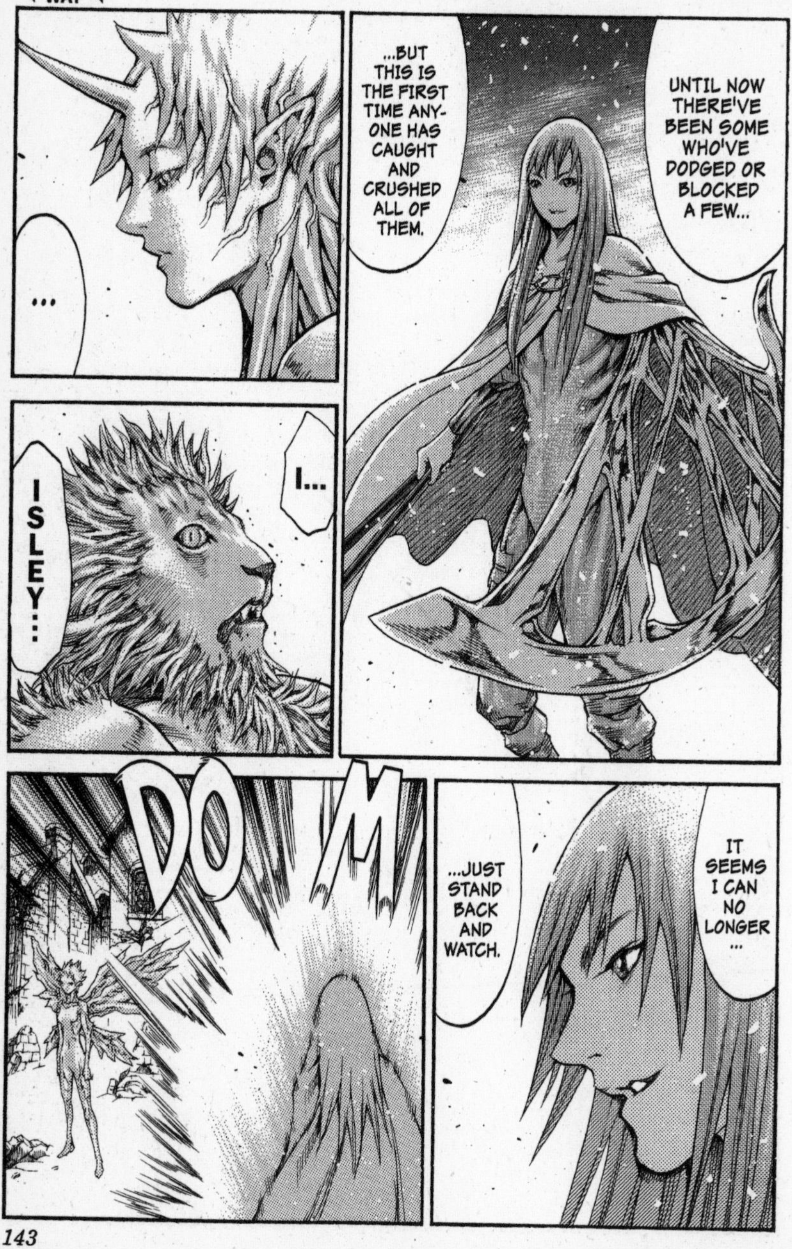
UNTIL NOW THERE'VE BEEN SOME WHO'VE DODGED OR BLOCKED A FEW...
...BUT THIS IS THE FIRST TIME ANY-ONE HAS CAUGHT AND CRUSHED ALL OF THEM.
...
I...
ISLEY...
IT SEEMS I CAN NO LONGER ...
...JUST STAND BACK AND WATCH.
DOM

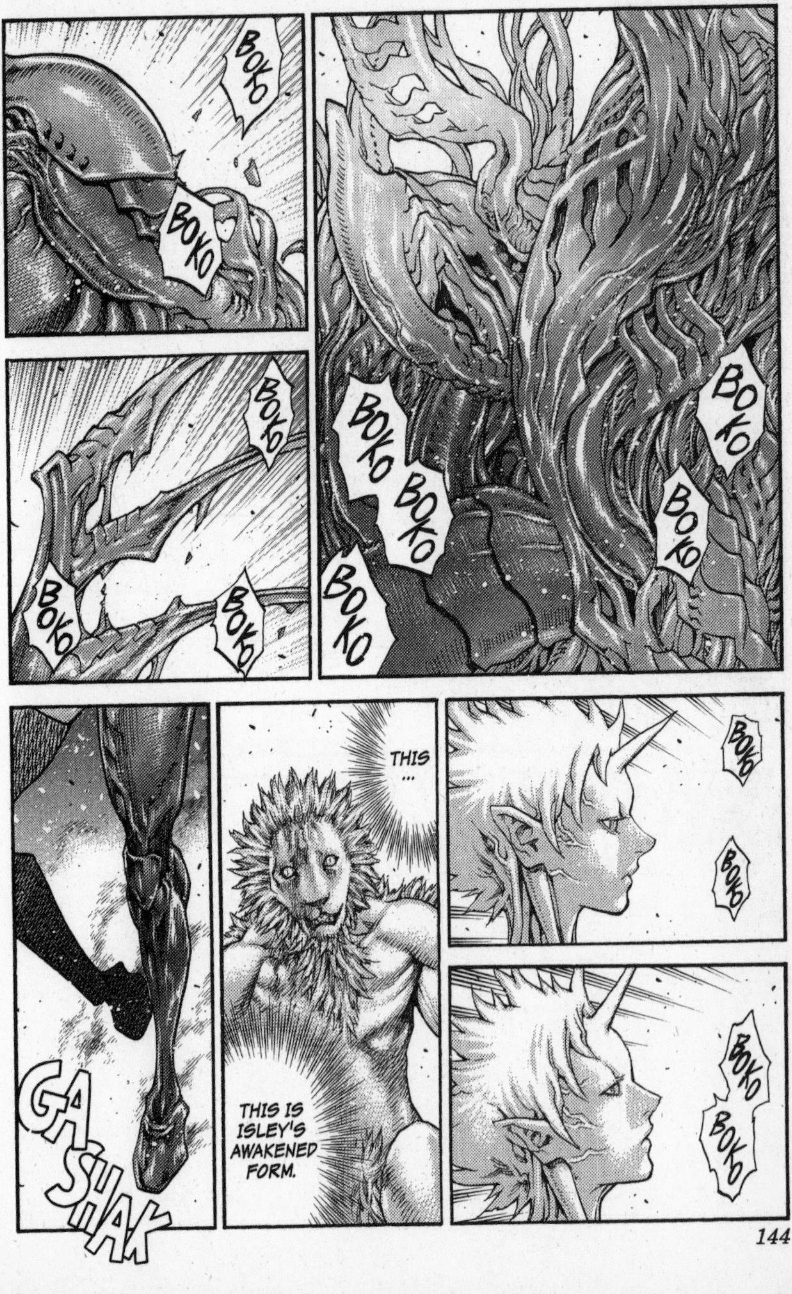
BOKO
BOKO
BOKO
BOKO
BOKO
BOKO
BOKO
BOKO
BOKO
BOKO
BOKO
BOKO
THIS ...
THIS IS ISLEY'S AWAKENED FORM.
GASHAK

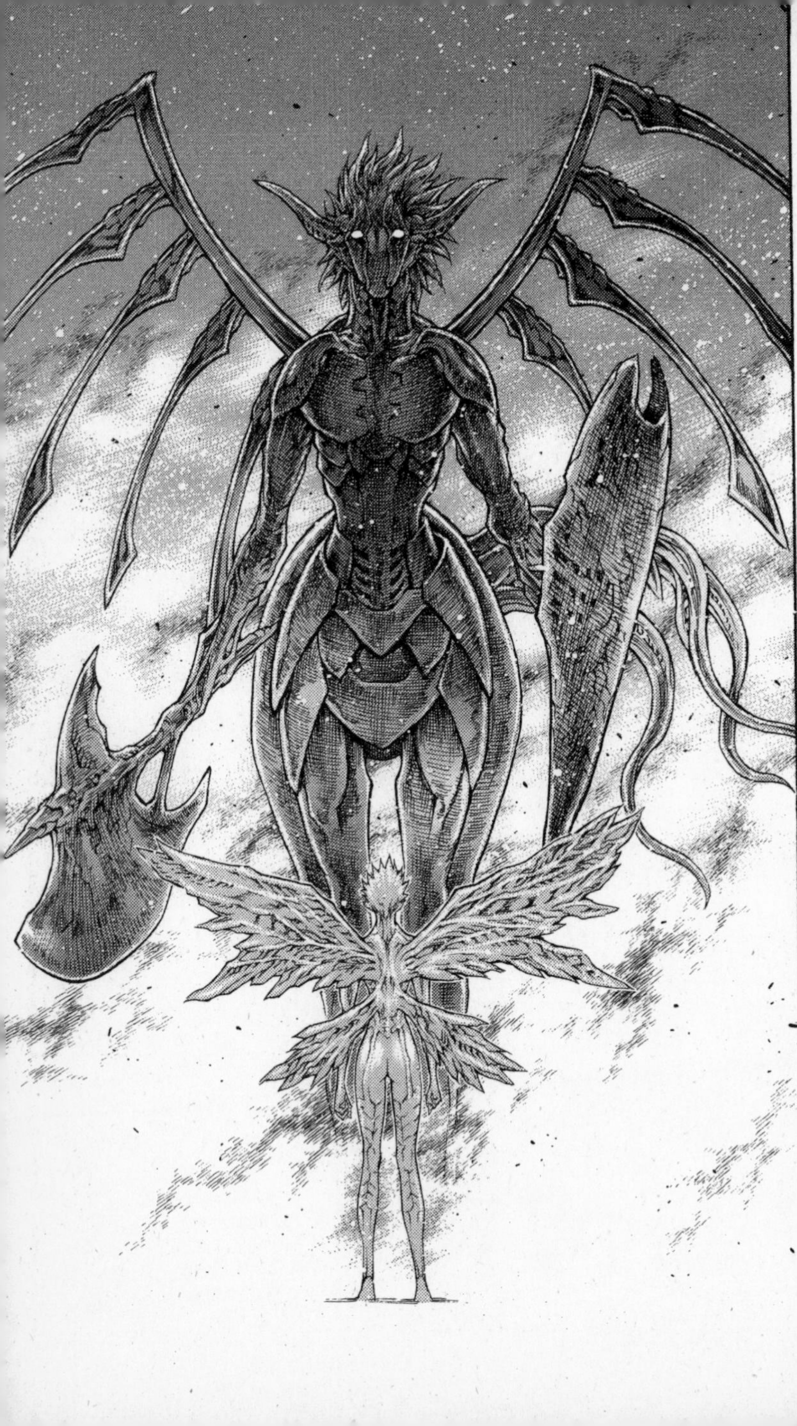

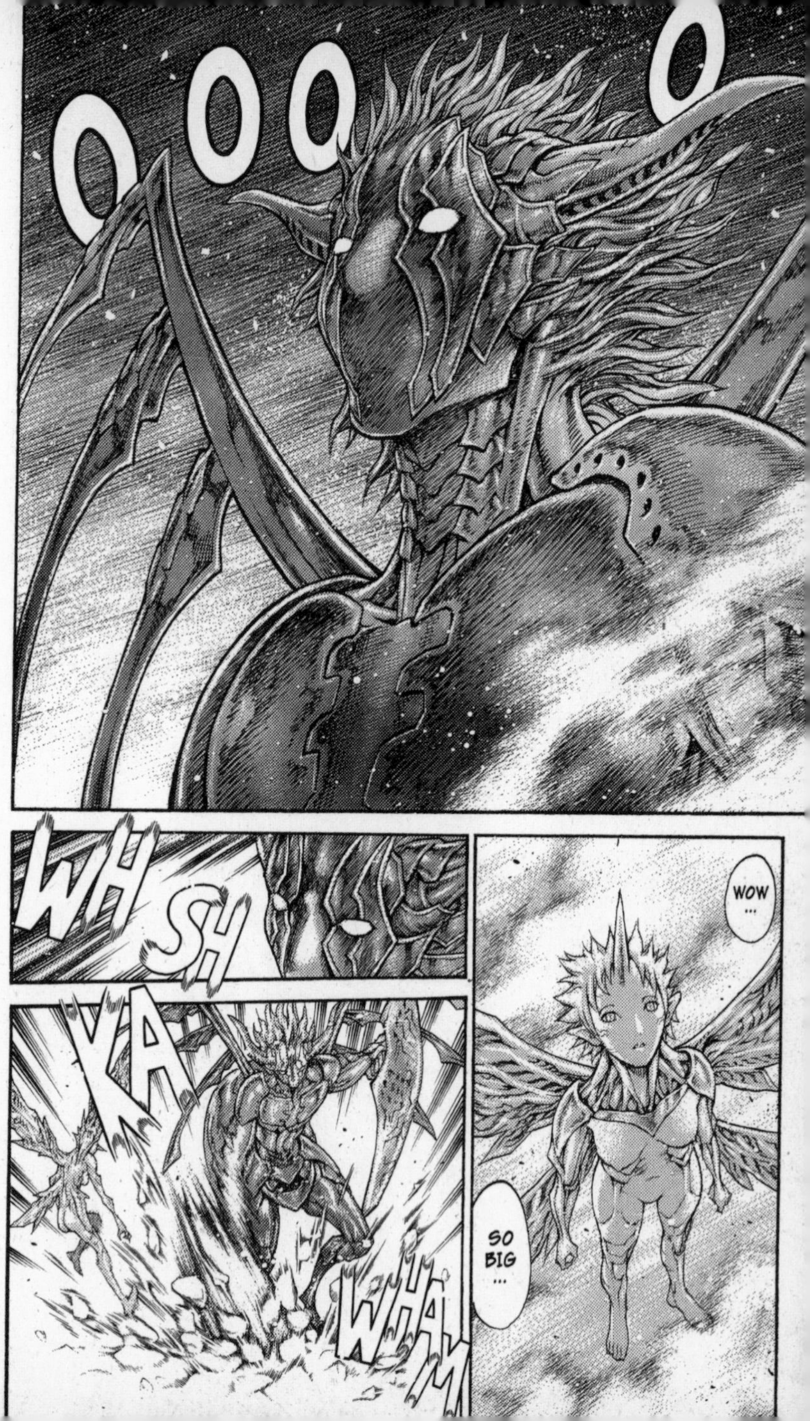
OOOOO
WOW ...
SO BIG ...
WHSH
KA
WHAM

READ THIS WAY

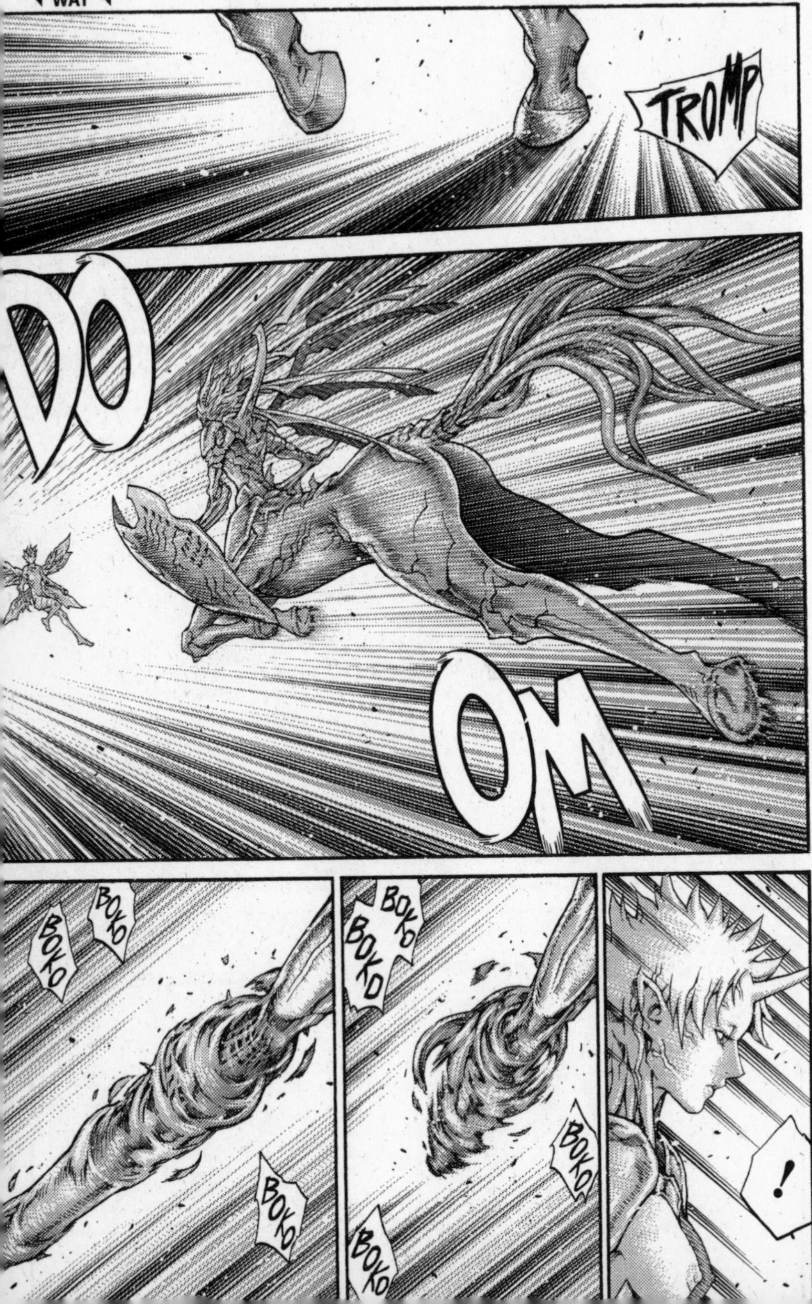
TROMP
DO
OM
BOKO
!
BOKO
BOKO
BOKO
BOKO
BOKO
BOKO
BOKO

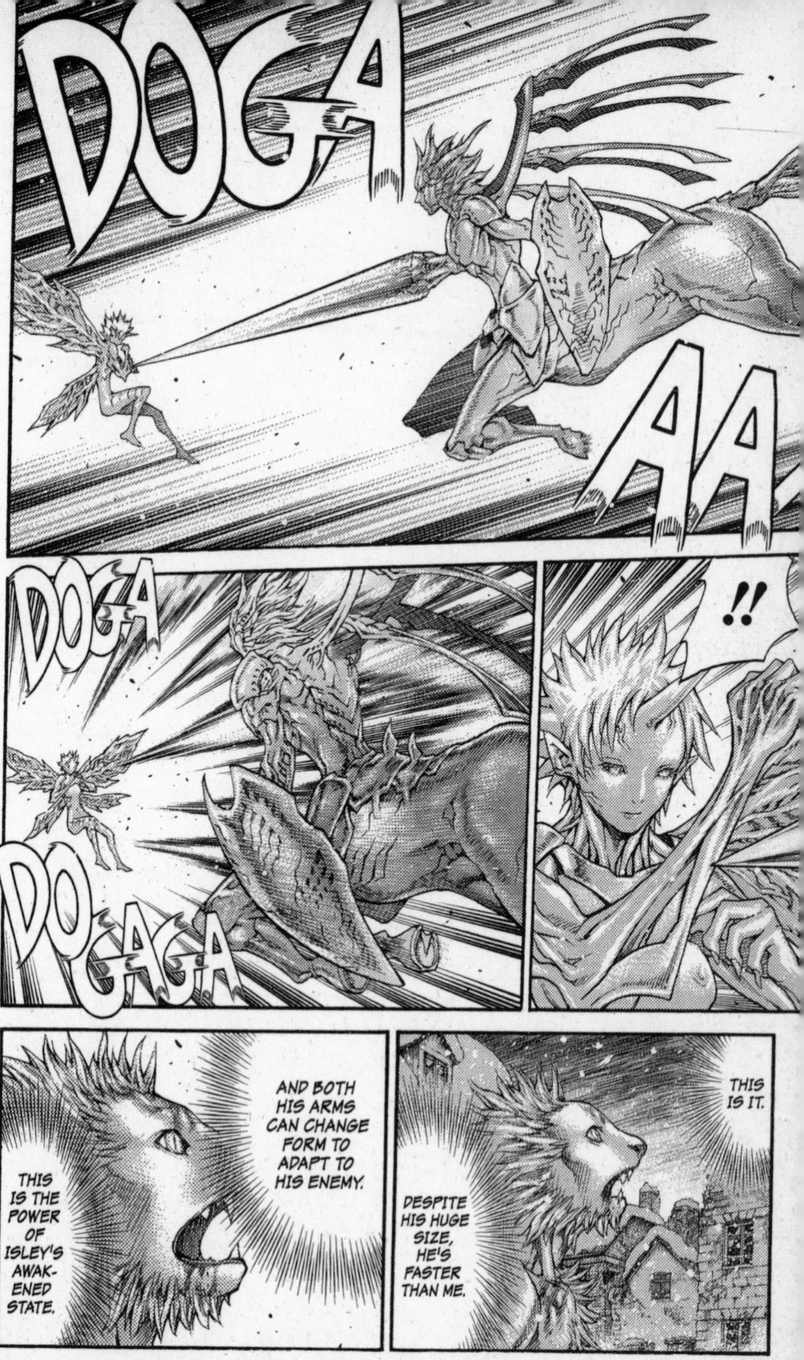
DOGA
AA
!!
DOGA
DOGAGA
THIS IS IT.
DESPITE HIS HUGE SIZE, HE'S FASTER THAN ME.
AND BOTH HIS ARMS CAN CHANGE FORM TO ADAPT TO HIS ENEMY.
THIS IS THE POWER OF ISLEY'S AWAKENED STATE.

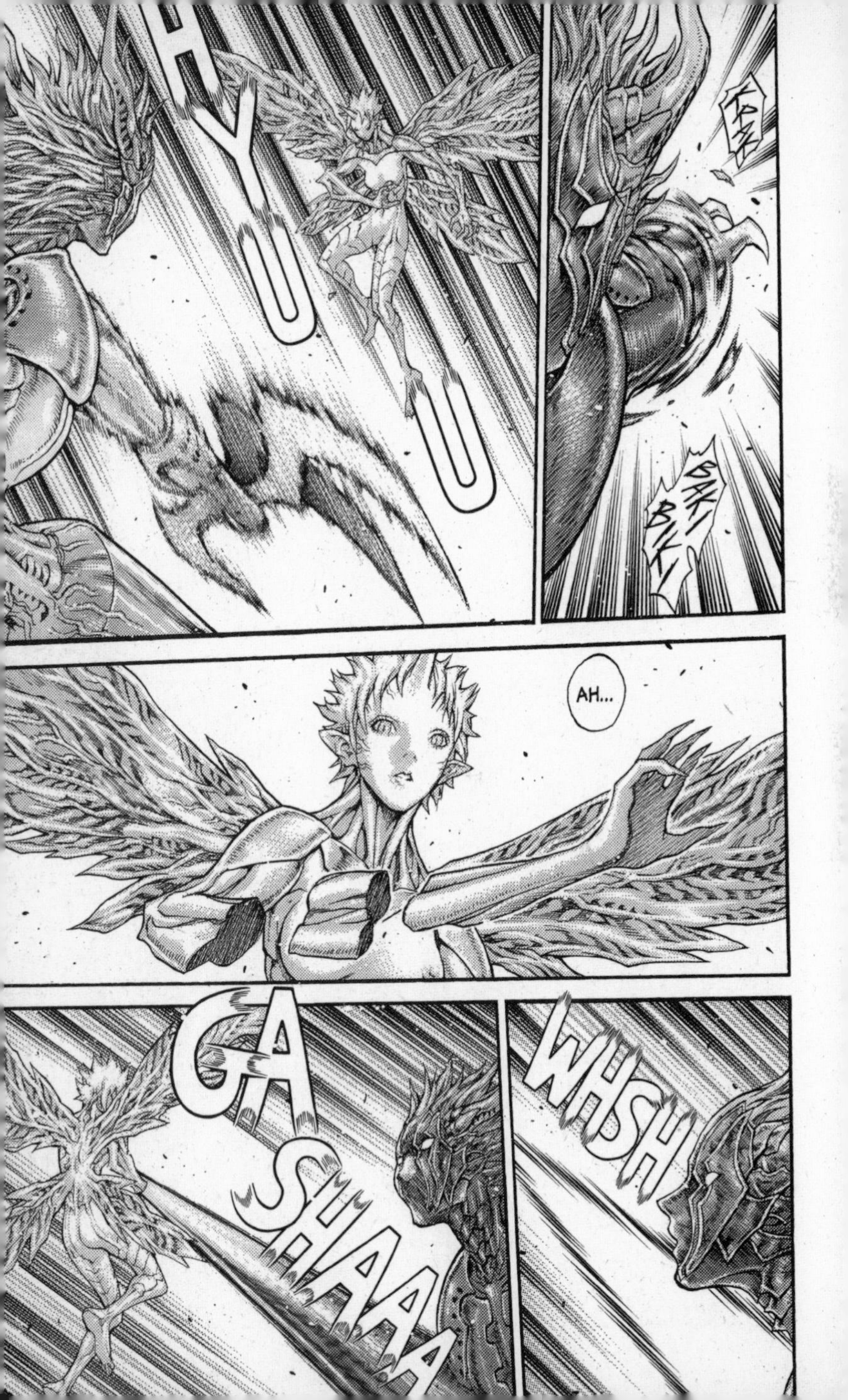
KRSK
BAKI BIKI
HYUUU
AH...
WHSH
GASHAAA

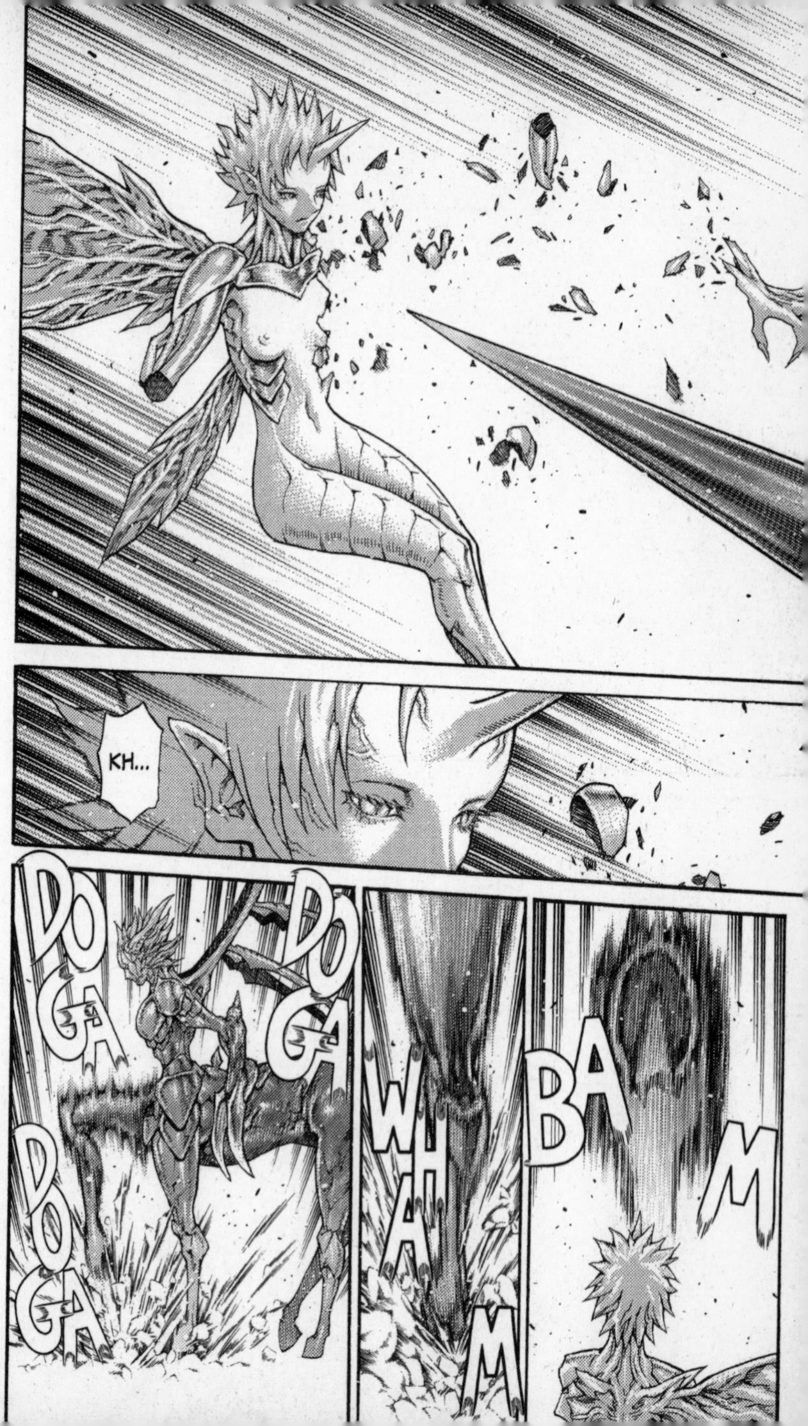
KH...
BAM
WHAM
DOGA
DOGA
DOGA

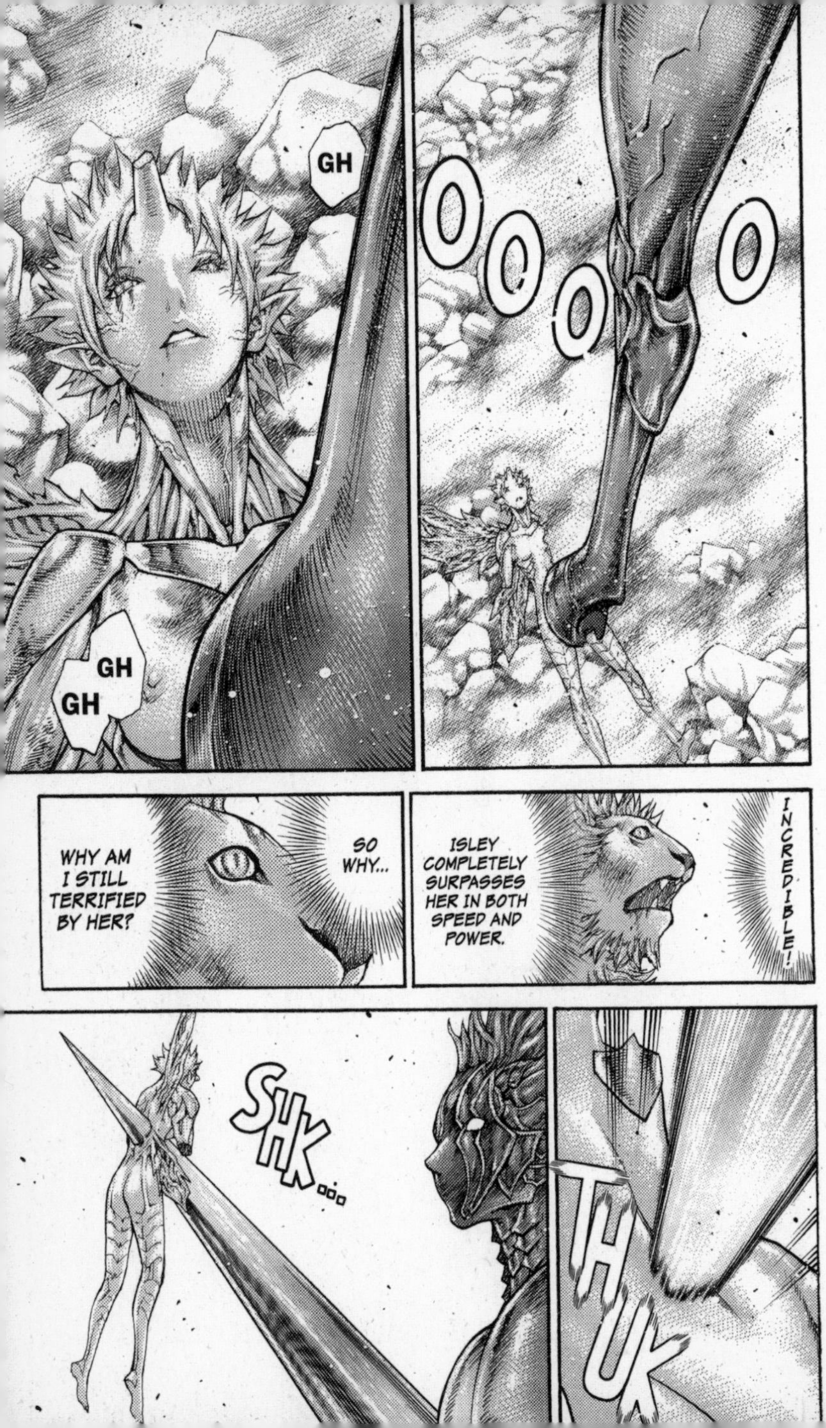
OOOOO
GH
GH
GH
INCREDIBLE!
ISLEY COMPLETELY SURPASSES HER IN BOTH SPEED AND POWER.
SO WHY...
WHY AM I STILL TERRIFIED BY HER?
THUK
SHK...

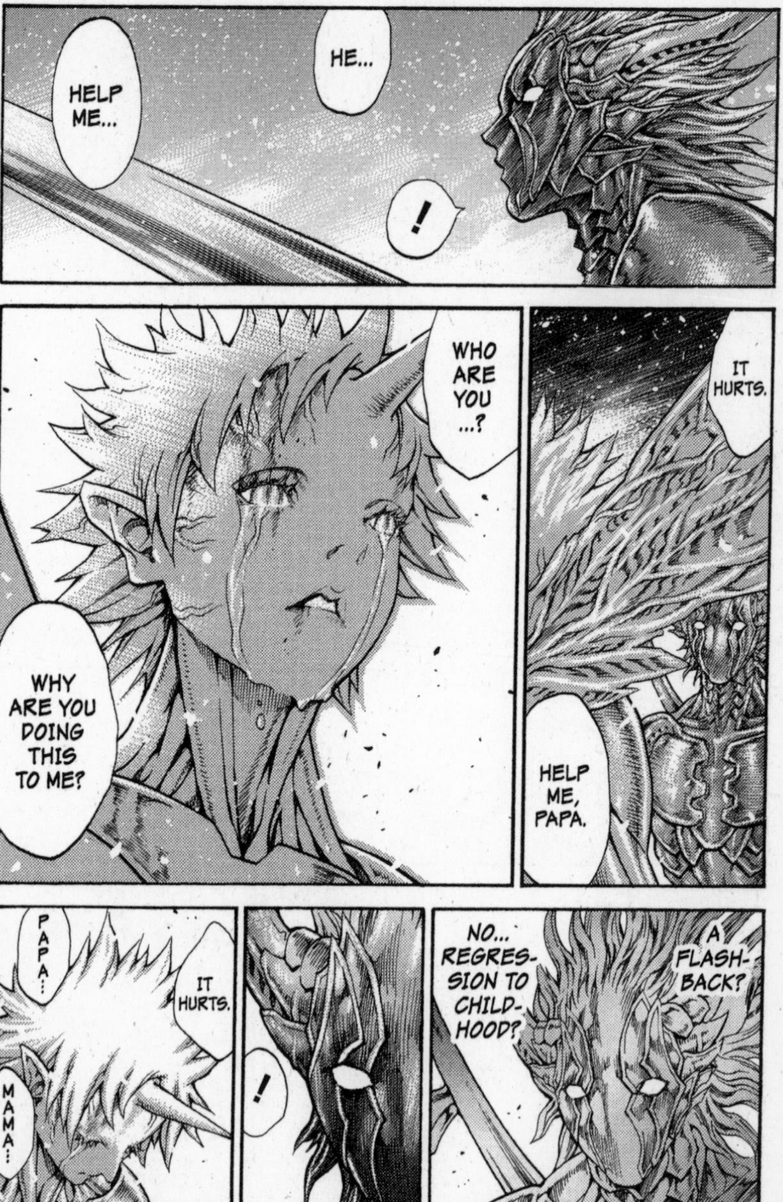
HE...
HELP ME...
!
IT HURTS.
HELP ME, PAPA.
WHO ARE YOU ...?
WHY ARE YOU DOING THIS TO ME?
A FLASH-BACK?
NO... REGRES-SION TO CHILD-HOOD?
!
IT HURTS.
PAPA...
MAMA...

READ THIS WAY

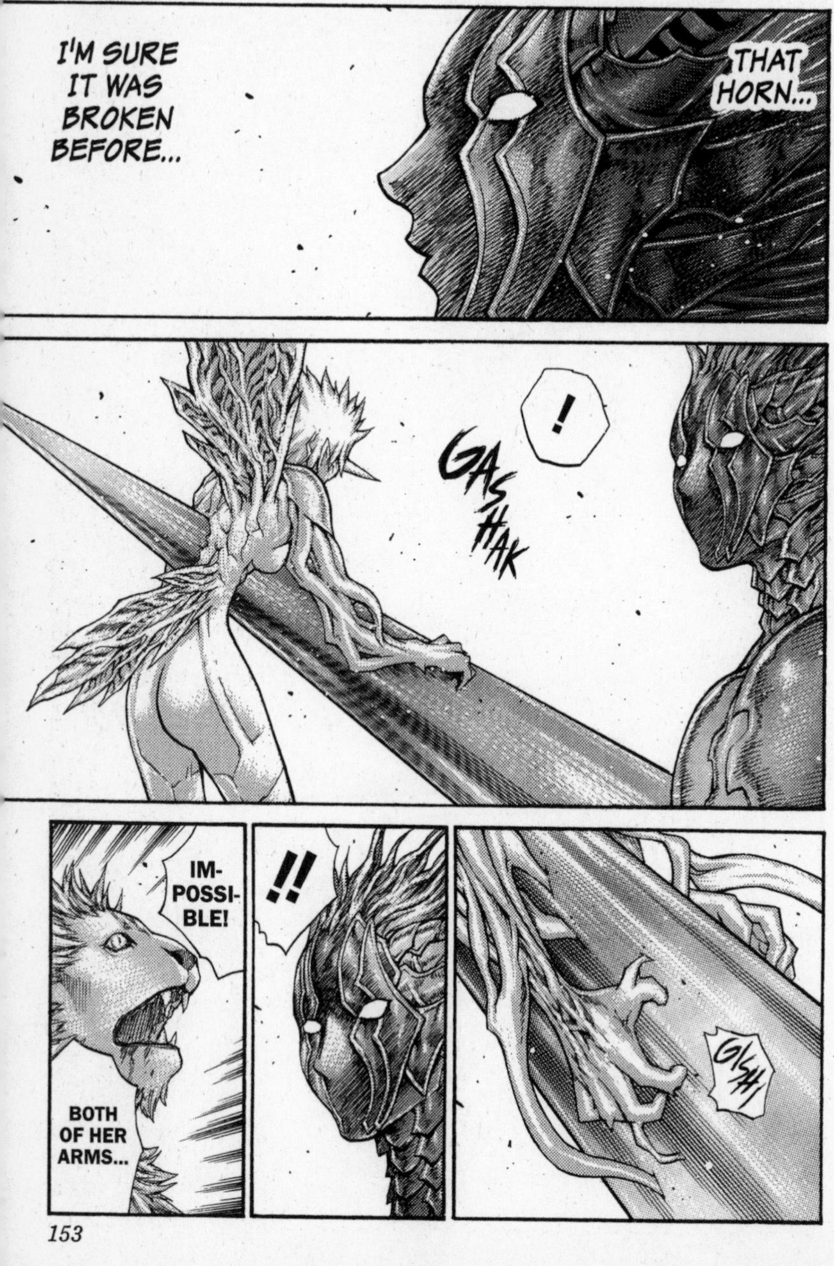
THAT HORN...
I'M SURE IT WAS BROKEN BEFORE...
!
GASHAK
GISH
!!
IM-POSSI-BLE!
BOTH OF HER ARMS...

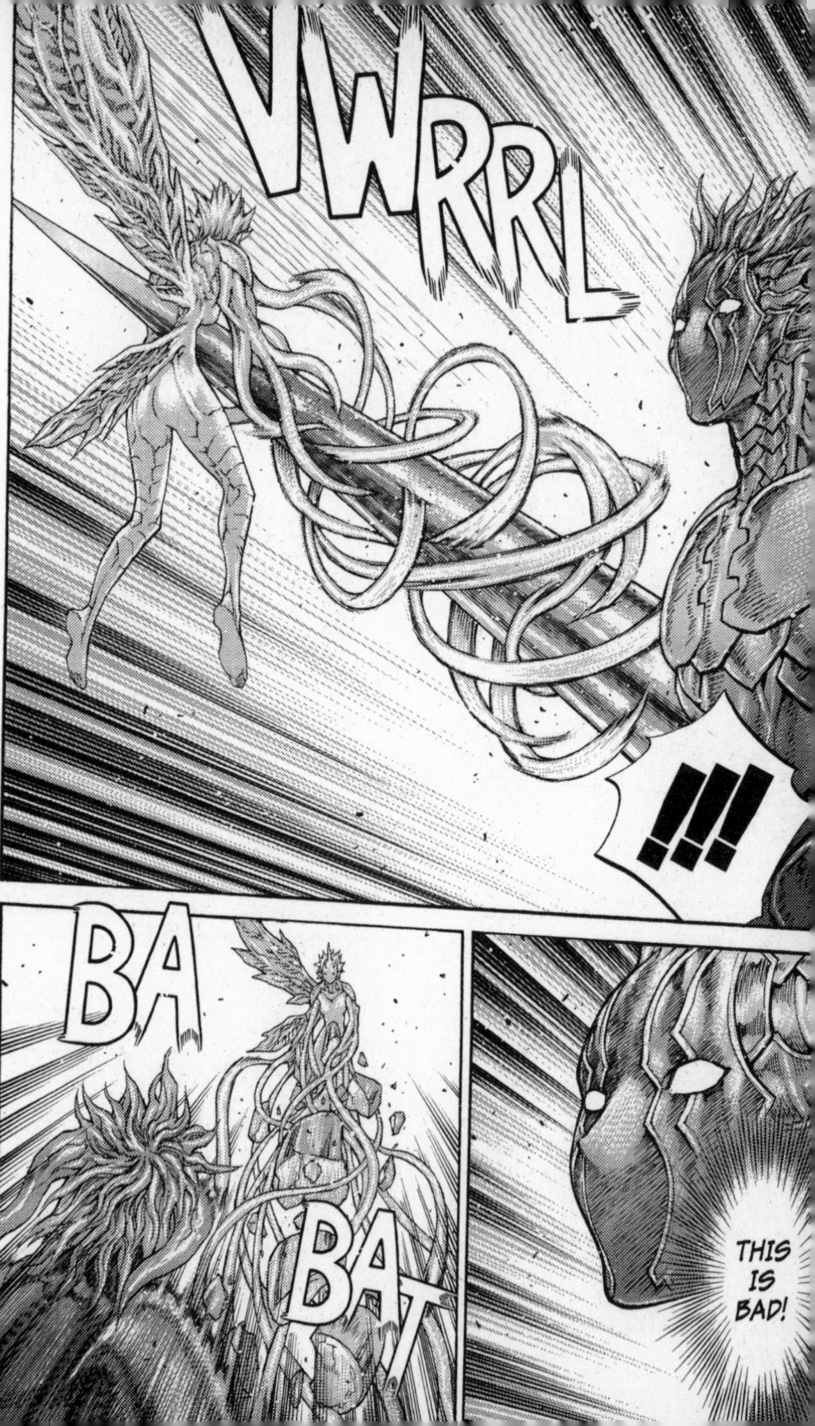
VWRRL
!!!
BA
BAT
THIS IS BAD!

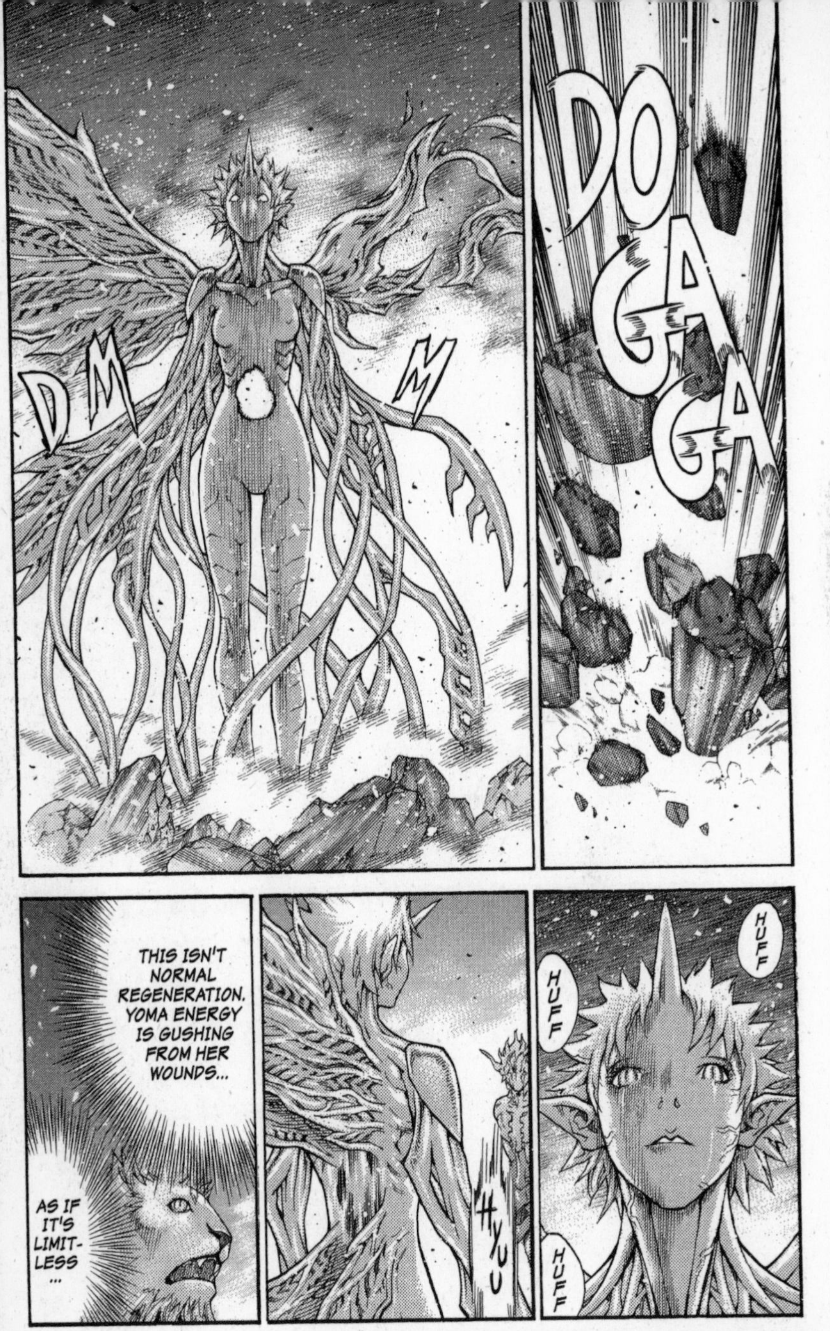
DOGAGA
DMM
HUFF
HUFF
HUFF
HYUU
THIS ISN'T NORMAL REGENERATION. YOMA ENERGY IS GUSHING FROM HER WOUNDS...
AS IF IT'S LIMIT-LESS ...

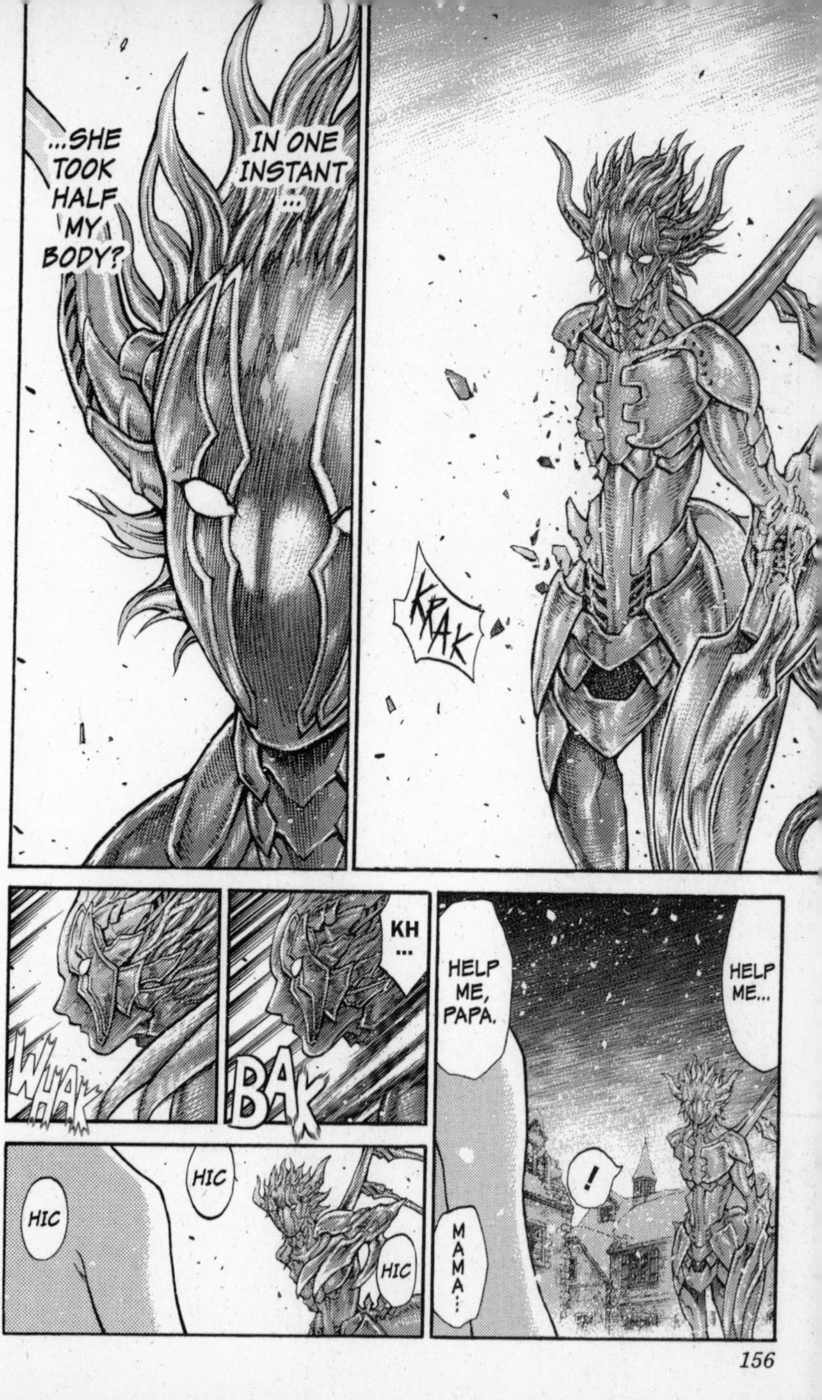
KRAK
IN ONE INSTANT ...
...SHE TOOK HALF MY BODY?
HELP ME...
HELP ME, PAPA.
!
MAMA...
KH ...
BAK
WHAK
HIC
HIC
HIC

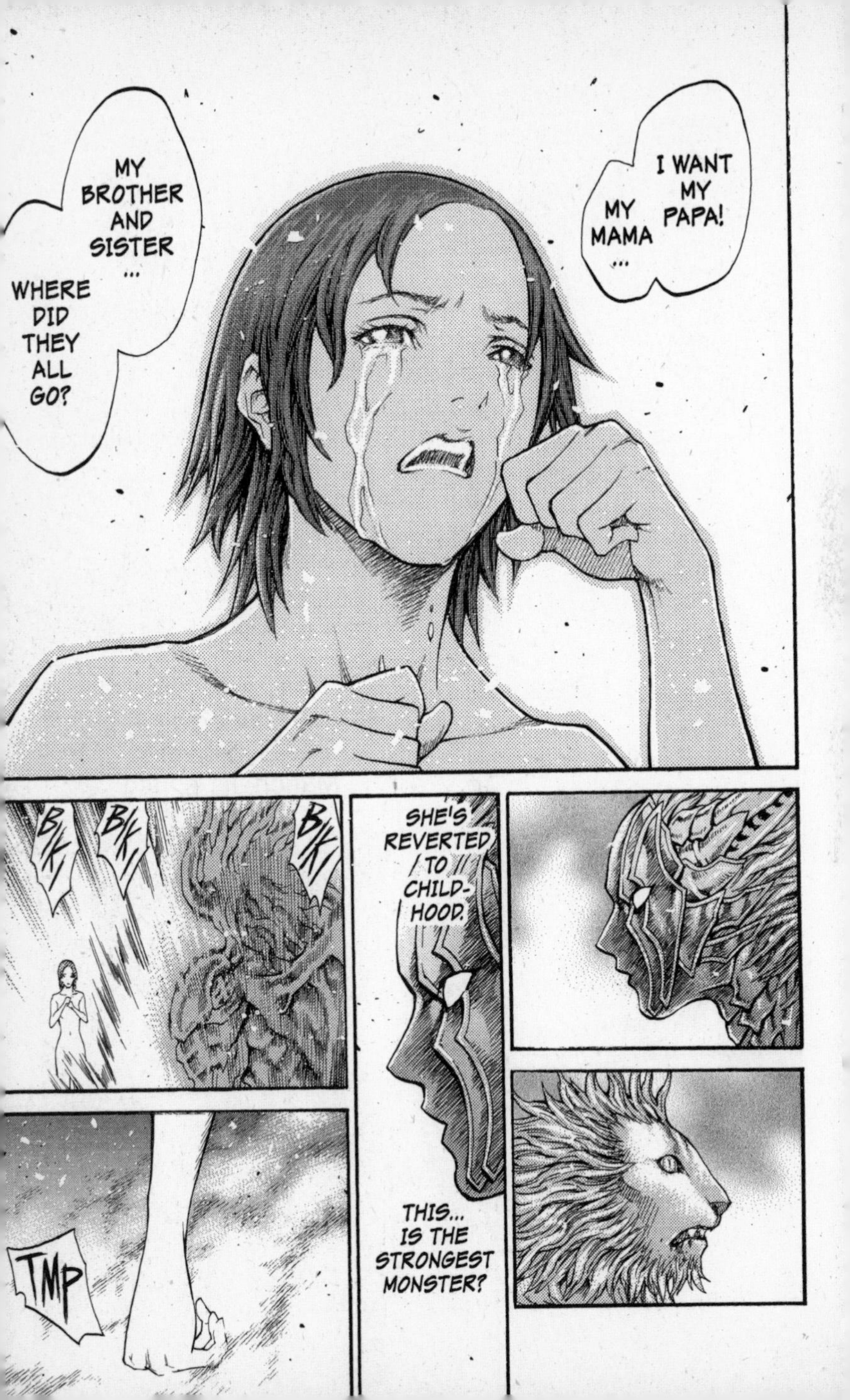
I WANT MY PAPA! MY MAMA...
MY BROTHER AND SISTER... WHERE DID THEY ALL GO?
SHE'S REVERTED TO CHILDHOOD.
THIS... IS THE STRONGEST MONSTER?
BIKI
BIKI
BIKI
TMP

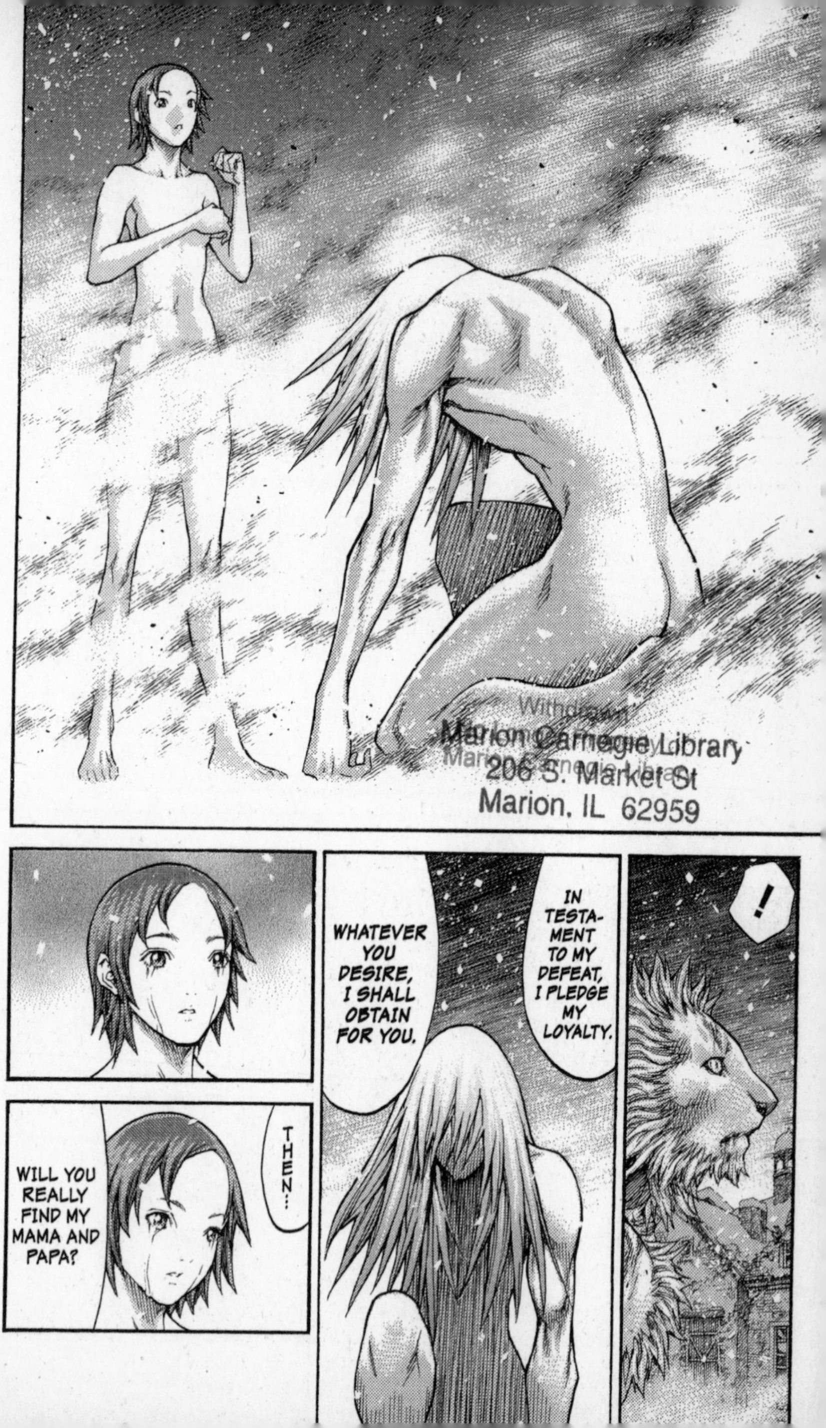
!
IN TESTAMENT TO MY DEFEAT, I PLEDGE MY LOYALTY.
WHATEVER YOU DESIRE, I SHALL OBTAIN FOR YOU.
THEN...
WILL YOU REALLY FIND MY MAMA AND PAPA?

READ THIS WAY

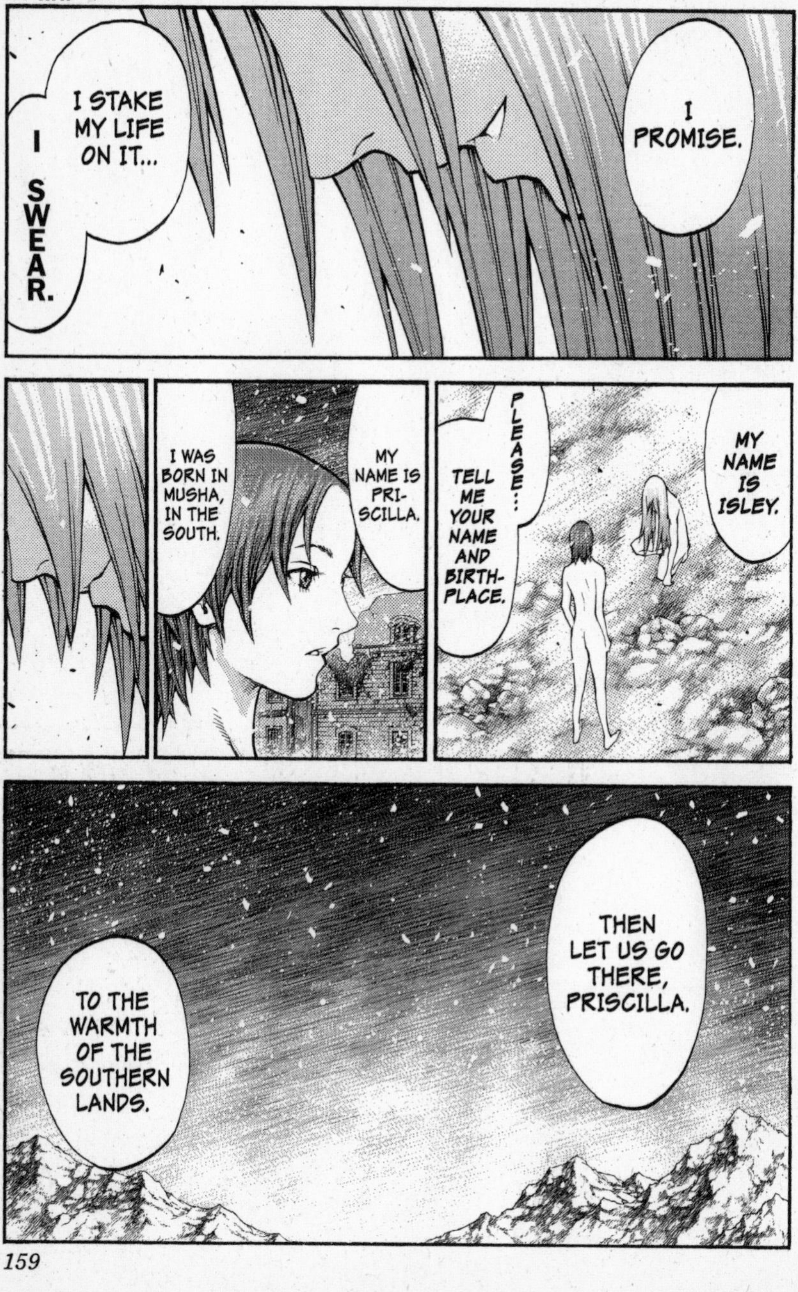
I PROMISE.
I STAKE MY LIFE ON IT...
I SWEAR.
MY NAME IS ISLEY.
PLEASE...
TELL ME YOUR NAME AND BIRTH-PLACE.
MY NAME IS PRI-SCILLA.
I WAS BORN IN MUSHA, IN THE SOUTH.
THEN LET US GO THERE, PRISCILLA.
TO THE WARMTH OF THE SOUTHERN LANDS.

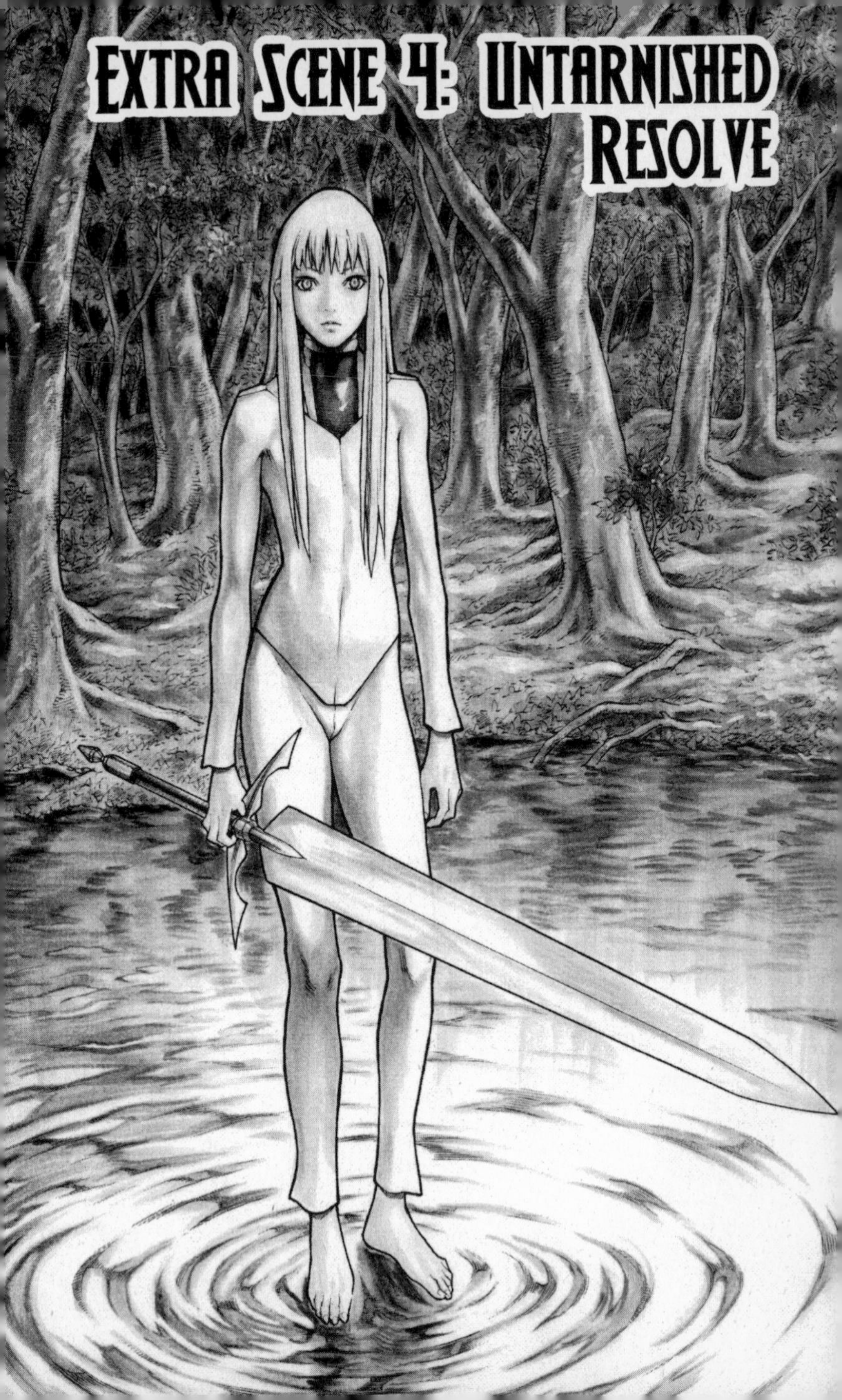
Extra Scene 4: Untarnished Resolve

READ THIS WAY

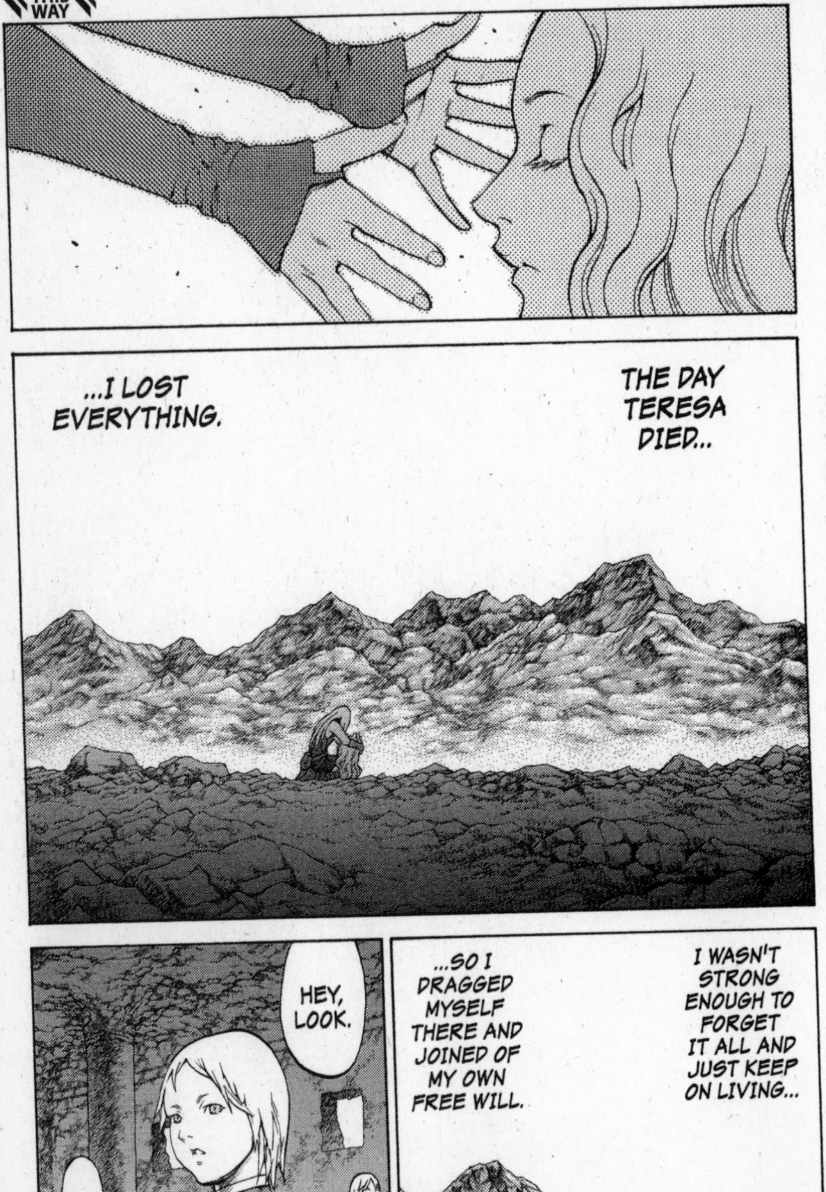
THE DAY TERESA DIED...
...I LOST EVERYTHING.
I WASN'T STRONG ENOUGH TO FORGET IT ALL AND JUST KEEP ON LIVING...
...SO I DRAGGED MYSELF THERE AND JOINED OF MY OWN FREE WILL.
HEY, LOOK.

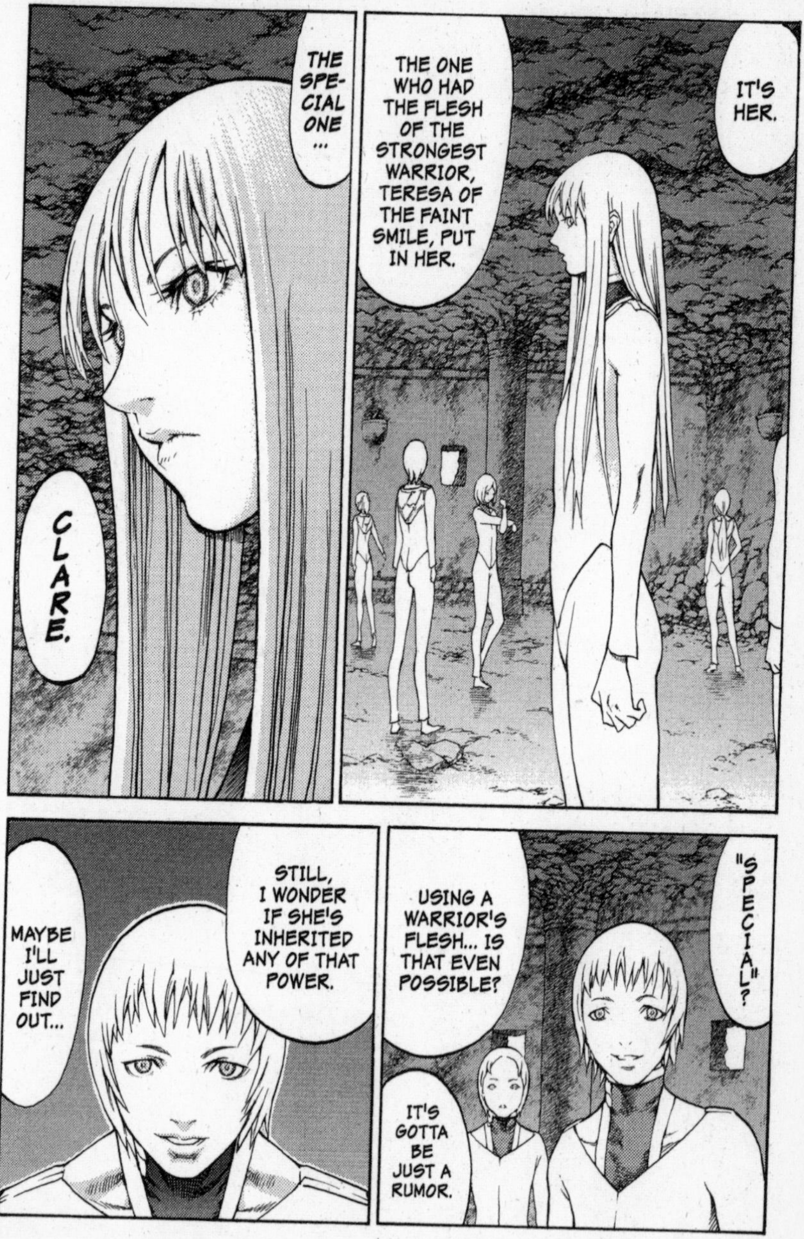
IT'S HER.
THE ONE WHO HAD THE FLESH OF THE STRONGEST WARRIOR, TERESA OF THE FAINT SMILE, PUT IN HER.
THE SPE- CIAL ONE ...
CLARE.
"SPECIAL"?
USING A WARRIOR'S FLESH... IS THAT EVEN POSSIBLE?
IT'S GOTTA BE JUST A RUMOR.
STILL, I WONDER IF SHE'S INHERITED ANY OF THAT POWER.
MAYBE I'LL JUST FIND OUT...

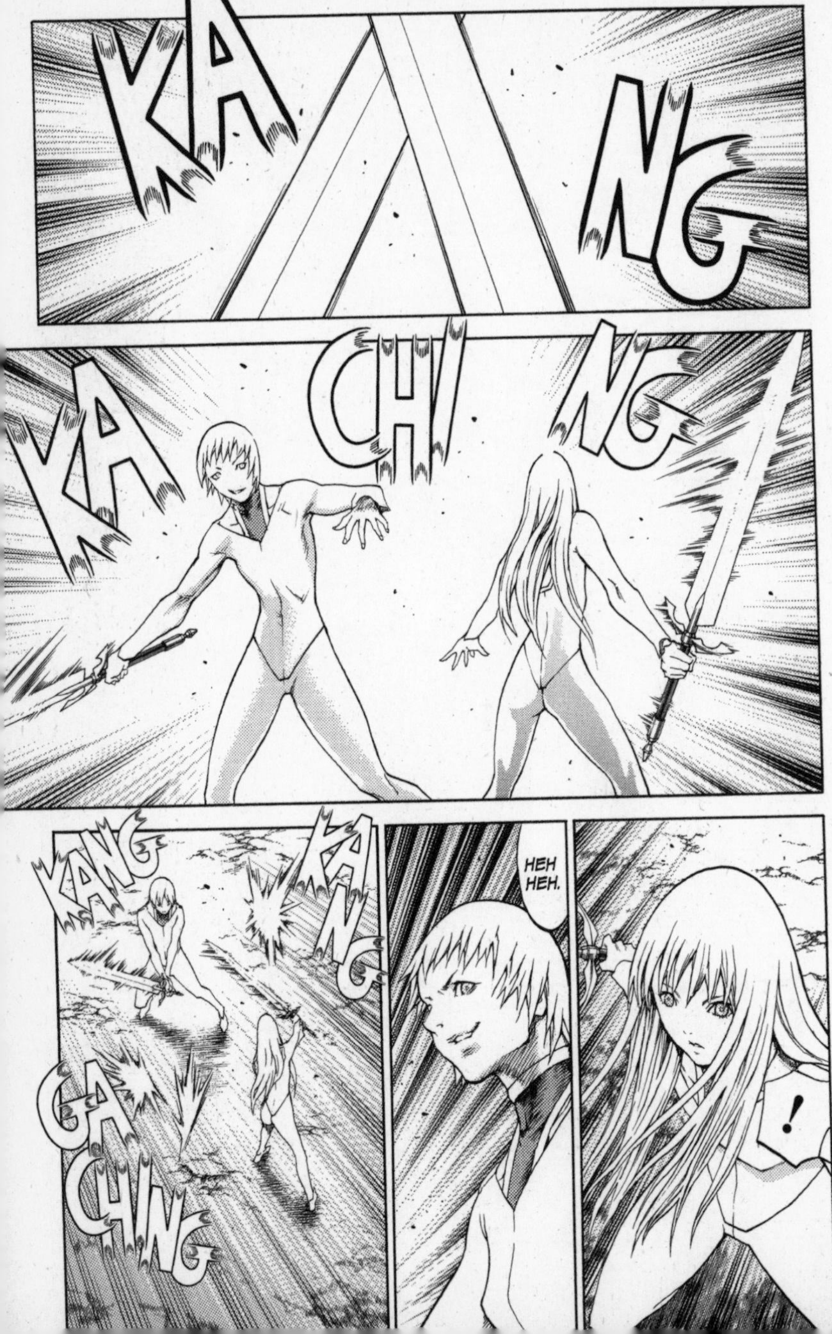
KA NG
KA CHI NG
!
HEH HEH.
KANG
KANG
GACHING

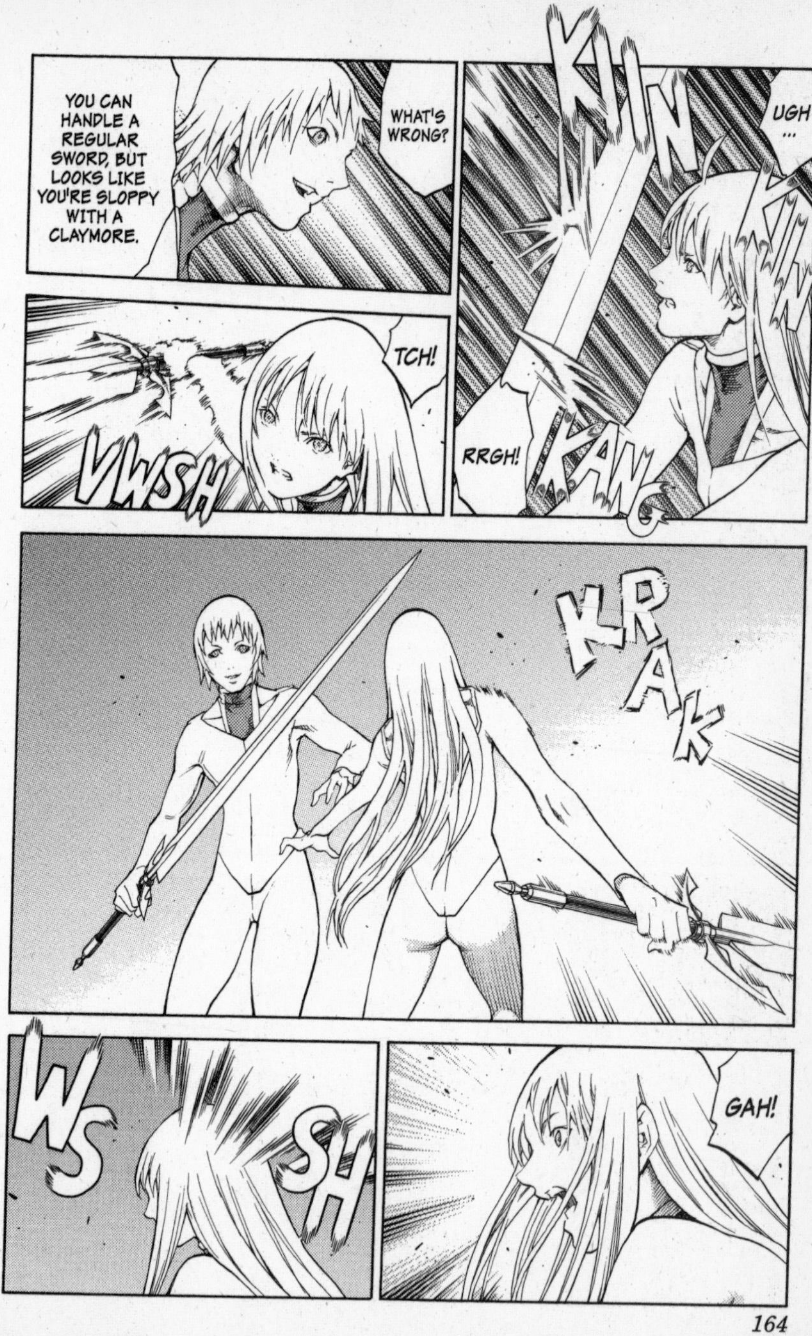

KLIN
UGH ...
RRGH!
KANG
WHAT'S WRONG?
YOU CAN HANDLE A REGULAR SWORD, BUT LOOKS LIKE YOU'RE SLOPPY WITH A CLAYMORE.
TCH!
VWSH
KRAK
GAH!
WSSH

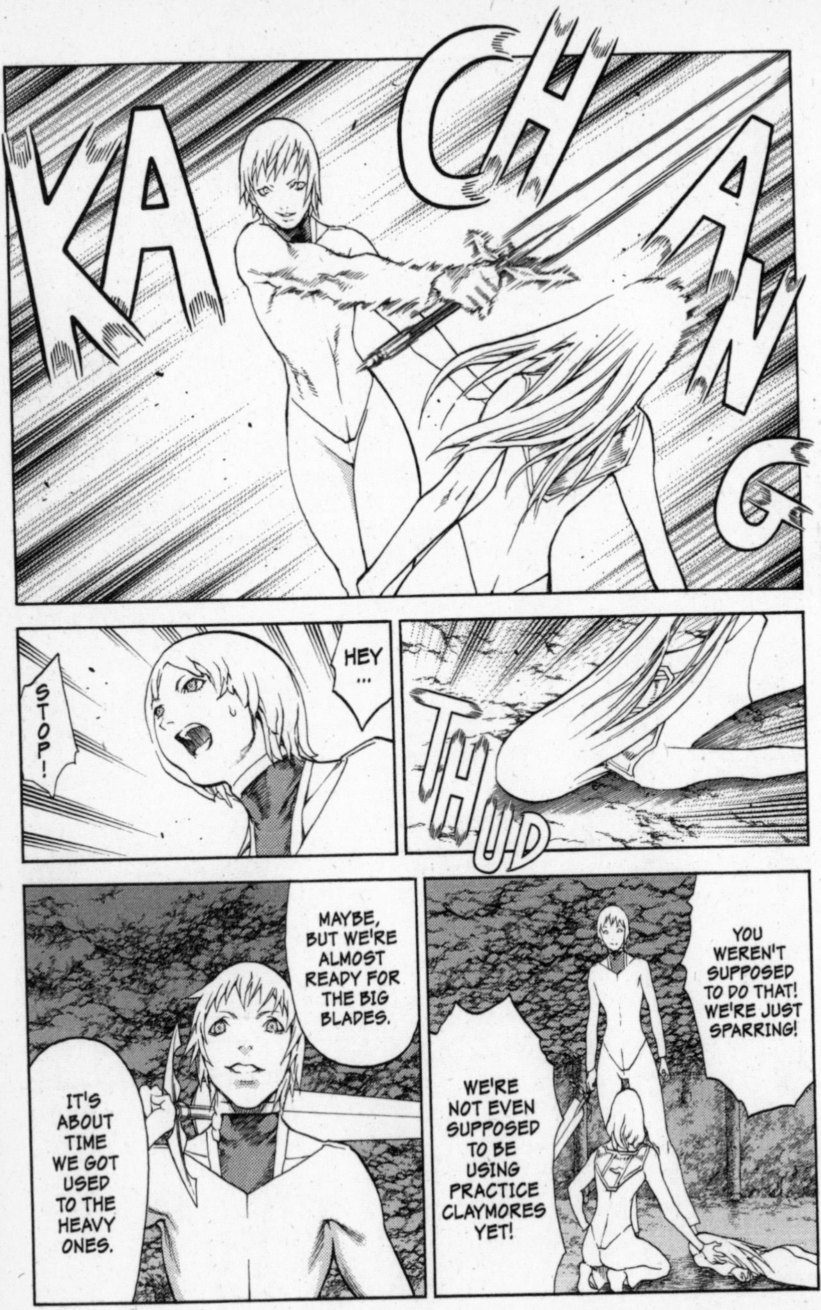
KA CHANG
THUD
HEY ...
STOP!
YOU WEREN'T SUPPOSED TO DO THAT! WE'RE JUST SPARRING!
WE'RE NOT EVEN SUPPOSED TO BE USING PRACTICE CLAYMORES YET!
MAYBE, BUT WE'RE ALMOST READY FOR THE BIG BLADES.
IT'S ABOUT TIME WE GOT USED TO THE HEAVY ONES.

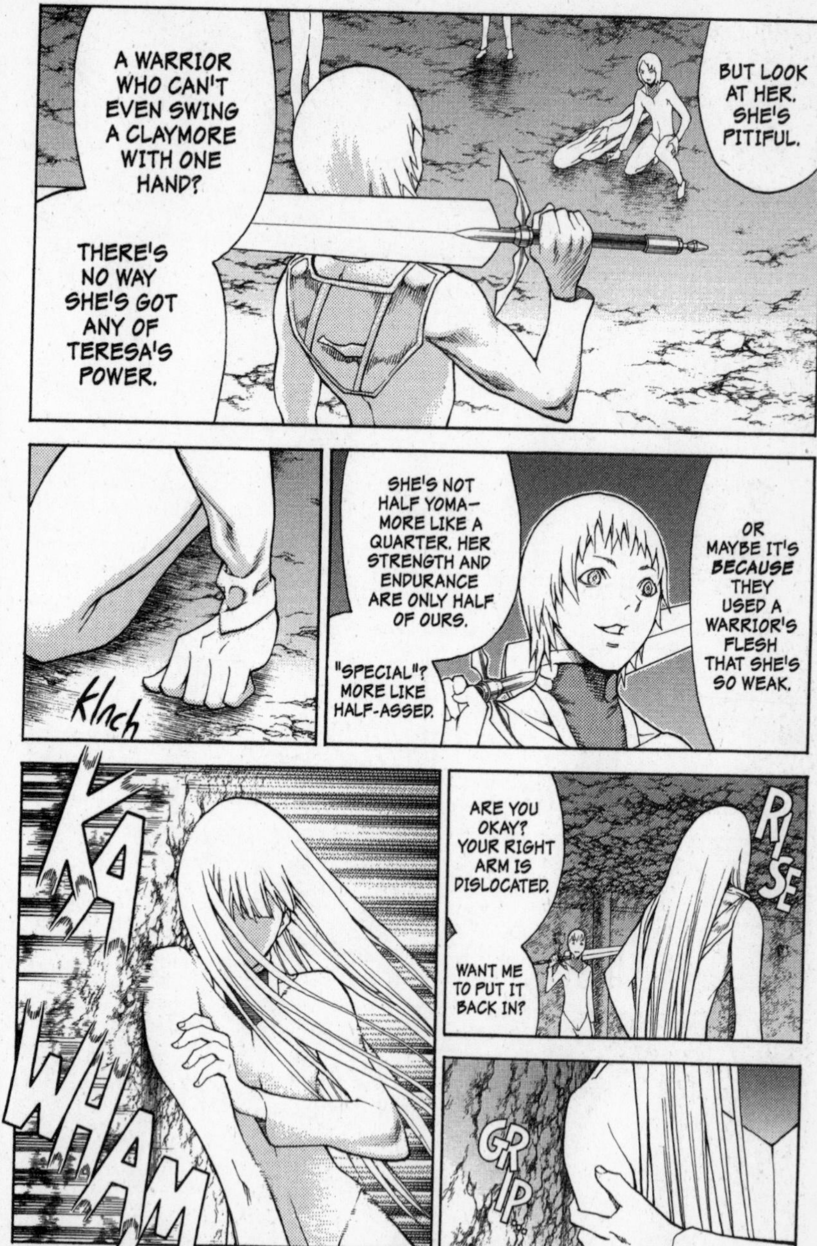
BUT LOOK AT HER. SHE'S PITIFUL.
A WARRIOR WHO CAN'T EVEN SWING A CLAYMORE WITH ONE HAND?
THERE'S NO WAY SHE'S GOT ANY OF TERESA'S POWER.
OR MAYBE IT'S BECAUSE THEY USED A WARRIOR'S FLESH THAT SHE'S SO WEAK.
SHE'S NOT HALF YOMA— MORE LIKE A QUARTER. HER STRENGTH AND ENDURANCE ARE ONLY HALF OF OURS.
"SPECIAL"? MORE LIKE HALF-ASSED.
Klnch
RISE
ARE YOU OKAY? YOUR RIGHT ARM IS DISLOCATED.
WANT ME TO PUT IT BACK IN?
GRIP...
KA WHAM

READ THIS WAY

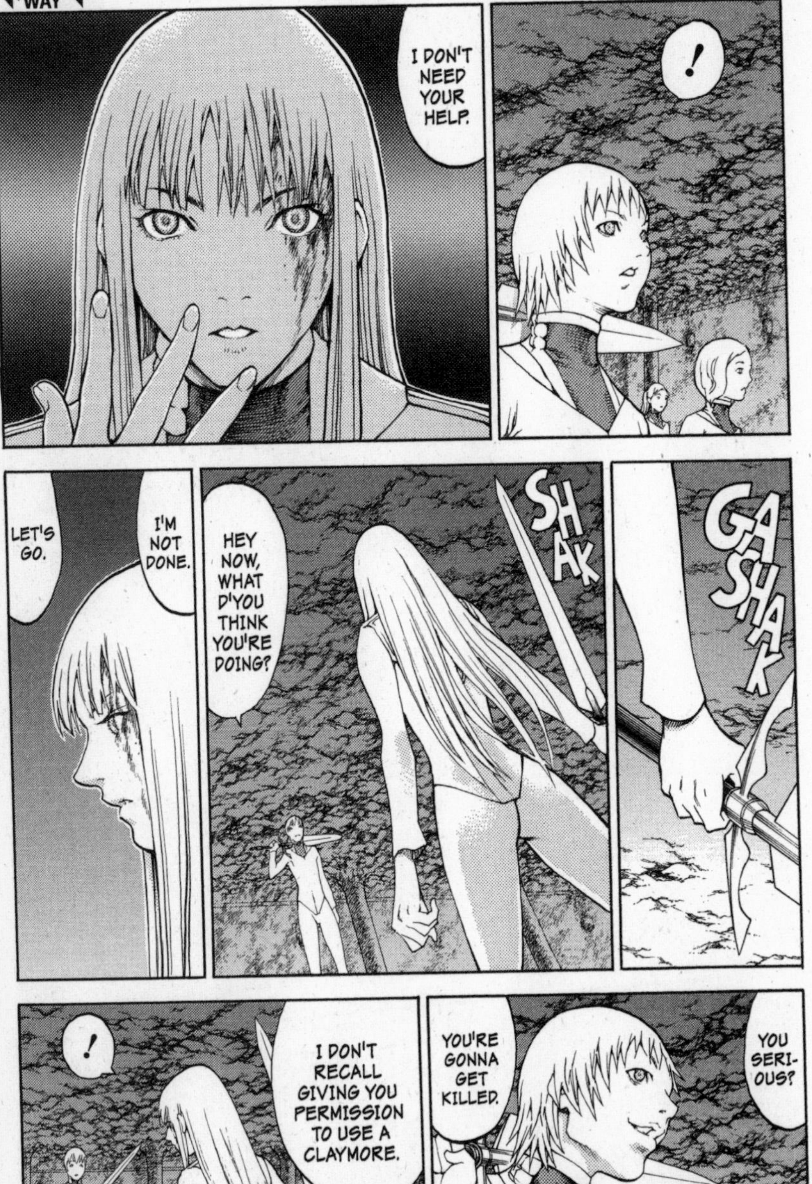
!
I DON'T NEED YOUR HELP.
GASHAK
SHAK
HEY NOW, WHAT D'YOU THINK YOU'RE DOING?
I'M NOT DONE.
LET'S GO.
YOU SERI-OUS?
YOU'RE GONNA GET KILLED.
I DON'T RECALL GIVING YOU PERMISSION TO USE A CLAYMORE.
!

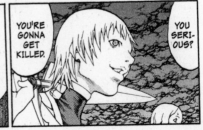

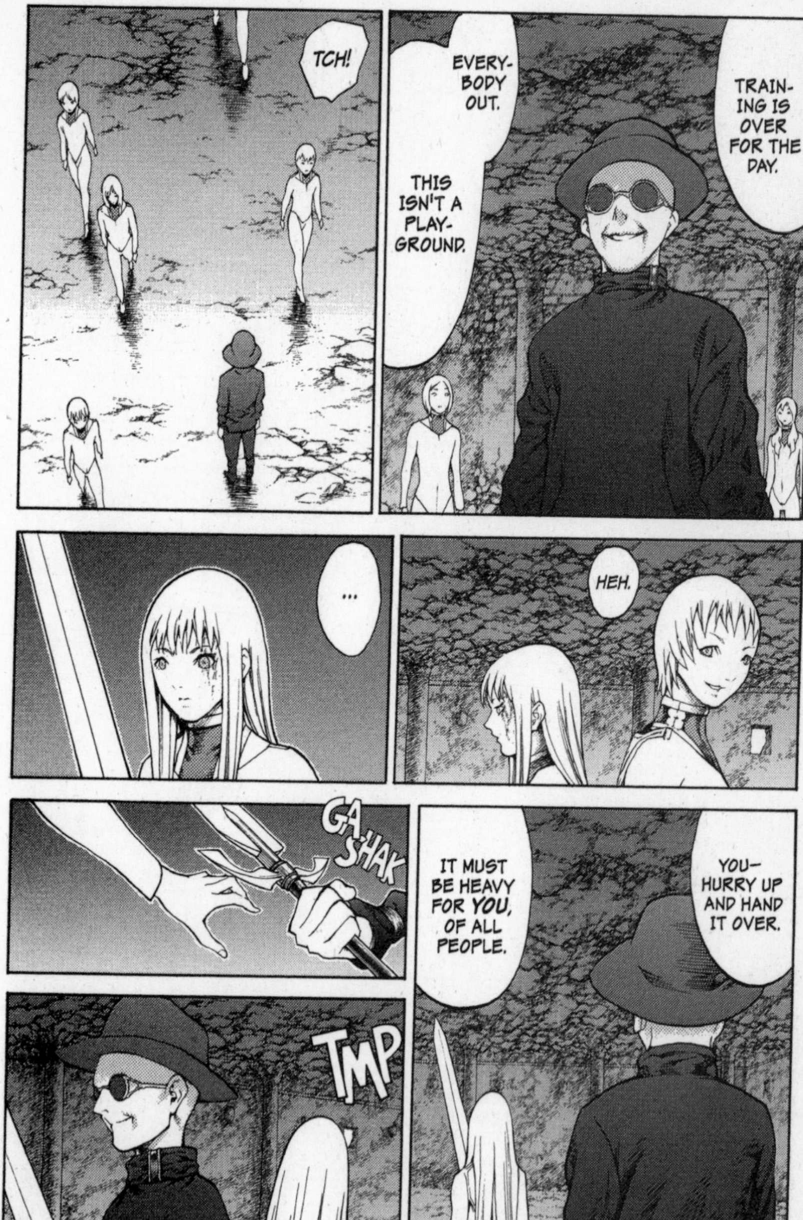
TRAINING IS OVER FOR THE DAY.
EVERYBODY OUT.
THIS ISN'T A PLAYGROUND.
TCH!
HEH.
...
YOU—HURRY UP AND HAND IT OVER.
IT MUST BE HEAVY FOR YOU, OF ALL PEOPLE.
GA-SHAK
TMP

READ THIS WAY

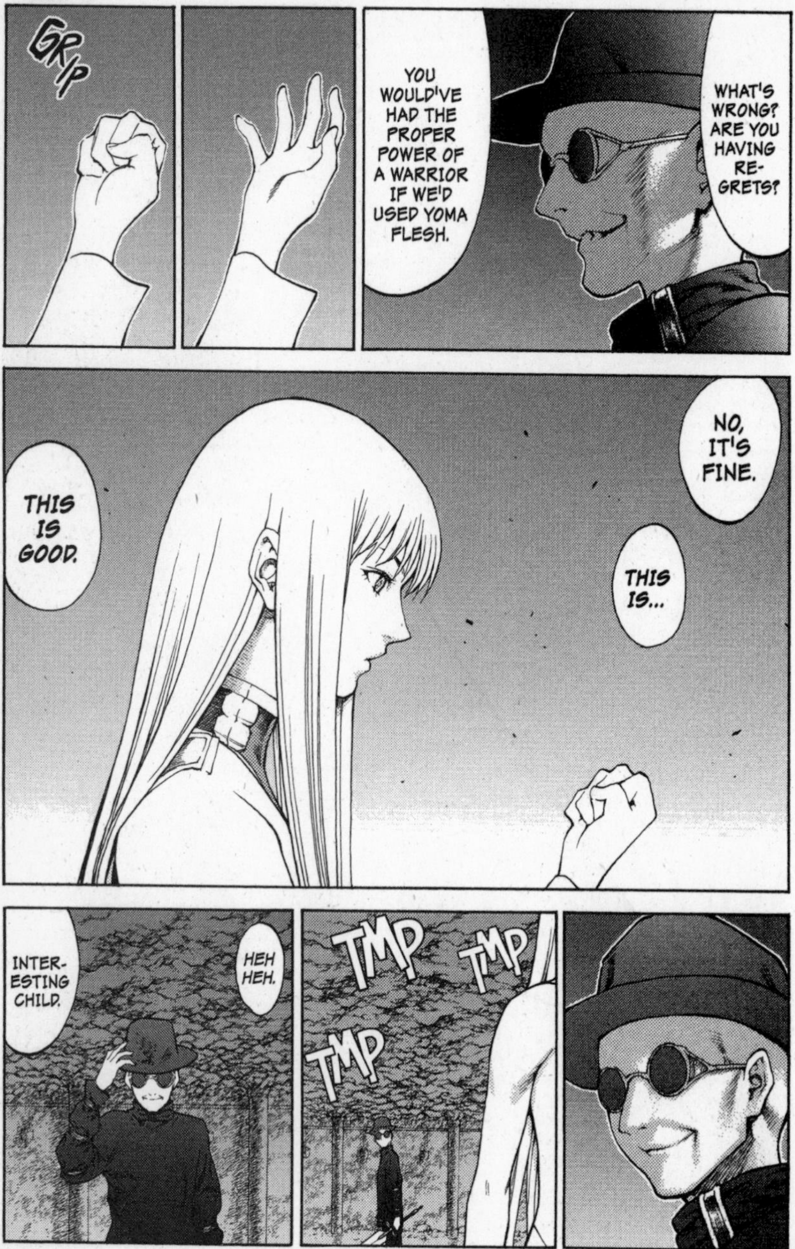

WHAT'S WRONG? ARE YOU HAVING RE-GRETS?
YOU WOULD'VE HAD THE PROPER POWER OF A WARRIOR IF WE'D USED YOMA FLESH.
GRIP
NO, IT'S FINE.
THIS IS...
THIS IS GOOD.
TMP
TMP
TMP
HEH HEH.
INTER-ESTING CHILD.

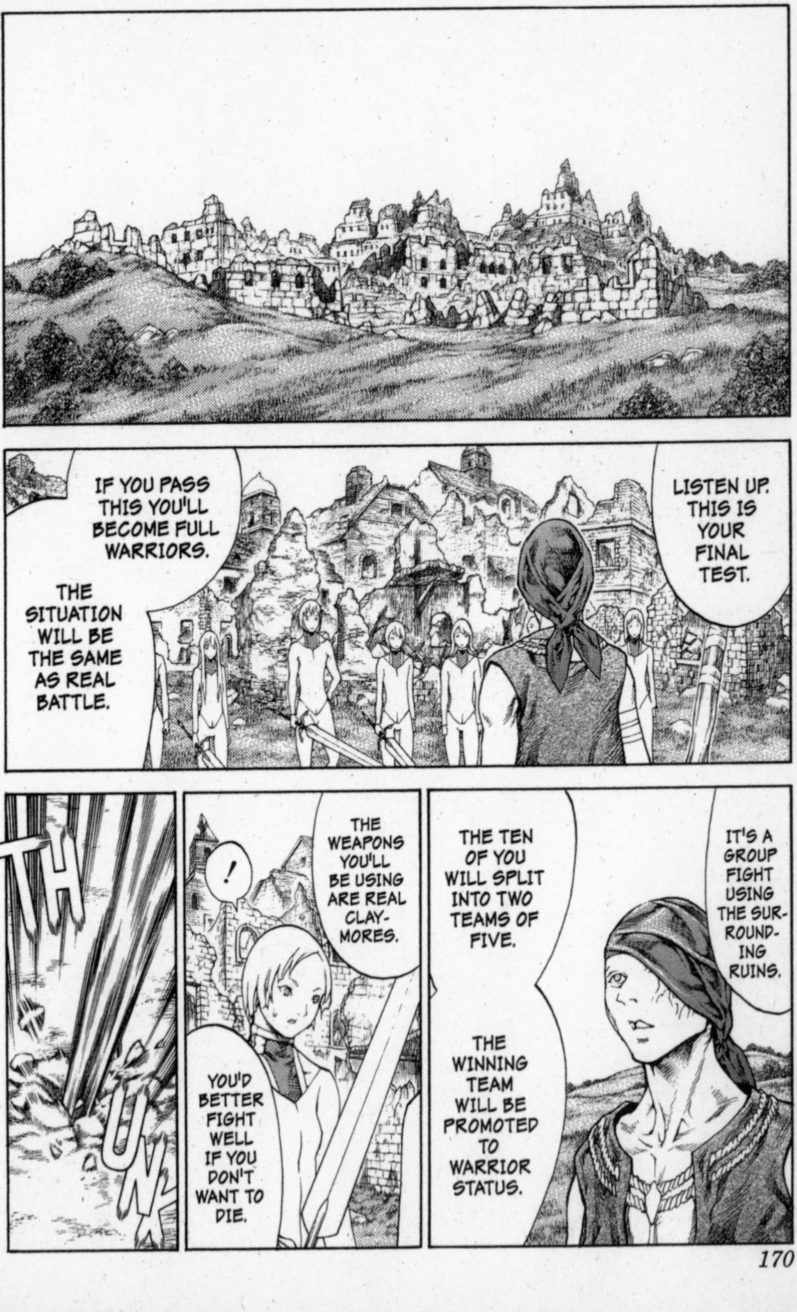
LISTEN UP. THIS IS YOUR FINAL TEST.
IF YOU PASS THIS YOU'LL BECOME FULL WARRIORS.
THE SITUATION WILL BE THE SAME AS REAL BATTLE.
IT'S A GROUP FIGHT USING THE SUR-ROUND-ING RUINS.
THE TEN OF YOU WILL SPLIT INTO TWO TEAMS OF FIVE.
THE WINNING TEAM WILL BE PROMOTED TO WARRIOR STATUS.
THE WEAPONS YOU'LL BE USING ARE REAL CLAY-MORES.
!
YOU'D BETTER FIGHT WELL IF YOU DON'T WANT TO DIE.
THUNK

READ THIS WAY

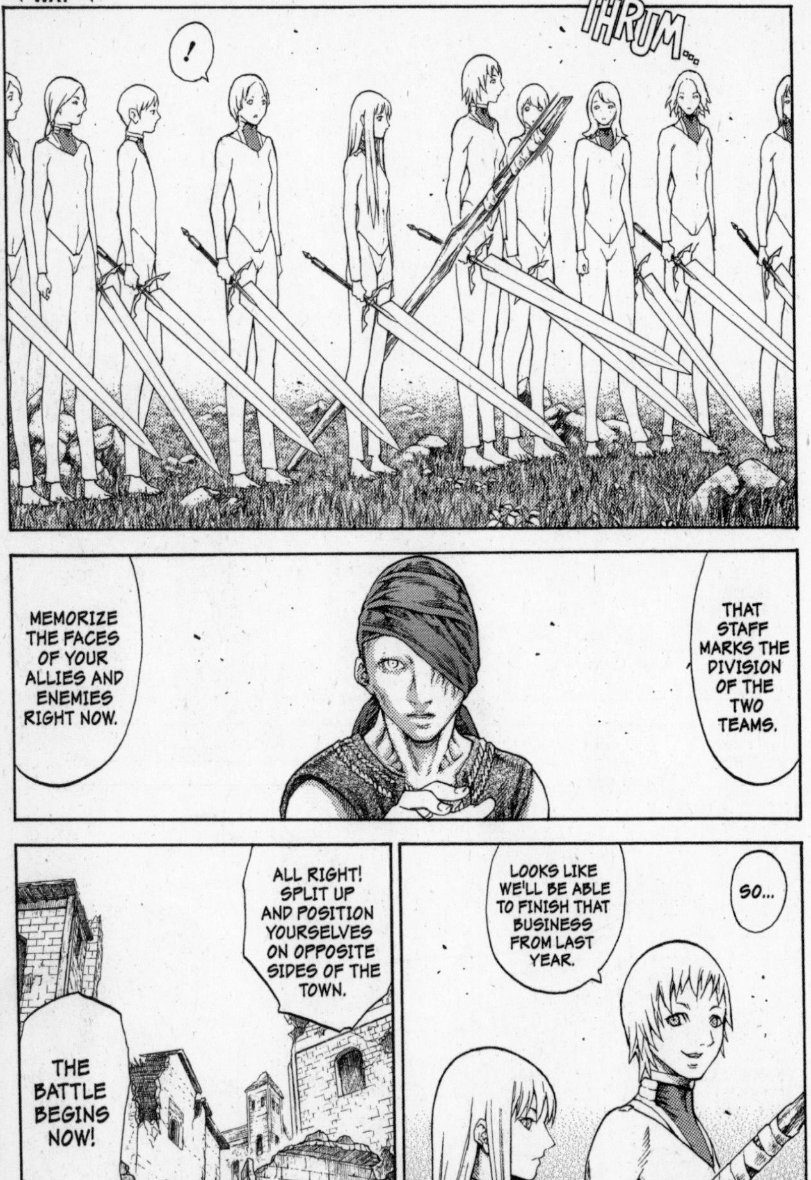
THRUM...
!
THAT STAFF MARKS THE DIVISION OF THE TWO TEAMS.
MEMORIZE THE FACES OF YOUR ALLIES AND ENEMIES RIGHT NOW.
SO...
LOOKS LIKE WE'LL BE ABLE TO FINISH THAT BUSINESS FROM LAST YEAR.
ALL RIGHT! SPLIT UP AND POSITION YOURSELVES ON OPPOSITE SIDES OF THE TOWN.
THE BATTLE BEGINS NOW!

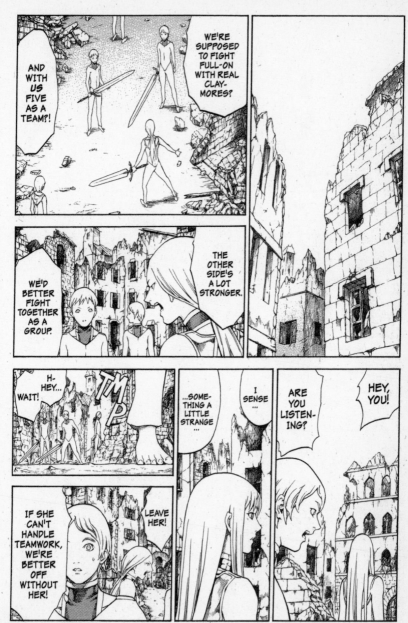

WE'RE SUPPOSED TO FIGHT FULL-ON WITH REAL CLAY-MORES?
AND WITH US FIVE AS A TEAM?!
THE OTHER SIDE'S A LOT STRONGER.
WE'D BETTER FIGHT TOGETHER AS A GROUP.
HEY, YOU!
ARE YOU LISTEN-ING?
I SENSE ...
...SOME-THING A LITTLE STRANGE ...
TMP
H-HEY... WAIT!
LEAVE HER!
IF SHE CAN'T HANDLE TEAMWORK, WE'RE BETTER OFF WITHOUT HER!

READ THIS WAY

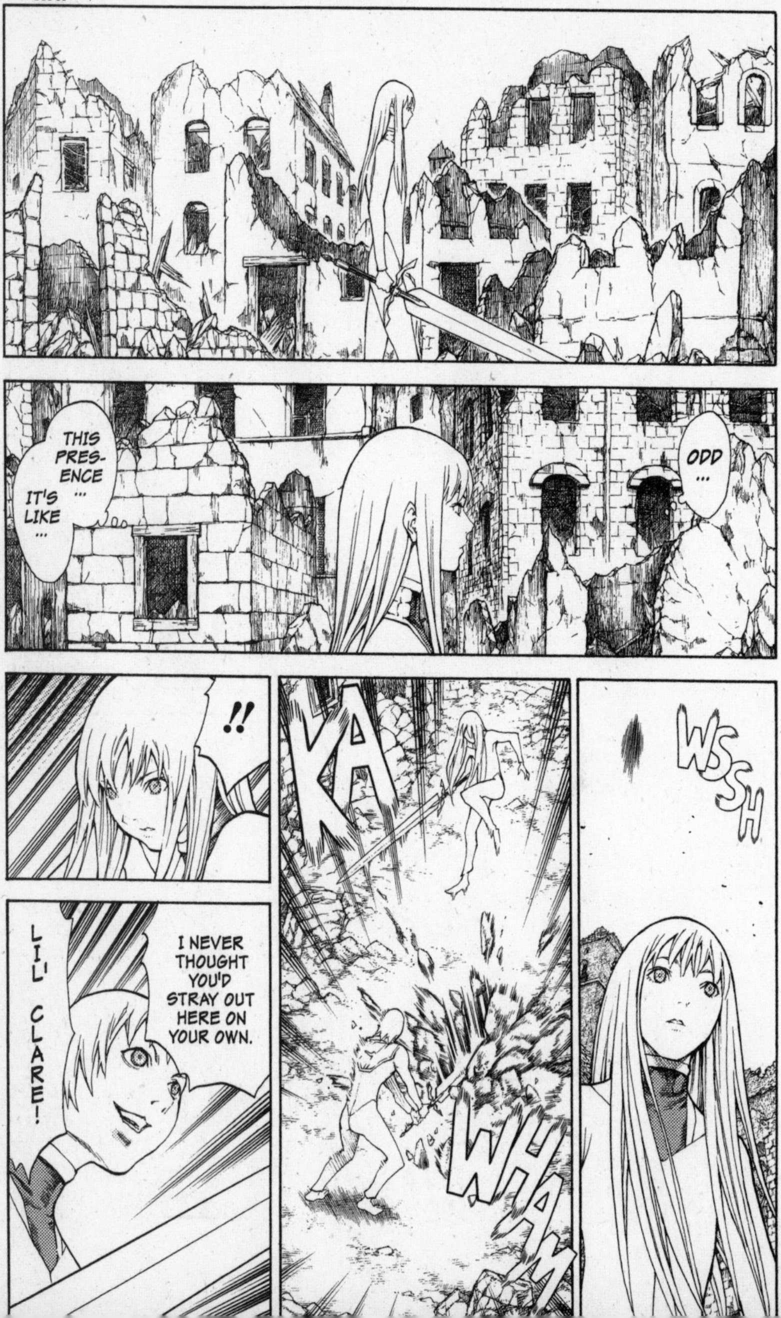
ODD...
THIS PRESENCE... IT'S LIKE...
WSSH
KA
WHAM
!!
I NEVER THOUGHT YOU'D STRAY OUT HERE ON YOUR OWN.
LIL' CLARE!

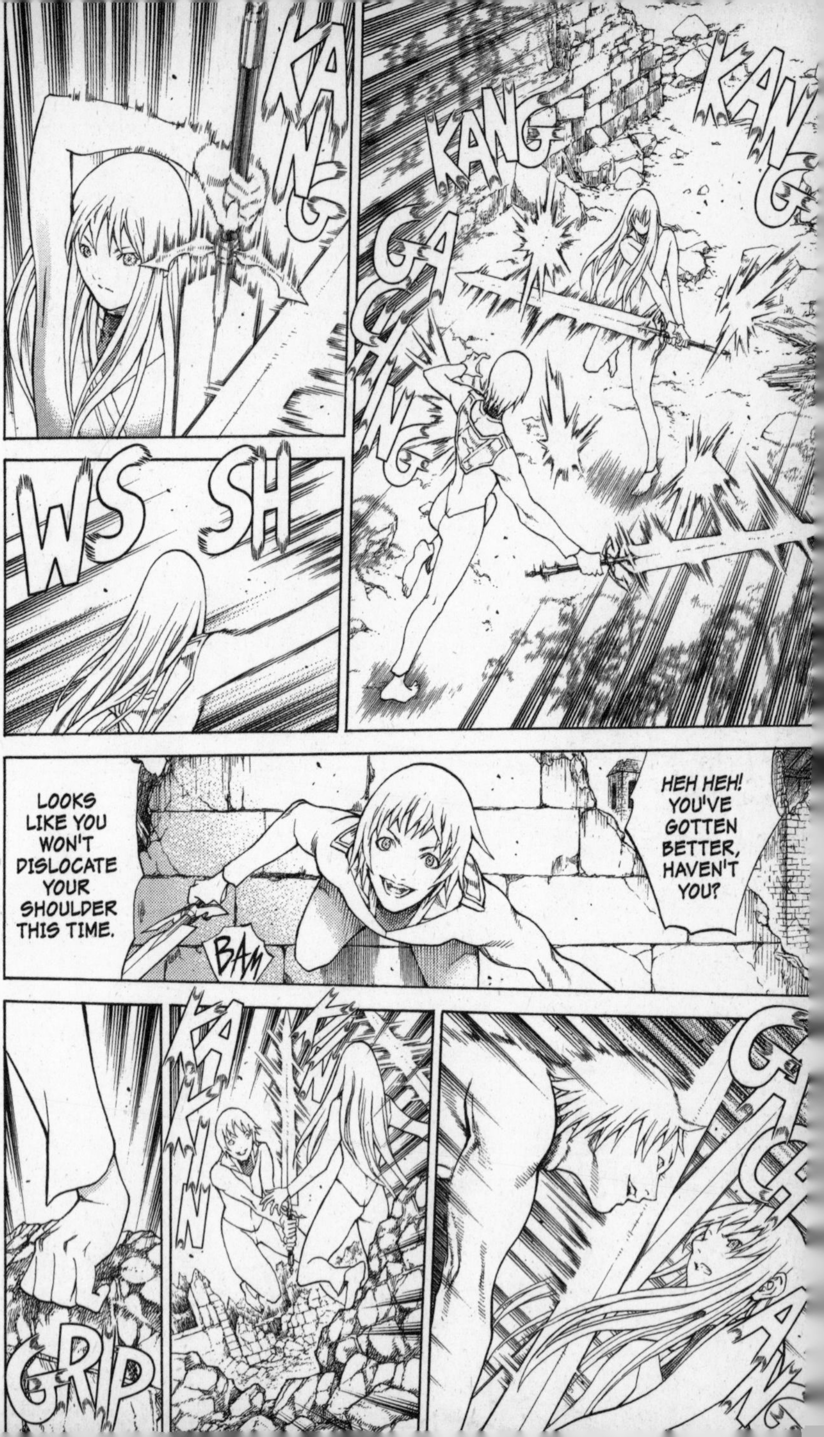
KANG
KANG
GACHING
KANG
WSSH
HEH HEH! YOU'VE GOTTEN BETTER, HAVEN'T YOU?
BAM
LOOKS LIKE YOU WON'T DISLOCATE YOUR SHOULDER THIS TIME.
GACHANG
GRIP

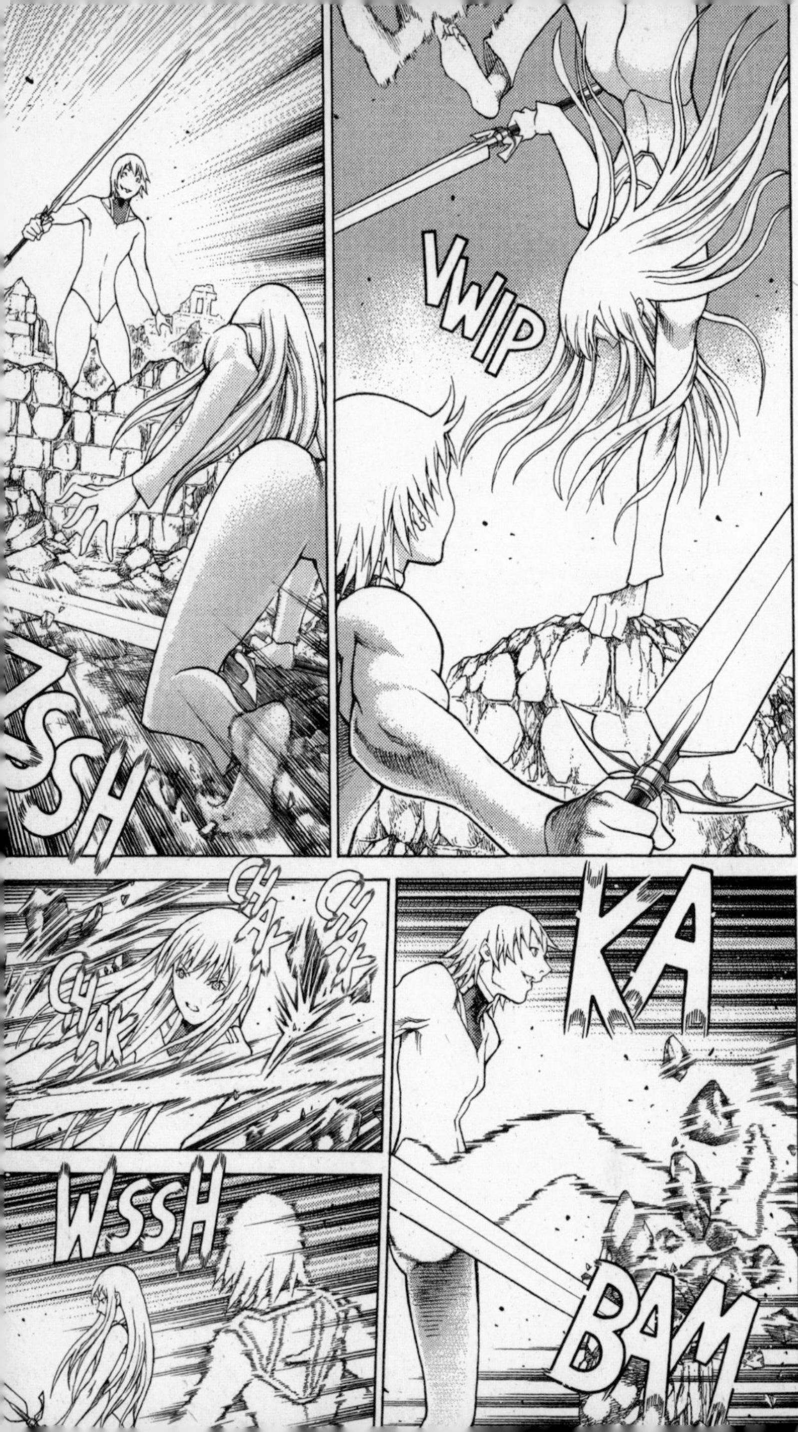
VWIP
SSH
KA
BAM
CHAK
CHAK
CHAK
WSSH

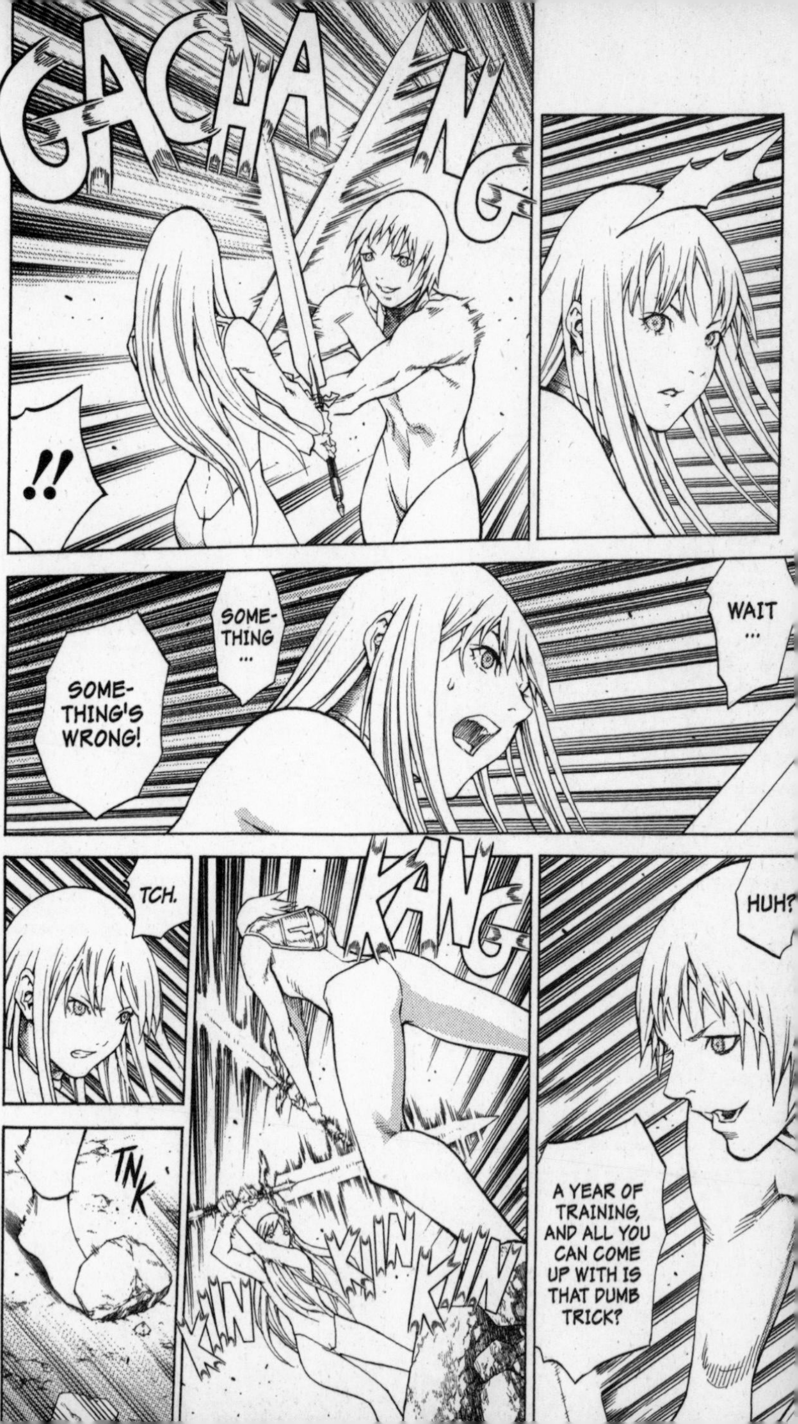
GACHANG
!!
WAIT...
SOME-THING...
SOME-THING'S WRONG!
HUH?
A YEAR OF TRAINING, AND ALL YOU CAN COME UP WITH IS THAT DUMB TRICK?
KANG
KIN KIN
KIN
TCH.
TNK

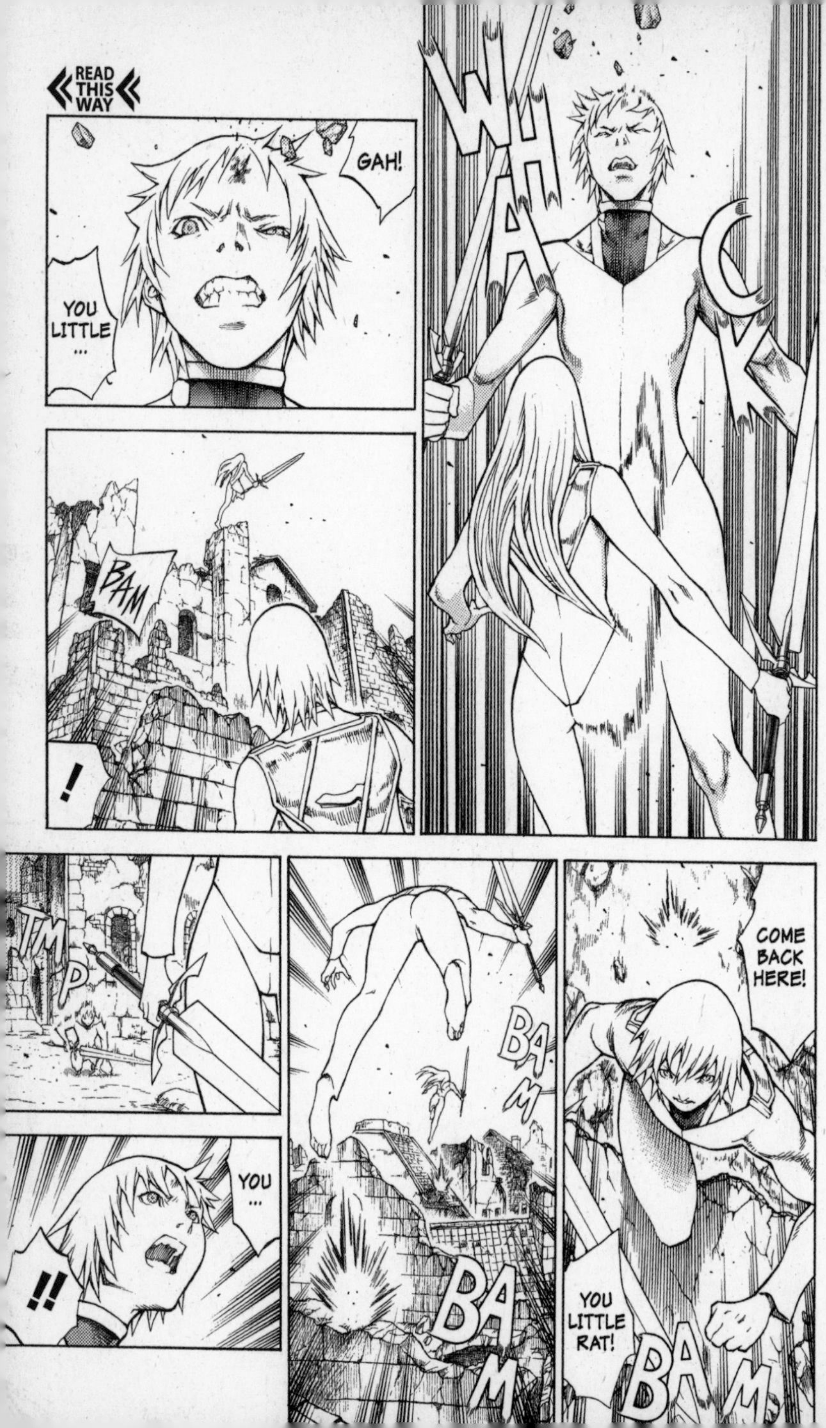
READ THIS WAY
WHACK
GAH!
YOU LITTLE ...
BAM
!
COME BACK HERE!
YOU LITTLE RAT!
BAM
BAM
BAM
TMP
YOU ...
!!

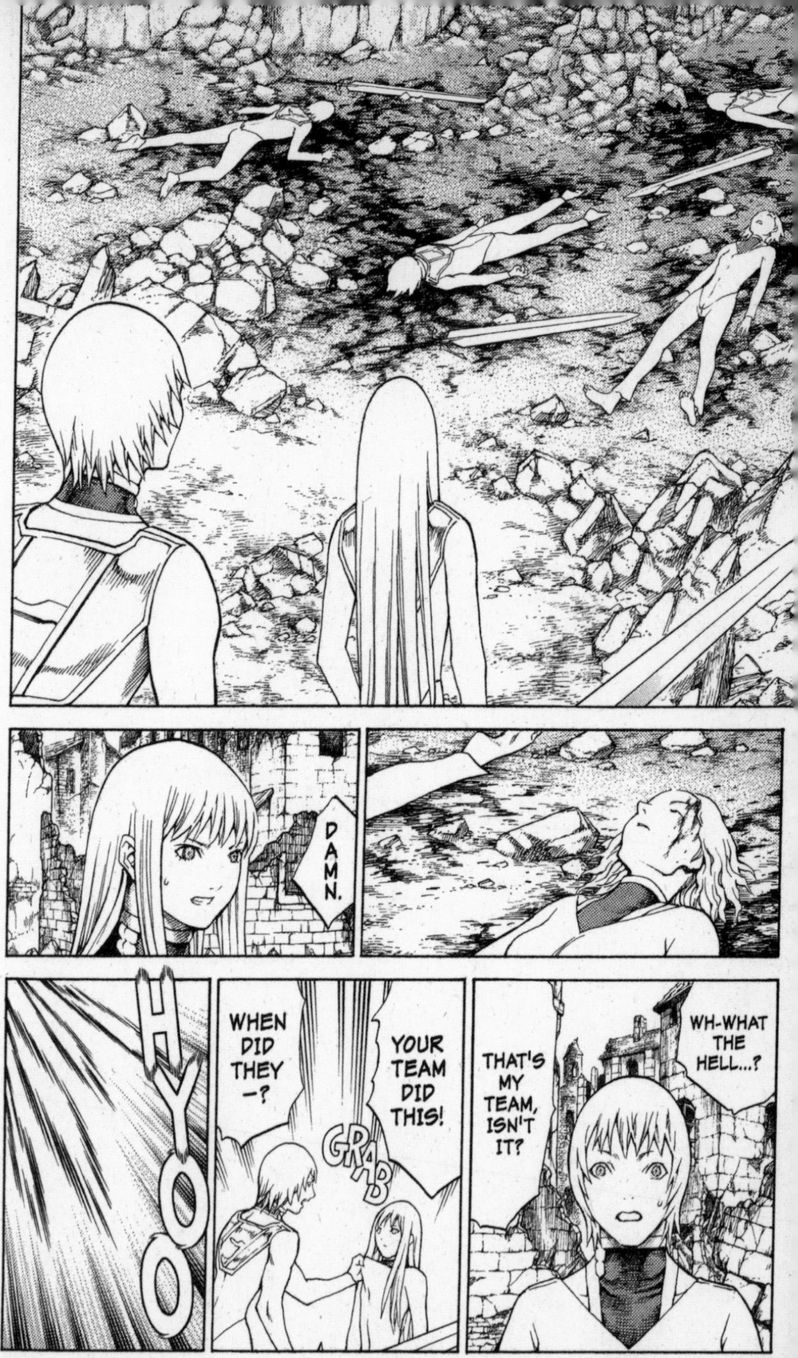
DAMN.
WH-WHAT THE HELL...?
THAT'S MY TEAM, ISN'T IT?
YOUR TEAM DID THIS!
WHEN DID THEY—?
GRAB
HYOOO

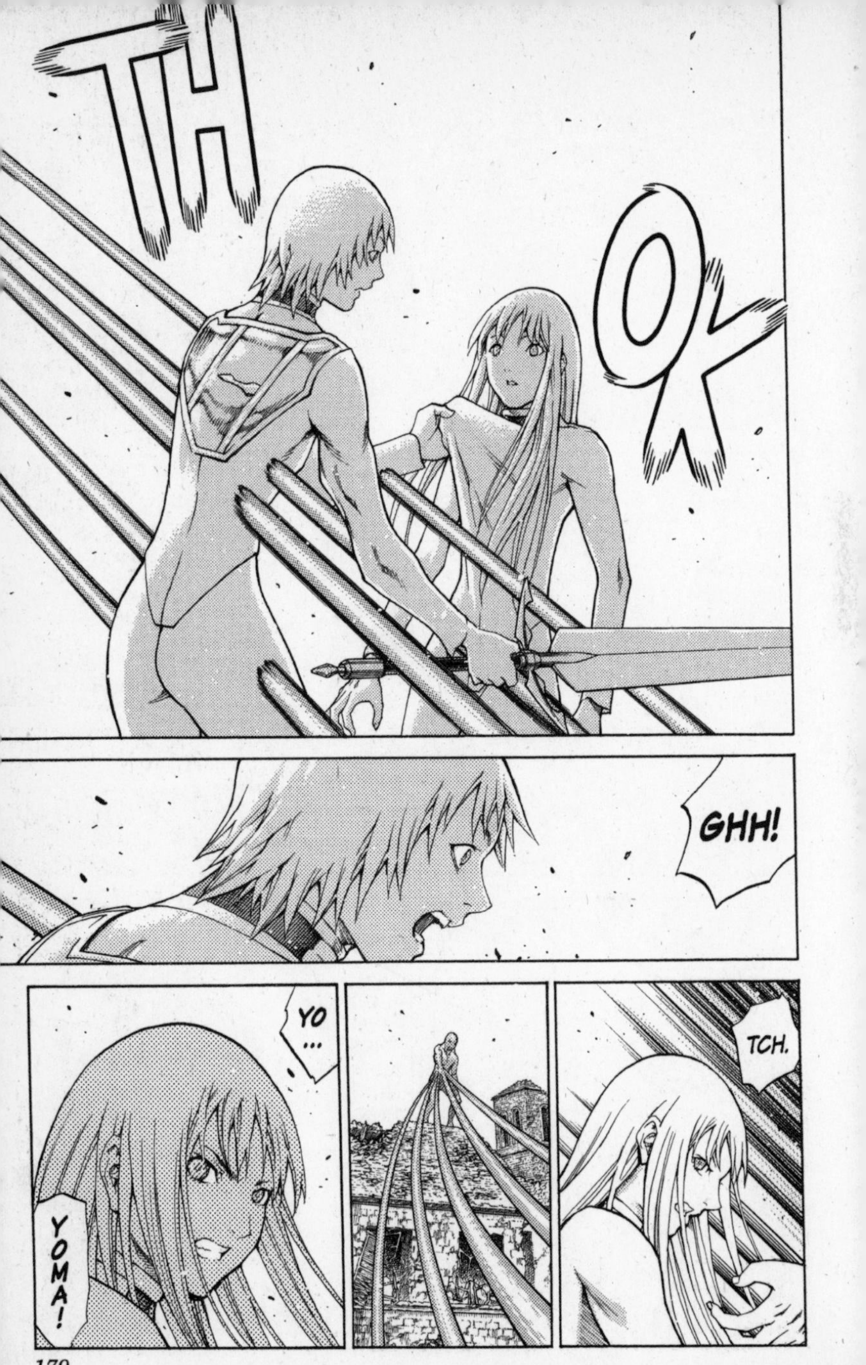
TH
OK
GHH!
TCH.
YO ...
YOMA!

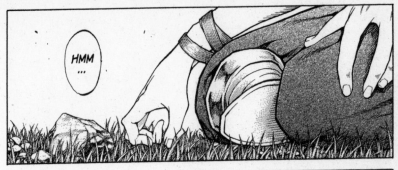

HMM...
I TOLD THEM THE FINAL TEST WOULD BE THE SAME AS REAL BATTLE.
DID ANY OF THEM ACTUALLY LISTEN?
I WONDER...
HOW MANY WILL SURVIVE THIS TIME?
GRAB

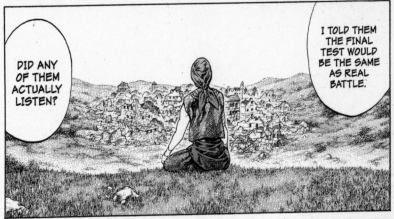

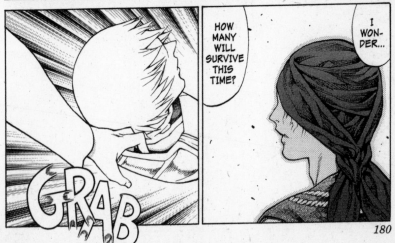

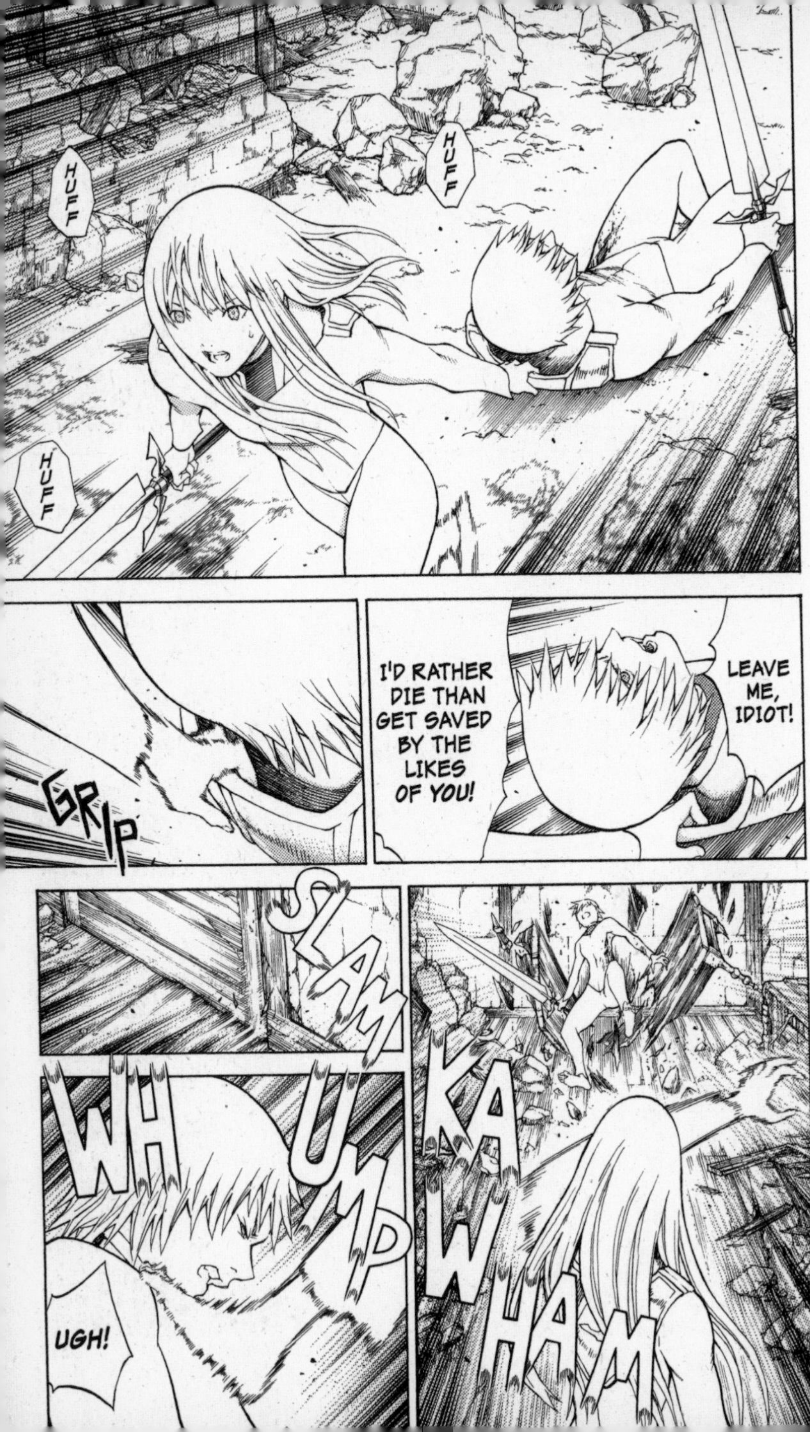
HUFF
HUFF
HUFF
LEAVE ME, IDIOT!
I'D RATHER DIE THAN GET SAVED BY THE LIKES OF YOU!
GRIP
KA WHAM
SLAM
WHUMP
UGH!

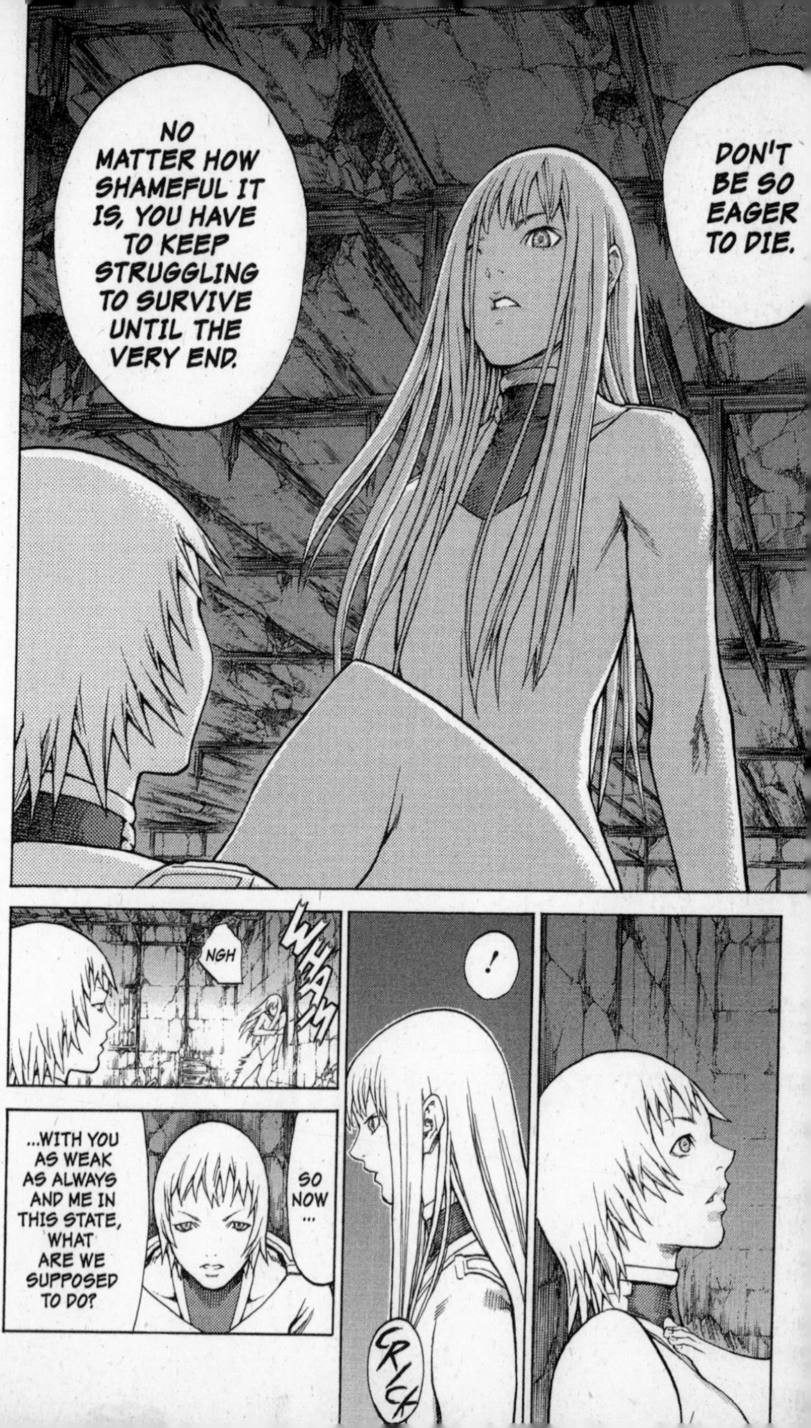
DON'T BE SO EAGER TO DIE.
NO MATTER HOW SHAMEFUL IT IS, YOU HAVE TO KEEP STRUGGLING TO SURVIVE UNTIL THE VERY END.
!
CRICK
WHAM
NGH
SO NOW...
...WITH YOU AS WEAK AS ALWAYS AND ME IN THIS STATE, WHAT ARE WE SUPPOSED TO DO?

READ THIS WAY

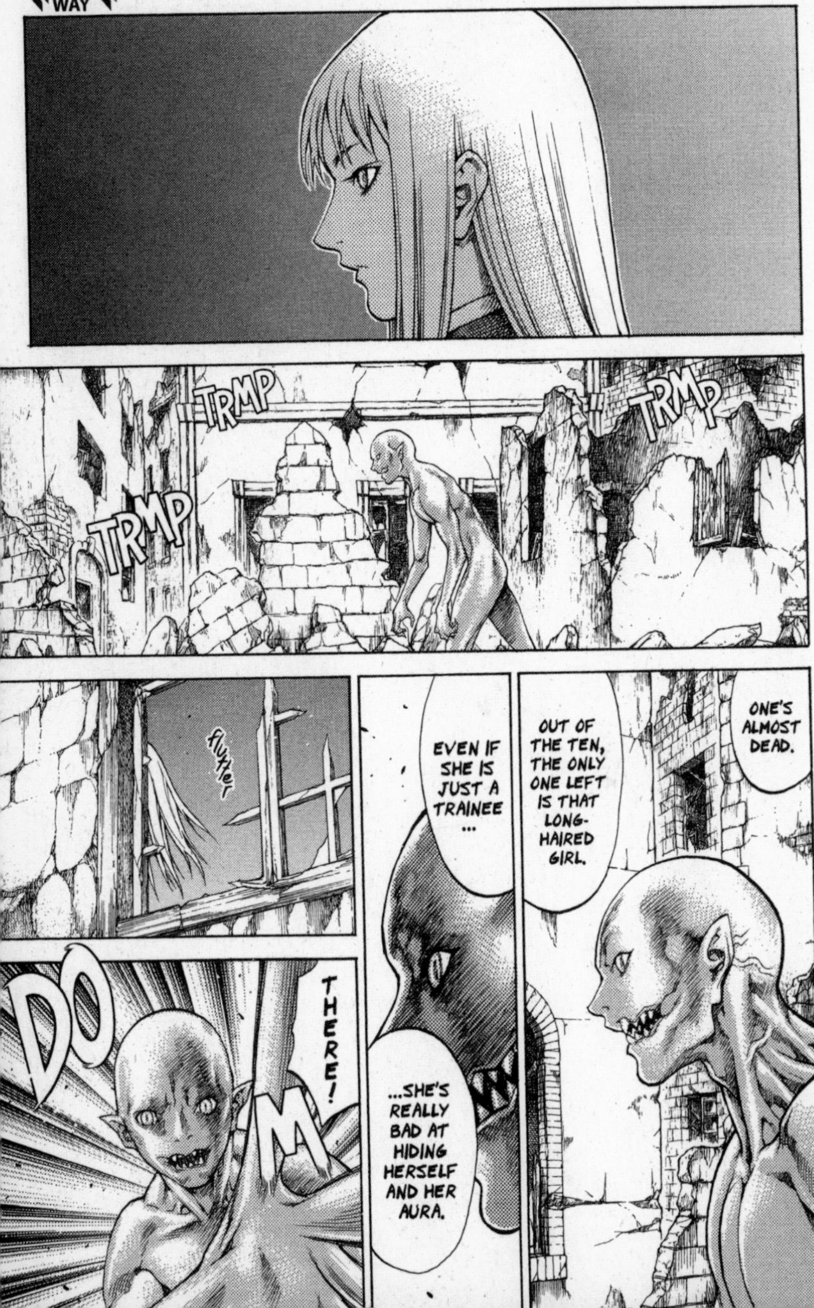
TRMP
TRMP
TRMP
ONE'S ALMOST DEAD.
OUT OF THE TEN, THE ONLY ONE LEFT IS THAT LONG-HAIRED GIRL.
EVEN IF SHE IS JUST A TRAINEE...
...SHE'S REALLY BAD AT HIDING HERSELF AND HER AURA.
flutter
THERE!
DOM

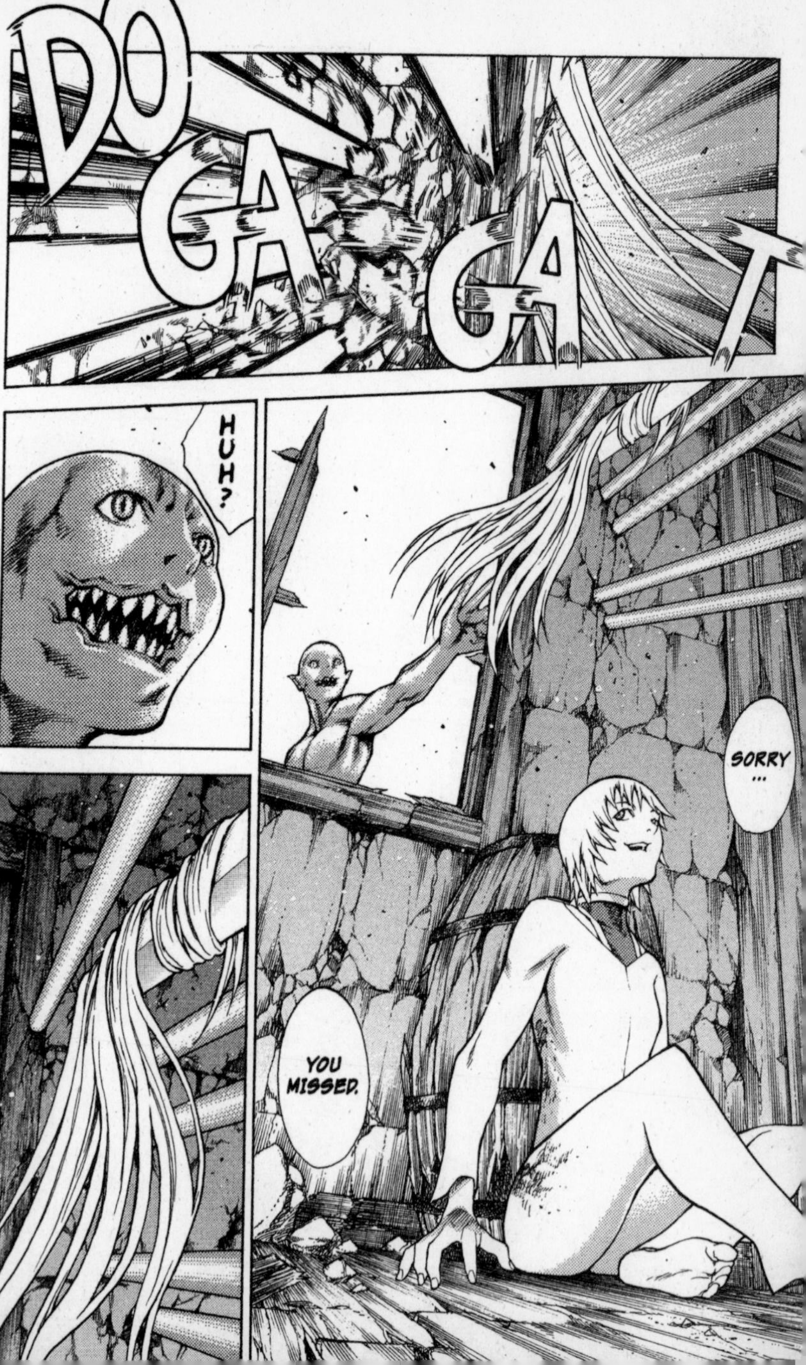
DOGAGAT
SORRY...
YOU MISSED.
HUH?

READ THIS WAY

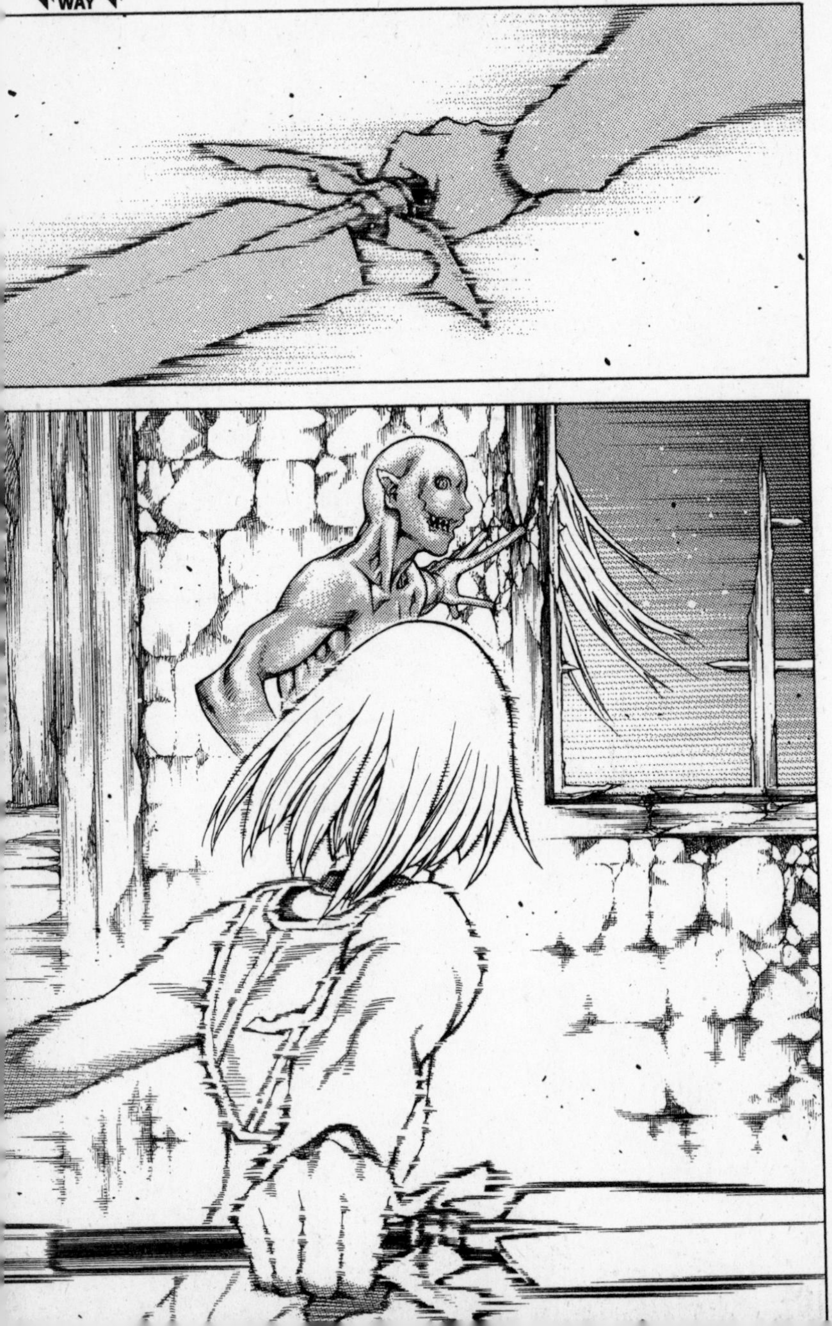

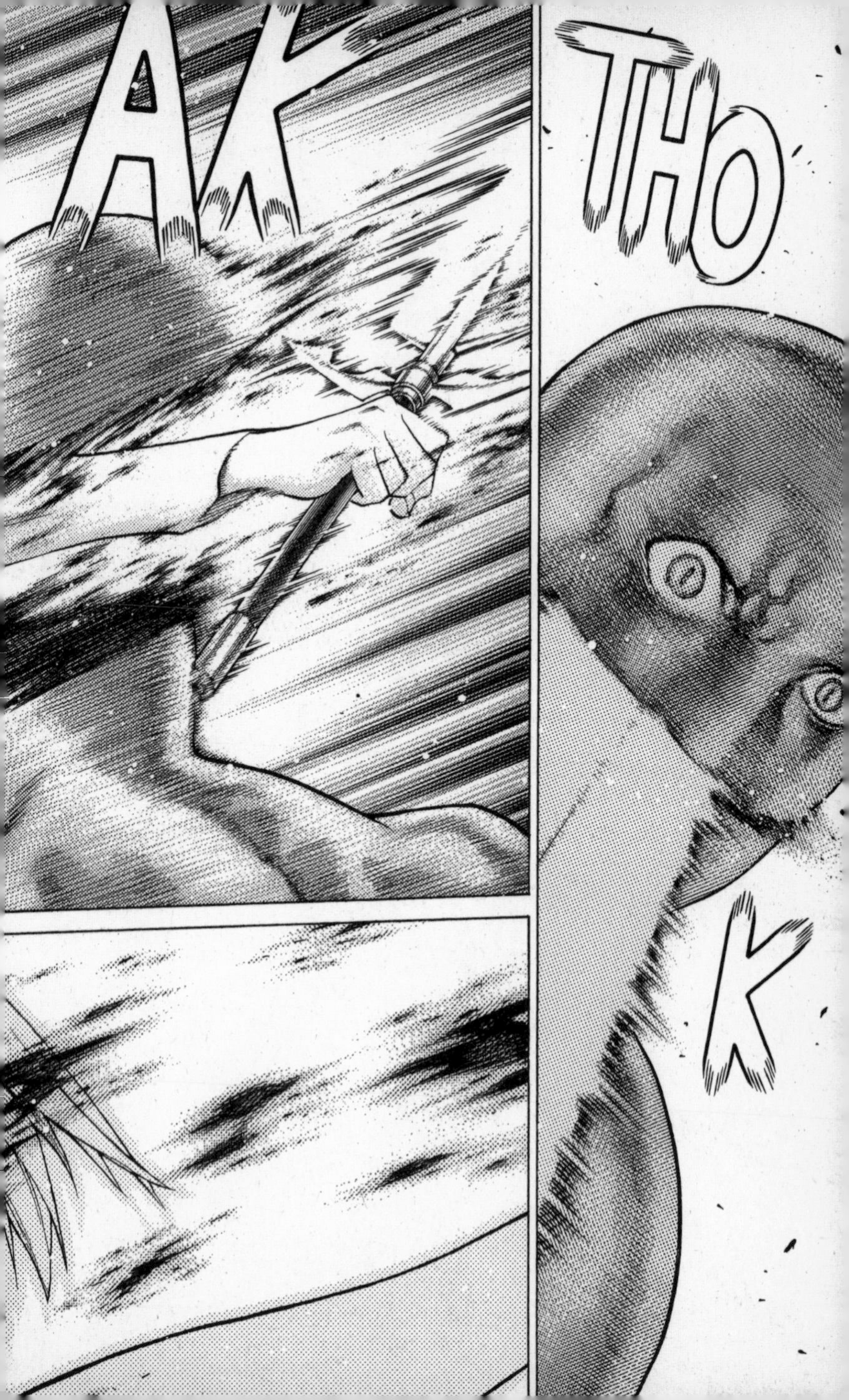
THOK
AK

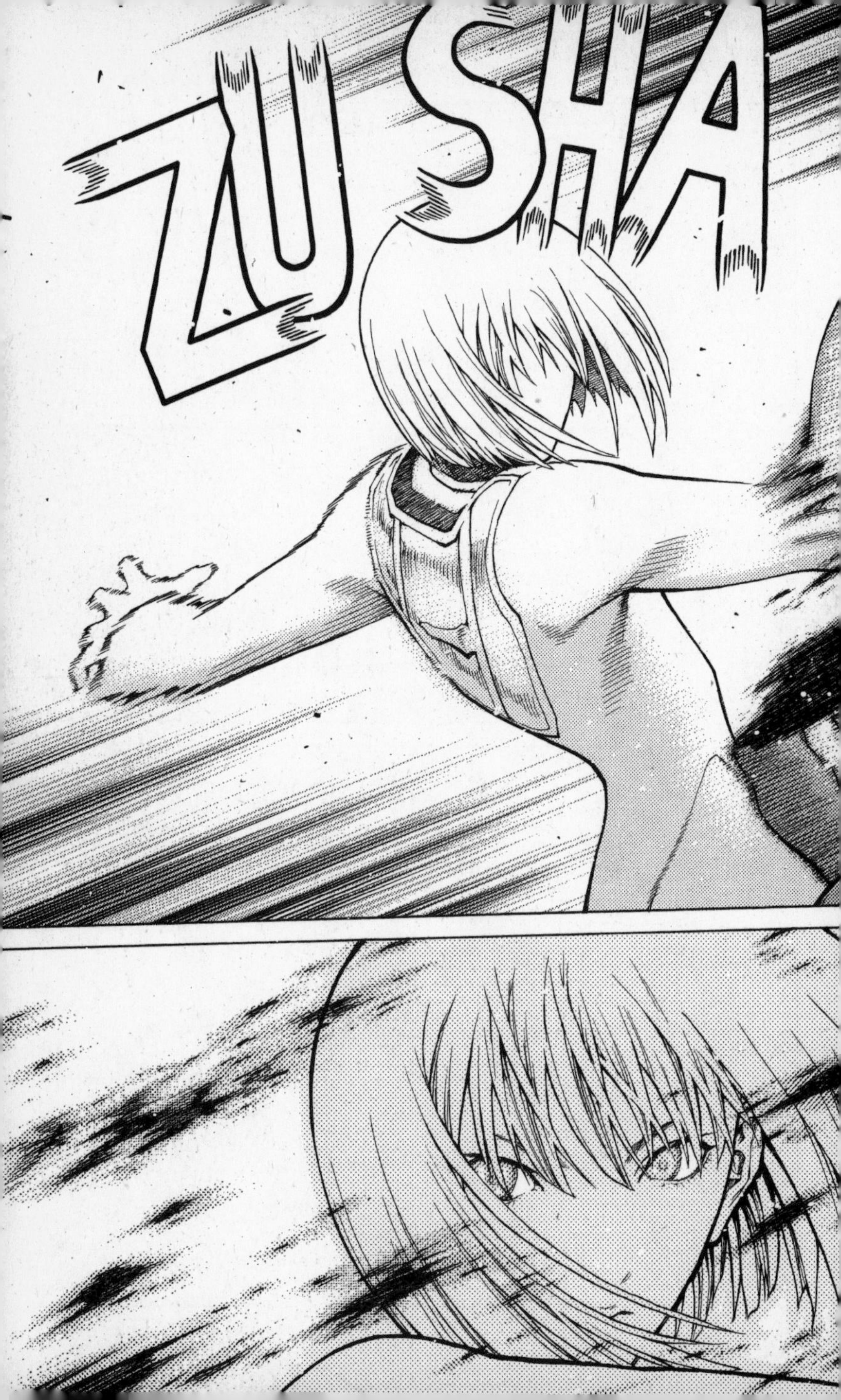
ZU SHA

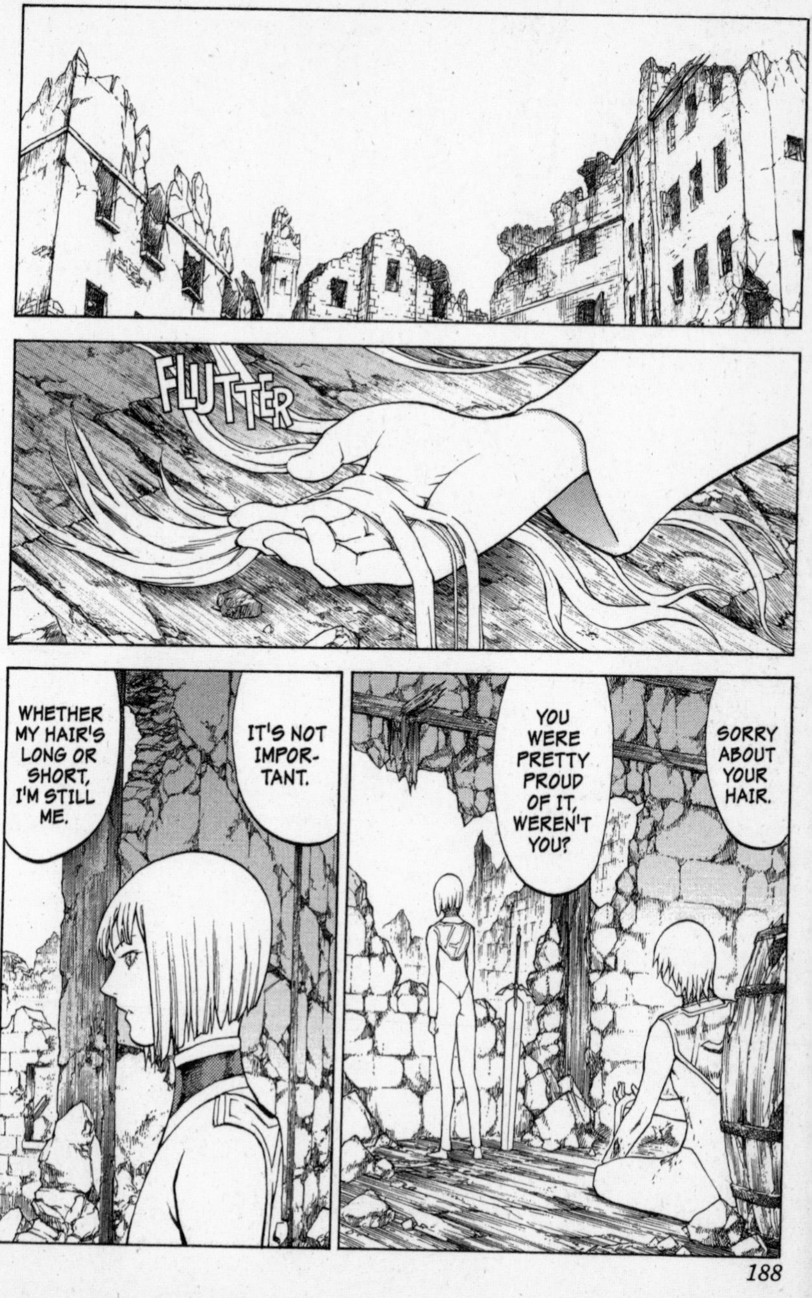
FLUTTER
SORRY ABOUT YOUR HAIR.
YOU WERE PRETTY PROUD OF IT, WEREN'T YOU?
IT'S NOT IMPORTANT.
WHETHER MY HAIR'S LONG OR SHORT, I'M STILL ME.

READ THIS WAY

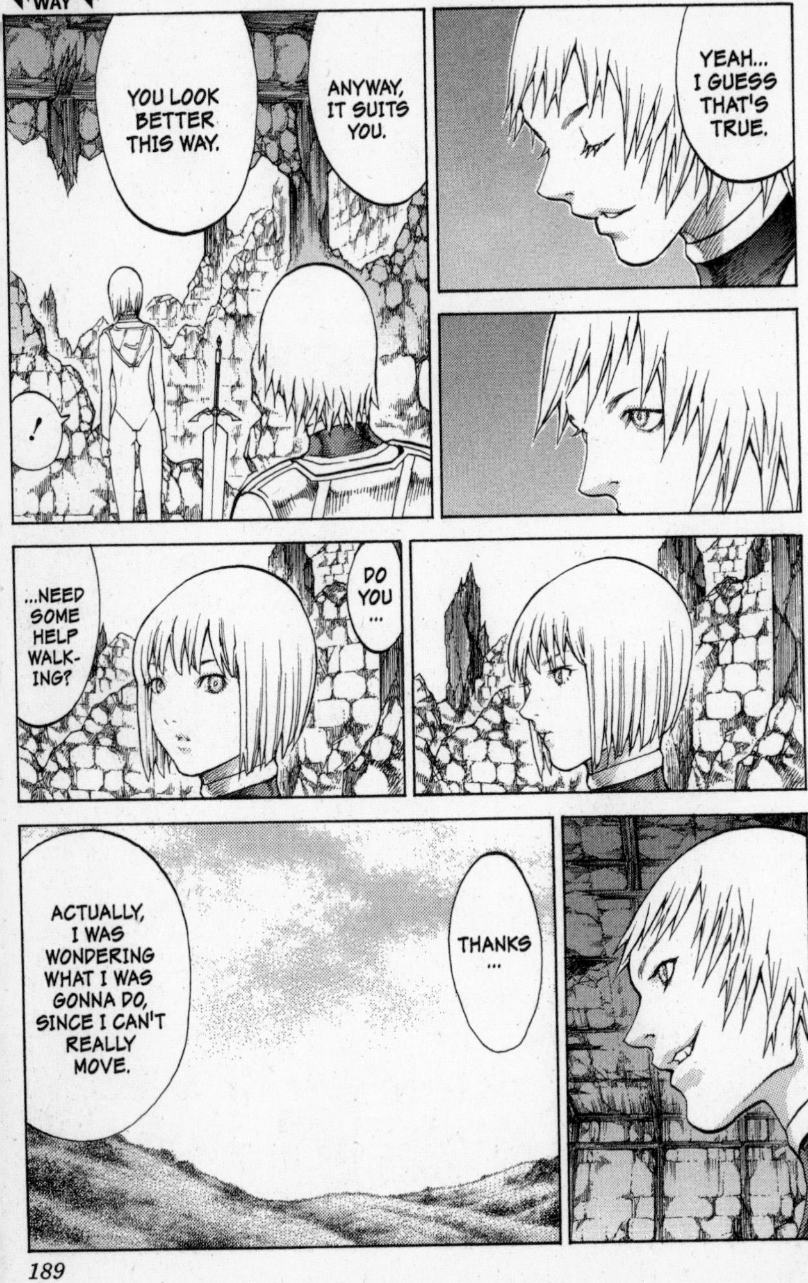
YEAH... I GUESS THAT'S TRUE.
ANYWAY, IT SUITS YOU.
YOU LOOK BETTER THIS WAY.
!
DO YOU ...
...NEED SOME HELP WALKING?
THANKS ...
ACTUALLY, I WAS WONDERING WHAT I WAS GONNA DO, SINCE I CAN'T REALLY MOVE.

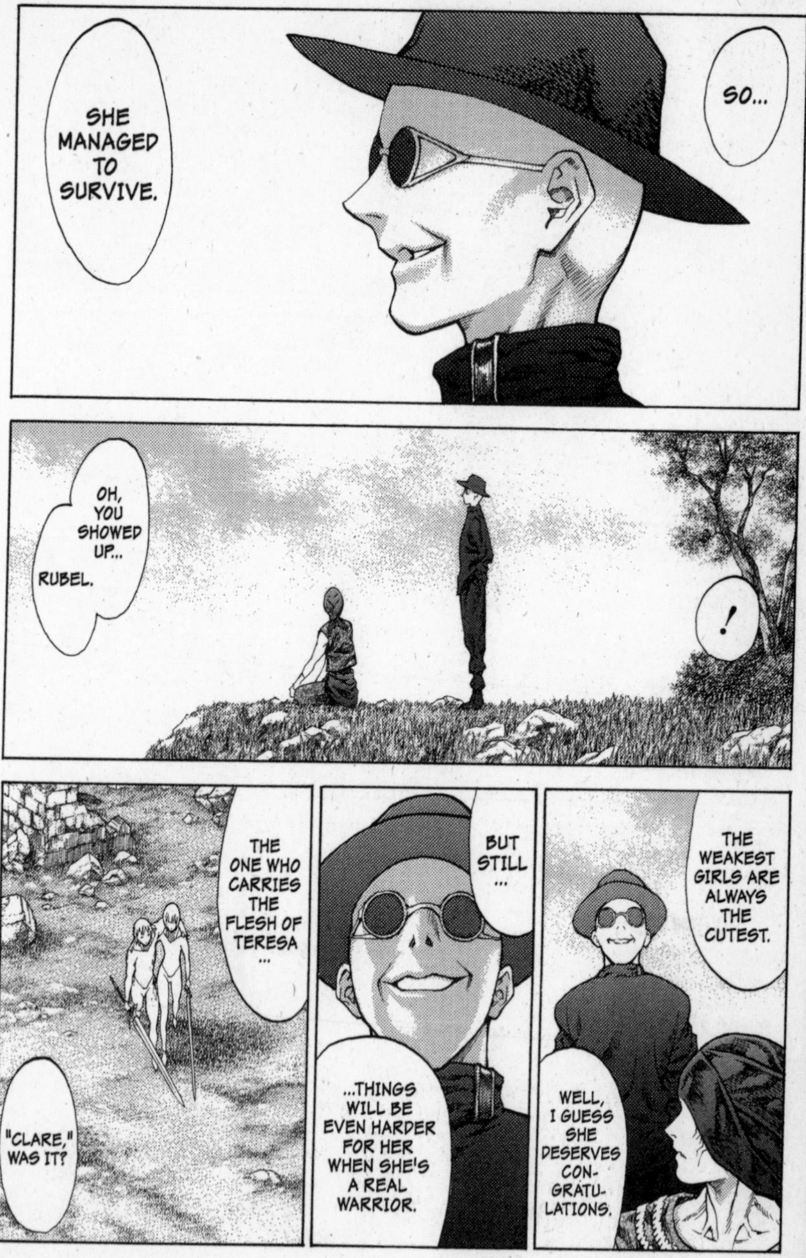
SO...
SHE MANAGED TO SURVIVE.
!
OH, YOU SHOWED UP... RUBEL.
THE WEAKEST GIRLS ARE ALWAYS THE CUTEST.
WELL, I GUESS SHE DESERVES CONGRATULATIONS.
BUT STILL ...
...THINGS WILL BE EVEN HARDER FOR HER WHEN SHE'S A REAL WARRIOR.
THE ONE WHO CARRIES THE FLESH OF TERESA ...
"CLARE," WAS IT?

READ THIS WAY

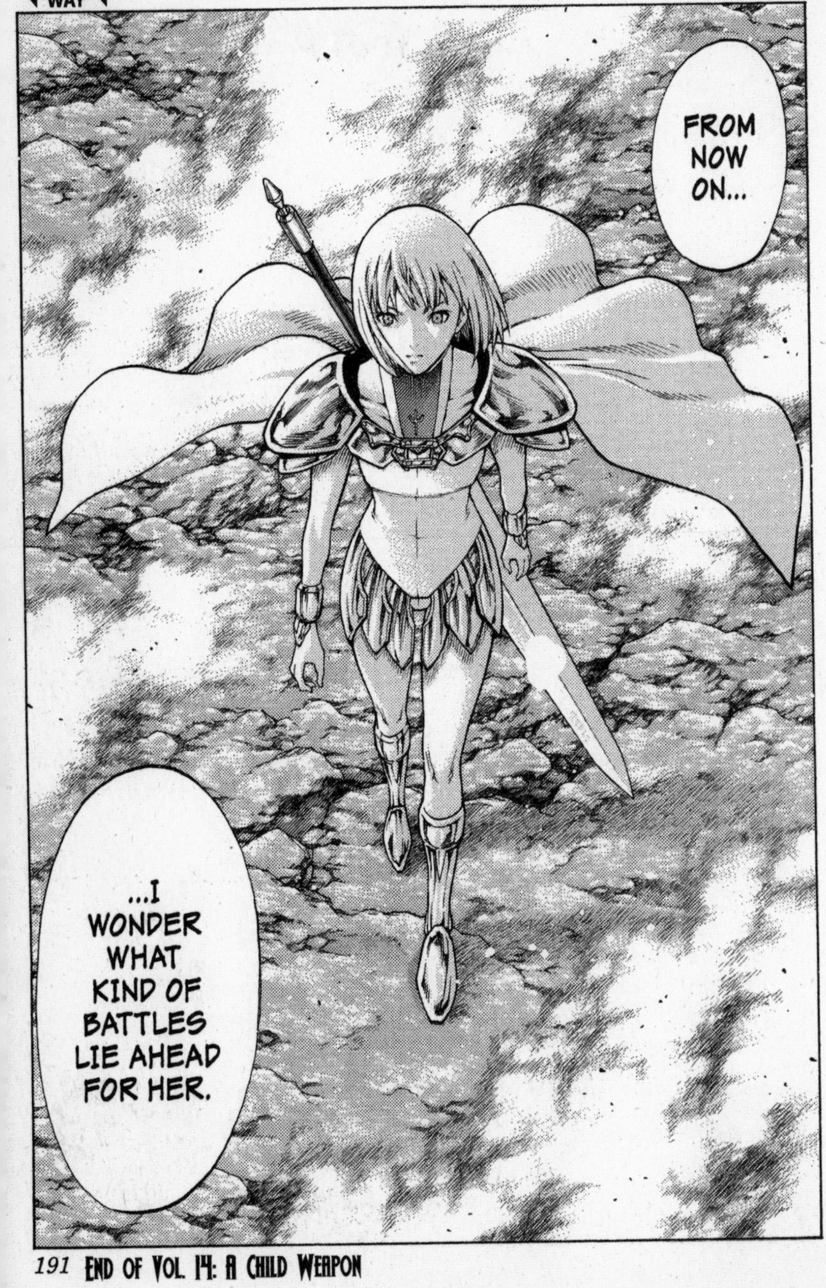
FROM NOW ON...
...I WONDER WHAT KIND OF BATTLES LIE AHEAD FOR HER.

E NEXT VOLUME

a's plans to eliminate the Awakened former number
ly" Agatha, have failed, but the arrival of Clare and
mrades turns the tide of battle. In the aftermath, Mi
s to finally share her shocking discoveries about the
of the Yoma, of the Organization and of the Claymor
elves.